Learning and Development

Processes, practices and perspectives at work

STEPHEN GIBB
University of Strathclyde

First published 2002 by
PALGRAVE MACMILLAN
Houndmills, Basingstoke, Hampshire RG21 6XS and 175 Fifth Avenue, New York, N.Y. 10010
Companies and representatives throughout the world

PALGRAVE MACMILLAN is the global academic imprint of the Palgrave Macmillan division of St. Martin's Press, LLC and of Palgrave Macmillan Ltd. Macmillan® is a registered trademark in the United States, United Kingdom and other countries. Palgrave is a registered trademark in the European Union and other countries.

ISBN 0–333–98446–3 hardback
ISBN 0–333–98447–1 paperback

This book is printed on paper suitable for recycling and made from fully managed and sustained forest sources.

A catalogue record for this book is available from the British Library.

10   9   8   7   6   5   4   3   2   1
11   10   09   08   07   06   05   04   03   02

Printed and bound in Great Britain by
J.W. Arrowsmith Ltd, Bristol

Dedication

To Mary and John; for being so great, so often, in so many ways

Chapter Outline

Preface

The consensus is that Learning and Development (L&D) at work is now a prominent and central part of Human Resource Management (HRM). This text is designed in structure, style and content to provide a complete and integrated introduction to the processes, practices and perspectives of this important area of people management. The structure is to explain and explore L&D at work as a process which is an integral part of the overall performance management of organisations. Selected, representative and prominent aspects of L&D at work are then explored, illustrating through case studies what this process involves in practice. Finally a number of different key contemporary concerns, concepts, arguments and evidence are explored by considering different perspectives on L&D at work. The text is thus an 'all in one' view of processes, practices and perspectives.

It is hoped that this approach does justice to the subject. The subject of learning and development has animated, both fascinating and frustrating, people from time immemorial. No doubt the first thoughts on learning and development occurred when an early ancestor found that the joy of passing on their wisdom about making axes from flints to keen and enthusiastic learners, who got it all, had to be tempered by the pain of dealing with recalcitrant and dismissive learners, who did not get it at all, and would rather be somewhere else doing something else. If only this learning and development thing could be sorted out, the first stone age trainer must have thought, then my life would be so much better. And, it is probably fair to assume, the thoughts of the learners 'not getting it all' would have been the same.

Yet the answers are still elusive, despite millennia of further thinking and analysis of learning and development. As the 21st century gets out of first gear, we are still uncertain about how best to promote L&D, we are still reviewing practices and processes, generating new ways of looking at and thinking about learning and development. Why do they still frustrate as well as fascinate? Learning and development are fun and exciting, the keys to success and good fortune. They are, one survey found, considered by many to be more satisfying and gratifying than sex. Learning and development are what animate us, they bring us to life, inspiring, challenging and invigorating. But learning and development also involve toil and trouble. They are hard work. And if they can make us they can also break us; they raise hurdles that can become barriers and involve being exposed to harsh judgements. There is no gratification in this. Instead of facing up to hard work, and the risks of encountering failure and setbacks, people seek other means to success and good fortune; or, which is worse, they just give up. They seek animation and gratification elsewhere.

These general uncertainties about learning and development are found in the context of performance in work and organisations. The promised ends are tantalising; L&D for individuals to gain entry to work and occupations with career success, L&D to achieve greater and higher standards of performance and organisational success, and L&D to compete and prosper as a nation. These are the promised ends of L&D, and while achieving them can bring the greatest gratification, they also involve the greatest work that many individuals, organisations and nations will encounter.

One frustration facing an author in this field is that the current nature of the subject of L&D at work can be described as exhibiting a lack of 'content stability'. Texts are out of date almost as soon as they are written, never mind being published and put to market, as new institutions, practices and initiatives bloom and old ones fade. Take three examples. As I write this the concept of 'blended learning', mixing e-learning with conventional training, is in the ascendant. Another concept discussed here, 'emotional intelligence', may be showing signs of decline. Yet another concept, 'lifelong learning', is being defined in quite different ways by the UK and by the European Union; this is the L&D equivalent of the euro, as everyone else in Europe uses it, but the UK retains its own 'currency'. Organisational practices evolve and change with bewildering frequency, Government policy is subject to constant review, and even the apparently established rocks of learning theory are but a thin crust floating on a molten core that may erupt anywhere, anytime. It can be difficult to even define a basic vocabulary and language for L&D that remain stable from one year to the next. This is a general problem with HRM, but it is acute in the field of L&D. This is something that other authors of texts in this area have struggled with over the last decade.

The structure, style and content of the text as a support for learning are based on a specific view of learning which provides one way of working around this problem of a lack of content stability. This is the constructivist view of learning. Constructivism recognises that the construction of new understanding requires a combination of things. It involves evoking a readiness to learn by animating people, connecting with their prior learning to allow new learning to be built up, as well as providing new ideas and information. Just concentrating on providing new information and ideas in themselves is not enough. Individuals who are not animated, and who cannot make connections with existing ideas are as likely to evade or misconstrue new ideas and information as they are to absorb them.

In this respect the subject of L&D presents a real challenge. Learners come with a rich array of different backgrounds and ways of thinking about learning and development. It is a subject where many preconceived ideas will be present. Myths, taboos, things people learn from their families, friends, and past teachers will all have shaped their prior understanding, providing some solid and some insecure foundations upon which to try and build anew. This is when learning needs to be based on the learners' active participation in problem-solving and critical thinking, through activities which they find relevant and engaging. Only by testing ideas and approaches that challenge their prior knowledge and experience, and applying these to a new situation, can learners 'construct' sound new knowledge.

Hands-on activities and observations of a real organisational world provide the best source of experiences to enable such constructions. In lieu of that this text is styled to combine coverage of processes, practices and perspectives drawing on both the practicalities of L&D at work and the more academic analysis of L&D at work as a subject of scholarship and research. Models, concepts, text references and illustrations are available as resources; but learners should always treat these as the results of others' observations and speculations, not authoritative conclusions. Such references are actually the 'constructions' by others of their current understanding of the world around them; and those are open to challenge and change.

Adopting such an approach is meant to avoid the pitfalls of providing an introduction to managing L&D at work that is either too practically oriented and

prescriptive, or insufficiently set in the wider performance and organisational management context. The solution is an introductory text for students that combines an
introduction to the core elements of the L&D processes at work with an analysis of
these in the context of contemporary practices and perspectives. This text aims to
provide just such a blend, a blend for the thoughtful performer, and a blend that
enables the development of the thoughtful performer. Bringing together these aspects
of L&D at work, the core elements of L&D processes and practices at work and the
perspectives which animate and enliven arguments and debate about L&D at work,
was my goal. But, as a constructivist, all I can really hope is that I have provided a
resource that will animate, not a text that provides the first and last word on everything to do with L&D at work.

Acknowledgements

Many colleagues and students have been instrumental in providing insights into L&D processes, practices and perspectives over the years. David Megginson has been a font of wisdom unparalleled over the years. Carol Pease has helped enormously with insights into the work of consultants. Special mention must also be made of students whose work with me has helped me learn: Sandy Wilkie, for insights into mentoring, Lynne Fitzpatrick for insights into IiP, and Greig Aitken for insights into Corporate Universities.

Copyright permissions from the Health & Safety Executive (The Cullen Report), and the 'e-learning network' for the concluding case study in Chapter 9, were kindly given.

While this book is dedicated to my parents, John and Mary, the encouragement and support of Jennifer has been the foundation of all my work.

I've left others' value excluded; you've offered unbeatable learning, affected untold reflections, all implicitly or naturally acknowledged.

Introduction

This first chapter aims to provide a foundation for describing, analysing and exploring L&D at work. It does this by first outlining the main concepts associated with L&D at work. At the centre of these is the idea of performance management, and a process of observation, planning, action and review. The major kinds of practice of L&D at work that are found, based on empirical evidence, are described. The good and the bad experiences that people have in the course of these practices are also described and analysed. Together this outline of concepts, process, practices and a perspective of what people find to be good and bad provide an overview of L&D at work. To illustrate the relevance of these matters a detailed case study of one organisation is provided in conclusion. The mistakes that the organisation made can be analysed with the concepts and the process model.

chapter one

Learning and Development in Work and Organisations

Learning outcomes

- Define the key concepts associated with Learning and Development (L&D) in work and organisations
- Describe a model of the core process and elements of performance management
- Analyse the connections between the contemporary performance management concerns of organisations and L&D at work
- Define and discuss five major practices associated with L&D in work and organisations
- Explain the importance of L&D in work and organisations with reference to work and organisation case studies

FRAMEWORK CASE STUDY: LADBROKE GROVE

After the standard two hundred and fifty hours instruction, on 26 September 1999, Michael Hodder qualified as a train driver with Thames Trains. Thirteen days later he was driving a train on a route out of Paddington station in London, with one hundred and forty seven passengers on board, when he failed to see a red stop signal, signal SN109. He went through the signal. Thirty three seconds after that his train collided with another passenger train at Ladbroke Grove. Thirty one people were killed and over four hundred were injured.

Nearly two years later, in June 2001, after a major public inquiry, Lord Cullen (Cullen 2001) produced a report on the Ladbroke Grove crash. A whole range of problems had been uncovered by the inquiry. There were technical issues about the positioning of signals which made them hard to see. There had been organisational problems, with 'institutional paralysis' in Railtrack, the body responsible for the track that the trains ran on; they had failed to deal with health and safety issues in the railway effectively over a number of years. The poor performance of regulatory bodies, who were meant to oversee standards, was also identified as a factor contributing to the accident. There was no doubt, however, that it was significant shortcomings in Michael's training which meant that these chronic problems, which had been contained up till then, were to have such dreadful consequences. The inquiry found that his instructor had not recognised it as part of his job to teach routes in and out of Paddington. Michael was not taught to pay particular attention to 'signals passed at danger' (SPAD), such as SN109, which had regularly been 'passed at danger' in the past. Indeed the instructor involved in his training was quoted as telling trainees, when they asked about route knowledge, 'This is Paddington, and sort of make the best of it really'.

As a consequence of this accident, soon to be followed by others which would equally dramatically expose the chronic problems facing the railway industry, the whole railway system in the UK came under intense scrutiny, criticism and review. The consequences of these accidents, and other problems with performance standards on the railways, mean that widespread organisational change and significant investments over the coming years will be necessary. But equally important to learning the lessons of Ladbroke Grove, and the future performance of the industry, will be the improvement of driver training.

INTRODUCTION

The reason for beginning with such a stark and tragic example is that it illustrates how and why Learning and Development (L&D) at work is such a major concern for organisations. It is a truth widely acknowledged that mistakes provide an opportunity for effective learning. The Ladbroke Grove case provides a salutary example of this. The Cullen inquiry into the events preceding the Ladbroke Grove disaster offers a rare opportunity; the opportunity to scrutinise in great detail the mistakes in L&D practices of a major organisation. Analysing how and why L&D at work went wrong in this case requires the application of basic concepts and models. This introductory chapter will describe those concepts and models. This will provide you with the means to begin to explore the range of challenges of attaining effective L&D at work. The details of the events leading to the Ladbroke Grove case will be described at the end of the chapter. By exploring that case using the concepts and models introduced here the foundation for developing a broader and deeper knowledge of L&D at work will be established.

DEFINITIONS AND CONCEPTS

L&D at work is a subject where the areas of human science, management and professional practice overlap. Each of these constituent areas has its own concerns about L&D at work, and its own 'way of talking' about L&D at work. These differences can sometimes lead to people using different terms for the same thing, or using the same term to mean quite different things. The central terms whose meaning needs to be fixed for use in this text about L&D at work are;

- Learning & Development (L&D)
- the three dimensions of L&D: cognitive capacity, capability and behaviour
- performance management

■ the L&D process
■ human resource management

Learning and Development

There is a good pragmatic reason and a good academic reason for the use of the term 'Learning and Development' (L&D) for a subject that can also be described as either plain 'training', or 'workforce development', or 'human resource development'. The pragmatic reason for using the term L&D is that, in the redesigned professional education scheme of the Chartered Institute of Personnel & Development (CIPD), the subject area that was called 'employee development' is now called L&D. As the CIPD, an influential voice in people management matters, has set the precedent by using the term it makes sense to follow what will no doubt become common usage.

But there is more to it than that, to there having been a change in fashion. There is a substantive reason. This is illustrated by the contemporary initiative within the UK Government to modernise policy in this area, where defining the boundaries of what they termed 'workforce development' (PIU 2001) became a taxing exercise. Depending on how 'workforce development' was defined it could include or exclude a range of aspects of policy. The review group concluded that 'workforce development' had to be considered as being broader than 'training' but narrower than 'education'. It was to be defined as part of, but not the same as, 'lifelong learning', encompassing as it did both formal and informal learning. It was to be defined as focussed on those in or near the workforce. And it was to be defined in a way that acknowledged and included inequalities arising from race, gender and disability as relevant and important issues. In conclusion the PIU defined workforce development as being

> activities which increase the knowledge, skills and abilities of the workforce necessary both to ensure sustainable economic success and to contribute to social inclusion (PIU 2001 p 1).

This is in one sense clear enough. But such a definition of 'workforce development' is actually very much like any definition to 'trainine' that has been used in the past. Yet the care taken with this exercise to definine the core term does reflect serious concerns, rather than representing the splitting of hairs over fine distinctions that make no difference. It is symptomatic of there being an awareness of the need to move on from past ways of thinking, and embrace new ways of thinking (Gibb and Megginson 2000). The underlying issue is that, in the past, there were different spheres in which the development of knowledge, of skills and of abilities have traditionally been managed. Such divisions were reflected in definitions and distinctions being made about the kinds of learning involved in the spheres of training, education and development.

Training was the term that had dominated discussion of learning at work in the past, and is the 'narrow' term that the PIU definition of workforce development was trying to supersede. Training set the boundaries narrowly by seeming to be concerned only with learning undertaken for the development of skills for work and in work, to enable effective performance in a job or role. Training was then something different from, separate from, education and development. The connotations of training were of specific kinds of formal learning provided in the workplace (see Box 1.1).

Box 1.1

Spending on training in the UK

According to one recent survey the annual cost for UK employers of training is £23.5 billion. This includes £14.5 billion on 'off the job training' and £9 billion spent on 'on the job' training. Of the £14.5 billion spent 'off the job' £11.8 billion is spent on courses. The largest single cost in this is trainee labour; so higher wage costs in a sector mean higher training costs. Annual costs per employee in training then vary from finance and business (£1400) to manufacturing (£600).

   With a workforce of just under 24 million these figures suggest that an average of £1000 is spent per employee per year on training.

Source: Keynote 1998

Box 1.2

UK education facts

34.6 thousand schools*	16.1 million pupils	500,000 teachers
88 universities, 58 other HE institutions	2 million students 880,000 part time 400,000 postgraduate 1 million first degree	74,000 FT lecturers
516 further education colleges	4 million students 3 million part-time	58,000 FT lecturers
Total Pupils and students	*22.1 million*	*632,000 teaching staff*

   *28,500 public schools, 2456 private schools, 1523 special schools

   Total managed education expenditure on services by public authorities in the UK in 1998/99 was £38.4 billion. £1.8 billion was directly on under fives, and £22.5 billion was on schools. This represented 4.5 per cent of Gross Domestic Product. In 1998/99 average spending per pupil in nursery and primary schools in the UK was £1880. The figure for secondary schools was £2530.

Source: DfEE 2001a

Education, the broader term the PIU was seeking to distinguish workforce development from, was in the past differentiated with respect to training by being defined as learning undertaken in educational institutions in the pursuit of qualifications in advance of employment. The audiences for education were consumers of bodies of knowledge, typically children, young people and mature entrants being taught subjects by professional teachers in institutions (see Box 1.2). The role and evolution of educational institutions and opportunities in a time of economic and social change is a critical concern for all. That is why 'education, education, education', is for the current UK Government, in all its forms, the subject of much reform. Some of this is related to learning at work, but not all of it. Education still seeks to promote learning for life and in aspects of life not connected with work and organisations.

Figure 1.1   *From past separate spheres to the present integrated L&D*

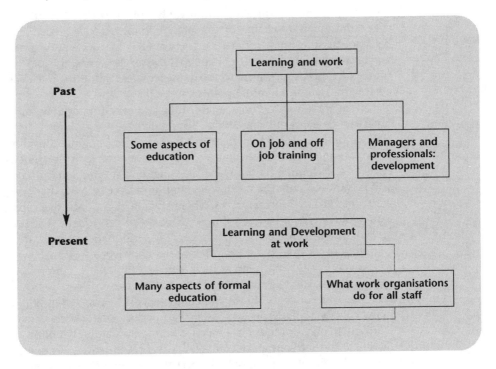

Finally, in the past, *development* was often differentiated from training and education but also related to both of them. Development was considered to be about the
change of the whole person, not just their knowledge or skills, in the course of their
experience and growth through a career and lifespan. In the work and organisation
'training' context, development was most often used to describe learning for managers
and professionals; employees were trained, managers and professionals were developed. Development had connotations of superior and more elaborate learning. More
recently, with personal development becoming relevant to all kinds of effective performance, not just that of managers and professionals, the concept of development
was also applied more broadly to learning for all employees.

These past definitions of education, training and development, with their essentially sequential division of learning, are no longer useful or acceptable. They would
be deemed to draw the boundaries around the subject, in theory and practice, too narrowly, and also inaccurately; they would not capture and deal with the practice and
theory of contemporary work and organisations (see Figure 1.1). Alternatives, such as
those offered by the idea of 'workforce development', need to combine and include
aspects of contemporary concern.

L&D at work is about more than the provision of training courses in workplaces.
The definition here is that L&D at work involves

processes of observation, planning, action and review to manage the cognitive capacities, capabilities and behaviours to enable and improve individual, team and organisational performance in work organisations.

The three dimensions of L&D

Effective performance in work and organisations is taken to require, to some degree, the establishment or change of a combination of cognitive capacities, capabilities and behaviours. All of these different aspects of L&D at work will be more fully discussed and explored in the following chapter, as their significance, use and relevance in identifying L&D needs, planning L&D experiences, and delivering and evaluating L&D are dealt with. Here some initial points can be made.

L&D at work involves both establishing and evolving *cognitive capacities*. Cognitive capacities range from being able to accumulate 'bodies of knowledge' through to the elaboration and use of analytical and higher order thinking. This dimension of L&D at work has previously been more commonly referred to as the dimension of 'knowledge'. But accumulating 'knowledge' is just one specific kind of cognitive capacity, and it is indeed only the most basic kind. It cannot be treated as being synonymous with what L&D at work involves, where a whole set of cognitive capacities are significant and relevant if people are to be 'thoughtful performers'. The brain is capable of far more than memorising knowledge, and performance at work involves aspects of cognition other than the use of memorised knowledge.

Capabilities are what people have and use to achieve performance in work and organisations. The two terms most commonly used in the past in this dimension of L&D were the concepts of skill and competence. The concept of skill, though, has too many connotations of physical aspects of performance, when much performance at work and in organisations now depends upon information handling and interpersonal qualities. And the concept of competence has been increasingly questioned as a useful and valid concept. The concern in L&D at work should be squarely with the kinds of capability required for and involved with employability, occupational realities and the contemporary organisation's effectiveness.

In the third dimension, here defined as *behaviours*, L&D at work involves establishing or changing patterns in the ways that people act so that desired and expected performance is achieved. The term 'behaviours' is favoured rather than 'abilities', which is often found in other tripartite taxonomies of learning to define this aspect of L&D at work. This is because the relevance of this third dimension of learning is to take into account the affective dimension of performance and L&D at work, with an analysis of attitudes, emotions and values. People behave in ways that make sense in the context of their individual backgrounds, what is involved in their work, and what is required in the organisation. These ways of acting may be consistent with performance expectations, or they may present an obstacle to achievement. Behaviours, how people actually act, can vary significantly despite the same levels and kinds of cognitive capacities and capabilities being present. That is because behaviours will be influenced by the emotions, values and attitudes that individuals experience in work settings and organisations. These influence actions, what people do in practice.

Performance management

While L&D at work, as it will be described here, involves a range of processes and practices and can be interpreted from a number of perspectives, these are all, in the work and organisation context, to be made sense of in the context of performance management. A definition of performance management (Armstrong 1994, p 397) is that it involves

Figure 1.2   *The performance management process*

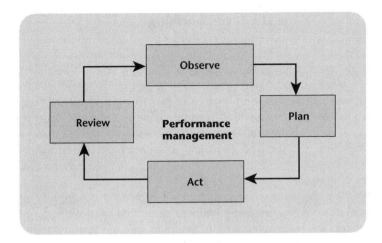

a means of getting better results from the organisation, teams and individuals by understanding and managing performance with an agreed framework of planned goals, objectives and standards.

L&D in work and organisations is one means to the ends of these goals, objectives and standards. These goals, objectives and standards can be seen to be established as the result of a process, a series of phases or steps. It is a process which involves the phases or steps of observation, planning, action and review (see Figure 1.2).

The L&D process

L&D at work can be modelled as a parallel process, following the basic phases and steps of observation, planning, action and review. Therefore the L&D process is defined as involving a set of observational, planning, action and review activities undertaken in a sequence. It involves observation through assessing L&D needs at work at various levels and in various ways. It involves planning through setting objectives for L&D interventions at work to achieve specific kinds of outcomes and results. It involves action in professionally delivering L&D at work using a range of methods and techniques. And it involves review, through evaluating L&D experiences and outcomes; from testing what learners have learned to assessing costs and benefits. It is this series of steps, this basic cycle (see Box 1.3), that will be referred to as the L&D process.

Because this view of process, with its association with a cycle analogy is illuminating in some ways, but limited and in some ways misleading, it has drawn criticism (Hallier and Butts 2000). These critiques usually make the point that the reality of L&D at work does not reflect the ideal model of the L&D process. In real organisations the notion that a smooth and logical accomplishment of steps and phases characterises L&D at work is untenable. The ideals of the L&D process are either not to be found or are not followed smoothly and logically. There seem to be two main problems that cause this. One is that each stage, and therefore the overall L&D process, is not properly dealt with. But to try to impose or enforce the ideals of the L&D process would be to introduce a bureaucratic template that would strangle rather that enable L&D at work. The other concern is that factors other than objective demands derived from performance management-validated

Box 1.3

The 'cycle' analogy

The analogy between the L&D process and a 'cycle' is worth reflecting on. The analogy is with the phases of natural cycles, such as the 'water cycle'. There is no strict beginning or end to such cycles, as each phase could be taken as a beginning or an end. From the human point of view, however, the water cycle is seen to begin with rain falling over the land, providing the fresh water needed for life. It proceeds with that water running off and into underground stores or flowing through streams to the sea. The sun acts to evaporate the sea water, which then forms clouds. These come over the land where they once again provide rain and fresh water. Completing one phase begins the next, and so on, until the initial stage is reached again; and then it happens all over again.

In L&D at work the cycle analogy is that each phase leads naturally and inevitably into the next, until the initial phase is reached and it happens all over again. Beginning with an observation of needs enables and leads into planning, which enables and leads into the provision of L&D, which leads into and enables evaluations, which returns the cycle to again identifying needs.

However natural cycles are driven by the impersonal and objective forces of the physical world; there is no choice involved, no deviations allowed. In work and organisations the L&D cycle is entirely driven by human forces. It is choice, not necessity, which drives the L&D cycle. As these choices are made so may the 'L&D cycle' deviate from completion, or cease altogether. It depends on the choices which emerge from and are part of the individuals', groups' and organisation's economic and social beliefs.

goals and standards determine what kinds of L&D at work occur; and who gets L&D. What actually happens in L&D is a matter of choice in conditions of uncertainty, influenced by power and politics rather than the objective application of an L&D process. Despite these reservations about the realities of L&D at work such a model of the L&D process serves to provide some boundaries within which the pieces that make up L&D at work can be placed and interrelated.

Human resource management

In some texts the term HRM is used to define a particular approach to the management of people at work, in contrast with other approaches such as conventional 'personnel management' or traditional systems of 'industrial relations' (Mabey *et al* 1998). The existence and significance of such variations in forms and philosophies of people management, and the extent to which there has or has not been a shift from previously dominant systems to new HRM systems, have attracted much debate and research. However, the term HRM is used here in a neutral sense, to mean the whole of people management, the combination of employee resourcing, employee relations, employee reward and L&D concerns in business and management that together constitute the field of HRM. L&D at work is always an aspect of the broader HRM of an organisation, not an isolated and stand alone activity. The strategies and policies organisations have for attracting and retaining staff, and the ways that stakeholders define their different and common interests at work, can have a great impact on what

L&D at work involves. The scope of this text is to consider the L&D process, the practices associated with it, and perspectives relevant to exploring in more detail the nature of L&D at work.

L&D IN CONTEXT

An increasing interest in effective L&D at work over recent years was, in general, an outcome of more positive analyses of the connections between L&D and effective organisations (Johnson *et al* 2000) rather than an outcome of an analysis which suggested that mistakes of the kind made by Thames Trains were too commonplace. Instead we were entering an era where adaptations to the onset of a 'learning society' and a 'knowledge economy' (Richardson and Unwin 2000, NACETT 1999, NACETT 2000) seemed to mark the way ahead for many organisations as requiring more effective L&D than in the past. Learning societies can be thought of as communities dependent on the lifelong learning of all their members, in contrast with industrial societies which only required most of the community to participate in basic education. Knowledge economies can be thought of as economies where wealth creation is dependent upon the creation and use of information, rather than on the manufacture of goods and provision of services. In this context L&D at work becomes more than a minor part of HRM, and is rather one of the more essential and critical tasks confronting Government and management.

This was a slow rise to prominence. A consensus that L&D at work was a 'good thing', an essential concern, has been manifest in exhortations to employers to invest in their people, and for Government to invest in new schemes and initiatives to improve workforce development, and for all individuals to embrace 'lifelong learning', in one form or another since the 1960s. But it was overshadowed by greater concerns. The 1970s were an era when industrial relations problems dominated social and economic thinking, and subsequently people management. The 1980s were dominated more by employee resourcing concerns, with changes in organisational and employment structures such as the rise of flexible firms, and the establishment of 'new deal' employment practices and policies. It was only in the 1990s that the importance of L&D gained the prominence it merited. The 1990s saw many employers embrace L&D, and be accredited as 'Investors in People' (IiP): it saw a host of Government schemes and initiatives launched whose goal was to improve workforce development for those in work and those preparing for work; and it did see many more people participating in learning, formally and informally, more or less continuously, as part of their lives.

The quantity and quality of L&D at work are now acknowledged as key factors in adapting to change; economic change, social change, organisational change and technological change. As the old traditional industries with their old forms of knowledge and skill base declined, new knowledge and skill bases had to be established, to enable job creation and growth. That required a great interest in L&D at work. In the context of dealing with unemployment, and aspirations to eliminating historical discrimination and inequalities, the foundations for the 'social inclusion' intent and concern with L&D at work were established. And as work organisations changed, from the standard bureaucracies with classic divisions of labour, to flatter structures for lean, world class manufacturing or service delivery, so a new agenda for L&D at work was needed, as a means of effecting such change and as a consequence of it. Finally, but not least, as new technologies, most prominently information technologies, were invented and adopted, so a whole range of other changes to organisations and jobs required new L&D at work.

This convergence of various forces leading to a critical role for L&D at work shows no signs of abating. There are rather signs that the importance of L&D at work is still increasing, and that L&D at work in the future will be even more important than it has been. From being overshadowed it has now come centre stage, and looks like staying there. The proponents of the era of the learning society, of knowledge economies, of flexible organisations and careers, and the developers of new technologies all concur that the future will see greater demands being made upon employers, governments and individuals to participate in and improve L&D at work. It is in this context that L&D at work can claim to be a significant and challenging aspect of the future of HRM, much more than in its past where its status was one where L&D at work was of concern only to specialist trainers who had to learn 'how to train' people.

In an era that is characterised by the volatility of change to being a learning society and a knowledge economy, there is of course a logic to this. Effective L&D at work promises to provide the levers that can be manipulated so that the future of work and organisation can be controlled to assure individual career and success and competitiveness for those currently prosperous, and a route to prosperity for those currently struggling to 'get by' or 'going nowhere'. L&D at work seems to offer the ultimate win-win outcomes for everyone.

And that, of course, sounds all too good to be true. Certainly there are rival perceptions of both the actual state of L&D at work, and its potential to realise these hopes and aspirations. Establishing the truth, a more balanced view, requires an analysis of L&D at work that delves into related fields, arguments and issues. It will involve looking at what the human sciences have to offer, what the problems of L&D strategies in organisations are, how National Vocational Education and Training (NVET) policy is important, what the potential of information and communication technologies (ICT) is, and the theory and practice of 'knowledge management'.

PRACTICAL MATTERS

The context then is one emphasising the value and significance of L&D at work. The evidence about, and facts of, L&D at work need to be explored as well. The areas in practice where L&D themes and concerns are encountered in work and organisations can be analysed. Table 1.1 provides data on the main subjects of L&D in work organisations. Individual and organisational performance, it appears from these snapshots, involve managing cognition, capabilities and behaviours in a range of areas: from health and safety, through customer care, to technical training in new processes or services.

These are the practical frontiers where the rhetoric of lifelong learning is being explored. L&D interventions on these matters are typically managed by the design and delivery of L&D using a range of methods. Table 1.2 gives an overview of these. There are a range of options available, though some clearly dominate and others are less frequently used. 'On the job' training is defined here as training given at the desk or place where the person usually works. Both surveys show this is an important method of L&D at work. 'Off the job' training is defined as training away from the immediate work position, at the employer's premises or elsewhere, including all forms of courses as long as they are funded or arranged by the employer. The Learning and

Table 1.1   *L&D provision by subject in active organisations*

Industrial Society survey	%	LTW survey	%
Health and safety	68	Information technology	45
Communication skills	61	Managing own development	42
Customer care	53	Working with others	40
Teamworking	53	Communication	35
Computer/IT	47	Problem solving	32
Quality	44	Application of number	20
Product knowledge	38	Basic numeracy	10
Equal opportunities	34	Basic literacy	10
Legal/regulatory	15		
Technical	17		
Management of people	13		
Business/finance	14		
Leadership	6		

Sources: Industrial Society (1998); DfEE (2000)

Table 1.2   *L&D techniques in organisations*

CIPD survey (of regularly used methods)	%	LTW survey	%
On job training (OJT)	87.3	On the job only	35
Face to face (training facility)	84.3	Off the job only	10
Coaching/mentoring	59.4	Both on and off job	31
Formal education	49.6	Neither	24
Conferences	43.4		
Non electronic open learning	34.7		
CD-ROM	28.9		
Video	26.1		
Intranet	23.7		
Other computer	22.7		
Action learning	14.7		
Internet	16.5		
Audio based	8.4		
Extranets	7.4		

Sources: CIPD (2001); DfEE (2000)

Training at Work survey (DfEE 2000) suggests that this method of L&D at work is less dominant, though the CIPD (2001) survey suggests that most of the organisations they surveyed are using a variety of off the job L&D methods. The design of L&D then seems to include and involve the use of these methods.

Looking at L&D delivery, at the typical structure of off the job training experiences within and outside the organisation, Table 1.3 shows that L&D at work is dominated by the delivery of short courses, of 1–3 days duration. Where organisations make use of external delivery and 'off the job' L&D interventions it is clear that most also use 1–3 day courses (Table 1.4), while some use a variety of other modes of delivery. These then are the basic and most frequently used means of delivery.

This overview of survey data suggests that L&D at work in organisations typically involves five major kinds of practice. Their management is the key to developing effective performers in work and organisations. These major methods are:

■ [on] the job' learning experiences at the workplace
■ being on an organisation-managed short training course
■ attending a short external course or learning event
■ using information and communication technologies (ICT) systems; computer based or learning in a 'learning centre'
■ being involved in a 'learning partnership', like mentoring

Table 1.3   *Length of training courses received by employees in employment*

Length	% of learning experiences
1 day	21
2–3 days	15
4 days–2 weeks	8
2 weeks–6 moths	9
6 months–3 years	19
3 years or more	11
Ongoing	17
Total	100

N = 1529
Source: DfEE (1995)

Table 1.4   *Training approaches used regularly for external training*

Approach	%
2- to 3-day courses	82
Up to 1 day courses	79
Day release	69
Residential training	63
Evening classes	55
Distance/open learning	42
Computer-based learning	24
Outdoor training	24
Coaching/mentoring	12
Video based learning	9
Learning resource centres	6
Action learning sets	7

Source: Industrial Society (1998)

Exercise 1.1   The L&D process and typical practices

Read the cameos of good and bad experiences in Boxes 1.4 and 1.5. Describe and analyse what makes the good effective and the bad ineffective, using the four phases of the L&D process:

■ identifying real needs
■ planning and designing L&D
■ professional delivery
■ effective evaluation

> ## Box 1.4
>
> ## Some good L&D experiences
>
> John cited a total customer satisfaction (TCS) course as being effective. This was a company wide course that used well trained facilitators. A lot of thought was put into the course environment and room layout. There was good use of different media, and a blend of thinking and doing. There were many group exercises involving team working. There was even an after course reception dinner, and follow up involving developing and swapping action plans.
>
> Paul experienced an induction process when moving from one retailer to another, where one of his new key objectives was to understand the store financial report. He arranged a one to one meeting with his line manager, who explained it step by step, line by line. He could relate this to what he knew from his previous experience, and understand the new to him method of reporting financial information. He could get immediate clarification of any questions from an experienced person.
>
> Chris described learning how to do the 'store walk' as a manager in a supermarket. This was an experience with his store manager, who did this every day. He explained the benefits of doing this store walk daily; for Chris's own awareness, staff awareness and ultimately to benefit the customers. The walk was structured at a good pace, and he summarised each stage and referred to relevant issues. The manager got Chris's input by asking 'what if' questions. Chris was encouraged to take notes and afterwards he was asked to communicate these to the manager, and the manager clarified issues Chris had misunderstood. On the next occasion Chris had to lead the store walk, with the manager asking him questions.
>
> Jill talked about the importance of relationships. As someone thinking about aspiring to promotion she had an opportunity to shadow a senior manager on the job for two days, who was also female. She was prepared to discuss, almost like 'mentoring', general issues rather than just go through the tasks. She was very self aware and was able to highlight 'good' and 'bad' characteristics of her own management style which Jill found very useful and informative. It also dispelled some of the fear that Jill had about aspiring to promotion.
>
> Simon had the near universal experience; learning to serve food in a restaurant and work behind a bar for the first time as a student was effective. He had no experience of either, and was thrown in at the deep end, getting coaching from other members of staff. The best way to learn was actually to do the tasks in the real environment. It was stressful, but he felt that he could learn at a faster pace this way.

Figure 1.3 organises the points you might have identified from the cameos outlined in Boxes 1.4 and 1.5 in relation to the phases of the L&D process discussed earlier: assessing needs, planning events, professional delivery, and effective evaluation. Strengths and weaknesses are not confined to one type of L&D at work. They are equally spread over all kinds of L&D: in house courses, external courses, on the job, using ICT, or self managed learning in specific partnerships. Why are some experiences effective and positive, while others are clearly ineffective and negative? In essence it seems that the L&D process has not been managed in some or all of its phases where L&D is poor, and it has been followed in most or all phases where L&D is good. Understanding the strengths and overcoming the problems encountered in these typical L&D practices, the challenge of being able to duplicate effective L&D and

---

Box 1.5

Some bad L&D experiences

For Fiona an ineffective learning experience was an evening course she enrolled on to learn typing. She was at university at the time and did not have either the motivation or the time to complete the course. She was not really interested in the subject, although she could see benefit in knowing how to type. She paid for the whole 12 week course, but lasted only three weeks.

For John an in-organisation course was poor. The materials used were out of date, and there was only one facilitator delivering the course with a limited style. The pre-course objectives were unclear, and there was not a mix of thinking and doing on the course. There was no time for delegates on the course to mix, and the facilities were cramped and uncomfortable. There was limited connection to his work role, and no follow up after the workshops.

For Jim an ineffective course was one with a senior manager delivering a course on a specific topic relevant to his job as a senior civil servant: 'drafting for ministers'. The course had been promised for a number of years, but was delayed time and again. This constant delay meant that training on the topic became a source of ridicule, which was vented against the senior manager who eventually gave the course because of his behaviour. He was late for the course at the start, ill prepared, and allowed himself to be interrupted by phone calls during the course, and he delivered confusing information. He constantly 'lost the thread' resulting in attendees feeling they had learned nothing. The delayed course had been worse than no course at all.

For Lorraine attending a one day course (in house) on basic employment law, delivered by an employment lawyer, was ineffective. The course content was devised in house but was aimed at managers with no HR background, so she found the course to be of little use as an HR experienced person. She learned very little as the course was not for someone with her experience.

For Paul an ineffective experience was when his company got a new computer system. A course was given on using this. A lot of information was rushed or missed as the trainer felt the trainees ought to know it anyway. The trainer was unfamiliar with the materials, and jumped about from subject to subject. The trainees felt they could not ask questions as there was no time, and because of a fear of looking stupid. It left them with no confidence at all about using the system, and having no faith in the trainer.

For Simon ineffective learning was in the use of the front of house computer system. This was learned on the job, with reference to a training manual. He learned how to do each task, but often not until he had made a mistake; and then had to phone a very expensive helpline to fix it. A few hours with someone trained in the system would have helped him to learn the basics.

---

avoid ineffective L&D to improve individual and organisational performance, requires a broader and deeper analysis of the L&D process as a whole.

CONCLUSION

The Ladbroke Grove case illustrates the fact that making mistakes with L&D at work can have dreadful consequences. There is a responsibility to assure that 'sort of making

Figure 1.3   *Perceptions of L&D interventions: summary of effective and ineffective experiences*

In house training courses

Effective

Have clear structure and objectives
Are relevant to the employees in the organisation
Have well prepared and informed trainers
Are effectively delivered
Use learner participation and a mix of learning methods
Include action planning and follow up
Have clear value back in the workplace
Learners develop a rapport with the trainer

Ineffective

Too much information on a brief course
Great differences in ability among the participants
On-site interruptions distract from learning
Poor design and or inappropriate timescales
Materials in use are well out of date
Trainers are not properly prepared

Learning partnerships

Effective

Doing it in own time; flexible
Self motivated and rewarding
Widens knowledge base
Increases confidence
Onus on self
Control over own career development
Preferred learning style

Ineffective

Maintaining self motivation
Doing it in own time if it is for work
Having unclear or ill defined outcomes in mind
Measurement/comparability

On the job

Effective

The benefit of others' experience
Is a relaxed and informal setting
The characteristics of the situation are real
'Trainers' have an interest to help learners
Happens in a supportive environment
Customise to individual learning concerns

Ineffective

Trainers' inaccurate perceptions of learners
Training readiness of the trainee
Poor communication between these
Threatening; getting it wrong

External training events

Have clear objectives to be achieved
Have realistic timescales for the training
Give a good balance of theory and practice
Provide feedback and learning reinforcement
Are interesting, useful, relevant, realistic, enjoyable

Gap in identifying need and delivery
Lack of opportunity to consolidate learning
Proof of 'learning' is a test of short term memory
Compulsory; doing training for training's sake
Workload at work still waiting to be done

ICT

Going at own pace
Freedom to make mistakes
Applied to work-frequent practice
Specially suited to own needs/competence

Haste/time constraints
Poorly targeted on training needs
Not applicable
Lack of motivation

the best of it really' is never accepted as an attitude or allowed to influence practice. Yet Thames Trains as an organisation is by no means unique; the factors that contributed to Michael Hodder being ineffectively trained exist, either evidently or not far under the surface if it is scratched, in many places at many times. Had the L&D process in Thames Trains been better managed, with better needs identification, design, delivery and evaluation, could the Ladbroke Grove disaster have been prevented? Of course there were other factors, regarding the technical systems in use, management problems more generally, and the structure of the whole industry. Better L&D at work, the effective use of people performance management, could not offset those. Effective L&D is not a substitute for the right work systems or effective performance management as a whole. But a proper concern for professional L&D at work can often bring to light, before it is too late, problems with the performance that is required for an effective organisation.

The equation of investment in L&D with effective performance, not just in theory but evidently in practice, should secure the relevance and importance of L&D. This is the consensus, though the evidence is that for individuals, organisations and governments it is still debated whether, and how much, L&D brings advantage. Commitment to L&D has to be argued for, not asserted. Even then, commitment is not enough. That this is an integral part of effective business and management is a conclusion that few reading this text are likely to take serious issue with. Providing effective L&D, getting it right, is what matters. The next problem though is that, even though effective L&D is a necessary element of success, it is not in itself a sufficient precondition of effective performance or success (see Box 1.6).

The argument that is threaded through this text is that L&D at work has to be analysed in the context of performance management, and that the L&D process runs parallel to that. Where the L&D process is well managed, through the major forms of L&D in practice, performance management will be an integral part of dealing with threats and opportunities, building on strengths and overcoming weaknesses. Then the promised returns of L&D at work (boxes 1.7, 1.8 and 1.9) can be realised.

Box 1.6

Motorola at Bathgate

Motorola is a US based major multinational manufacturer of, among other things, mobile phones. It established a large plant at Bathgate in Scotland, which at its peak was employing around 3000 people manufacturing mobile phones. Consistent with its reputation as a leading innovator and employer of excellence, Motorola invested heavily in training and development, with some of the best systems, facilities and training professionals in the UK. The Bathgate plant was very successful, consistently being more productive than other European plants. When economic troubles hit the electronics and telecoms sectors in 2001 the company had to review its operations. The company accepted that the plant at Bathgate was efficient, with a loyal and skilled workforce. But it elected to close it in favour of retaining European production at a plant in Germany. Despite being a model skilled workforce other factors entered the equation, and the net result was closure of the whole plant, the largest single job loss in the area since the decline of traditional manufacturing industries some decades earlier.

Box 1.7

Learning pays for individuals
Who wants to be a millionaire?

It has been estimated that the difference in earnings, over a lifetime, between a person with low level qualifications and one with high level qualifications is over £500,000. So, while a broad general knowledge might make you a millionaire by answering 15 questions on a game show, it's actually more likely that getting specific knowledge and skills and qualifications will make as big a difference, if not quite so suddenly.

Box 1.8

Learning pays for companies

A study of the benefits of learning for companies was equally stark. This suggests that organisations deemed to be effective in employee development, by which is meant those that are accredited as Investors in People (IiP), make significant gains on all key performance indicators.

	Average company	IiP accredited company	Gain
RRC	9.21%	16.27%	77%
Pre tax profit margins	2.54%	6.91%	172%
Average salary	£12,590	£14,195	13%
Turnover/sales per employee	£64,912	£86,625	33%
Profit per employee	£1815	£3198	76%

Source: NACET (1999)

Box 1.9

Learning pays for countries

Governments throughout the world seek to support knowledge and skills development to adapt to economic change and pursue social policy goals. Employee development has become a key lever for this. In the UK the current goal is to achieve a highly skilled, inclusive economy to grasp the opportunities of a 'new learning age'. The 'power of learning' is the key to prosperity and 'the workplace must become a faculty of learning and personal development' (DfEE 2001b, p 15). To pursue this now involves a web of agencies, policies and partnerships with common goals to improve learning and skills among students, the unemployed, and most critically organisations small, medium and large in all sectors, 'new' and 'old'.

Source: DfEE (2001b)

CONCLUDING CASE STUDY

Driver training in Thames Trains

Introduction

The framework case for this chapter described how a train driver, Michael Hodder, passed a signal at red, leading to an accident with many fatalities and injuries at Ladbroke Grove. As a result of this an inquiry was set up. The material provided here is based on Chapter 9 of Cullen's (2001) report on this inquiry. In that chapter Cullen examined evidence about the adequacy and the performance of the systems within Thames Trains for driver training and management. The case is structured with the following sections:

- Background to driver L&D in Thames Trains
- A warning and response: the Royal Oak accident
- Communications
- Route knowledge
- Associated matters
- 'No blame' culture
- Human factors

Case instructions

You should read and analyse the case material with the following questions in view, also bearing in mind the ideas and concerns raised in the first chapter about performance management and the core L&D process: observing, planning, acting, reviewing.

1 In what ways was L&D inadequate?
2 What should be done to improve L&D in the organisation in the future?

Background to driver L&D in Thames Trains

In the days of British Rail, before privatisation, a trainee driver usually came from within the established workforce, and brought with him or her a basic knowledge of the railway system developed from experience. They were given a period of a year or so to travel with, and learn from, a qualified and experienced driver. The trainee then progressed through a training process, known latterly as 'Driver 2000'.

Initially in Thames Trains drivers were trained according to the existing British Rail Driver 2000 syllabus, but changes, reducing the amount of training, were made to this by the company. This was done to reflect the fact that Thames Trains had only one type of locomotive, and no freight operations. An internal investigation into the company's driver training, conducted by the parent company of Thames Trains, the Go-Ahead Group, discovered that much of the early documentation on how and why the training had been changed could not be found. The evidence before the inquiry did not yield a clear account of the development of the L&D process as a whole through these changes.

The system of L&D at work was that driver training and driver management within Thames Trains were carried out by 'driver standards managers', who in turn reported to a senior driver standards manager. They in turn reported to the operations manager at Thames Trains headquarters. Each driver standards manager was meant to lead approximately 35 drivers, and he or she was the key person responsible for ensuring that drivers kept their equipment, documentation, traction knowledge and route knowledge up to date. However, in practice, due to a shortage and a high turnover of driver standards managers, they shared their duties amongst the workforce of the depots as matters arose. The system in training was described by Mr Chilton, Thames Trains' operations manager, as 'driver standards managers conducting their own classes as they thought best, based loosely on what had been the practice in British Rail days'.

Mr Cox, a driver standards manager who taught Mr Hodder traction, said that he was given no structure to the course. 'One didn't exist, to my knowledge . . . I was given four weeks and told to teach them how a Turbo works and how to get by when things go wrong, faults and failures'. This section of the training was not validated. Mr Lyford, a senior driver standards manager, described how he taught rules and regulations. He himself was responsible for allocating to each of the six weeks the particular subjects available for this element of training. It was a matter for him, based on his own discretion: 'It was also based very much on my own experience and what was considered previously to have been best practice amongst colleagues'. Again this material was not validated.

The L&D process continued to evolve, with the driver trainers using their own initiative to modify existing practices in the light of the needs as they saw them. This undoubtedly left some gaps in the training. The most obvious lacuna of which the inquiry heard was the fact that driver instructor Adams did not recognise it as part of his job to teach route knowledge in and out of Paddington. He said, 'This is Paddington and sort of make the best of it really'. This contrasted with the evidence of Mr Chilton who said that route knowledge was an integral part of train handling training.

The fact that this confusion existed in the training team as to what should or should not be taught to trainee drivers, combined with the specific admission of failures in the system as accepted by Mr Worrall, director and general manager, and the lack of a validation process, led Cullen to conclude that the safety culture in regard to driver training was slack and less than adequate.

At a meeting on 20 August 1996 an HMRI inspector told the company that he 'was very concerned about driver training', and believed that Thames Trains could be prosecuted if an incident occurred where driver error was partly to blame. He said his concern extended towards driver leaders, who were too young or too inexperienced to deal with at risk drivers.

Mr Baird, a driver standards manager at Thames Trains between 1997 and January 1999, described to the inquiry how he was asked by his line manager to redesign the driver training scheme with a view to modifying the inherited Driver 2000 programme to make it more specific to Thames Trains' operations. But there was little communication between Mr Baird and Mr Chilton when the latter took over as operations manager in February 1999. Mr Chilton was unaware of much of Mr Baird's work on training. He was not aware of Thames Trains' previous poor performance, or of the details in two memoranda, of 17 December 1998 and 19 January 1999, which described driver performance problems and proposed a course of remedial action. This shows a lack of 'corporate memory'.

A factor which may have affected the quality of driver training could have been the strain of the speed and scale of the recruitment in 1998 and 1999. Mr Dunglinson, human resources director of Thames Trains, said in evidence that over 80 employees were recruited and trained in 1999, out of a total complement which rose to 259 drivers.

CONCLUDING CASE STUDY (cont'd)

A warning and response: the Royal Oak accident

In an accident at Royal Oak on 10 November 1995 a Thames Trains driver passed Signal SN74 at danger, an incident termed a 'signal passed at danger' (SPAD). The formal inquiry into this incident made 14 recommendations, all of which were accepted by the industry Safety Review Group on 20 March 1996. Three of these recommendations were directed to train operating companies (TOCs) such as Thames Trains and related to the subject of driver management and training. The response by Thames Trains to the recommendations on driver management and training was described to the inquiry by Mr Franks, who was production director of Thames Trains from May 1996 for two and a half years and responsible for operational safety. He described how weekly team meetings, monthly safety meetings and the production of a video and posters were used to educate drivers. The inquiry was also told of information prepared by Thames Trains about SPADs, such as a defensive driving pack in June 1996, and their 'SPAD strategy'.

Mr Franks undoubtedly had some success with these programmes. The inquiry was told of a 70% improvement in SPAD performance between June 1996 and June 1998. However, more could and should have been done to organise driver training and management in a systematic manner.

Mr Worrall, who joined Thames Trains in May 1999 after having previously worked with them as a consultant (employed by Halcrow) from November 1998, said he asked Mr Chilton (operations manager) to prioritise driver issues, to examine staffing levels and to ensure that competencies matched needs. As a result he increased the number of senior driver standards managers and driver standards managers.

He commissioned the company Halcrow to examine driver training practices. He received their report on the 'Validation of driver training process' in May 1999. It confirmed that the SPAD problem still needed to be managed and that the driver training program had still not been validated. Halcrow also pointed out that the training system did not meet a Railway Group Standard, GO/RT 3251.

The company addressed the poor SPAD performance, and in a SPAD review in August 1999 Mr Waters of Halcrow discussed SPAD management. He said: 'It is evident from the review the company is currently focusing considerable attention and resources on this subject in an attempt to reduce and mitigate the consequences of such incidents. The review has not identified any single area of significant concern'.

The inquiry also heard how the number of driver standards managers had been increased from seven to nine at each of the three train driver depots, and that an operations manager had been added in May 1999 to match the increase in the driver establishment and to cover the increased workload in training, assessing and monitoring the new drivers. However, despite these efforts driver Hodder and driver instructor Adams had not been made aware of the SPAD history of SN109.

The inquiry was told of the inadequacy of driver Hodder's training in regard to route knowledge and briefing on signals at which multi-SPADs had occurred. These failures to implement fully the Royal Oak recommendations were acknowledged by Mr Worrall.

Communications

Cullen dealt with the question of 'corporate memory' in Thames Trains. This might also be thought of in terms of how well communications flowed within the company, and how well these communications were recorded and, in particular, understood. The inquiry heard a number of examples of how poor communications had hindered good performance on driver training.

At senior management level, for example, the inquiry heard evidence from Mr Worrall about how in March 1999 he had attempted to investigate what had prompted a driver restructuring initiative. 'I expected to find that there would have been some evidence as to what had prompted the project . . . I found no such evidence'. Mr Worrall said that until November 1999 he was not aware of a video which had been produced in 1996 to show the driver's cab view of the approach to Paddington. Neither he nor anyone else could find a copy of the video or evidence that it had been used.

In another example of poor communications at driver level Cullen heard how the one day SPAD avoidance and awareness training had not been given to the current group of drivers in training.

A report to the board of the parent company for Thames Trains, the Go-Ahead Group, in November 1999, following the investigation of Thames Trains' management processes, found that 'records are vague'. Mr Baird, who devised the revised driver training package, said that whilst he was aware of the video for driver training which had been produced in 1996 and recommended its use, he had never actually seen it. When Mr Chilton took over he did not meet him or give him a formal handover. Mr Chilton said: 'When I arrived . . . I could not put my finger on what was happening'.

With regard to drivers and signallers, there appeared to be little or no formal communication or joint training between signallers and drivers.

The inquiry heard evidence about the system of team briefings within Thames Trains, whereby each driver received a written brief every four weeks covering operational matters and local issues. This written briefing process was reinforced by a rostered face to face meeting between the drivers and a driver standards manager. These meetings were held every eight weeks and it was expected that no driver would miss more than two consecutive briefings.

Route knowledge

Route knowledge is an important part of a driver's training. It was admitted by Mr Worrall that Thames Trains' training, which failed to ensure that Mr Hodder's route learning assessment questions specifically covered the area between Paddington and Ladbroke Grove, was inadequate.

Mr Chilton told the inquiry of the methodology that Thames Trains employed in teaching route knowledge. He explained that there was no formal system. Drivers learned by driving the route with qualified instructors and drivers. The company did not provide route maps to help drivers learn this aspect of their job, or require drivers to prepare maps themselves, although there was evidence that some drivers did this on their own initiative, and on occasions shared the maps informally with each other.

Mr Chilton explained that a key part of the teaching process was an ad hoc questioning process between the driver standards managers and the trainees, but drivers were given no specific information on difficult aspects of the route (which would include, for example, multi-SPAD signals). Mr Winkworth, a driver assessor for Thames Trains, described the process which he used to test a driver's route knowledge. He asked verbal questions relating to the route and then filled out a route assessment card. Drivers were advised in advance of some 80% of the questions to be asked, and of the correct answers to these questions. The remainder were asked spontaneously and without warning. Mr Winkworth explained that most drivers answered all of the questions correctly, and he had never found that a driver failed this part of the test. He said that there was no set pass mark given as a guide by management, but he never had any doubt in his mind as to what was a satisfactory pass performance.

Mr Adams, who was largely responsible for the training of driver Hodder, said that he did not consider the teaching of route learning to be part of his job. He explained that he taught drivers to drive from signal to signal. It was apparent that Mr Chilton was unaware of this gap in the teaching process until the day he gave evidence. He said that it was his belief that driver instructors were carrying out route training as part of the training in practical handling.

Professor Groeger gave evidence about such training practices. He said that a lack of objective standards made it impossible to validate the assessment process. He was concerned that no specific criterion was being used by the examiners to determine whether a driver had competently handled a situation. He was also concerned about the lack of definition as to how frequently a driver should have to perform a task appropriately before being assessed as competent. He also stressed the need to define very specifically a level of deviation which was to be tolerated.

Associated matters

Defensive driving

In guidance produced by Railtrack and the train operating companies (TOCs) in November 1999, defensive driving was described as being about thinking ahead: 'Know what you are driving; where you are driving; how you are driving; and how you are braking'. It was also about reading conditions, knowing black spots and multi-SPAD signals, not taking chances by anticipating signals or other actions, stopping well short of signals or obstructions, and 'killing' speed to maintain total control.

The inquiry heard from Mr Adams that he instructed his pupils in the principles of defensive driving. The inquiry was also shown excellent training material used by Thames Trains to promote the principles of defensive driving. Driver instructors said that they did in fact use this material. Drivers were given, for example, appropriate instructions in training material about the effect of sunlight. If a driver was unsure of the aspect of a signal because of sunlight, the advice was clear – stop and ask the signaller: 'Do not take a chance'. The inquiry heard from Mr Adams that he gave these instructions clearly to driver Hodder.

Driver licensing

The inquiry heard a considerable body of evidence regarding the training and certifying of drivers. According to guidelines issued in December 1999 drivers must be tested on the Rule Book, on traction knowledge and route knowledge. They must also be trained in defensive driving techniques, addressing as a minimum potential hazards arising from cautionary and stop signals, weather and environmental conditions, approaching stations, buffer stops and other rail vehicles, and the failure or isolation of warning or protective systems. TOCs are also required under this Group Standard, at a frequency determined by the individual TOC, to review the effectiveness of the systems in place to deliver this level of competence.

The Association of Train Operating Companies (ATOC) is carrying out a study on driver licensing which has indicated the scope for some central licensing, for example on the testing on the

Rule Book and other areas of common interest. This process would have the benefit of being open to independent verification against the national standard, and might provide some cost benefits and improve the efficiency of the training.

The inquiry was also informed that ATOC had retained Halcrow to review driver training. Recommendations from this review are to be incorporated into guidelines which the Railway Safety and Standards Directorate will issue as codes of practice. Standards relating to driver competence and training are being developed, with particular attention to safety briefings and defensive driving techniques. It is understood that after the Ladbroke Grove crash every TOC carried out detailed briefing of drivers on multi-SPAD signals. Railtrack has now issued guidelines to ATOC about driver training and has provided a CD-ROM to assist in the briefing of drivers about SPADs, and the Safety and Standards Directorate is to ensure that driver training is covered in future audits of every TOC.

The use of simulators

Simulators are extensively used for the training of airline pilots, and in many countries for that of train drivers. However, only limited use appears to have been made of them in the UK railway system in recent years. Mr Worrall's attention was drawn to page 139 of the Thames Trains drivers' manual, which stated that: 'particular attention should be applied to rules, infrequently applied emergency skills and procedures . . .'. Mr Worrall agreed that simulators would be an appropriate way to address this requirement and indicated that Thames Trains would be proceeding with their use. The inquiry also heard from Mr Carroll, managing director of First Great Western, that his company agreed with the use of simulators and that their introduction would be progressed.

'No blame' culture

The Health and Safety Executive (HSE) has for many years encouraged a 'no blame culture' within the rail industry, as elsewhere, in an endeavor to ensure that all incidents, including near misses, are reported so that they can be investigated thoroughly without concern about punishment or criticism. Mr Worrall said that a no blame culture had been developing on the railways since the late 1980s, aimed at encouraging employees to report all incidents so that they could be properly investigated. He said that this had been supported and developed by Mr Franks at Thames Trains and that he himself had continued with it. He stressed that it was not only for drivers but applied to all staff.

Mr Worrall referred to the review by Mr Waters of Halcrow in October 1998, which analysed reports of the nine SPADs that had occurred with Thames Trains between 18 March and 11 October 1998. Eight of the nine instances had been classified after investigation at the time as having been caused by 'driver distraction'.

There is a potential drawback in a 'no blame' culture. The inquiry heard evidence that to most drivers a SPAD is a traumatic incident and that there is a possibility that they accept blame in order to conclude the investigation as quickly as possible. This belief is reinforced by the fact that 85% of SPADs are reported as 'driver error'. In an examination of the SPAD investigation process, Mr Waters questioned whether the SPAD investigators were getting to the root cause of the incidents. He said: 'Basic and underlying causes need to be identified and recommendations [made] more meaningful . . .'

CONCLUDING CASE STUDY (cont'd)

The inquiry heard from Dr Lucas of the HSE of her interpretation of an acceptable no blame culture. Rather than a blanket assertion of no blame, she preferred the phrase 'justifiable blame'. She made the point that if someone had broken a serious rule they should not be able 'to get away with it'. This is an important point: people must be accountable for their actions. I agree with this, and commend to the industry the development of a culture in which information is communicated without fear of recrimination and blame is attached only where this is justified.

A confidential reporting system is now in place across the industry. This allows employees to report safety-related incidents confidentially. This enables 'near miss' incidents to be reported and receive attention. It also enables incidents to be categorised by type and location, and trends to be measured.

Human factors

Human factors can be thought of as the interplay between the operator, the machinery and the working environment. Professor Groeger gave evidence of his concerns about the appreciation of the human factors in driver training and performance.

Considering the human factor of memory, he referred to a comment made by Mr Chilton that training requirements dictate that there should remain a great deal of discretion and flexibility in the way training is conducted. Professor Groeger's concern was that this flexibility might involve the risk that a driver might not be trained in how to perform in particular circumstances. He went on to question the criteria used during the testing of trainee drivers, and especially how frequently a driver had to perform an operation successfully before he or she could be considered competent.

The inquiry also heard from Professor Moray about how visual attention is distributed amongst a number of tasks which have to be performed at the same time. He explained, for example, how drivers must at the same time look out for signals, monitor their speed, observe the track, look for speed restrictions and look at their documentation. Using a well established statistical analytical technique, and assuming drivers could switch their visual attention every second, he said that on about half of the occasions they were carrying out these tasks they would return to any point of observation in about four seconds, and that on a quarter of the occasions more than seven and a half seconds would elapse. He also pointed out that since these times were averages, on occasions the time interval could be considerably longer.

Under these conditions there was a possibility that a driver's attention would be elsewhere when a significant event occurred. He suggested that it was important, therefore, during training, to give drivers instruction on how to assess priorities in complex situations. He also stated that to ensure that a driver would always stop at a red signal, and considering the many human factors involved, the driver should be given technical assistance by automatic braking devices.

Case study points

In what ways was the training inadequate?

There was no formal system for learning routes, a crucial part of the knowledge needed for the job. There were not even maps of routes, though staff developed their own. Learning about routes was through an ad hoc questioning process. The company did apparently test knowledge; but trainees were told the questions beforehand and given the answers.

There was a shortage and high turnover of trainers and driving standards managers. They were young and inexperienced, and expected to conduct their own classes as they thought best. This led to no clear job description for trainers and gaps in the training. There was poor record keeping and communication.

Some training was good, for example on defensive driving. Materials were prepared and systems were in place. But, for example, no one could find the training video that had been made, or evidence that it had been used.

Evaluations were either not done properly or their lessons were not implemented. There was a lack of corporate memory.

All these factors combined meant that, despite plenty of concerns about the training process, and attention given to it, it failed in providing effective training for Hodder. There were clearly also problems with management development and training, not just driver training.

What should be done to improve training in the organisation?

Cullen made several recommendations:

Examples of poor communication and poor record keeping are of considerable concern. It is essential that an organisation has a system to record what it has learnt, and a process to pass those lessons on to its employees. This is especially the case in a period of considerable business expansion and staff changeover, such as Thames Trains was experiencing. The need is for an effective corporate memory.

Joint training for drivers and signalers; this is a major concern as they have to cooperate closely. Cullen supported the suggestion that has been made that signallers and drivers should jointly attend away days and other training processes to develop their mutual understanding.

Team briefs; a driver should have a face to face meeting with his or her driver standards manager at least monthly, if not more often, and safety should be the first item on the agenda of these meetings. Thames Trains should ensure that it adheres to this frequency.

Defining trainers' responsibilities; there was a significant problem in the management processes for setting out the job descriptions appropriate to the trainers in Thames Trains.

Assessment criteria; there were concerns with regard to the need for specific, relevant and validated criteria for testing trainee drivers. Thames Trains and other TOCs should ensure that these are adequately covered by their driver training and testing programmes. Drivers should be tested against these criteria, and a definite pass standard should be established. Consideration should be given to how often drivers should repeat key steps in their training before submitting themselves for testing.

Licensing reviews should be conducted at least once every three years, and the TOCs should retest the driver against the revised systems at the same frequency.

While a confidential accident reporting system has great merit, it was to be hoped that in the longer term the culture of the industry would be such as to make confidential reporting unnecessary. That situation may be a long time in coming to pass in the industry. In the meantime it is essential to support and encourage the further use of the confidential reporting system.

Further research should be carried out to develop the understanding of human factors as they are related to train driving. This should take into account the view that 'most of us, whatever walk of life we are in, would be uneasy if we were expected to perform at our absolute maximum on every single occasion'.

In sum, these recommendations provide clear action points:

CONCLUDING CASE STUDY (cont'd)

Needs

- Modify the 'no blame' culture; this requires a change in attitudes and values
- Analyse information from confidential reports on accidents
- Research human factors studies to set standards for driving training and guidance

Planning

- Training should be handled more systematically
- Have better communication about who does what

Design

- Improve and validate the assessment of drivers
- Issue codes of practice
- Consider the use of technologies, such as simulators

Review

- Keep records and evaluate training properly
- Implement continuous improvement systems for ongoing training

These were the main ways in which Cullen concluded that the industry could redouble its efforts to provide a system of direct management and training that is secure against ordinary human error whilst endeavoring to reduce the incidence of such human error to an absolute minimum. The report also clearly suggests much more than these action points, and the revision of some training courses, though the quality of basic training is an essential part of effective L&D. It is also being argued that the TOCs as organisations need to become 'learning organisations'. Management needs to instil and attain a culture of safety before all else, rather than being paralysed by a 'blame culture' which makes staff defensive rather than proactive.

REFERENCES

Armstrong, M. (1994) *A Handbook of Personnel Management Practice*, London, Kogan Page.

CIPD (2001) *Training and Development in Britain 1999*, CIPD.

Cullen, W.D. (2001) *The Ladbroke Grove Rail Inquiry*, Health and Safety Executive.

DfEE (1995) Training statistics, *Employment Gazette*, October.

DfEE (2000) *Learning and Training at Work*, Department for Education and Employment.

DfEE (2001a) *Education and Training Statistics 2000*, Department for Education and Employment.

DfEE (2001b) *Opportunity and Skills in the Knowledge Economy*, Department for Education and Employment.

Gibb, S. and Megginson, D. (2000) 'New employee development: successful innovations or token gestures?', *Personnel Review*, Vol. 29 No. 4.

Hallier, J. and Butts, S. (2000) 'Attempts to advance the role of training: process and context', *Employee Relations*, Vol. 22 No. 4.

Industrial Society (1998) '*Training Trends*', May/June.

Johnson, S., Campbell, M., Devins, D. and Gold, J. (2000) *Learning Pays: The Bottom Line*, National Advisory Council for Education and Training Targets.

Keynote (1998) '*Training*', Keynote Marketing Report.

Mabey, C., Salaman, G. and Storey, J. (1998) *Human Resource Management: A Strategic Introduction*, Oxford, Blackwell.

NACETT (1999) *Learning Pays and Learning Works*, National Advisory Council for Education and Training Targets.

NACETT (2000) *The Learning Society and the Knowledge Economy*, National Advisory Council for Education and Training Targets.

PIU (2001) *Workforce Development Project: Executive Summary*, Cabinet Office, Performance and Innovation Unit.

Richardson, W. and Unwin, L. (2000) The Learning Society and the Knowledge Economy, National Advisory Council for Education and Training Targets.

part one

Processes

A process is a series of operations used in making or achieving something. The overall L&D process is illustrated graphically in Figure P1. It shows the four main phases:

- ■ Observing: Assessing L&D Needs
- ■ Planning: Designing L&D Experiences
- ■ Acting: Developing and Delivering L&D Experiences
- ■ Reviewing: Evaluating L&D

Each of these phases is explored in sequence in Chapters 2 to 5. Within each of the major phases there are other series of operations that are usually required to complete each major phase. These can be described with regard to two relevant themes. First is what is involved in professional performance, the techniques and practical operations in use. Second is what is involved in the organisational environment, which requires these techniques to be applied thoughtfully rather than mechanically.

Figure P1   *The L&D process*

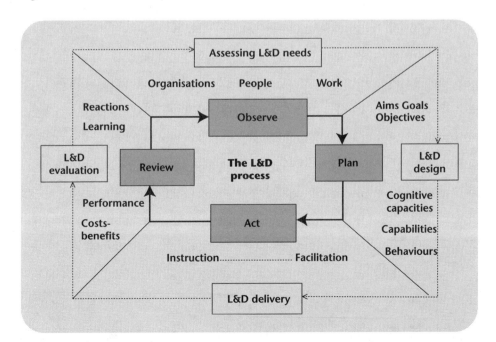

chapter two

Observing:
Assessing L&D Needs

Learning outcomes

■ Develop a more elaborate analysis of performance management and the concerns of business and management organisations

■ Describe and explore three levels of assessing L&D related performance gaps: the organisational level, the work or occupational level, and the individual level

■ Describe and use models and techniques to identify L&D themes in gaps between expected and actual performance

■ Differentiate between performance gaps related to L&D needs and other kinds of performance gap and support systems

FRAMEWORK CASE STUDY: CHASE ADVANCED TECHNOLOGIES LTD

When Chase Advanced Technologies won a major contract to provide electronic components for gambling 'fruit machines' across the UK the future looked bright and profitable. But rather than assuring the future the contract brought problems for the company. Poor pass rates for the components being made and a need for high levels of reworking meant that the profitability of the contract was being threatened. At one point things were so bad that internal 'pass rates' for work fell to 38%. There were clearly major performance gaps, gaps between what was desired and expected and what was being achieved.

An intensive training programme to tackle the immediate crisis was devised. This involved 60 employees undertaking basic training in printed circuit board assembly. Quality levels began to rise, reaching 80% in a few months. The company then introduced further initiatives: skills training related to staff gaining National Vocational Qualifications (NVQ) and the development of an in-house workmanship training culture. These were established with support from a local college and electronic training centre. A multimedia computer based training package to support the delivery of the NVQ was also developed. By doing this the management team were conscious of laying the foundations for a genuine training culture. They therefore made a commitment to attaining the Investors in People standard.

After two years of heavy losses Chase returned to profit and the company was once again a thriving organisation, with a better skilled and committed workforce. Managing director Eugene Martinez concluded that 'The training programme has led to a new spirit of enthusiasm among our staff. Having been given an opportunity to learn many have developed a real hunger for knowledge. A working grandmother was one of the first people to gain an NVQ and has recently gained a level 3 qualification in manufacturing support. Many staff are so keen that they are even undertaking NVQ work in their own time'. Source: DfEE (2000), p 5

INTRODUCTION: THE PERFORMANCE MANAGEMENT CONTEXT

That an organisation which had worked hard to win a contract, such as Chase Advanced Technologies, could then face such substantial problems in achieving the performance required to deliver on it is salutary; it was unwelcome but it produced beneficial effects. The success of winning the contract exposed problems with performance throughout the organisation. There were gaps in performance in various areas: in the quality of work being done, leading to waste and losses that threatened the company's profitability and survival. The need for L&D at work to be improved, both immediately and over time, was the solution. Figure 2.1 provides an overview of the performance management context. It models the context, the possible causes of performance gaps and interventions to deal with them. It clearly illustrates a range of causes and possible interventions. Some aspects of a performance gap can be attributable to deficiencies in L&D at work. In the case of Chase these kinds of gaps existed, and had to be dealt with to get the current work done to the desired quality. This phase of observation also led the company to review their whole L&D culture and provision throughout the company as a whole.

For this case study organisation L&D was a means to an end, not an end in itself. It was a means to the end of achieving the expected and desired levels of performance. It was one of a number of interventions that could have been used to move from ineffective performance to optimum performance management (see Box 2.1). This is the context within which the first phase of the L&D process, the phase of observation and the assessment of L&D needs, is to be described and analysed.

Identifying performance gaps that are worth closing, and the kinds of L&D need that will be associated with them, may take different forms depending on how an organisation perceives what performance management involves. Box 2.2 highlights some different ways of thinking about performance management within an organisation. These reflect and embody assumptions about management and changes in organisation which will influence how causal analysis and interventions will be managed.

The way that performance management is constructed depends upon how the problems of performance are conceived of in the first instance. This is important as it will influence the way and the extent to which L&D needs come to be observed and assessed. In practice a variety of frameworks for performance management have been proposed in theory and can be found to some extent in practice. These frameworks offer different ways of defining and translating the fundamental goals of the organisation into unit, team and individual performance terms.

The set of frameworks identified in Box 2.2 offers different ways of thinking about and approaching the question of planning goals, setting objectives and agreeing standards in organisations. These ways of thinking about organisational performance will shape the way that L&D needs are to be observed and assessed. That is, they define

Figure 2.1   *Performance management analysis (based on Ford (1999))*

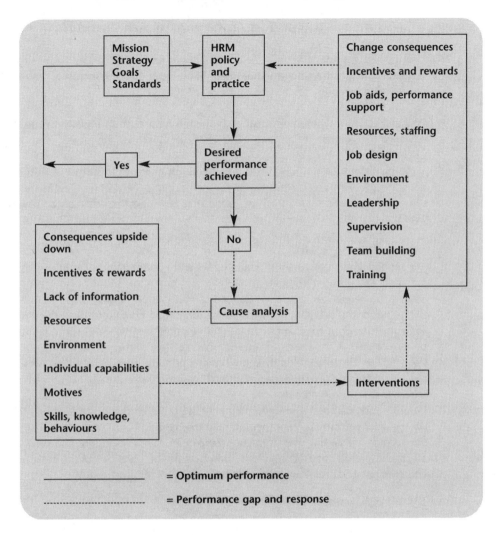

the type and 'shape' of the gaps that will be identified as desired levels of performance not being achieved. By using these frameworks, explicitly or implicitly, organisations will observe and identify certain kinds of gaps between their desired performance and their actual performance.

The implication is not just for the kind of gap that is identified at the analysis of causes stage. It is also connected to how gaps in performance will be seen to be symptomatic of different underlying causes requiring certain kinds of intervention. Depending on the framework in use gaps will be interpreted differently; as problems of 'quality' requiring quality oriented interventions, or as problems of 'business process' requiring business process interventions, or as problems of 'learning' requiring L&D interventions and so on. It is by analysing the extent to which, and in what ways, these gaps in performance relate to L&D that the L&D process comes to be an

---

Box 2.1

Are the performance gaps worth closing?

Performance gaps do not necessarily mean that actions have to be taken. Mager suggests a ten point structure for determining whether observations lead to the conclusion that a gap exists where L&D needs might be involved.

1 Define specifically whose performance is at issue. Which person, which group?
2 What is the actual performance discrepancy? Describe the actual and the desired performance.
3 Is the problem worth solving? Is it a big enough problem to bother about? How much does the problem cost? What happens if you ignore the problem? Estimate the cost in some way so that a solution can be found that costs less than the consequences of living with the problem.
4 Is it possible to apply a fast fix? If the light goes out try changing the bulb rather than calling out an electrician.
5 Are expectations clear and are resources adequate, is performance quality visible, and is feedback on performance being given?
6 Are the 'consequences' properly balanced? Or are people in some way rewarded for doing things wrong? (For example, if someone does not complete their work properly will someone else do it for them?) List all the negative and positive 'consequences' of poor performance that are evident, from the point of view of the people involved.
7 Do the people involved already know how to perform effectively? Could they perform in the past? Are the tasks performed often? Perhaps better feedback is needed, or some refresher practice or job aids.
8 Consider task changes as solutions; simplify the task, remove obstacles to performance.
9 Do the poor performers have the potential to change?
10 If it seems after all this that the performance gap is worth closing, and L&D is appropriate, then describe the L&D solutions and calculate the costs. Select the most practical and cost effective L&D solution and implement it.

Source: Mager (2000)

---

integral part of management (Chiu *et al* 1999). Where it appears that there is a gap and that L&D is the best way to deal with a gap in performance the first phase of the L&D process is being initiated: the observation of L&D needs.

Having broadened the modelling of performance management in this way the focus can be sharpened again. The essence of performance management is that 'what gets measured gets done', that what is subject to scrutiny and observation will determine what people take to be important. There are various ways of thinking about, observing and measuring organisations and their goals. Variations occur in terms of sectors; private sector profit making organisations observe and measure different things in comparison with public sector and non-profit organisations. Variations will occur according to strategies, such as 'quality' versus 'price' led strategies.

> ### Box 2.2
>
> # Frameworks for performance management
>
> **Identifying key performance indicators;** this involves setting specific, measurable, attainable, realistic, time bounded (SMART) objectives for core activities. This is the dominant image of performance management that many people have, and which indeed many organisations adopt. It is associated with conventional 'top down' strategic management in the private sector and 'value for money' initiatives in the public sector.
>
> **Kaizen, TQM;** this involves developing, planning and monitoring systems to achieve continuous improvement. This is most associated with the lessons of successful manufacturers, with origins in Japanese companies.
>
> **Becoming 'excellent' or 'world class';** adopting, or establishing, the standards of the best in order to compete. Associated with, for example the work of Peters and Waterman (1990) on 'excellence' and in the contemporary context with standards such as the European Quality Management Foundation (EQMF).
>
> **High commitment organisation;** this involves ensuring that the workforce is fully and enthusiastically engaged in achieving the tasks of the organisation. It is associated with trends in organisations to develop organisational cultures which embody this concern, focussed often on customer service.
>
> **Business process re-engineering;** this involves reviewing organisational structures to achieve tasks faster with less resources. It is associated with the 'flattening' of hierarchies, 'downsizing' of workforces and 'outsourcing' of activities.
>
> **Developing balanced scorecards;** this involves identifying measures across a broad range of areas to monitor and evaluate. Associated with the work of Kaplan and Norton (1996). They identify four areas that need to be balanced: 'translating the vision', 'feedback and learning', 'business planning' and 'communicating and linking'.
>
> **Learning organisation;** this involves keeping abreast or ahead of the competition by ensuring there is an effective collective learning process that enables change and innovation. This is associated with, in the USA the work of Senge (1990), and in the UK with the ideas of Pedler *et al* (1994).
>
> **Organisation development;** this involves using behavioural sciences to diagnose and solve organisational problems. This is most associated with the 'academic' literature on management and organisations (eg Robbins (1993)) and the use of 'action research' projects, where researchers and managers work together.

Without a clear sense of relevant and specific performance improvement outcomes desired from undertaking L&D, no matter how much is to be spent on L&D, or how professionally L&D may be delivered, the prospects for effective L&D are poor. The focal concern is to identify areas for investing in L&D which will help establish and maintain expected and desired performance, so that the organisation gets the results it seeks and wants. To reiterate, the L&D process can be mapped onto the core performance management process (see Figure 2.2). The phase of 'observation' becomes the phase of observing and assessing L&D needs. The underlying question is about

Figure 2.2   *The L&D process mapped onto performance management*

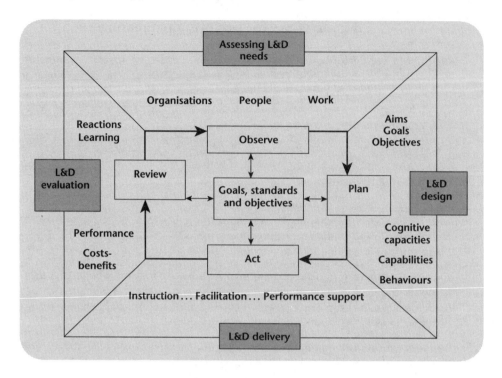

Figure 2.3   *Three kinds of performance concern (based on Boydell and Leary (1996))*

Goals	Standards	Objectives
Implementing	Doing things well	Competence
Improving	Doing things better	Excellence
Innovating	Doing new and better things	Pioneering

how best, professionally and scientifically, to observe and assess L&D needs (Bartram and Gibson 1994).

OBSERVING AND ASSESSING L&D NEEDS

Observing and assessing L&D needs is the first phase of providing the learning opportunities required to achieve the goals, standards and objectives of the organisation (Boydell and Leary 1996). Boydell and Leary provide an analysis of performance management concerns that relate specifically to L&D at work. One aspect of their analysis is to define the goals, standards and objectives of the organisation in terms of performance management concerns in three categories (see Figure 2.3).

Exercise 2.1   Performance management concerns

Identify an industry sector, for example food retailing, fashion, banking, universities. Using the categories in Figure 2.3, identify an example of an organisation from each sector which represents each of these kinds of performance management goals, standards and objectives. Are there examples in the sector of pioneers, the excellent and the competent? By identifying such concrete organisations it should be easier to visualise how these different performance management goals result in different kinds of standards and objectives.

One interpretation of these different performance management goals is that they are a hierarchy; the more demanding they get the more L&D will be needed. To be competent requires a degree of L&D, so a certain level of need will be observed; to be excellent requires further and greater L&D, so a greater level of L&D need will be observed. To be pioneering requires the greatest investment in L&D of all; so substantial amounts of L&D will be observed.

An implication is that this distribution will not be stable; there will usually be, in the context of competition, an imitation and escalation which leads some to observe increasing L&D. As certain organisations pioneer then the others who are excellent will follow, and those who are just 'competent' will also have to change and adapt. Equally an organisation that has been pioneering or excellent, but which neglects L&D, can find itself backsliding. These performance goals and associated issues can be applied to units within the same organisation as well; certain units or parts of an organisation may be competent, others excellent, and others pioneering, having different performance management concerns and degrees of observation of L&D needs.

Boydell and Leary also discuss observing and assessing L&D needs in relation to another form of analysis: three different levels of L&D need. They call these the organisational, team and individual levels of need. Whether an organisation is seeking competence, excellence or to be pioneering there will be L&D needs at these different levels. These are associated with the L&D needs that apply to everyone in the organisation, those related to specific kinds of work and occupations, and those particular to a specific person. This kind of observation of L&D needs was first suggested by McGehee and Thayer (1961), and has been in common use since then (Buckley and Caple 1990).

If the assessment of L&D needs is needed to identify gaps between expected and actual performance then at any of these levels the first step in analysis has to be 'what is expected performance?'. Defining what expected performance should be requires the determination of both objective and subjective 'facts' and measures (McClelland 1994). Objective data about expected performance are data which can be obtained by measuring that which is tangible and can be quantified. These will be aspects of the organisation, group or individual performance. These data may be based on financial results, levels of productivity or the quality of service or product (see Box 2.3).

Difficulties are encountered in measuring tangible and objective productivity criteria, reflecting general problems with defining what to measure and obtaining accurate information efficiently. There are also problems specific to sectors, where productivity may be too dependent on external factors. Even overcoming these problems, collecting objective data is on its own of little use. It can only be meaningful when set in a relationship to and compared with some standard. It is this comparison rather than the data in themselves which provides useful information for assessing L&D needs. For example, the level of sales a person achieves will not indicate if there are or are not performance gaps; it is only when compared to other people's sales, or the

Box 2.3

People and productivity

Productivity is the average output produced by inputs, a combination of human and capital resource. Productivity can be described in economic terms, for example in manufacturing measuring the number of goods produced per hour, or in terms of customer satisfaction. One survey found that 36% of organisations formally measured productivity, 22% measured it informally, 21% used both formal and informal measures, while 22% did not measure it all, as shown in the table.

Productivity measure	Organisations using it (%)
Customer satisfaction	24
Output per head	16
Output per hour per head	13
Sales/turnover per head	12
Profit per head	11
Output	10
Output per £ invested/ROI	10
Other	2

The UK is viewed as a poor performer in productivity terms in comparison with other countries. This reflects poor capital productivity, a lack of investment in L&D and structural differences such as having more part-time and temporary staff.

Lack of L&D can be seen as a principal barrier to increased productivity.

Source: NOP World (2001)

sales of other similar companies, that any difference will be seen. Therefore norms for performance have to be established. Means and deviations from these provide the control limits and thresholds of acceptable performance. If the organisation as a whole is outside these thresholds its viability will be threatened; if a retailer is failing to make as many sales as its close competitors then something is clearly wrong. It is these comparisons which can be identified and analysed to explore where performance is not as expected or desired.

Another complication is that accurate judgement about levels of performance is best made over time. Tracking trends over time rather than simply analysing snapshots of norms, means and deviations in time is the most secure and certain source of information about objective gaps in performance. In relation to financial measures that is what stock markets are doing for private sector companies, and what 'value for money' analyses attempt to do for public sector organisations and public spending. In relation to measures of levels of productivity that is what comparative economic data provide. In relation to measures of quality that is what ongoing customer surveys provide.

Defining objective measures for norms and observing deviations from these which embody performance gaps is not the sole or even primary source of assessing L&D needs. This is because it may be difficult to find tangible aspects to measure which tell the whole story. Subjective data can also be collected and analysed. Subjective perceptions of performance are formed by establishing and interpreting attitudes and feelings about the organisation's, groups' or individuals' performance. Such perceptions may be formed by managers in the course of their work or through conducting staff surveys. These perceptions of intangibles and attitudes may be checked through surveys of customers or other stakeholders. They may also be derived from focus group discussions among managers, staff and customers on important performance themes and issues. The need for comparability rather than a description of perceptions in themselves also applies here. Norms for subjective perceptions need to be referred to, not just perceptions in isolation. Trends over time rather than snapshots are the most valuable. Unlike much 'objective' data, subjective perceptions remain 'private', being generated within and confined to the organisation. Where information is publicly available it can provide some basis for identifying norms. An example would be the findings of Baillie (1996) on employee attitudes in the UK. These would enable an organisation to evaluate if there were gaps with the extent to which its workforce was as committed as others, or as satisfied with work as others.

ORGANISATIONAL NEEDS

Using either objective or subjective measures organisational L&D needs can be defined in various ways. First, organisational L&D needs may be defined as those that are common to all members of the organisation. Everyone, from top to bottom and across all units may need L&D of a particular kind. It may be that new technologies are to be introduced, and therefore all staff need to be trained in the use of the new systems. It could be that an organisation wide restructuring is proposed, and in the course of that jobs and job specifications will change; therefore aspects of the cognitive capacities and capabilities required will have to be changed. It may be that a change of 'culture' is sought, and the behaviours expected and required of all staff will have to be realigned with that culture; an example would be creating a new equal opportunities culture in the light of new legislation and social change.

Secondly organisational L&D needs may be defined in terms of a performance gap that is seen to affect the organisation as a whole. Closing that performance gap through L&D will then be critical to the future success of the organisation as a whole, not just to a group or individual. At this organisational level gaps between desired performance and actual performance can come in many shapes and sizes. In pursuit of effective performance, which may as Boydell and Leary defined it mean doing things well, doing them better or doing them differently, an L&D issue becomes a central strategic issue, of major concern to the organisation. The design and promotion of the Investors in People (IiP) initiative, which is outlined in detail later in Chapter 8, was premised on arguing that there were often organisational level L&D needs in this sense, but these were often neglected or ineffectively dealt with. L&D had to be a pervasive concern for the organisation as a whole, not an infrequent and ad hoc concern. Bramley (1991) offers one way of classifying the kinds of concerns about organisational effectiveness that may lead to identifying L&D needs at the organisational level (see Figure 2.4).

The case of Chase Advanced Technologies illustrates how these organisational level needs may arise. A lack of effective L&D did not stop the company winning a big contract, but it did confront them with circumstances where identifying and dealing with L&D needs became critical to delivering that contract and building the business. They

Figure 2.4   *Organisational effectiveness (from Bramley (1991))*

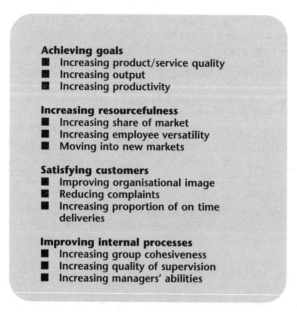

Achieving goals
- Increasing product/service quality
- Increasing output
- Increasing productivity

Increasing resourcefulness
- Increasing share of market
- Increasing employee versatility
- Moving into new markets

Satisfying customers
- Improving organisational image
- Reducing complaints
- Increasing proportion of on time deliveries

Improving internal processes
- Increasing group cohesiveness
- Increasing quality of supervision
- Increasing managers' abilities

had not done the 'ideal' in identifying organisational needs in advance of the contract; they reacted to the needs that arose as the organisation developed.

In discussing and analysing these areas of organisational effectiveness managers and others can consider the extent to which L&D provision can and will help. An integration of these views provides an overview of what the L&D function can do at the organisational level. In dealing with the identification of L&D needs at the organisational level the point has to be stressed that this is a particular example of a general activity; conducting research to inform problem solving and decision making. The methods and techniques of data collection and analysis involved are not unique to identifying L&D needs.

Much existing information may already be available, in the form of plans and data sources that already exist within the organisation, limiting the need for new observation and research. The need to make specific observations in order to identify L&D needs can be circumvented by using existing data sources. Bee and Bee (1994) provide an analysis of such existing plans and data in relation to what they call training needs analysis (TNA), but what is here being called the assessment of L&D needs. They emphasise, in a prescriptive way, that in undertaking a TNA it should be the business needs that provide the rationale for what is to be done, not what a training manager or anybody else with a personal view thinks might be useful. They emphasise this as they argue that in too many instances trainers and training managers are too committed to providing a catalogue of courses, as apparently ready made solutions to performance problems. This is a consequence of the 'popularity' of such easy to manage catalogues or menus of courses, with both managers and staff. But they stress that TNA should be bound up with, and be part of, the general analysis of environmental factors impinging on the organisation and its development.

In pursuing a TNA there are some existing sources of information and other HR systems that are relevant. These involve interconnections with other plans and systems that could already exist in the organisation. These are given in Box 2.4.

Box 2.4

Existing plans and data

1 **Human resource plans and data;** looking at future demands for staff and ensuring there is a supply of the right kinds of people, whether that means maintaining a steady state, expanding or rationalising. From this some perceptions of the extent and kind of L&D needs can be derived.

2 **Succession planning data;** identifying concerns with flows related to promotion, retirements, leavers.

3 **Reviews of critical incidents;** organisations often experience and then analyse unforeseen events that they see to be of great importance, that were not planned for. From reviewing 'accidents', good or bad, and discrepancies they develop a database of experience.

4 **Management information systems;** data from various sources are collated and can be integrated to support analysis for decision making. In manufacturing, for example, there is the development of Enterprise Resource Planning (ERP) systems, where data on real time performance are made available to managers.

5 **Individual performance appraisal systems and records;** performance review based on attainment of targets offers a potentially rich source of information about L&D needs. It is though quite possible to have the trappings of a performance management system, particularly an individual appraisal system, without the data from that being collated and processed for the management of L&D.

On the other hand, if the analysis of organisation level L&D needs is required and undertaken and these plans and data are not available, then the L&D needs analysis exercise raises a concern with them. If there are performance problems which seem to require L&D, but there are no current measures of productivity with which to gauge the impact of any L&D that is to be done, then such measures may be developed as a response. Thus analysing L&D needs may lead into evolving better performance management.

WORK AND OCCUPATIONAL ANALYSIS

L&D needs can also be observed for certain kinds of work and occupations. Where HRM plans and systems exist in an organisation the centrepiece will usually be some kind of job specifications. Job specifications typically identify roles, key tasks, competencies and performance standards. The methods of job and task analysis (Wolfe *et al* 1991) will have been used to create these, and L&D needs can be simply derived from them. On the one hand this is logical and means a range of pre-existing reference points are available. On the other hand there is an inherent problem with these kinds of job specifications. One view is that the traditional form of scientific job and task analysis which leads to the specification of work defined in boxes called 'jobs' or 'competencies' continues to be appropriate. These job specifications are therefore useful. The other is, however, a contemporary view of changing organisational circumstances where flexibility in teams and roles is more important, making the notion of discrete jobs that can be thoroughly specified in these ways seem outmoded and inappropriate.

Table 2.1 *Occupations and employment*

Major work groups	% share 1999	Projections to 2010
Managers and senior officials	13.2	72,000 increase
Professional occupations	11.1	864,000 increase
Associate professional and technical occupations	12.5	789,000 increase
Administrative, clerical and secretarial occupations	14.7	56,000 increase
Skilled trades occupations	13.7	196,000 decrease
Personal services occupations	5.8	645,000 increase
Sales and customer services occupations	6.6	178,000 increase
Process, plant and machine operatives	8.9	103,000 decrease
Elementary occupations	13.5	177,000 decrease

Source: IER (2001)

Certainly at a national level specifications for occupational categories are well defined (see Table 2.1), with sub-divisions in these categories (see Table 2.2). These categories can be used to analyse supply and demand issues at a national level, providing the context for a national L&D at work needs analysis. Note that the figures here are projections based on certain assumptions.

Exercise 2.2   Occupational data

Analyse the data in Table 2.2. What leaps up at you when you consider these data? Is there anything in the data that surprises you, or that you would want to know more about, or that you might want to challenge?

The L&D needed to provide the year by year replacements in these occupations, depending on expansion or contraction in the occupational area, is managed by various institutions. Government provides funding for L&D in educational institutions, and organisations provide their own L&D to those pursuing careers in these occupations. The interest here is with the observations being made by organisations to identify L&D needs at this level.

Within organisations job, task and occupational analysis is required to support HRM systems in diverse areas of practice, from templates for recruitment processes through to performance appraisal systems. Bee and Bee suggest that, even where job specifications already exist, doing a TNA may raise issues about the validity and reliability of these existing job specifications. It can be dangerous to assume that existing models of work and occupations can be adopted for L&D needs analysis. Thus the ultimate goal of assessing L&D needs may generate a prior task: to review or develop existing job specifications. This then means that L&D analysis may involve the use of, and therefore requires familiarity with, methods of job analysis.

Job analysis is defined broadly as any systematic procedure for obtaining detailed information about a job. While the methods may vary they should all produce as outcomes the following:

■ specifications which have 'face validity'; that is that they are acceptable to current job holders and their managers
■ clear role definitions; defining the purposes and main functions of the job
■ specified key tasks; describing the main the parts of the job

Table 2.2   *Sub categories of occupational groups*

Occupational categories	1999 % share	Projections to 2010 net req's (000)*	Replace per year (000)
Corporate managers	9.7	657	55
Managers/proprietors in agriculture and services	3.5	498	41
Science and technology professions	3.2	552	46
Health professionals	0.9	199	17
Teaching and research professionals	4.4	821	68
Business and public service professionals	2.6	423	35
Science and technology associate professionals	1.5	142	12
Health and social welfare associate professionals	3.2	546	45
Protective services occupations	1.0	88	7
Culture, media and sports	1.8	408	34
Business and public services associate professionals	5.1	791	66
Administrative and clerical occupations	1.5	1338	111
Secretarial and related occupations	4.1	422	35
Skilled agricultural trades	1.2	115	10
Skilled metal and electrical trades	5.6	452	38
Skilled construction and building trades	3.6	324	27
Textiles, printing and other skilled trades	3.3	456	38
Caring personal services	3.8	1144	95
Leisure and other personal service occupations	2.0	475	40
Sales occupations	6.2	1111	93
Customer services occupations	0.4	49	4
Process, plant and machine operatives	5.4	455	38
Transport and mobile machine drivers and operatives	3.4	425	35
Elementary; trades, plant and machine related	3.7	458	38
Elementary; clerical and services related	9.8	1172	98

* Net requirements = expansion demand (or decline) + total loss (replacement demand due to retirement, mortality and outward occupational mobility
Source: IER (2001)

■ specified competencies; what people need to know and be able to do to perform the tasks
■ specified performance standards; what will be measured and reviewed

All these aspects of job analysis can help identify what L&D will be relevant and where L&D efforts might need to be focussed. As will be discussed in the next chapter these outcomes of job analysis can be used to structure the planning of L&D; by suggesting areas where specific aims, goals and objectives for L&D activities will be needed. It is quite possible though that a performance gap seen to be associated with the way that a task or occupation is managed is not relevant for L&D needs analysis at all. Box 2.5 provides one set of explanations of and response to gaps in performance at a task and occupation level which are not related to L&D needs. Other means of performance support can be used to address performance gaps caused by these kinds of factors (Mager, *op cit*).

Where there is a need to review jobs or tasks with a view to identifying L&D needs a framework for analysis is needed. Ford (*op cit*) provides an overview of models for the tasks involved in assessing needs at the level of jobs (see Figure 2.5).

For instance, examples of job outputs could be to take orders over the phone, to assemble a piece of furniture, to write marketing reports. Duties related to these kinds

---

Box 2.5

Non L&D related causes of occupational performance gaps

Reasons why people do not perform	Closing job and task performance gaps
They've forgotten how to do it	Job aids; remind people how to do what they already know how to do, for example checklists
They don't know what is expected	Information; provide clarity on what is expected in the job
They do not have the authority, tools, time or space	Giving permission to perform; provide not just responsibility for results but also authority to achieve these
They don't get feedback	Feedback; people need specific feedback on how they are doing, to help them attain what is desired and expected
Documentation is poorly designed, inaccessible or non-existent	Improved documentation; manuals and materials to help people do their jobs
Work station is badly designed	Changing the workplace; from being 'just assembled' to being carefully designed for optimum performance
Punished or ignored for doing it right Rewarded for doing it wrong Nobody notices if they do it right or wrong	Ensuring no 'upside down' consequences; provide rewards for desired performance and punishments for failing to perform. These 'consequences', as the individuals concerned see them, can be upside down; where doing it right gets the person punished (embarrassment, ridicule, more work, frustration, boredom) and failing to do it right gets rewarded (peer approbation, less work, easier life)
Organisation makes desired performance difficult or impossible	Changing organisational structure; deal with boundaries which are producing 'turf wars' or confusion

---

of outputs can be described. These descriptions may vary from the general and broad, to the highly detailed and specific. In the examples cited here the 'titles' resulting would be 'call centre operator', 'furniture maker' and 'marketing manager'. 'Boundaries' are the limits to the job; where responsibilities stop. These are the interfaces with other jobs in the organisation, requiring interactions between job holders to achieve overall outputs. Call centre operators will not manage budgets, someone else will. Furniture manufacturers will not sell the product, someone else will. Marketing managers will not design the products, someone else will.

Behaviours are defined here as the observable actions involved in performance, while competencies are defined as the underlying capabilities made manifest in effec-

Figure 2.5   *Job analysis and links to occupational L&D*

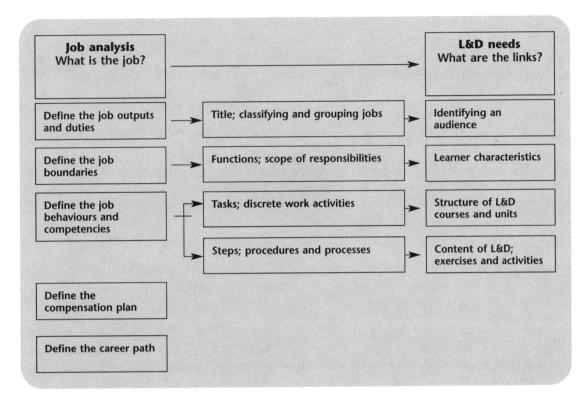

tive performance. There can be an emphasis on, or balance between, behaviours and competencies in describing jobs. Some jobs can be described using behaviours alone, if they involve directly observable activities, such as making furniture. Others, such as management and professional roles, are more often described in terms of competencies as they involve the application of capacities that are not directly observable. An example to illustrate this is that of a doctor. A doctor cannot guarantee to produce the outcome of a 'successful' operation or course of treatment, that is a healthy or 'live' patient. What can, and should be, guaranteed is that in the course of dealing with a patient the doctor competently follows the procedures that should be followed.

Job analysis in itself does not provide a direct link to L&D needs. What it does is produce a framework in which work tasks and steps can be articulated. The tasks involved in an occupation or area of work still need to be analysed. The structure for task analysis can be thought of as being about branching out to define steps (see Figure 2.6).

The methods to be used for achieving task analysis can include interviewing task experts, interviewing job holders, observing experts at work, or surveying job holders and/or experts. Ford also suggests that some kind of learner analysis is required at this stage. Learners should never be thought of at any stage as blank slates to be written upon. How the people who are in this area of work or this occupation may best learn can be considered here, as this has implications for how learning will be designed and delivered (Box 2.6).

Figure 2.6   *Task analysis rationale*

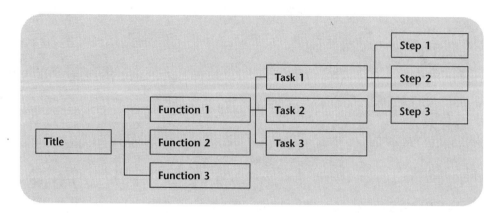

Box 2.6

Aspects of learners relevant to occupations

Demographics	Age range, gender, typical existing qualifications
Learning style preferences	Auditory, visual, or kinaesthetic
Kind of audiences	Current knowledge and skills; will they be experts learning something new or novices? What are the attitudes and motivations of those doing the tasks?

Exercise 2.3   HR Services Co

HR Services Co is an outsourcing provider for HR services using information technology, founded in 1998 in the USA. It provides HR services across the board, through the use of ICT, for large blue chip organisations. Using an 'e-hr' delivery model it assumes complete ownership and management of the entire HRM process, including administration of areas like training, compensation and recruitment. To do this it uses a range of general and in house web based tools and systems. It currently has four 'client service centres' (CSC) in various locations worldwide and around 1000 staff. Its latest CSC was to be developed in a UK city, employing 150 staff.

Being a young organisation it had been focussed on getting and dealing with contracted services. Internal company policies and plans of its own were still in their infancy; a classic case of the 'cobbler's children being poorly shod'. Ironically for an organisation managing others' training it had not yet developed its own training plan. There was a map of competencies in use in the organisation. These competencies were:

- contribute to team success
- customer focus
- quality orientation
- innovation

- organisational skills
- assertiveness skills
- flexibility
- communication skills

No formal assessment of L&D needs had been done in the company itself. It was thought that the most urgent concerns existed at the occupational level, to ensure that employees could carry out the requirements of their jobs.

Task: Given a short lead time and limited resources what would you advise this organisation to do to pursue an analysis of the occupational L&D needs of its staff?

INDIVIDUAL LEVEL L&D NEEDS

Having or developing organisational training plans, job specifications, completing task analysis or maps of competency are all aspects of ensuring that observation and assessment of L&D needs are managed in a way that fits with the performance management concerns of the organisation as a whole. Yet L&D needs assessment confined to a generic analysis of organisational or task needs would be a blunt instrument. Not everyone whose work includes common tasks, whether new or existing staff, will have the same kinds or degrees of L&D need. The pejorative term for L&D that characterises this kind of situation of just analysing organisational level and task needs and subjecting all employees to the same L&D because of that, is 'sheep-dip' training; everyone is processed through the same course regardless of their individual needs.

In the cameos of effective and ineffective L&D experiences in Chapter 1, a clear theme was the actual extent of need the person involved in L&D had for learning. Where there was great individual need, the L&D provided was usually a success. Where there was little or no individual need the L&D, no matter how well designed and delivered, was a waste of time and resources. The scope for reducing waste and concentrating resources properly for establishing and improving performance for the organisation and the individual through L&D means that at the individual level needs have to be accurately identified and accommodated.

Where clear organisational, task or occupation descriptions and standards have been defined then individuals can be assessed against them. Some individuals may need more development in some aspects of the organisational need or task need than in others. This individual analysis of needs is typically done at a number of points. One is when exploring the experience and qualifications of applicants in selection. Another is when undertaking some form of performance appraisal during employment. On other occasions assessment centres may be used for identifying L&D needs, for either selection, placement, appraisal or career development purposes during employment. A crucial area is managing career development, both up the promotion ladder and across posts and tasks. Great variety exists in performance appraisal methods, but this should not obscure their common purpose: to identify the extent to which the individual satisfies expected and desired performance standards.

The aim is to try to provide L&D that deals systematically with individual performance issues, over at least an annual cycle, rather than reacting as and when individual issues arise. In practice in the past this depended upon line managers being concerned with L&D provision as they discussed and planned the work of their staff. Increasingly the expectation is that employees themselves will take responsibility for identifying their own L&D needs.

Figure 2.7   *Performance concerns and assessing L&D needs (based on Boydell and Leary 1996)*

		Area of need		
	Aspect	**Organisational**	**Group/ occupation**	**Individual**
Level of business benefit	1. Implementing; doing things well	Meeting current organisational objectives	Working together to meet existing targets and standards	Being competent at the level of existing standards
	2. Improving; doing things better	Setting higher objectives and reaching them	Continuous improvement within teams	Having and using systematic continuous improvement skills and processes
	3. Innovating; doing new and better things	Changing objectives and strategies	Working across boundaries to create new relationships and new products and services	Being able to work differently and more creatively with a shared sense of purpose

OBSERVING L&D: SKILLS AND ISSUES

The assessment of L&D needs in the context of performance management is then the first step, the phase of observation, to ensuring that resources for L&D are directed so that people can either do things well, or do them better, or do new and better things. By combining these categories of performance concern and these different levels of L&D need, Boydell and Leary produce a matrix (see Figure 2.7). This maps the whole range of areas where an assessment of L&D needs may be attempted to ensure comprehensive and complete foundations for L&D in the organisation.

Boydell and Leary conclude that effective L&D will be based on exploring all these aspects of assessing L&D needs. To achieve this they emphasise that the assessment of L&D needs by managers or HRM professionals can be analysed as a challenge and activity involving the particular application of a range of generic skills. They call these generic skills 'process skills', 'content skills', and 'relationship skills'.

- **Process skills** are capabilities in setting goals, making plans, reviewing and evaluating the progress of an assessment of L&D needs.
- **Content skills** are capabilities in getting information, analysing it and making sense of it. Boydell and Leary themselves seek to provide a guide to using tools derived from the 'quality movement' to help collect and analyse objective data about performance.
- **Relationship skills** are about capabilities in maintaining relationships with people as the L&D assessment is undertaken. In regard to relationship skills they suggest

Table 2.3 *Personnel with primary responsibility for establishing training needs*

Personnel	1997 %	1998 %
Line managers	54	65
Training function	22	19
HRM/personnel function	22	14
Employees	9	8
Board/directors	3	4
Chief executive	2	3
Other	1	1

Source: Industrial Society (1998)

that there are dual skills involved. These are the skills of being empathetic, with learners and managers and others, and also the skills of being assertive, to confront and challenge people in the course of assessing L&D needs.

These then are the skills needed by HRM professionals, and also by line managers, when observing and assessing L&D needs. Line managers are apparently increasingly responsible for establishing training needs within a company or organisation (Table 2.3). This reflects trends in which line managers are given more responsibility across a range of issues directly related to HRM.

This emphasis on the abilities involved in observing and assessing L&D needs has many merits and implications. One is to emphasise that the ability to conduct an assessment if L&D needs is a particular application of generic skills; it is not a special and arcane activity with mysteries that only the initiated can understand. These skills include using methods such as benchmarking, undertaking learning climate surveys, and relating L&D to strategic change and models of organisational development (OD). Secondly, while observing and assessing L&D needs does include the use of data collection techniques, there is much more to it than that. In approaching the identification of L&D needs there can often be an over emphasis on the 'technical' side of research and data collection; but this is only a part of it. The political and relationship aspects are as important.

Yet such assessments of L&D need have to be undertaken bearing in mind the importance of making optimal use of often limited resources to deal with a range of diverse and relevant L&D concerns. Few organisations have the luxury of what can be called 'over investment' in L&D, being able to meet all the L&D needs that might exist and then some. Many organisations have to struggle with what others would see as 'under investment', where constraints on resources mean that identified needs cannot be dealt with. As it is important to deal with diverse and relevant concerns, and not waste limited resources, it is essential that L&D needs are accurately identified.

What is particular and challenging about identifying L&D needs at the organisational level is that the process can be sensitive; for the organisation as a whole, for groups within it, and for individuals. These sensitivities arise because identifying L&D needs always involves investigating gaps between expected performance and actual performance. Anxieties about being adjudged to be falling short of expected performance can interfere with and offset the forces pushing for gaps to be properly identified and dealt with.

The typical difficulties that beset effective assessment of L&D needs are that the time, effort and skills required to collect data and make of it useful information are not available. It is not often that no needs are observed and assessed, it is that gaps in identifying gaps exist. There may be a good organisational level analysis (for example, identifying strategic objectives and needs) but not good enough operational analysis (expected and actual performance) or assessment of individual needs (personal performance review). Errors in needs observation and assessment process at all these levels can exist, as with any observation based research process. The consequences of errors are either over training, under training or meeting perceived rather than actual needs of individuals.

The solutions to these errors are evident. They include assessing L&D needs in a systematic way while remaining proactive; to have written plans but also to be flexible; to have central organisation but also to support local action in observing and assessing needs. In the occupational/job area the concern is keeping up with changes, continuous development, standards and certification. In the individual domain the concern is ensuring that positive developmental relationships exist between employees, managers, and others, so that L&D needs can be analysed and explored openly.

A CAVEAT AND CAUTION

Even where such prescriptions for observing L&D needs are followed there may be problems with L&D. Rainbird (2000) identifies five challenges for L&D, among which are two that are particularly relevant to thinking about performance management and the assessment of L&D needs. First is the challenge of deconstructing what she calls the contemporary consensus on L&D, which is that training and skills should be made responsive to employers' needs for increased productivity and flexibility. The rationale of performance management accounts of L&D needs assessment is precisely to fit L&D with employer needs. But are the steps being taken to interpret L&D needs from the perspective of employers warranted, and even becoming part of the problem? Rainbird questions the extent to which there is in fact a link between training, skills and competitiveness that justifies the obsession with defining L&D needs in terms of the needs of current businesses. The emphasis on defining and meeting 'business needs' for L&D, through training and skills, may be distorting investments in L&D to bolster short term profitability at the expense of longer term change, which might generate a quite different assessment of L&D needs. That distortion may be seen in meeting the short term needs of existing businesses, rather than providing for the longer term future. It in effect marginalises the 'needs' of employees, to be able to operate in an era of lifelong learning as free agents. L&D needs may have to be defined in the context of being responsive to employers' economic demands, but what about social concerns such as equity and equality? This interpretation of a subtext of assessing L&D needs within optimising performance management is an expression of a stream of thinking which sees the workplace as an arena in which different interests, within a balance of power, are contested.

Second, Rainbird argues there is a need to acknowledge and critically analyse assumptions about the modernisation of work, setting as it does the agenda for arguments about the content and quality of learning at work. The assessment of L&D needs sits in this wider context, not just within the performance management concerns of individual organisations. This requires assessing L&D needs in order to focus on influencing the investment decisions of multinationals. It also requires matching L&D to the changing nature of work in a post 'Taylorist' era, where employee autonomy rather than close control is the hallmark of many jobs.

CONCLUSION

As the initial phase of the L&D process the quality of what happens in observing and assessing L&D needs sets the foundation for all that follows, for good or for ill. The observation and assessment of L&D needs should take place within a context of performance management in the organisation. If this is done then ideally L&D needs will relate to business development, tasks will be clearly mapped, and individuals will be accurately reviewed. If all these three levels of assessing L&D needs are given attention then the subsequent phases of the L&D process are more likely to provide positive outcomes for investments in L&D; that is to address real and important gaps between expected performance and actual performance. Success in the L&D process depends upon the quality of analysis of what is involved in organisational performance, task performance and individual performance. It depends, that is, upon a coherent and integrated performance management system as a whole.

The ability to analyse organisations, tasks, jobs, occupations and professions requires being able to access or develop data sources: business plans or competency profiles of occupations, or individual performance reviews. It also involves being aware of how changes in structure and culture, or the introduction of new technologies and processes, will change the learning needs of those currently in the role and those who will in future be in the role. The design and implementation of effective performance appraisal systems should include fit with L&D needs assessment requirements. The dual concern is to manage the 'bottom up' assessments of need, from individuals in dialogues with their managers, with 'top down' thinking about future needs, from the strategic analysis of business L&D needs. Reconciling these can then produce the best plans to make optimum use of limited resources to satisfy both individual and organisational interests. See Box 2.7.

Box 2.7

The relativity of performance

Two hikers are deep in the woods when they notice a bear slowly approaching. While they watch it approach, one of the hikers starts to take off his walking boots and put on running shoes. 'What are you doing that for?', his friend asks. 'No shoes in the world are going to let you run faster than a bear!'. 'I don't have to run faster than the bear', he replies. 'I just have to run faster than you'.

What is the bear? The threat, the performance problem
Who do you have to run faster than? Competitors, or challengers
What are the shoes? L&D things to do to get an edge

Exploring observations of the 'performance management' of students

Questions to be addressed

How clear are you on your learning needs as a student on your current course? If you know and can define clearly the expected performance of the ideal student and analyse your own performance in regard to that, you should be able to identify the development needs you face to do well or to do better. Are you aiming to be competent, excellent or a pioneer? Exploring the organisational context, the 'tasks' and the individual context of being a student can help you to review the ideas outlined here about assessing L&D needs.

First, remember that performance management was defined as

> a means of getting better results from the organization, teams and individuals by understanding and managing performance with an agreed framework of planned goals, objectives and standards (Armstrong 1994, p 397)

The first step to explore then is how performance management is defined by the organisation, and the extent to which it has defined L&D needs for students. Is the organisation, the institution in which you are studying, aiming to be competent, to be excellent or to be pioneering? What are the agreed frameworks of planned goals, objectives and standards that are applicable to you in the organisation in which you are a student? Have you agreed these goals with anyone? Have you agreed objectives with anyone? Have you agreed standards with anyone? If you have not, then what is there that you use to identify how well you are performing?

The next step is to think about what the equivalents are of the following for you as a student in an organisation pursuing their studies. Where possible identify equivalents for:

- job specifications which have 'face validity'
- clear role definitions; the main functions of the job of being a student
- specified key tasks and steps; the main parts of the job of being a student
- defined competencies; what you need to know and be able to do to perform the tasks of being a student
- specific performance standards; clear objective measures that are reviewed

Finally, what equivalents are there for individual performance appraisal and the identification of personal needs as you perform through your career as a student? What are the equivalents of individual needs assessment, such as appraisal interviewing and assessment centres? When do these happen, and what is involved in them?

Exercise 2.3 answers: HR Services Co

A pilot exercise was suggested as the starting point. This was to identify the occupational training needs of a specific group in HR Services Co, and to provide a template for conducting further analysis of the needs of other groups. The specific pilot group was explored in detail.

The methodology was to use a questionnaire and semi-structured interviews. The questionnaire was chosen because it was efficient, to be completed by employees. Interviews with selected respondents were also conducted. These enabled issues in the questionnaire to be further discussed, to help evaluate the accuracy of the questionnaire and to discuss line manager interview guidelines.

The survey showed that most, but not all, had completed an induction course. It also showed that many staff were involved in activities that they had had no training for. Staff also highlighted a number of available courses relevant to their jobs but which they had not completed. The survey highlighted 'good communication skills' as a key. In relation to the map of competencies, the survey respondents did not identify any needs; but this was considered to be an overestimation on their part of their abilities.

Interviews with some of the survey respondents were completed. The staff were motivated to learn, and had developed expectations because the needs identification exercise was being undertaken. They were keen to differentiate between 'essential' and 'desirable' training. Questioning them on their competencies did result in changed answers, with an initial overestimation of ability being modified. The interviews also brought to the surface an underlying dissatisfaction with the amount of training being given, and the quality of that which was being given. Line managers for these staff agreed that the model used for assessing needs should be linked into the staff's appraisal process. The need for more and better training was accepted.

Having validated the methodology the intention was to replicate the survey with all staff, but with the process being organised by managers themselves rather than by a surveying specialist from the HR department. The intention was to make the survey available on a website, to save on distribution and analysis time.

Specific recommendations were also made about the need for particular kinds of training for this group as a result of the survey, on technical systems as well as communication and assertiveness. While the survey was quite comprehensive it did not include or cover health and safety training. This was felt to be a discrete area that required a separate treatment.

Case study answers: learning needs of students

Knowing learning needs

It would not be uncommon for the answer to this to be 'No, I cannot clearly define what my learning needs are to improve my performance as a student'. Many students will be all too aware of performance gaps, demonstrated by getting grades and marks they feel are not good enough for competence or excellence, or indeed getting grades and marks which indicate failure. But in the absence of clear standards it is virtually impossible to identify how the gaps can be closed by L&D; always assuming that it is such an L&D gap and not something else (a motivational problem, or inconsistent assessments, for example) that is the issue.

Organisational context

The organisation will have defined some common learning needs for all students, and have taken steps to provide for those. Those might be about study skills, about using technology, or about using the library system. The goals, objectives and standards of your organisation will share the common ground that higher education covers, but also specific goals and so forth the institution and department have. Some of these will be about being competent, some about being excellent and some about being pioneering. In many institutions that provide HRM, that includes providing courses which meet the requirements of accreditation by a professional body (namely the Chartered Institute of Personnel and Development, CIPD).

The sense in which these goals and so forth have been 'agreed' with actual students is minimal. There is no process of agreeing goals, objectives and standards; they are simply applied. The context for exploring a student's performance is confined to applying these generic standards to assessed work in as 'objective' a way as possible; no mean feat in a discipline like HRM that has no 'right answers', and where the tension between providing academically robust critiques and professionally relevant analyses of HRM faces HRM students.

Task analysis context

The organisation has to plan its intake of students, depending on Government funding, and competition among institutions for the 'best'. In doing so it has to review what it expects of student applicants, and therefore what the entry criteria are going to be and what it may need to do to close 'gaps' in performance among some of those it recruits. Many employers now complain about the lack of skills among graduates, and universities need to respond to this.

The obvious flows are those through the different years or phases of a programme. In the course of this different students may enter at different points and leave at different points. Problems with completion of courses are uppermost in many institutions, and steps to close gaps between expected and actual performance to ensure completion may involve a host of agencies, from providing counselling services to offering additional classes. And while there is no 'promotion' the management of superior performers to top grades is clearly an issue; though much tutor time in practice is spent with the 'problem' students, not the superior performers.

Many institutions will have review processes, involving existing students, to monitor and deal with performance issues as they arise. These will vary from staff-student committees concerned with common issues to systems of providing personal tutors to deal with individual concerns. Incidents of apparent plagiarism are one example of responding to discrepancies.

As students study various classes, perhaps across various departments and even across different faculties, and increasingly across different institutions (perhaps in another European university), there is a need to collate information about their performance. But this tends only to be done at the end of the academic year, in the course of reviewing performance at exam boards. It is, of course, by then too late to do anything about gaps between expected and actual performance. They just become a matter of record.

The individual context

There is usually no formal individual appraisal equivalent. On entry to university there may be an advisor or supervisor of studies; but their role is limited and often 'one off'. Many students take care to develop a relationship with a tutor who takes the trouble to discuss their performance with them.

The system for most institutions, given the resources they have, is one designed around large scale lecturing, with brief periods in group tutorials, assessed by assignment and anonymous examination.

The extent to which you will find equivalents of the following elements of 'job specifications' will vary; they certainly all could be specified in principle:

CONCLUDING CASE STUDY (cont'd)

■ specifications which have 'face validity'; this would include generic capacities to obtain degrees and qualifications through writing assignments, passing exams, and the ability to study independently

■ clear role definitions; purposes and main functions of the 'job' (being a student); this would include ideas about general development of 'graduateness' and professional development in specific disciplines

■ specified key tasks; the parts of the 'job' (being a student); these would be tasks such as attendance at lectures and tutorials, reading and independent study, completing assessed work. Steps within that might be, for example for lectures: active listening, effective note taking, contributing to discussions, participating in exercises

■ specified competencies; the things you need to know and be able to do to perform the tasks. These are often to be found in course descriptors, to varying degrees of specification

■ specified performance standards and clear measures for them; this is often what most confuses students. Pass marks are clear, but what is the difference between a good exam answer and a bad one, between an excellent exam answer and a good one? The system of 'double' marking and external examiners used in many institutions to decide these matters often reveals that staff themselves have different views on this. And feedback from this is provided at the end of the year, not in a way that enables development before formal assessment.

REFERENCES

Armstrong, M. (1994) *A Handbook of Personnel Management Practice*, London, Kogan Page.

Baillie, J. (1996) *Employment Attitudes in Britain*, London, IPD.

Bartram, S. and Gibson, B. (1994) *Training Needs Analysis: A Resource for Identifying Training Needs, Selecting Training Strategies, and Developing Training Plans*, Aldershot, Gower.

Bee, F. and Bee, R. (1994) *Training Needs Analysis and Evaluation*, London, IPD.

Boydell, T. and Leary, M. (1996) *Identifying Training Needs*, London, CIPD.

Bramley, P. (1991) *Evaluating Training Effectiveness*, London, McGraw-Hill.

Buckley, R. and Caple, J. (1990) *The Theory and Practice of Training*, London, Kogan Page.

Chiu, W., Thompson, D., Wai-ming, M. and Lo, K.L. (1999) 'Re-thinking training needs analysis: A proposed framework for literature review', *Personnel Review*, Vol. 28, Nos 1/2.

DfEE (2000) 'National Training Award winners' *Employment News*, December/January.

Ford, D. (1999) *Bottom Line Training*, Houston, Gulf Publishing Company.

IER (2001) *Projections of Occupations and Qualifications; 2000/2001*, Institute of Employment Research.

Industrial Society (1998) *Training Trends*, May/June.

Kaplan, R. and Norton, D. (1996) 'The balanced scorecard', *Harvard Business Review*, January/February.

Mager, R. (2000) *What Every Manager Should Know About Training*, Chalford, Management Books.

McGehee, W. and Thayer, P.W. (1961) *Training In Business and Industry*, New York, Wiley.

McClelland, S. (1994) 'Training needs assessment data-gathering methods: Part 1, survey questionnaires', *Journal of European Industrial Training*, Vol. 18, No. 1.

NOP World, (2001) *People and Productivity*, Investors in People.

Pedler, M., Burgoyne, J. and Boydell, T. (1991). *The Learning Company: A Strategy for Sustainable Development*, London, McGraw-Hill.

Peters, T. and Waterman, R. (1990) *In Search of Excellence*, London, Harper & Row.

Rainbird, H. (2000) *Training In the Workplace: Critical Perspectives on Learning at Work*, London, Macmillan (now Palgrave Macmillan).

Robbins, P. (1993) *Organizational Behaviour*, London, Prentice-Hall.

Senge, P. (1990) *The Fifth Discipline*, New York, Doubleday.

Wolfe, P. (ed.) (1991) *Job Task Analysis: Guide To Good Practice*, Englewood Cliffs, NJ: Educational Technology Publications.

chapter three

Planning: Designing L&D Experiences

Learning outcomes

- Define the themes and issues involved in planning L&D experiences
- Define and develop aims, goals and objectives for L&D experiences
- Analyse cognitive capacity, capability and behavioural objectives
- Critically evaluate the options available and used for responding to a variety of L&D needs
- Reflect on how the principles of design can be applied to planning L&D experiences

FRAMEWORK CASE STUDY: 'TRANSFUSION'

A company employed around 1500 people in the production and bottling of alcoholic drinks at various sites throughout the UK. There was a history of adversarial employee relations in the company. In an increasingly competitive environment they adopted a strategy based on what they called a 'change agenda'. This involved a change to flexibility, shared responsibility, continuous improvement, a customer focus and team working. These were the characteristics that they needed to be a pioneering and innovative organisation. Associated with this was a process of intensive and extensive L&D. 'Transfusion' was the name given the major L&D event they planned and designed to meet the demands of their broader change agenda.

The L&D was planned and designed as a series of three day workshops for all staff. These workshops would use dramatic techniques to challenge and break old norms of 'rule following' and 'task orientation'. They were designed to help staff develop a more holistic view of and commitment to the new organisational culture, along with a new entrepreneurial ethos in the company. This training event was seen as being almost 'evangelical', requiring staff to confess their weaknesses before moving on to embrace the new values. At each event up to 50 people drawn from various locations attended. On day one as participants entered the room loud music was playing, and during the day learning points were illustrated with clips from major motion pictures. These were intended to stir up a fervor, providing a quite different experience to the way that previous company seminars had been run. The other sessions included guided fantasy exercises, Tai Chi exercises and the use of forms of dramatised group interaction.

It was an event that was planned to engage with the 'whole person'. The days started at 7.30 am and went on until late at night. Only healthy food and drinks were made available for refreshment. There were 'spotlight sessions': participants were put on a stage in a room in darkness, and were then asked to tell the group their values, hopes and fears. This encouraged many to reveal 'astonishing disclosures'; items discussed were divorce, deaths and serious illness. And at the end of each day there was a 'ho' session, mimicking traditional North American Indian practices. Participants sat cross legged and had to access a symbolic stick to be able to talk; when they were finished they called 'ho' to signal that, and everyone else had to respond likewise.

At the end of all this the directors of the company felt that 'Transfusion' had 'done it'; it had broken down barriers, taken away inhibitions and given people a real buzz. Young team leaders were more ready to talk and interact. The HR manager commented that 'people who would have been seen as cynical were jumping and singing and dancing and whooping because they thought it was brilliant'. Apparently nobody had a negative view. Research done 18 months later confirmed this overall positive assessment of the L&D event. The planning and design had worked. The need to fulfil the demands of the change agenda, in a company which had had severe employee relations problems, had been met.

Source: Beech *et al* (2001)

INTRODUCTION

Having identified L&D needs the next phase of the L&D process is to plan and design L&D experiences which will deal with those needs. Because planning is a generic activity the project management aspects of developing L&D experiences have a lot in common with other aspects of management. But in the specific context of planning, allocating resources and designing L&D, the L&D process can go awry (Chiu *et al* 1999). This is because it is challenging to design the aims, goals and objectives needed to structure L&D experiences.

The planning phase as a whole is concerned with 'the preparation of a blueprint for a training program' (Ford 1999, p 73). The preparation of a blueprint can also be thought of as a design activity, following on from the specification of need. The need for a building, a product or a new service may be established and specified. But blueprints for buildings, products or services are needed to guide their actual construction. Designs in this sense are abstract two dimensional models, using drawings to prefigure the construction of real world three dimensional objects. Their design is about specifications being made manifest, ideas being translated into reality. For 'social products', such as L&D events, the 'blueprints' that are created are made up of statements rather than line drawings. But they serve the same purpose: to make ideas manifest so that they can be discussed and refined in advance of being implemented.

Planning and design tasks will range from the straightforward to the highly complex; from how to plan and design a single on-the-job training experience through to developing events like the 'Transfusion' event described above. Starting with fairly conventional L&D needs and specifications, including concerns such as better team working, can lead to the planning and design of L&D that is unusual and challenging. The core of the planning phase, whether the outcomes will be conventional forms of L&D or experimental ones, is the same. It requires the establishment of aims, goals and objectives to structure the design and construction of a learning experience. This requirement for planning raises conceptual and practical questions about how to model the content of 'what is to be learned and developed'. This involves two kinds of analysis. First is the craft of determining and writing aims, goals and objectives. Second is the determination of a balance and unity in the L&D experience among these goals and objectives, so that the L&D provides for the elements of cognitive capacities, capabilities and behaviours involved in effective performance, but in an engaging way.

CRAFTING AIMS, GOALS AND OBJECTIVES

Planning and design in L&D is then about the preparation of statements to act as blueprints. These statements provide the structure for form and content; the form and content of course and lesson plans for classroom instruction programmes, or what a mentoring program involves, or what should be contained in a multimedia simulation. On the one hand each of these methods presents a unique kind of planning and design challenge. On the other hand the same principles of planning and design will apply. For, as with all design in context, there is a general structure for good practice that is particular to the context, and those elements of principle can be mastered. In L&D this context and structure entail developing and specifying statements in the form of aims, goals and objectives. These are the blueprints that allow learning events to be constructed and refined in advance of then building, or delivering, the actual learning events.

This good practice structure for L&D design has to be seen, as all elements of the L&D process should be seen; as an ideal (UDACE 1992). The rigours of this kind of planning and design may not always seem to have been followed in practice. Certainly there are not the requirements for such planning and design as there are with the creation of physical products, such as buildings or machines. And rather than providing a structure for the form and content of effective L&D, well identified L&D needs can become lost in a mist of 'word smoke', of vague and 'fuzzy' statements and definitions, rather than being converted into well founded plans for learning.

Errors in defining aims, goals and objectives can undermine the effort invested in assessing L&D needs effectively. To ensure that effective learning experiences are not compromised by failures in design the dual conceptual concerns are with both analysis and synthesis. Analysis entails breaking down the 'whole', the definition of an aim, into parts; into goals and objectives that flow from these and can be translated into the form and content of L&D experiences. Such definition of statements about L&D to improve human performance is ultimately an exercise in effective communication. But synthesis is also required, to put together from all these parts an integrated L&D experience that deals with the aim which has been determined. The result of this synthesis is the construction of a practicable and high quality learning experience, whether that is off job training, mentoring or a multimedia programme (see Figure 3.1).

The first element of analysis is to identify the right aim. Aims are general statements of intent, which provide the broad boundaries for what should follow. They form the outer boundary within which analysis of the form and content of learning should be confined. They are often a single sentence. Aims are not directly measurable, and the use of amorphous terms such as 'learn', 'know', 'understand' is acceptable. If the wrong aims are established, then whatever follows will not be taking everyone on track towards closing the performance gap. For example, if a performance gap in an organisation due to a lack of staff motivation has been identified, an aim

Figure 3.1   *L&D planning and design*

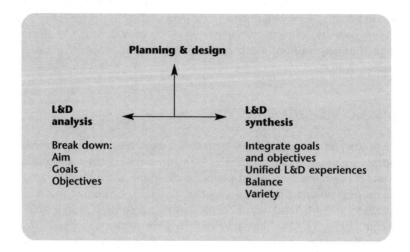

for L&D at work might then be for managers to learn to motivate staff. If the lack of motivation is a consequence of some other factor, planning and designing L&D to meet this aim will not lead to improved performance. Perhaps staff are not motivated because they do not have the technical skills to do their job well, and that is the problem; the lack of motivation is a symptom, but the aim of managers learning about motivation will not resolve it.

Having confidently identified an appropriate aim, the next step is defining goals. This second level of analysis is needed to translate an aim into discrete and manageable parts which can then be further analysed. Following the example above, of a concern with a problem in staff motivation, some examples can be given, First, some 'vague and fuzzy' versions of badly expressed goals that might become the focus of L&D in this context would be 'make managers able to fix employees' poor attitudes' and 'make staff more motivated'. These are too 'vague and fuzzy' to provide a template for the structuring of an L&D experience. Goals themselves have to be more clearly defined than this. A process for doing this is outlined in Box 3.1.

This process of defining goals can result in anything from a single goal statement for an aim to several interrelated goal statements, depending on the complexity of the performance issue and the scale of the L&D required. A planning and design ideal is to have no more than seven goal statements for any particular learning and L&D event. More than this is inadvisable as it impedes communicating with others about the L&D, and means the further analysis of specific objectives becomes too complex an exercise. Developing a myriad and complex set of goal statements is a substitute for good design, not an expression of good design. The identification of up to seven goals related to an aim can, then, provide the entry point for the third level of analysis.

The final step, the third level of analysis, is to craft objectives. Objectives are 'statements of the specific outcomes to be achieved by training stated from the point of view of the learner' (Ford 1999, p 74). Objectives are needed for planning and design for three main reasons. They are needed to provide the focus for detailed L&D design, to communicate the purpose of the L&D to learners and others, and to establish the context for measurement and evaluation (Box 3.2).

Box 3.1

Defining goals clearly

1 State the goal which is currently vague and fuzzy in terms of *outcomes* rather than *processes*. This means describing the end result of learning, what will happen as a consequence of learning and focussing on that. This is to be contrasted with specifying 'processes', for example, fix their attitudes. Trying to specify goals in this way is putting the cart before the horse. It often leads to people becoming entangled in thinking about 'how to get there' (how to fix people's attitudes) when they don't even know where 'there' is (what will happen as a result of the fixed attitude). Clearly phrasing goals in terms of outcomes is also effective for communicating with potential learners, who should be able to see by reading the goals what the benefits of the L&D will be for them. For example:

Unclear goals
Fix their attitudes
Be more motivated

Clear goals
Staff will have a responsible attitude towards their work
Levels of absenteeism will be reduced

2 Next, list the performances which may still at this stage be somewhat 'fuzzy'; this can be done by brainstorming or mind mapping, thus for staff having a responsible attitude towards their work these performances might be:

- ■ deal with customers courteously
- ■ get work done on time
- ■ keep work area uncluttered

3 Then sort this list of performances that has been generated to select the primary goals; identify those items on the list that will be too abstract to be measurable and scratch these from the list, or revise them again until they are in some way measurable.

4 Finally, having done this process of selection and refinement, test to see if you are finished defining goals. Do this by asking 'if someone did all these things (that the L&D event will cover) would that provide the expected performance?

The final concern with this level of analysis is that, having generated a number of objectives, there is a sorting process required. This is needed to sort objectives into a hierarchy for the form and content of the L&D experience. Ford suggests the following framework of enabling, terminal and application objectives (see Figure 3.2).

As a result of this whole process an L&D learning experience whose aim is to help managers motivate staff could now be designed around these enabling, terminal and application objectives. *Prerequisites* define the kinds of learning learners must already have, or which they will need to undertake before engaging with the primary learning. The focus of design and construction is either then to be seen as concerned with dealing sequentially and separately with the *enabling objectives* through separate L&D events, or dealing with them all together in one L&D experience along with the *terminal objective*. In the former case different L&D events might be designed and developed for appraisal and team building, whereas in the latter case a single event that included something on all of these might be designed. The best approach to take is partly to be determined by resources and practicability. Finally, the culmination of this stage of analysis is that some criteria for measurable evaluation have been determined; the *results objectives* will be the focus of evaluation.

Box 3.2

Crafting objectives

Objectives are the specific statements of intention which define outcomes for the learner that can be measured. They indicate the specific cognitive capacities, capabilities and behaviours that need to be demonstrated for learning to have occurred. Formulas for developing L&D objectives from goals are:

■ Specifying the target behaviours involved, using an action verb,

  eg   *not*   'understand how to motivate people'
       but   'be able to *motivate staff*'

■ Specifying a statement of content, using a noun describing a task,

  eg   *not*   'to motivate staff'
       but   'to motive staff and *reduce customer complaints*'

■ Providing a statement of conditions and standards; quantity (how much), quality (how well), time (how long),

  eg   'to motivate staff and reduce customer complaints by 10%'

If there is no direct and apparent explicit target behaviour, perhaps because the goal involves objectives related to more abstract learning, then a behaviour which requires performance of an activity that enables application of the theory should be determined,

  eg   for health and safety awareness, 'list and explain safety rules'

Figure 3.2   *Organising objectives: the example of 'managers motivate staff'*

Objectives	Examples
Prerequisites	Communication skills, knowing quality
Enabling objectives ↑	Appraise, lead, handle conflict, build teams
Terminal objectives ↓	Motivate staff
Application objectives	Meet customer requirements for quality of service
Results	Reduce customer complaints by 10% Increase customers by 10%

Figure 3.3   *Aim, goal and objective statements*

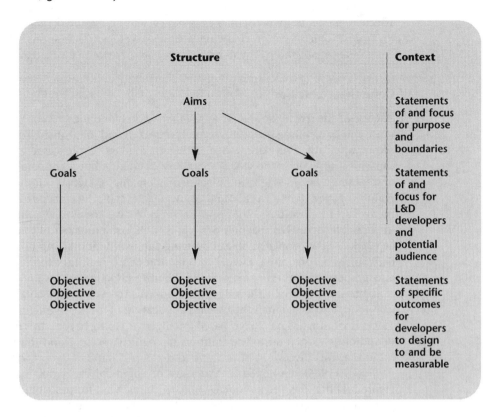

In sum then, Figure 3.3. provides a graphic overview of the planning and design process.

COGNITION, CAPABILITIES AND BEHAVIOURS

This structure for determining an aim, goals and objectives is the general analysis process. But there are a variety of kinds of objectives that can be determined, and there is usually a need to have some balance among these. There are a number of ways of mapping or modelling the variety of kinds of objective and balance needed to support L&D. Academics and practitioners writing on learning and L&D have long discussed the role of a tripartite division of the constituent parts of performance and learning. The terms used can vary, but the basic division and structure is the same. Some use the terms 'knowledge', 'skills' and 'abilities', while others use variations on these parts. The model of a tripartite division is therefore sound, analytically, but the concepts of knowledge, skill and ability are a problem.

Here three models will be presented and analysed as frames of reference, one for each main aspect of L&D. In planning for cognitive capacities the cognitive categories and levels suggested by Bloom (1965) will be the frame of reference. These will be critically evaluated by discussing constructivist interpretations of knowing and learning. In the planning for capabilities in learning and performance a tripartite model of employability, vocational and overarching capabilities will be given. This particular model is related to but builds on previous discussions of skill and competency. Finally, in regard to planning for 'behaviours' in learning and performance, a model of the affective elements involved in performance will be explored. The options here are to analyse objectives for changing attitudes, values or emotions. The concept of emotional intelligence (EI) will be described and critically evaluated.

Cognitive capacities

The use of the term 'knowledge' as the definition of a dimension of L&D, as common sense and in common use as it is, is both mistaken and inadequate. For what is usually meant when the term 'knowledge' is used in the L&D context is a range of cognitive capacities, of which 'knowledge' narrowly defined is but a constituent part. In this narrow sense knowledge is to be defined as organised, factual information about the realities of the external world. Such 'knowledge' is typically embedded in verified statements and propositions. What is mistaken is to take knowledge as being the set that includes all cognitive capacities when it is itself just a member of the set of cognitive capacities. How people go about knowing the world, and acting in it, is not dependent solely on organised, factual information about realities expressed as statements and propositions. Human knowing and acting also involve creativity and imagination; they involve making judgements and decisions where factual information is uncertain, and they entail the use and application of 'multiple intelligences' (Gardner 1993), not a single 'knowledge' based intelligence. Going beyond this narrow and basic definition is to step up to the frontiers of cognitive science and the mapping of the mind that this involves. This is done in detail in Chapter 10, on L&D in theory.

Bloom (1965) developed a taxonomy of cognitive capacities for education (see Figure 3.4) that has been a long established framework for describing a range of such capacities. The model has a number of benefits, though it suffers from being a 'content' model of cognitive capacities. One benefit is the simple modelling of a hierarchy, a hierarchy that can be simply applied to a range of performance domains and learning contexts. Knowledge is the most basic foundation, with 'evaluation' being the most complex. Some kinds of performance rely only on knowledge, some rely on a capacity to evaluate; the performance of a call centre operator can be pre-programmed and scripted, the performance of a surgeon in the midst of an operation has to be based on evaluation as they go along.

Figure 3.4   *Bloom's taxonomy of cognitive capacities*

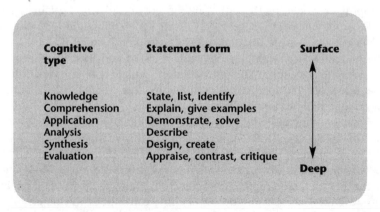

Cognitive type	Statement form	Surface
Knowledge	State, list, identify	
Comprehension	Explain, give examples	
Application	Demonstrate, solve	
Analysis	Describe	
Synthesis	Design, create	
Evaluation	Appraise, contrast, critique	Deep

- **Knowledge** is demonstrated by recall of previously learned material; able to define, identify, list
- **Comprehension** is demonstrated by being able to grasp the meaning of new material; able to explain, discuss, review, interpret
- **Application** is demonstrated by the use of learned material in new and concrete situations; able to relate, show, demonstrate
- **Analysis** is demonstrated by being able to break material down into component parts; able to analyse, compare, contrast, investigate
- **Synthesis** is demonstrated by being able to put parts together to form a whole; able to design, formulate, develop, organise
- **Evaluation** is demonstrated by being able to judge the value of material for a given purpose; able to assess, evaluate, argue, validate, criticise

In Bloom's taxonomy 'knowledge' is a term for the baseline or entry level cognitive capacity involved in performance; the capture and retention of information as a prerequisite of being able to do something. But as is well understood the capture and retention of information are necessary but not sufficient conditions for effective performance; there is more to doing than knowing. Often the immediate leap is to having capabilities, being able to do things. But this is in part because there is often more to performance than the possession of information. There is an increasing degree of difficulty and complexity associated with effective performance that draws upon other cognitive capacities. It is not enough, for example, for a doctor to 'know' that certain symptoms may indicate the presence of a specific disease; otherwise there would be automatic diagnosis machines that could respond to descriptions of symptoms, rather than doctors. Instead there are long queues at general practitioner practices; because real doctors have to be able to analyse various sources of data and symptoms, and put those together to diagnose and then evaluate an appropriate course of action. No machine can do this, though the development of call centres and interactive websites for heath related queries can provide a degree of service without the usual full cognitive capacities found in trained doctors.

However, as a 'content' model of cognitive capacities there are problems with the Bloom model. Content models suggest a fixed and set hierarchical structure; in this case of the kinds of cognitive capacity involved in performance, from the simplest to the most complex. This whole model of cognitive capacities assumes that for humans information is passively received by the senses, and that the more complex cognitive capacities are restricted to certain kinds of activity, tasks and situations. The overall function of cognition is assumed to be to help people discover an objective reality; that is a reality that exists 'out there', independent of the person sensing it. Both these assumptions about cognitive capacities inherent in the Bloom model are contestable. For people are not just passive cognition machines, passively receiving information through the senses; rather they may be seen as agents actively building up and constructing a view of reality based on their own experience and interests. The functions of cognition can then be interpreted as adaptive and serving to help manage the person's experience of the world, rather than being about accessing an 'objective reality' that is 'out there'. And this kind of sense making is not confined to some professionals undertaking difficult and complex tasks; it is an inherent feature of all human action. If that is true then such a view of cognitive functions means that learning even the simplest task is always being achieved by sense making, active agents, not cognition machines trying to memorise knowledge.

The former assumptions about cognition embody what can be termed an objectivist view of cognitive functions, whether they are simple, in the form of knowledge, or complex, in the form of critical evaluation; cognitive capacities are for obtaining the 'truth', codifying and packaging the truth. Cognition is a passive reflection of an external, objective reality. This then implies that a process of 'instruction' is needed to support L&D: in order to obtain such an image of reality, the subject, the person, must somehow receive the information from the environment, they must be 'instructed'. People are like cameras, that capture an image of how the world 'really' is in the brain. But such a view runs quickly into a host of conceptual problems; human brains do not act like mirrors or cameras at all. People can be seen as always actively generating a number of different models of the 'world out there', and the role of observing the actual outside world serves to reinforce some of these models while eliminating others. There is then a process of selection in the brain rather than a process of mirroring. That process of selection can have productive or problematic effects. On the one hand it can lead to new insights as people check and test the versions of the world they have and come to useful and insightful conclusions. On the one hand there may be a reinforcement of delusions. What cognition cannot do is establish the one and only, best and true way of perceiving reality.

A constructivist view of cognitive capacity (see Box 3.3) means that knowledge and all other aspects of cognitive capacity arise from what is internally constructed by a person, a learner, not what is impressed upon them by external authorities. Such construction serves in the first place an organic and natural purpose: that the individual person seeks to control what they perceive in order to eliminate any deviations or perturbations from their own secure, existing and preferred model of the world. Thus people always consider that which is relevant to their individual goals and actions and their own 'status quo', and tend to ignore that which is not felt as relevant. The individual person does not care about the truth of the knowledge which an expert may try to communicate to them; they are concerned primarily to compensate for perturbations they sense in their existing models of reality as they face up to and adapt to changed ideas about the world that come with new knowledge. Trying to 'pack in' more and more new knowledge in order to develop a person's cognitive capacities is then wrong, because it creates information overload. It is also wrong because people need to have time to adapt and adjust their whole model of the world as they go along a learning and development curve. If they are overloaded in this regard they will almost inevitably reject the new knowledge that others have been trying to instil. On the more positive side a sign of such a qualitative change in their constructed model of the world arises with 'Aha!' learning, when it seems that a person suddenly gets something that has previously eluded them.

Constructivist views of learning suggest that people do not accept verification of new knowledge by judging it as providing a 'better constructed model' of the outside world, more valid than their own. Experts may indeed be right, and their information and knowledge may be valid, but people will still not adapt or change their own models, their own validated kinds of information and knowledge. The most important L&D issue is then to help the individual choose between different constructions, to help them select the 'right one' rather than to enforce the correct one. This though is much more difficult to manage; it is easier by far to try to enforce a correct model, by citing authority, by asserting and imposing.

But too often this approach fails; it fails to engage adults with learning and indeed alienates them, and it fails to have the desired effect. The individual's criteria for selection of the kind of information and knowledge they will accommodate may be coher-

Box 3.3

Cognitive capacity L&D: more than cramming facts into brains

Constructivism has roots in philosophical debates about rationalism and empiricism. Rationalists argue that the individual human has no direct access to external reality, only to impressions of external reality. Thus people can only obtain information and use it through in-built cognitive principles which actively organise their experience rather than being like machines that neutrally process it.

The psychologist Piaget, for example, developed a theory of the different cognitive stages through which a child passes while building up an increasingly complex model of the world.

In a neuropsychology context it is noted that the nervous system cannot distinguish between a perception and a hallucination as both are merely patterns of neural excitation.

The cognitive principles evident in change in child development or in people not being able to tell the difference between perceptions and hallucinations suggest that there is active construction of information and knowledge. The analysis implies that when trying to structure and direct learning that involves establishing or developing cognitive capacities there is much more to doing it well than cramming facts into brains.

ence related; that is, if there is agreement between their existing patterns of information and knowledge and the new information and knowledge. Or the criteria may be consensus related; that is, if there is agreement between different individuals about accommodating the new information or knowledge. This latter process connects learning with 'social construction' ideas, which see cognition as shaped by social processes of communication and negotiation, part of the person's larger 'social construction of reality' as the member of a group (Berger and Luckmann 1979).

A pragmatic interpretation of this constructivist view is to be sensitive to the ways that the process and adequacy of cognitive capacity development in practice require more than specifying information and knowledge profiles. In some areas of L&D there are expert validated and accepted bodies of information and knowledge and the kinds of cognitive capacities required for jobs and tasks. It is nonetheless often difficult to help people learn and develop these, in part because of the learners' pre-existing models of the world and the perturbations to these which new information and knowledge bring, rather than because people lack the capacity to learn and develop. Equally there are areas of practice, and general management for instance seems to be one of those, where there is little or no agreement with others about the range and kinds of cognitive capacity in use. Here people may use many 'incoherent models' in the absence of an agreed body of information and knowledge.

Capabilities

The fact is that 'knowing how' does not always translate into 'being able to'; cognitive capacity, from knowledge through to critical evaluation capacities does not ensure effective performance; the individual must have constituent capabilities as well. Capabilities are to be defined as the discrete abilities involved in effective performance. Figure 3.5. provides one framework for mapping capabilities.

Figure 3.5   *A framework for mapping capabilities (Parsons 1997)*

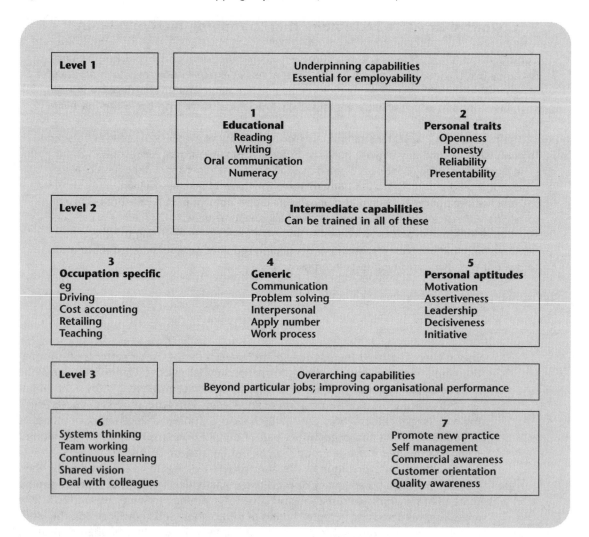

This map of capabilities suggests that capability related objectives for L&D can be considered at three levels: as underpinning capabilities, as intermediate capabilities and as overarching capabilities. Underpinning capabilities are those which, broadly speaking, are expected as a consequence of primary and secondary education. As such they may seem to be irrelevant for L&D at work. However, there are widely acknowledged problems with the success of education in establishing these underpinning capabilities; meaning that many enter the workforce lacking in both numeracy and literacy and personal traits. Intermediate capabilities are those most usually associated with L&D at work, L&D in occupation specific roles, in generic capabilities relevant to most jobs, and in personal development.

The final level is one that is increasingly most prominent: of overarching capabilities that are associated with productive people and productive organisations. Their essence is that they all relate to people taking responsibility rather than being instructed. They are capabilities that need to be developed in concrete workplace sit-

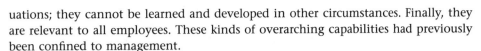

uations; they cannot be learned and developed in other circumstances. Finally, they are relevant to all employees. These kinds of overarching capabilities had previously been confined to management.

Such maps of capabilities have to be analysed in terms of validity. Validation is a process of estimating the extent to which correct and accurate inferences can be derived from the scores or profiles generated by using a model. Such models may be of the classical psychometric test type, or of the more general kind such as a framework for performance appraisal based on an annual review of objectives between a manager and an employee. The former tend to be subject to formal validation studies while the latter are simply evaluated in terms of 'being useful to get results'. A model that provides correct and accurate inferences is valid; for example a selection test is said to be valid in allowing inferences about the potential job performance of an applicant to be derived from its use. An instrument that does not allow correct and accurate inferences is invalid. A psychometric test used in selection that does not allow inferences about potential job performance of the applicant is invalid. Maps of capabilities like those outlined in Figure 3.5 have to be considered in terms of their validity. Do such maps of capabilities provide a way of defining objectives that are accurate and useful?

In principle the simplest division possible of capabilities is into three categories: capabilities with data, with people and with 'things'. Finer sets of distinctions can be and are made. These may elaborate upon differences between types of data, types of people, and types of 'thing'. Thus there may be quantitative data (numerical) and qualitative data (statements, meanings); there may be people in the form of external contacts (customers) and internal contacts (staff); simple things (use of basic computing applications) and complex things (the control of a complex machine). More and more distinctions can be made; there is no obvious limit to this.

One practical limit to the enumeration of capabilities is the problem of measurement. From a measurement perspective, it becomes increasingly difficult to collect reliable and valid data as the number and degree of abstraction of capability categories increase. One study in the 1980s grouped over 12,000 occupations using highly abstract data and people capabilities, and concluded that only five occupational clusters, five different kinds of job, existed. But within each of these mega-clusters of occupations there was a tremendous degree of variability in actual work activities, rendering the description of any specific job using these terms effectively useless for any practical purpose, such as advising people on career paths or developing training plans to prepare people to work in those jobs.

The issues are of accuracy and verifiability; what kinds of information can be reliably and validly rated directly by either occupational analysts, job incumbents or managers about capabilities? Harvey (1999) argued that several problems existed with developing accurate and verifiable information about the tasks involved in jobs. First was a problem of communication; frameworks were often described in a style that meant that the reading level needed to use them so high that they precluded incumbent completion. They also used items and rating scales that were so abstract that it was difficult to collect accurate and verifiable data about the presence and significance of work activities in jobs. In addition there were deficiencies in content coverage, making them poor tools for use in analysing, for example, managerial jobs. Finally, the fact that most instruments rated jobs using a small number of highly abstract items made them largely unusable for a number of personnel functions; for example, developing job descriptions and related employee performance appraisal forms requires relatively detailed data. Worker-oriented instruments were not really fit for such purposes.

Behaviours

The identification of a third dimension of development, in addition to cognitive capacities and capabilities, is a standard feature of models of L&D. The model of capabilities in Figure 3.5, for example, refers to 'aptitudes'. The reason for this inclusion of a third dimension is that effective performance is a consequence not only of what people know and think, and what they can do, but also of how they actually behave because of how they feel (Le Doux 1996). The affective influences on people and therefore performance can often make the critical difference between effective performance and poor performance. This is because the affective influences are the prime controllers of behaviour and therefore of performance (see Box 3.4). If the affective side is so critical for performance it is then essential that it has to be addressed in the design of L&D experiences and the setting of objectives. In this context, of learning experiences and performance, affective factors influencing behaviour are commonly discussed in regard to three constructs:

- **Changing attitudes**; defined as patterns of personal likes and dislikes which can be measured and changed
- **Developing values**; defined as basic beliefs about right and wrong which will influence what people will pursue and what they will or will not do
- **Emotional intelligence**; defined as the effective handling of emotions to enable effective interpersonal relations

Changing attitudes

Psychology, if it only studies an abstract isolated individual with no social context, and sociology, if it studies people only as parts of systems without any individual agency, are of limited use in analysing performance and L&D at work. The human

---

Box 3.4

Changing perspectives on the affective

During the nineteenth century and early twentieth century, psychology gave primacy to 'affect' in explaining much human behaviour. People were thought to be at the mercy of various drives and passions, which might erupt and overwhelm reason and rationality.

As behaviorism became more dominant in the field of psychology, affect was more and more discounted. There were those who wished to exclude affect from the 'scientific' study of people altogether. Even recently, with the ascendancy of cognitive psychology, humans have still been viewed as essentially problem-solvers whose thinking processes operate rather like a computer.

Often in such a view, affect is seen to matter, if at all, as a regrettable flaw in an otherwise perfect cognitive machine. With the current rise in popularity of ideas about multiple forms of intelligence, including the concept of emotional intelligence, the full cycle is completed, as once more affect is seen to be a primary factor in human behaviour which can be studied scientifically.

science that applies most directly to L&D at work is, in this sense, social psychology; the study of human behaviour in interpersonal relations and groups. The construct of attitudes is one of the major connections between social psychology and performance and L&D. The concept of attitudes was established as the heart of early social psychology, as a focus for research and discussing the interface between psychological and sociological processes, between interaction and persuasion or group membership and prejudice (Fishbein and Alzen 1975). Attitudes are mental states of positive or negative evaluations, likes and dislikes, regarding self, others and the world. Attitudes provide for patterns of behaviour based on the interaction of three elements:

- *Cognitive* components; elements of perceptions
- *Affective* components; elements of feelings
- *Conative* components; elements of patterns of action and experience

Attitudes are formed either from general experience through exposure to situations in the course of life, or by direct conditioning, where others structure associations and reinforcements. They come to be subject to dynamics of balance and dissonance. People seek to have attitudes that are consistent, and feel troubled if there is dissonance between what they perceive, what they feel and what they do.

In principle then to shape or change attitudes is to influence one or a combination of these elements: what people perceive, what they feel and what they do; behaviour will tend towards removing any dissonance. However, there are problems with the concept of and shaping of attitude. First, measurement is a problem; as attitudes are not directly observable there is a need to use scales and questionnaires to define and explore attitudes. The validity and reliability of these scales and questionnaires are questionable. Second there are concerns based on evaluating arguments about managing attitude change. There is often agreement on the 'ideal' behaviours; that, for example, it is right to try and reduce attitudes such as prejudices. But there is far less agreement on what 'works' to effect such change. For changing attitudes is it best to use the central route, which is providing for people to be exposed to and weigh up arguments? Or is the peripheral route better, which involves using emotion to arouse dissonance and change behaviours? Recent examples of anti-drug attitude change campaigns provide examples; is it better to provide information about drugs and let people weigh up the arguments, or should emotive messages about the dangers of drugs be promoted more forcefully?

When attempting to change attitudes the following variables are all important and of great relevance to effective L&D:

- **Communicator credibility**; whether they have expertise and are trustworthy; if L&D experiences are managed by people who are not perceived as experts and trustworthy any attempt at attitude change is likely to fail
- **Communicator attractiveness**; that is there to the person whose attitudes are to be influenced. The ability to have rapport with a person or group is essential in L&D
- **Extremity of message**; greater attitude change requires more extreme messages. Think back to the 'Transfusion' case example. The organisation sought a great change, from an old culture and old attitudes to the new; hence the extreme and evangelical methods adopted

- **Using one sided only or two sided, debate style, forms of argument**; many L&D experiences need to be given a structure where either one sided presentations (of instruction) or scope for debate and discussion is needed. Using the wrong method in the wrong circumstances will frustrate and confuse
- **The use of fear**; people will change their attitudes if threats can be articulated to favour attitude change
- **Different social situations**; group situations are better at eliciting attitude change than interpersonal face to face settings, and public situations are better than private. This is one reason why many L&D experiences are organised with groups when attitude change is involved
- **The influence of prior events**; for example, being forewarned that attitudes will be confronted can lead people to self inoculation against change. In the management of attitude change through L&D it should not be kept 'secret', but the potential for self inoculation can mean that time is needed to open people up in L&D events.

If it is hard to measure attitudes, and to influence them, what is the point of including them in the L&D planning process? The answer is that attitudes matter as and when they affect behaviour. See Box 3.5 for a profile of the kinds of attitudes that might seem to influence the behaviour of one kind of professional. Yet it is also the case that people's avowed attitudes can be only loosely related to their actual behaviour; for example there are those who may hold prejudicial views but not actually act in prejudicial ways. As people's behaviour is limited by laws and rules, by knowing others' attitudes, by the relative importance of the issue at hand, and by perceptions of social pressures, the existence of an attitude may not actually be a good guide to how people will behave. Someone may demonstrate all the attitudes expected of a chartered accountant, but still then behave in an unprofessional way; or they may fail to have these attitudes, but still act in a professional way. These kinds of concerns all act to negate 'attitude' as a potential force on behaviour, and restrict the scope for and usefulness of attitude change as a part of L&D at work.

Box 3.5

Attitude and occupation: chartered accountants

Caution	A preference for certainty, predictability, and avoidance of risk
Exactitude	A preference for the maximum attainable precision
Anti-theoretical pragmatism	A preference for convention-based rather than analytical approaches to problems, and for experience rather than theory
Professional exclusiveness	A preference for the qualities of chartered accountants compared to other kinds of accountant
Quantification	A preference for numerical methods of working
Rationality	A preference for systematic, logical approaches rather than intuition in problem solving

Source: McKenna (1987)

Developing values

The role of values provides an alternative perspec___ ___ ___ ___ ___ ___ ___ ffect in behaviour which is relevant to performance ___ ___ ___ ___ ___ ___ ___ of objectives. A value is 'an enduring belie___ ___ ___ ___ ___ ___ ___ e of existence is personally or soci___ ___ ___ ___ ___ ___ ___ ___ ___ duct or endstate of existence' (___ ___ ___ ___ ___ Values ___ ___ ___ ___ ___ is right and what is wrong, expre___ ___ ___ ___ ___ ___ ___ ___ ___ ___ ture require for stability within t___ ___ ___ ___ ___ ___ ___ ___ ___ ___ place also requires people to acc___ ___ ___ ___ ___ ___ ___ ___ ___ business context would be the i___ ___ ___ ___ ___ ___ ___ ___ honesty. In the absence of these ___ ___ ___ ___ ___ ___ ___ ___ and be dishonest. As members o___ ___ ___ ___ ___ ___ ___ ___ values, or define alternative valu___ ___ ___ ___ ___ ___ ___ ___.

Values impact upon o___ ___ ___ ___ ___ ___ ___ ___ (IRS 2000). There is often an ex___ ___ ___ ___ ___ ___ ___ identified and propagated; orga___ ___ ___ ___ ___ ___ lues to staff and others. Professio___ ___ ___ ___ ___ ___ t to guide many in their occupati___ ___ ___ ___ ___ others should abide by these above a___ ___ ___ ___ ___ barred from practising. Personal values about w___ ___ ___ ___ about duty and virtuousness, are invariably at the core of peo___ ___ ___ personal identity and self. In the context of L&D the concern is with con___ ___tency among the values relevant to the organisation, the job and the individual which can affect performance. Honesty, equity, fairness, reasonableness, efficiency, effectiveness, quality, satisfaction, trust, respect, and so on are values to be welcomed and upheld. Justifying cheating, acting harmfully, promoting conflict, harassment and aggression, malingering, dishonesty, discrimination, slackness, and duplicity are values to be excluded or confronted.

According to Rokeach (*op cit*) values have a 'transcendental quality' that guides an actor's actions, attitudes and judgements beyond immediate goals to more ultimate ends. While values are easy to identify and promulgate the problem is that they are not necessarily mutually supportive. For example there are potential contradictions in being both thrifty and charitable. They are both worthy behaviours in the right context at the right time, but may come into conflict at some times and in some contexts. It is as these value conflicts are resolved, either consciously or unconsciously, that a hierarchical arrangement is established and evolves as a value system (Davidson 1972). A value system is a rank ordering of values that serves to resolve social and personal conflict and direct the selection of alternatives where choices have to be made.

Values may be about self or other people (Reich and Alcock 1976), about ways of living (Morris 1965), or about any other aspect of being that bears on how people should live and what ends they should pursue. The analytical interest in values has been inspired by exploring different value systems, by the emergence of different value systems within specific cultures and between different cultures. Values were also explored because they were perceived to be important in social conditioning and ensuring social relationships. Rokeach describes value systems as being organised around two different concerns. Some values, which he calls terminal values, embody what people think and feel about desirable end states. Other values, which he calls instrumental values, embody what people think and feel about modes of conduct.

There are many challenges in dealing with values in L&D at work. One of the most obvious problems in organisations is the espousal of certain values and the use of others in practice. This may involve espousing, for example, honesty in the form of open communication but then practising secrecy and duplicity. Or it may involve claiming to be an organisation that subscribes to values of equality but then failing to act on that. There are also potential conflicts between value systems; between, for example, those seeing the workplace as a domain for achieving progress in equal opportunity and those who see the imposition of legislation on organisations as a burden. There are also potential conflicts within value systems. What happens, for instance, when the values of 'respect' and 'efficiency' are in conflict? For reasons of efficiency a proposed 'downsizing' may be required, but the workforce are hardly going to feel that is consistent with 'respecting' them.

The connections with L&D are that planning for and designing objectives related to values matter. Core organisational values are identified and propagated; examples are 'teamwork', 'quality', 'creativity'. Occupational values are relevant and necessary for competent performance of a specific job, as are professional values in the form of ethical guidelines. Personal values, and their fit with the organisation and occupational role, may provide areas where L&D is required.

Emotional intelligence

The emotional aspects of work and performance have been long acknowledged as important for performance in many jobs and organisational settings (Hochschild 1983, Fineman 1993). The topic seems to be assuming greater prominence in business and management as a whole. In part this has been caused by the rise of stress as a prominent health and safety issue in many organisations. An analysis of the kinds of emotional demands being made on staff, and ways of mitigating these, have been relevant to responding to the 'stress epidemic'. Concern with emotion is also a reflection of a longstanding 'human relations' concern within effective teams and relationships at work (Strongman 1996). Emotion is not just an issue for work and performance where employees may be exposed to high degrees and kinds of trauma; there have always been emotional contexts for all forms of work and performance. There are emotional aspects to effective performance when working as an undertaker or as a Club 18–30 rep, and there are emotional aspects to effective performance in working in call centres as well as in nursing and care in hospitals.

At a simple level emotions are defined and manifest as feelings; of being 'mad, bad, sad or glad'. Finer distinctions can be made, of variations and expansions on these (see Box 3.6). The specifics of how and why people experience anger, elation, anxiety/fear, disgust, grief, happiness, jealousy/envy, love, sadness, embarrassment, pride, shyness, shame, or guilt can all be explained in terms of various theories of emotion, each with different ways of defining and modelling emotions. In the L&D at work context the concern is that performance may be affected if positive emotions are not activated and if 'negative' emotions are not contained and controlled. Effective performance may require people to get angry or embarrassed or disgusted, or to avoid getting angry, embarrassed or disgusted.

There are various perspectives on defining and analysing emotions (Strongman 1996), which are relevant to defining L&D objectives. One is to view emotions as physiological processes; emotions are then studied as involving physical changes in the physiology of organisms. These kinds of analyses explore the connections between, for example, fear and preparing for fight or flight, or love and making/breaking reproductive bonds and relationships. L&D involves helping people cope with these physiological processes. Another perspective is to view emotions as they influence

> ### Box 3.6
>
> ## Personal and interpersonal emotions
>
> ### Personal emotions; feelings of the individual alone
>
> | | | | |
> |---|---|---|---|
> | Joy | Suffering | Pleasure | Pain |
> | Content | Regret | Relief | Aggravation |
> | Cheerfulness | Dejection | Rejoicing | Lamentation |
> | Amusement | Dullness | Aesthetic | Taste |
> | Hopelessness | Fear | Courage | Cowardice |
> | Rashness | Caution | Desire | Indifference |
> | Dislike | Fastidiousness | Wonder | Pride |
> | Humility | Vanity | Modesty | Insolence |
>
> ### Interpersonal emotions; feelings in relationship
>
> | | | | |
> |---|---|---|---|
> | Friendship | Enmity | Sociality | Courtesy |
> | Love | Hatred | Resentment | Anger |
> | Sulleness | Benevolence | Malevolence | Threat |
> | Pity | Gratitude | Forgiveness | Jealousy |
> | Envy | Guilt | | |
>
> Source: Roget's Thesaurus 1987

thinking; emotions are studied as a feature of the information processing brain and mind. Here the concern is how emotions influence perception and thinking processes. L&D about emotion is needed to help people be aware of and take into account the way that emotions can influence thinking. There is also study of the patterns of emotion within social contexts, reflecting conditioning. Emotions are studied as facets of socialisation into patterns of role behaviour; for example with gender based and cultural variations in appropriate emotional display, or 'big boys don't cry' and 'women are nurturing' expectations. L&D at work can then be about challenging this conditioning and the stereotypes that go with it. Finally emotions have been studied in the context of clinical dysfunction; emotions are studied as causing or contributing to mental dysfunction, for example to the experience of depression. L&D is not appropriate if this kind of concern arises; health professionals are the proper people to investigate and deal with this influence of emotion on performance.

In the work and performance L&D context, current concerns arising from all these perspectives are currently focussed on the discussion of 'emotional intelligence' (EI) (Goldman 1996, Dulewicz and Higgs 1999). Intelligence is the ability to define and pursue goals and overcome obstacles to achieving them. Emotional intelligence is the ability to appreciate the interpersonal dynamics involved (see Figure 3.6) in defining and pursuing goals and overcoming obstacles to achieving them. Performance gaps and L&D objectives can be related to gaps in EI. One framework for structuring analysis of this is given in Figure 3.7. This suggests that EI requires as a minimum some awareness, complemented then by personal experiences enabling empathy; and further involves being able to express emotions oneself, and therefore ultimately enables the control of emotions based on this awareness, empathy and ability to express. Without awareness

Figure 3.6   *Some elements of emotional intelligence*

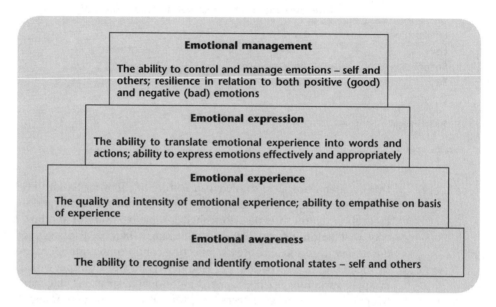

Effective relationships	Self esteem	Political awareness
Empathy	Self awareness	Influence
Service orientation	Emotional awareness	Adaptability
Accurate self assessment	Self confidence	Initiative
Conflict management	Self control	Developing others

Source: Goldman (1996)

Figure 3.7   *Emotional intelligence (based on Smith and Aufenast (2001))*

Emotional management

The ability to control and manage emotions – self and others; resilience in relation to both positive (good) and negative (bad) emotions

Emotional expression

The ability to translate emotional experience into words and actions; ability to express emotions effectively and appropriately

Emotional experience

The quality and intensity of emotional experience; ability to empathise on basis of experience

Emotional awareness

The ability to recognise and identify emotional states – self and others

there can be no experience, without experience there can be no expression, and without expression there can be no control (Smith and Aufenast 2001).

CONCLUSION

Planning and designing effective L&D require the establishment of aims, goals and objectives. These need to relate in a balanced way to the cognitive capacities, capabilities and the behaviours required for effective performance. Box 3.7 gives some principles of good design that can be applied to the synthesis of elements required to make a good learning experience. The opening case study can now be re-read with these concepts in mind, and it should help make more sense of why what was done was done, and it can explain why it seemed to work. In practice identifying and then developing deliverables provides the structure for project managing individual L&D experiences. It may be that aspects of the work environment need to be changed, rather

Box 3.7

The principles of good design

A design is a plan that shows the look or function of something that will be made. Principles of design have been suggested for many areas: graphic design, product design, building design. Some principles that emerge from all these areas of design that apply to the structure and content of L&D experiences are:

Balance: What is to be made will need to be balanced, and design should be the time when the right balance is gauged. How much of one thing, and how much of another, to ensure balance? What proportion of cognitive capacity, capability and behaviour is going to be right?

Contrast: Powerful images use high contrast. These may use high contrast of dark and light, shapes or materials. Another way to show contrast is with contradiction. This can provide muscle to get a message over. Powerful learning can use high contrast: before and after, bad practice and good practice, light humour and serious stories.

Direction: Trainers need to lead learners through their L&D experiences, without them getting lost or confused. Direction in learning is about managing going in circles, but still making progress.

Economy: Getting down to the bare bones of the design, once all extraneous elements are eliminated, are you sure the message is clear? If you are not, then the learners will not be either. And sometimes it is essential to send a large message with a small voice; there is no time or resource for anything else.

Emphasis: People are always telling stories that end with them saying 'And my point is this . . .'. Although the story might be interesting, the point could be made with less embellishment and more structure. When everything is emphasised, nothing is emphasised. When you create an L&D event what point are you making? Where does the emphasis need to be?

Rhythm: Following a rhythm, a pattern, is central to all forms of communication. Without rhythm communication is lifeless and drab. The principle of rhythm is as unavoidable as the element of contrast. Good learning experiences have rhythm.

Unity: If form and content don't match goals, it all ends up an agony of self defeat. Unity sounds like the crowning achievement of all the principles of design, but it's really no better than emphasis, no less than rhythm. Unity is judged on how well the event is received. Elements must be employed effectively within a format. A success depends on the appropriate relationship of content within the format.

Source: http://www.graphicdesignbasics.com

than the L&D focussed on the set goals and objectives of developing cognitive capacities and capabilities.

The problems with planning and design reflect challenges in three areas: in analysis, in synthesis and in communication. The challenges of analysis are about breaking needs down into discrete 'developable' units of learning. The challenges of synthesis are about balance and variety in putting together designs for dealing with cognitive, capability and behavioural dimensions of learning. Throughout it all communication is central: clarity and simplicity in definitions and statements.

Concluding exercise

If you were to organise a one day L&D course for undergraduate students with the aim of 'giving an overview of the occupation' for one of the following, what goals would you devise for it? From these goals what kinds of objectives would you derive?

■ Becoming an entrepreneur
■ Nursing in intensive care
■ Call centre customer care
■ An HR manager

What aspects of cognitive capacity, capability and behaviour would you want to be emphasising as being involved in the occupation to enable an effective performance?

REFERENCES

Beech, N., Cairns, G. and Robertson, T. (2000) 'Transient Transfusion; or the wearing off of the governance of the soul?', *Personnel Review*, Vol. 19, No. 4.

Berger, P. and Luckmann, T. (1979) *The Social Construction of Reality*, London, Penguin.

Bloom, B.S. (1965) *A Taxonomy of Educational Objectives: Handbook 1: Cognitive Domain*, New York, McKay.

Chiu W., Thompson, D., Mak, W. and Lo, K. (1999) 'Rethinking training needs analysis: a proposed framework for a literature review', *Personnel Review*, Vol. 28, No. 1.

Davidson, P. (1972) 'Value theory: toward conceptual clarification', *The British Journal of Sociology*, Vol. 23, March.

Dulewicz, V. and Higgs, M.J. (1999) *Making Sense of Emotional Intelligence*, ASE Evolution@work.

Fineman, S. (ed.) (1993) *Emotions in Organizations*, London, Sage.

Fishbein, M. and Alzen, I. (1975) *Belief, Attitudes, Interaction and Behaviour: An Introduction to Theory and Research*, Reading, MA, Addison-Wesley.

Ford, D. (1999) *Bottom Line Training*, Houston, Gulf Publishing.

Gardner, H. (1983) *Frames of Mind*, New York, Basic Books.

Goldman, D. (1996) *Emotional Intelligence*, London, Bloomsbury.

Harvey, R.J. (1999) 'Job analysis' in M. D. Dunnette and L. Hough (eds), *Handbook of Industrial and Organization Psychology*, Second edition, Palo Alto, CA, Consulting Psychologists Press.

Hochschild, A.R. (1983) *The Managed Heart: Commercialization of Human Feeling*, Berkeley, University of California Press.

IRS (2000) 'Added values', *Employment Trends*, 711.

Le Doux, J. (1996) *The Emotional Brain*, London, Weidenfeld and Nicolson.

McKenna, E. (1987) *Psychology in Business: Theory and Applications*, London, Lawrence Erlbaum Associates.

Morris, C. (1965) *Varieties of Human Value*, Chicago, University of Chicago Press.

Parsons, D. (1997) 'A qualitative approach to local skills audits', *Skills and Enterprise Briefing*, Issue 6.

Reich, B. and Alcock, C. (1976) *Values, Attitudes and Behaviour Change*, London, Methuen.

Rokeach, M. (1970) *Beliefs, Attitudes and Values: A Theory of Organization and Change*, San Francisco, Jossey-Bass.

Smith, P. M. and Aufenast, J. (2001) 'Emotional competence at work: implicit theories, a new model and supporting data', *Proceedings of the British Academy of Management Conference, Cardiff, September 2001*.

Strongman, K. (1996) *The Psychology of Emotion: Theories of Emotion in Perspective*, New York, Wiley.

UDACE (1992) *Learning Outcomes in Higher Education*, Department of Employment.

chapter four

Acting: Developing and Delivering L&D Experiences

Learning outcomes

- Describe and analyse the theory and practice of instruction and facilitation in delivering L&D
- Design L&D events using instruction and facilitation methods
- Critically evaluate the strengths and weaknesses of instruction and facilitation as methods of L&D support
- Apply the project management process to developing and delivering L&D experiences
- Describe and analyse other forms of performance support systems relevant to L&D

FRAMEWORK CASE STUDY: THE DEATH OF GEORGE

A mystery man was found at the edge of a road by a passing motorist after being struck by a hit and run driver, and was taken to an intensive care unit. Staff inserted a chest drain and a breathing tube. As he lay unconscious, covered in bruises, abnormal heart and chest sounds were detected. X-rays revealed eight fractured ribs and other tests showed that blood sugar levels were high. He was put on a ventilator and lines for fluids and drugs were inserted. For the next five days he was attended by more than 40 people; always in a coma, his condition fluctuated. His carers knew him only as George, and that he was 22, facts based on rifling through his pockets.

Despite their best efforts George died (again); because George is a mannequin who lives in a simulated intensive care unit, next to other mock wards. His carers had included student nurses who were even younger than he was. They had to break the news to George's parents and girlfriend; just as they will soon have to do in the real world. The clinical simulation laboratory allows student nurses to cover all the basics, from taking temperatures to giving injections, without having to leave the campus during the first months of their course. Near graduation they return to deal with more complex life and death situations involving George.

The university believes it is immoral to use genuine hospital patients as guinea pigs, and the student nurses find the training highly useful and confidence building. It is a safe environment in which to practise before facing real hospital wards. What is striking about this is that this is a return to an old method of learning that fell out of favour in the 1970s and 80s. It had been dismissed as artificial, ill equipped and bearing no resemblance to real care settings. It was replaced with direct training in hospitals. But students complained about inadequate preparation on wards for training, and staff complained about students coming in lacking basic skills. So the practice room and the simulation are now back in fashion.

Source: Wilson (2001)

INTRODUCTION

Having identified an L&D need, and having planned and designed objectives for cognitive capacities, capabilities and behaviours, the next step and phase is to develop and deliver an appropriate L&D experience. There are a wide range of options for delivery (see Boxes 4.1 and 4.2).

Any mode of delivery has its own strengths and weaknesses, in terms of the costs, quality, and the speed with which experiences can be delivered (Leigh 1991). In the first chapter five major options were described:

1 'on the job' learning experiences at the workplace
2 being on an organisation managed short training course
3 attending a short external course or learning event
4 using information and communication technologies (ICT) systems, computer based or learning in a 'learning centre'
5 being involved in a 'learning partnership', like mentoring

Box 4.1

Learning to lie?

A college of speech and drama has launched a company to help provide training in businesses on acting skills. They want to teach the 'tricks of the trade' so that business people can give better presentations. The course is not just about using the voice effectively, but a total package of self presentation skills. Learners will also be able to practise television and radio interviews in real studio facilities. The course is not about getting people to pretend to be other people, as actors do, but to 'be themselves', and communicate well.

'What we do is to help people understand that there are maybe habits they have picked up – in speech and body language which can get in the way of that communication. You can't teach someone to lie convincingly in a two day course. That is a much more serious long term project.'

Source: Clark (2001)

Box 4.2

Employee development and assistance programmes (EDAP)

Company sponsored EDAPs are complementary to formal training, allowing employees to choose from a wide range of learning experiences. They may offer personal effectiveness courses, academic options, computer skills and professional exams. They are often designed to encourage uptake from those with minimal qualifications and limited opportunities in the past. They provide an opportunity for employees to enhance their employability, improve their learning skills, and increase their effectiveness at work.

Lucas Automotive Electronics promotes such a scheme. It was launched in 1989 to encourage staff to realise their potential. The scheme is voluntary and employee driven. Funding is not given for hobby or leisure interests; but the scheme can fund courses within the company or with external providers. In 1997/98, 60 employees participated out of the 1200 workforce, or 5%. Most of these were shopfloor workers. It has a positive effect on morale and motivation. Some staff have achieved promotion through undertaking learning activities, but that is not the main goal. In fact some people's expectations may have been falsely raised in that respect. As the scheme matures so do its learners; some employees have recently enrolled on Open University courses, having completed basic courses within the scheme.

Source: IDS (1998)

Figure 4.1   *A delivery continuum*

Instruction	Facilitation
Programmed	Flexible
Scripted	Improvised
Directive	Participative

While these are quite different options they share common methods of delivery in action. These are the methods of instruction and facilitation. The methods of instruction and facilitation are different ways of delivering effective L&D. In this chapter delivery methods are outlined and described on a continuum (see Figure 4.1), with instruction at one end and facilitation at the other. Other aspects of delivery are covered in further chapters on perspectives and practices.

Further effective L&D development and delivery involve abilities in project management. L&D projects will range from a single person developing a single session for a small group of employees to many people developing complex courses which form a part of larger organisational projects. Control of costs, quality and time are essential whatever the scale of project.

INSTRUCTION

Instruction involves programmed learning, which requires the direct transmission and development of predetermined cognitive capacities, standard capabilities and explicit behaviours. The principles of such programmed instruction emerge from classical theories and classical practice in how to shape and influence human development; from the rote learning of 'crude' knowledge, through trial and error learning for capabilities, to the conditioning and reinforcement of behaviour patterns. Some synthesis of cognition, capability and behaviour development is present in most instructional experiences. Ford suggests a four phase model of L&D delivery by instruction in the classroom which outlines the most common 'recipe' (see Figure 4.2).

Delivery is about following these steps in instruction (Figure 4.3). Specifications which have involved determining in full and in detail what learners have to know, be able to do, and how they should act are applied. Learning is then delivered with these elements presented in the logical sequence, enabling practice. The instructor is required to play the role of showing and telling. Learners are then directly and formally tested on whether or not they have developed the cognitive capacity, capability and behaviours required.

For example, a retail organisation decided it needed to improve stock flows and safety in its warehouses. The pre-instruction level of performance was poor stock flow management and evidence of unsafe practices. They developed a program of instruction that involved the following elements:

■ **Cognition;** knowledge of set procedures, specifying what employees will do. Employees will store incoming stock in the right order in the right areas. Employees will know the correct procedures for lifting and using machinery
■ **Capability;** instruction in the one best way to do things, how they will do it. Employees will be shown how to manage stocks. Employees will be shown how to lift heavy loads following prescribed procedures

Figure 4.2   *Phases of the development and delivery of instruction*

Orient	Motivate Assess Prepare
Present	Demonstrate Explain
Practise	Simulate Coach Trial and error
Evaluate	Observe Feedback
Apply	Review Check standards Check skill transfer

Figure 4.3   *Instructional learning steps*

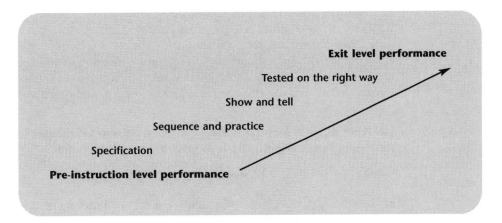

■ **Behaviour;** the organisation prescribed norms about why they should perform in these ways; employees will follow proper procedures to ensure the smooth running of restocking, ensuring efficiency on all shifts. Employees will behave safely to ensure there are no accidents or injuries with the impact this has on the efficiency of the organisation and to meet its legal obligations.

Learning delivery here depends upon including all objectives in a well sequenced learning experience which can be delivered by instruction. There are varieties of instruction. It may involve self instruction, from learning packs. It may involve instruction from managers, or instruction provided in specialist learning environments by trained instructors. The principles of instruction, whichever mode is to be used, are:

■ Having and sticking to set objectives for all the parts of the learning experience and the whole learning experience. This requires embedding instructional objectives in structured materials, experiences or class based sessions for one day or 2–3 day courses.
■ Instructional experiences must be both comprehensive and kept simple. Everything is to be included and dealt with, through confirmation stage by stage, until at the end the complete transmission of cognition, capability and behaviour is achieved.
■ Preparation is the largest task in instruction; developing materials, presentations, simulations, and appropriate tasks so that all objectives are covered.
■ In the delivery of instruction there has to be thought given to creating and maintaining interest for the individual or the group. Materials have to be engaging, experiences have to be motivating, and class based instruction has to be engaging.
■ Instruction requires an objective evaluation of the extent of L&D. As objectives have been tightly set, whether someone knows or does not know, is capable or is not capable, can behave appropriately or not, will be measurable. Trainees can be tested and deemed to be right or wrong in terms of performance related cognition, capability and behaviours.

Developing professional instructors has been an integral part of this approach to managing learning (Eitington 1984). The professional development of trainers, the training of trainers, has been largely concerned with this. Professional instructors are people who have a thorough knowledge of effective performance and the learning required for it; they understand the 'how' and the 'why' of the learning trainees are experiencing. They also understand and use the principles of structured and programmed instruction in design and delivery. They are able to perform consistently over many learning events and over time as instructors, to deliver and objectively assess learners.

Exercise 4.1 Is being or having been an excellent performer a necessary precondition for being a good instructor?

Good instructors have been characterised as:

- being consistent in their ability to manage repeated delivery of the same L&D event
- being meticulous and obsessively organised in order to ensure that all aspects of instruction are effective
- being sympathetic to learners of different abilities
- being patient with the process of showing and telling, trial and error
- being objective in assessing others' knowledge, capabilities and behaviour

Given these factors it is implied that the best instructors will be drawn from the ranks of those who are the best performers. But being the best performer is not a sufficient condition for being an effective instructor. Some of the best performers are unable to engage with supporting the learning of others, and cannot perform well as instructors. The best instructors may rather be those who best grasp the 'business' of learning, even though they themselves are not from the ranks of the top performers. Being, or having been, an excellent sports person, an excellent artist or an excellent manager is not any guarantee of being able to coach others in a sport, develop others' artistic talents, or develop other managers.

The principles of instruction (Forsyth 1992) that are to be embodied in learning events are clear enough (see Figure 4.4).

Yet some of the characteristics of adult learners present particular problems for instruction and the instructor following these ideals (see Figure 4.5).

Figure 4.4   *Principles of instruction*

- **Get attention; capture attention and keep it, get learners to respond**
- **Motivation; make it clear 'What's in it for me?'**
- **Modelling; provide learning through imitation; do it the way I do it**
- **Retention; manage retention of information and procedures**
- **Timing; keep everything on track**
- **Practice and feedback; enable and manage trail and error**
- **Relevant practice; ensure practice is realistic and performance related**
- **Reinforcement; reinforce the correct ways, extinguish the erroneous**

Source: Mager (2000)

Figure 4.5   *Instruction and adult learners*

Instruction	Adult learners
Get attention	Have different kinds and degrees of experience
Motivation	Can already perform many skills; get bored
Modelling	Seek to avoid pain and embarrassment; dislike feeling exposed
Timing	Pacing for different abilities; some bored, some lost
Practice and feedback	Feel exposed and vulnerable
Relevant practice	Through experience feel classrooms or cases are unrealistic
Reinforcement	Have own experiences to reflect on; dislike being 'taught'

Figure 4.6   *The experiential learning cycle*

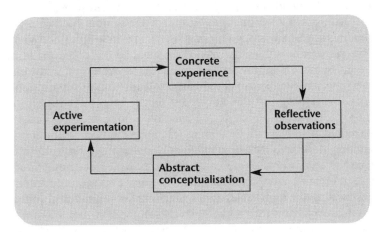

Tensions between the principles of instruction and the realities of adult learning present a challenge in delivery.

FACILITATION

Partly because of the nature of adult learners, and partly because of the kinds of L&D required, methods other than instruction have evolved and are in use to deliver L&D at work. Facilitation is the use of methods which require the participation of learners, and which enable 'constructive learning' through discovery. Facilitation is explained with reference to the operation of an 'experiential cycle' (see Figure 4.6.) of learning (Kolb 1984) rather than an instructional model to develop cognition, capability, and behaviour.

While facilitation is sometimes thought of as a recent development in learning, the origins of the principles and practice of facilitation are both ancient and modern. Socrates, in Greek antiquity, used to educate and infuriate in equal measure when he insisted that, far from being a font of all wisdom who could instruct others, he knew nothing; all he could do was question others who thought they knew. In reducing them to confusion he provided an opportunity for the critical exploration of ideas through dialogue, to improve understanding and develop knowledge.

In the modern context Rogers (1969) exemplifies best those who came to argue for facilitation and questioned the instruction based systems of learning that were common in many educational and corporate settings. The dominant approach was to see learning as a process of filling up empty vessels with prescribed and standardised bodies of knowledge, discrete predetermined capabilities and behaviours. But people had to be, in his phrase, 'free to learn'; to experience learning and change through having significant experiences which were meaningful to them. Classrooms in schools did not provide that environment, nor did training rooms in organisations. Schools, colleges and other learning environments had to be reformed to allow for and enable this freedom to learn. Like Socrates in his time, Rogers was issuing a challenge to people; to provide for and manage effective learning relationships which could overcome the 'disease' of the age. In Socrates' time that disease was the acceptance of unexamined assumptions about key ideas and concepts. In Rogers' time the disease was a climate where there was an endemic ' lack of purpose, lack of meaning, lack of commitment on the part of individuals' (*op cit*, p 271); a climate where people were alienated not just from learning and educational environments, but from their societies more broadly. Facilitating learning was one way of challenging these kinds of alienation.

The connection is there between these ideas about facilitating learning and organisational issues with improving performance at work. It is often the case that analysing specific problems with managing learning leads to a broader and bigger analysis of issues with learning, such as Rogers seeing the causes of problems with learning as being part of broader problems of alienation among young people.

Rogers' conclusion was that there was a need to create communities of learners, where the educator is facilitating change and learning, not instructing learners. They needed therefore to build on real problems, provide resources, and use 'learning contracts', to organise groups and stimulate inquiry. This meant, in educational contexts, doing away with formal classroom teaching, examinations, and grading systems. Facilitators would set the mood, enable learning, moving away from 'formal' teaching roles to being in learning relationships. A good review of facilitation relationships as expressing this kind of thinking and their applications in contemporary L&D with individuals, groups and organisations is to be found in Megginson and Pedler (1992). It is certainly the case that the use of 'action learning', involving people working with each other on real problems rather than sitting in classrooms, owes its genesis to those who promoted facilitation as a delivery method.

Underpinning the facilitative perspectives is an argument about the experiential learning cycle. Kolb was concerned, like Rogers, with reforming ideas about learning; learning was to be seen as a social process based on carefully cultivated and guided experience, implying a move away from instruction in the classroom to other modes of learning in other circumstances. In this he was adopting the earlier ideas of Kurt Lewin about experiences as providing the only firm foundation for developing useful knowledge.

Kolb adapted and applied this with a view to managing learning based on experience. He identified different aspects of what it means to talk about learning from experience, discussing two dimensions of how people interact with the world. One was a dimension of learning structured as apprehension-comprehension. The other was a dimension of knowledge structure as intention-extension. He derived from these dimensions four modes of learning; a person would have a preference for one or other of these modes of learning. The associated concept, developed by authors like Honey and Mumford (1982) in the UK, is that people have 'learning styles' (see Figure 4.7); they have a preference for learning based on one aspect of the experiential learning cycle. For Kolb the challenge of learning was one of integrative development; of people

Figure 4.7   The experiential learning cycle and learning styles

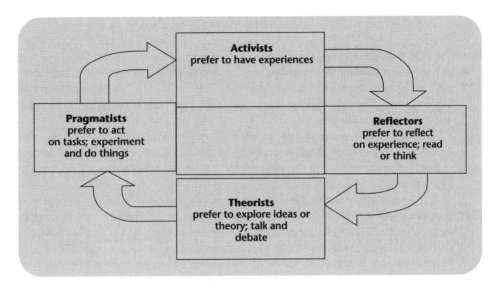

being able to deal with all these elements of experiential learning to complete their learning. For Honey and Mumford the significance was that learners ought to be aware of their preference, and therefore understand why some learning suited them and other kinds of learning were more difficult. Learning styles are the key to understanding these different preferences (see Box 4.3).

Learning delivery should involve encompassing the full learning cycle. For example, an organisation may seek to build more effective teams as problems with an absence of team work are causing performance concerns. It may seek to facilitate the development of teams by sending a group of people on an 'outdoors experience'. This would involve:

- **Cognition;** knowledge about how effective groups work. This will come from an experience of being in a group and reflecting on its development
- **Capabilities;** exploring what it takes to be a leader in a group by giving people an opportunity to experience that for themselves. As they practise it issues are raised, about options for leadership and their own abilities
- **Behaviours;** exploring how to encourage and maintain communication even where difficulties with handling conflict in the group arise

Facilitators are generally managing learning through the use of participative methods and reflection on experiences they are sharing with the learner (Bentley 1994). The learning happens as the experiential cycle is running, not in relation to a pre-set and fixed agenda scripted by the trainer. Learners are not empty vessels to be filled up, they come with already existing kinds of cognitive capacity and ideas, capability and behaviour. If these are to be changed through L&D, that involves either adding new and increasing ideas, capabilities and behaviours or the displacement of erroneous ideas, bad habits or dysfunctional behaviour.

There is a concern with delivering learning events to ensure maximum participation and involvement in the process by the learners. In delivery facilitators need to be sensitive to the obstacles which can impede involvement and therefore learning.

Box 4.3

Learning styles and delivery

Most people develop preferences which give them a liking for certain stages over others. Learning styles are the key to understanding these different preferences and each style 'connects' with a stage in the continuous learning cycle. The preferences lead to a distortion of the learning process so that greater emphasis is placed on some stages to the detriment of others. Here are some typical examples:

Preferences for *experiencing* can mean that people develop an addiction for activities to the extent that they cannot sit still but have to be rushing about, constantly on the go. This results in plenty of experiences and the assumption that having experiences is synonymous with learning from them.

Preferences for *reviewing* can mean that people shy away from first hand experiences and postpone reaching conclusions for as long as possible whilst more data are gathered. This results in an 'analysis to paralysis' tendency with plenty of pondering and little action.

Preferences for *concluding* mean that people have a compulsion to reach an answer quickly. This results in a tendency to jump to conclusions by circumventing the review stage, where uncertainty and ambiguity are higher. Conclusions, even if they are the wrong ones, are comforting things to have.

Preferences for *pragmatism* can mean seizing on an expedient course of action and implementing it with inadequate analysis. This results in a tendency to go for 'quick fixes' by overemphasising the planning and experiencing stages to the detriment of reviewing and concluding.

Source: http://www.learningbuzz.com

They can give feedback on ideas, capabilities and behaviour, but often not in a context where they can specify what is right and wrong in terms of there being 'one best way'; there is no one best way to develop a team, to lead it, or manage conflict among group members. There is a range of options which the people concerned will have to be able to think about for themselves. Effective facilitation requires effective facilitators. The qualities of good facilitators are that they will:

- Understand individual development and group process and dynamics as much as the actual 'subject' learners are learning. They need to know where and why people might get stuck in experiential learning, and how to encourage progress
- Create a positive environment for learning. They will do this by using participative methods and exercises from the beginning to the end of a learning experience. With individuals they will seek to maintain a supportive but also challenging relationship. For larger learning groups they will tend to rely upon using smaller syndicate groups
- Seek to manage the event towards achieving the performance related objectives. They will do this by keeping on track, through appropriate feedback, questioning, probing and challenging
- Have well developed interpersonal skills. To interact with learners using these methods requires empathy, emotional stability, responsiveness, integrity

Box 4.4

Difficult people in facilitated learning

Show-offs	Hogging the limelight
Hecklers	Undermining the trainer or others
Ramblers	Going on and on
Mutual enemies	Conflicts surface in the group
Digressers	Getting off the point
Professional gripers	Taking the opportunity to moan
Whisperers	Constant low level chatting
The inarticulate	Unable to express themselves
The silent	Not participating

Figure 4.8   *Principles of facilitation*

- **Establishing the right environment**
- **Ensuring participation**
- **Confronting difficult issues**
- **Maintaining a focus on achieving objectives**
- **Manage the pacing of tasks and exercises**

- If the OHP presentation is the hallmark of the instructor, the flipchart is the hallmark of the facilitator; as they set tasks, then listen and summarise on the flipchart; or get the groups to prepare their own flipchart presentations. Questioning and challenging matter as well
- Observing and responding with good feedback. Feedback is the gold dust of effective facilitation. The reason for this is the problems people can have with analysing their own knowledge, skills and behaviours

The use of facilitation principles and methods with adult learners can create an environment in which dealing with questions and responses, handling problem people (see Box 4.4) and maintaining rapport are key issues.

The principles of facilitation are presented in Figure 4.8.

Exercise 4.2   Having had the principles and practice of each end of the continuum outlined, reflect on your own experiences:

- What have been the problems with instruction in practice, in your experience? What causes these, and what could be done to avoid them?
- What have been the problems with facilitation in practice, in your experience? What causes them, and what could be done to avoid them?

When you have noted some, read Boxes 4.6 and 4.7.

Box 4.5

Facilitation: the use of role play

A group of personnel managers on a university course were invited to attend an event organised by a group of professional actors. They requested issues form the audience to improvise a scenario. Someone suggested informing a colleague that they had body odour (BO). The role play proceeded; the person who had to give the bad news was initially embarrassed; the person receiving the news was eventually tearful.

   The audience had been involved every step of the way in advising the actor bearing the bad news what to do. They were left with ideas about how to handle such issues. None of those watching could have acted out the scene so movingly; indeed when they found out they did not themselves have to participate in the role play there had been cheering and relief. It is punchy, but non-threatening, and captures people's attention. It is nonetheless only to be used as part of a wider programme, not in itself a sufficient base for development.

Source: Pickard (2000)

Box 4.6

Common problems with the delivery of instruction

Problems	Causes
Dull (tell, tell, tell)	Too much information
No buy in from trainees	Mandatory courses
Not real life	All theory no practice
Falling behind or racing on	Goes at instructor's pace
Only get instructor's point of view	Only one instructor
Little chance to question and consolidate	Time and nature of instruction
Pitched at one level	Lack of preparation
Not adapting to different styles	Lack of time
Too authoritarian	Not knowing audience
Boring; stand and deliver	Structure too rigid
One way; teacher-class	Lacking interactivity
Limited/no feedback from audience	Lack of time for review involving the audience
Lack of preparation/knowledge	Development of trainers
Poor presentation style and material and handouts	Project management of presentations and materials

For better instruction

Define and convey clear aims and objectives
Improve materials (ensure up to date)
Prepare, make time, know audience
Vary styles within class
Encourage intervention
Encourage participation (ice breakers, room layout, facilitation)
Work on presentation style

Box 4.7

Common problems with the delivery of facilitation

Problems	Solutions
Group dynamics	Need to know all types prior to start and be able to listen/observe
Some over talkative	Tactfully stop talkative people
Some very quiet	Get all to contribute
Fears, personality, attitudes	Create a safe environment for learning
Perception of the learning	Will not be the same for all
Experience and opinions can hinder agreement on solution	Accept and deal with different experiences, manage conflict
Keeping it focussed on objectives	Can involve questions before and at end of course
Facilitator is not competent	Facilitate for them, leadership in the group
Difficult to keep on track	Prior planning prevents poor performance; think about timings
Objectives not clear enough	Define clear objectives
Different levels/kinds of needs	Respond flexibly to these
Lack of control	Ensure that the learning rather than personal agendas prevails
Motivation	How does this translate back to work?

There are challenges inherent in delivering programmed learning. Some of these may be a consequence of inadequate needs identification or bad design, rather than flaws in the method itself. These problems where they exist are, in turn, often a consequence of inadequate resourcing. Assuming that adequate resourcing and effective needs assessment and design can be managed there are still inherent challenges of developing cognitive capacities, capabilities, and shaping behaviours using instruction. One option is to move to a better balance with structure and process incorporating elements of facilitation. The necessary filling up of 'empty vessels' can be made less dull, boring and irrelevant to many.

The analysis, and the fear, is that it seems that more can go wrong with facilitation if it is not done well (Berry 1993). Poor instruction can be redeemed by further learning in practice; poor facilitation can be really counter-productive and seem a total waste of time. Clearly one issue is knowing learners as individuals, getting and using information about them before and during the learning process. Anxieties about being in control of the process in order to attain objectives also feature. A lone facilitator has challenges in managing to coordinate small group work, and in providing feedback 'gold' to many individuals. The underlying issue with learning achieved by facilitation is often trying to close gaps in expected performance caused by the influence of past learning. Existing knowledge that impedes assimilation, routines, already established habits in behaviour that impede development, and values and attitudes that are already deeply entrenched, can all survive instruction. But facilitation can make a difference. The other option is to support learning away from classroom instruction, to move toward behaviour modification and performance support in work.

DELIVERABLES

Having identified the appropriate cognitive, capability and behavioural elements of the role and task there should be coverage for these in the development and delivery of any learning intervention. Development is the phase where the 'deliverables' need to be captured and defined. A deliverable is any end product of an instructional or facilitation development process. Deliverables are critical in project management terms as they need to be defined and approved in partnership with those who are concerned with the L&D activity: certainly managers, and often the learners themselves. This will require liaison about the schedule for developing the L&D activities and budgets for them. Estimates need to be made in order to agree what deliverables can and will be developed. Preliminary budgets are needed based on estimates to guide design. A final working budget should then be agreed before deliverables are actually worked up. See Box 4.8.

In the L&D context the essentials of project management are given in general in Figure 4.9 and more specifically in Box 4.9.

The steps outlined in Box 4.9 are not always needed. There is no need to use these procedures for some non-training L&D activities such as:

- orientation sessions
- information sessions; awareness only, not skills
- team building sessions; activities to get acquainted
- motivation sessions
- reward sessions; such as trips to desirable or exotic locations

For L&D activities in the classroom, using instruction or facilitation, the overall delivery structure is the same: to provide a beginning, a middle and an end (Box 4.10).

Box 4.8

Design time ratios for estimating costs

Design element	Content type	Design time ratio
Participant manual	Familiar, non-technical	3:1
Participant manual	Unfamiliar, technical	6:1
Leader's guide	Familiar, non-technical	2:1
Leader's guide	Unfamiliar, technical	4:1
Visuals/overheads	Simple, text based	1:1
Visuals/overheads	Complex, graphics based	5:1
Videos	Simple, voice over, one location	50:1
Videos	Complex, live audio, many locations	150:1
CBT	Simple, text based	50:1
CBT	Complex, graphics based	300:1
Multimedia	Simple, graphics based	150:1
Multimedia	Complex, video based	500:1

Source: Ford (1999)

Figure 4.9   *L&D and project management*

Element	Issues	Focus
Listing	All that needs to be included	Mind mapping
Sorting	The sequence and parts	Logical
Arranging	Producing a game plan and timings	Scheduling
Method	What trainer and learners will do	Learning
Materials	Required and available Visual aids: OHPs, flipcharts, whiteboards Equipment: OHP, etc Participant materials: pre course, notes	Creating
Reviewing	Completeness and fit	Checking
In delivery	Professionalism Personal: you and the learners	Appearance Relations

---

Box 4.9

Project managing L&D

1 Verify training need exists, which has usually originated with managers
2 Decide on a course of action, either obvious or requiring discussion
3 If training:
   - derive objectives and outcomes. Use analysis, or observe and ask
   - describe target audience; level, language, examples
   - draft skills hierarchies
   - review existing resources
   - determine scope of instruction
   - draft the skills checks; measure on objectives, not what is taught
   - derive the instructional content
   - select the delivery system; appropriate, not just the latest thing
   - draft the end first, then what needs to be done to get there
   - conduct tryouts
   - deliver; study and practice until demonstrate achievement – then move on
4 If there are shorter lead times use 'frameworking'; do one thing that will be useful

So verify training is needed
    Then do task analysis
      Then derive objectives
        Then develop units
          Finally consider audience

Source: Mager (2000)

Box 4.10

A template for training sessions

In the beginning learners are often uncertain, and can be distracted. There is a need to set the scene and state the topic, while creating and maintaining rapport

Gain attention through standard opening techniques: use a question, a quotation, a story, a factual statement, a dramatic statement, a curious opening, a checklist.

Use participative techniques: in the welcome use 'ice- breakers'

The middle; put over the content, using a structured approach. Maintain attention; stress relevance, use visual aids, involve people, be enthusiastic. Obtain acceptance; be clear, precise, demonstrate. Handle objections, and take questions. Use exercises; individuals, pairs, syndicates

The end; end on a high note, pulling the session together, identifying action points, and signing off (question, quote, story)

OTHER OPTIONS: DESIGNING AND DEVELOPING PERFORMANCE SUPPORT

Behaviourist psychology in business was, from the 1960s on, used to inform the design of programmed instruction which follows the ideals of setting aims, goals and objectives. Even so, discrepancies between effective L&D and job performance were still evident. Even well conceived and designed programmes appeared to fail. There was a pattern of regression to pre-training skill levels of performance. Initial vigour in performance soon lapsed, with performance problems again coming to the fore.

Instead of concentrating on writing better aims, goals and objectives for cognitive capacities and capabilities the concern shifted to more closely analysing expected behaviours and the environments that reinforced these. The argument was that organisations had not clearly enough defined expected behaviours and then built environments conducive to those, particularly by ensuring that consequences were congruent with what was desired. Behaviour in this sense is human activity that can be seen, measured or described. There was a concern to identify and deal with specific behaviours, not generic or abstract concerns in cognitive capacity, capability or affective factors. Results and the causes of results were not equally distributed. A few vital behaviours (see Figure 4.10) were seen as accounting for effective performance and results, not a wide span of cognitive capacities, capabilities and emotional intelligence.

The focus then was on an effective analysis of human performance problems based on identifying and reinforcing key behaviours and designing and developing environments that reinforced those. This can be called the 'behaviourist's ABC':

Antecedents; the causes of behaviour
Behaviour; people's overt actions
Consequences; what then happens as a result of the behaviour

For example, staff might be instructed in health and safety training to wear hard hats, they might then wear the hard hats when they return to work, but only to get the derision of their peers who do not wear them. This feedback does not reinforce the required behaviour, and indeed undermines it. It makes sense to the person not to

Figure 4.10　　*Key behaviours and results*

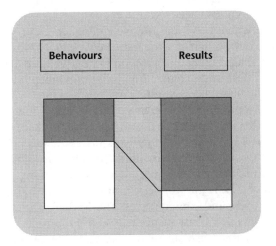

wear the hard hat to escape the derision of their peers. This kind of problem was taken as a paradigm for what was wrong with even the best designed training; it could not alter the dynamics of 'ABC' in the real world of the workplace. For the antecedents that applied were not the instructions people were given but the environments in which they worked. These caused behaviour, not the learning being provided on courses. So (Mager, *op cit*, p 89):

> Even well designed and carefully thought out training programs can fail because they are not supported on the job ... indeed many employee behaviours can be changed merely by systematically analysing and rearranging consequences.

A concern with dealing with performance gaps by developing interventions to modify behaviours in work rather than providing L&D was the result. Changing the consequences rather than L&D was what was needed in action; one of the origins of the organisational development (OD) perspective.

While behaviourists are renowned for denying the possibility of 'scientifically' studying 'mental events', what happens in people's minds as a cause of behaviour, the context is one where they have to accept that mental events do matter. People behave the way they do because 'it makes sense to them', even if it does not make sense to their managers or organisations. In particular the consequences of behaviours have to be seen as the individuals perceive them, from the eye of the beholder. What will or will not reinforce the desired behaviour has to be seen from their point of view. If the consequences are positive for them they will behave consistent with what is desired; if the consequences are negative for them the desired behaviour will diminish.

The problem was that the logic of the ABC was undermined in practice. Organisations would ask for one behaviour, but another would receive positive consequences. This would mean that the latter behaviour would occur. For example, the organisation might want to promote 'empowerment' by training their managers to involve teams in decision making. But if that newly trained manager was empowering their staff but not hitting targets they would be under pressure to do what matters most: achieving targets by being directive. Or, if a system where people are required to submit accurate reports of 'work done' is set up this makes additional work for staff.

If they find that failure to submit their reports has no consequences, because their manager corrects them if they are late and inaccurate, they will rarely bother to complete accurate and timely reports themselves.

Other problems arise where there are positive consequences in some conditions, but negative consequences in others, for the same behaviour. For instance, new ways of training in the Army based on self instruction were developed. The trials of this new system went well, with learners completing the courses much faster than had previously been the case. But when the new system was put into use more widely, beyond the trials, the results were the opposite. Learners were taking as long if not longer to complete the training. This was investigated, and it was found that because when the learners finished they were moved onto other work details, it was in their interest to delay finishing quickly to avoid being sent on those other work duties. The consequences did not favour the desired behaviour, to complete training quickly.

Another common problem in the work environment undermining the ABC is the distance between behaviours and consequences. The further in time a consequence is from a behaviour the less that consequence will have an impact. But for many employees the only time they were really being held accountable for performance was at their annual performance review; the distance between behaviours and consequences was too great. The ideal is to provide consequences at the time of behaviour: small doses of consequences, positive or negative, at the appropriate time, rather than large doses much later. In particular positive consequences ought to arise on an immediate basis.

If the ABC is to be used in the workplace to support effective performance it depends on feedback being given. Feedback is about providing information regarding performance on goals. Reinforcement is the desired effect of effective feedback. Performance gaps may be closed by appropriate reinforcement of desired behaviours using reinforcers rather than providing training. Effective feedback should be:

- immediate
- goal specific
- expressed positively not negatively

Feedback on performance problems will not work if it is:

- used as punishment
- delayed and too late
- given to someone not in control of the problem
- given on the wrong variable, for example on quantity not quality
- there is too much effort to record it

Using feedback and reinforcers will not have 'overnight' effects. Shaping people's behaviours to be consistent with what is desired is about changing in the right direction, reinforcing movement in the right direction, building upon success, noticing and reinforcing improvements. Intermittent reinforcement is, in theory, the best strategy. No or continuous reinforcement both fail to shape behaviours effectively. No reinforcement fails because without consequences the desired behaviours will diminish. Continuous reinforcement is not only impracticable and costly but fails because the apparent certainty of consequences means there is no credibility for it as a reinforcer. An example of classic intermittent reinforcement is the psychology of playing slot machines; people play them knowing that they will pay at some point, but not knowing when. The trick to designing machines that engage people is to reinforce their playing with intermittent wins. The work environment is analogous; people should want to 'play' the performance game, knowing they will get positive consequences, but not being sure exactly when.

Reinforcement of desired behaviour has to be complemented by the punishment and extinction of undesired behaviour. What is a punisher? It is that which diminishes undesired behaviour. This aspect of the ABC is more problematic than the provision of feedback for positive consequences. This is because use of punishment creates long term problems in relationships and can lead to their disintegration. And people learn to tolerate punishments. Punishment has temporary effects, but can extinguish other desired behaviours incidentally. Its use generates a culture of 'excuses', and escape and avoidance behaviour. The intermittent reinforcement schedule effect also arises; if punishment is intermittent the behaviour continues at a higher rate. Above all it cannot lead to the desired behaviour being established.

CONCLUSION

The development and delivery of L&D should follow the good practice outlines of project management. These help to establish what needs to be done across a wide range of possible options for development and delivery. The methods of instruction and facilitation are usually involved in some way in most development and delivery contexts, and the principles of these need to be understood. In addition some concerns about producing deliverables are also common. There is also a need to consider what is appropriate to influence behaviours even where L&D is not required; the behaviourist 'ABC' provides an overview and introduction to the kinds of developments in organisation that might be appropriate instead of the provision of training.

CONCLUDING CASE STUDY

What happened next?

Read the following case study of a facilitated learning experience.

■ What seems to have been well designed, good and useful about this form of delivering L&D?
■ What seem to have been the design flaws, leading to problems in using this mode of delivery of L&D?
■ What could be done to remedy these problems? Or should other modes of delivery be used?

An organisation, a University*, wanted some L&D on equal opportunity policies. The aim was to emphasise how important the policies were for the organisation's managers; in particular their heads of department. A day session was planned. The morning was to be taken up by instruction on the content of equal opportunity policies, exploring how they applied to staff, through recruitment, reward, and career management; and to relations with students as well.

Because the organisation felt an instructional approach was a bit dry, and because it did not provide an opportunity for these managers to reflect on the 'realities' of trying to make these policies work, the afternoon was to be devoted to an experimental use of experiential learning. The organisation invited a training company, who employ actors, to present a drama based

* This was not the author's institution

on an equal opportunity issue. The way the training company use theatre is to enact a drama. First they gave the audience some background information on an organisational scenario, and two characters whom they would then meet and see in action. The scenario was built around a fictional University and the characters were two lecturers, Philip and Angela, who were jointly supervising a PhD student. The audience were told some things about these people, and then allowed to interrogate them to explore aspects of their personality and background. Then these two characters were observed in a scene.

The scene involved a confrontation between Angela and Philip. They were both supervising a female PhD student. Angela confronted Philip with the fact that he had been having an affair with the student, which had now broken up. The effect on the student was that she was thinking about withdrawing from completing her PhD. Angela was infuriated that Philip had done this. Philip took the view that it was nothing to do with her, or the University, what happened between consenting adults; and he thought the impact of the end of the affair could be managed to ensure she did not withdraw from her PhD. Philip, by the way, was a married man, with children. The meeting ended with nothing resolved, and both parties clearly furious and upset.

Following the dramatic scene, the audience were expected to be able to discuss the behaviours of the characters involved, Philip and Angela, and explore the equal opportunity issues involved and how to resolve them. To do that they were expected to work in groups to discuss the issues, before being allowed to quiz the characters again, and explore some of their impressions of the characters' perceptions and motivations. They could ask the characters why they behaved in certain ways, how they felt, and suggest/discuss what could be done to resolve the matter.

The rationale for all this is that seeing a piece of theatre, a drama, a conflict between people, allows learners to view a problem as being 'over there'; they can get emotionally involved, and be disturbed, but still maintain a distance. The audience can reflect on what is going on, what the characters are doing wrong, why things are taking the turns that they do, and discuss among themselves what the alternatives are. They can then get the characters to demonstrate what happens if alternative strategies are used.

This is a very powerful method, having much more impact than reading a case study, or even seeing a professionally produced and acted video of the 'right' way and the 'wrong' way to manage a situation. Having real actors playing characters who are right there, right in front of you, and who can talk with you, disagreeing with you, responding to you as a person as you talk with them, is a powerful experience.

All this action is controlled by a facilitator, who is both stopping and starting the theatrical action, and managing the discussions that the group have about the issues raised. The facilitator's objective is to encourage people to explore the behaviours the characters are using which lead to problems, to appreciate the emotional aspects and conflicts involved in such interactions, and to seek insights that can be applied back to the managers' own jobs. What happens in the group as this is done is very important. The group can help each other learn, by providing insights and sharing ideas. The individuals involved can also reflect, quietly and to themselves, upon their own perceptions and ideas.

If the method is used well the learning that results can be great, in all senses of that word. Where it does not come off the risks are that, instead of learning, people will find themselves emotionally charged, in dispute with each other and the facilitator, confused about what they are doing and what they are learning.

On the afternoon that this session with heads of department from the University was run there was evidence of a mix of both these effects. Learning was achieved, but there was also conflict and confusion. Finding the reasons for that involves reflecting on a number of factors. First, the group was half male and half female. It was obvious to an independent observer that there were differences between the men and the women in their reactions to the drama they witnessed. The men all agreed that Philip was morally wrong to do what he had done. They chastised him for his behaviour. But one person who claimed to have a lot of experience in these matters hogged much of the discussion. He insisted that there was no point in heads of department taking these kinds of issues to senior managers, as nothing would be done about them. There could be no proof anyone had done anything wrong, and there would be no support for disciplining people who had behaved this way. He made this point time and time again. Heads of department were powerless.

Meanwhile the women were more concerned that there seemed to be a bad culture in the organisation, which meant that the woman, Angela, who was bothered by Philip's behaviour and affected by it, had no support. Indeed Philip had been her support in the organisation, against the others, prior to this incident. She was doubly let down, by his behaviour and by seeing him in a new light. The women, it seemed, could empathise with this kind of situation, of being isolated when it came to confronting such problems. The manner in which Angela had confronted Philip had been ineffective. They were concerned to explore with her what else she might do. But they still somehow felt that no other option would have had any different outcome; he would still 'get away' with it.

This was all, on the surface, very good for the facilitator. The group were engaging in debate and discussion, and the matters they were discussing were opening up questions about the realities of promoting equal opportunity policy that the morning's instruction had not. But, on the other hand, the facilitator felt the session was failing. Every time she tried to get the group to do a task, for example to split up into groups and talk about a specific issue, they resisted this and queried it. Some of this reflected the group; these were after all academics, albeit in a management role, nitpicking about the use of language, and the different meanings of words. They would spend their time in groups discussing these queries rather than completing the set task.

The facilitator felt this as a hostility towards herself, but could not see how to deal with that. And while the facilitator was aware that certain group members were hogging the discussion, and others were as silent as a sphinx, there did not seem to be time to deal with all these issues.

A culmination of this came half way through the afternoon. When quizzing the characters following seeing the scene, the characters responded to any questions true to their character, reflecting back to people how their behaviour impacts on the character; that may mean being nice or may mean being difficult. As a result of this one participant had his line of questioning taken issue with; the character of Angela took a 'how dare you' response to being asked if she had had an affair with Philip herself. The point is to allow people to see the impact of their behaviours, and to challenge the way that people in the audience are behaving. But the person who had asked this question and got this reaction got very upset themselves. After the character had left the room, he accused the facilitator of being unclear about what was happening, leading to him looking like a fool because the characeter had clearly taken strong exception to his line of questioning. He accused other group members of not participating properly, leaving it to him and a few others to be exposed in discussions. This had the effect of showing that this was not a safe learning environment for him, as he felt upset. And it then made it an unsafe environment for others to participate in; could they trust other people to listen to what they had to say without being challenged and put on the spot? Thereafter there was a tension about the session, and the earlier sense of people being engaged with what was happening had gone.

At the end of the day there were meant to be 15 minutes to review what people had learned, and how this could be applied to the workplace. Events ran over time, and there was literally only one minute for review. When the facilitator asked what people had learned the response from some of the dominant contributors was that such a scenario could not 'happen here'. If it did happen there would be nothing that a head of department could do, as they would get no support from the central management. Instead of time to discuss the points that were being made about the power, or lack of it, that heads of department had, the discussion petered out. People left. In the lift lobby, however, some of the participants mingled with the actors, who were now out of character; they thanked them for providing an excellent afternoon's stimulating learning.

Case points

What was well done and worked?

- The audience were initially engaged and involved; it worked
- Issues were being exposed by the use of theatre
- People had the opportunity to reflect on the problems of certain ways of behaving in confrontations
- People had the opportunity to discuss with their peers the realities of equal opportunities
- People could develop some ideas of their own about how their behaviour might be changed to avoid the problems witnessed

What problems were there?

- The environment shifted from being engaging to being threatening to at least some people
- Issues that could have been explored, for example, the power that heads of department do or do not have, were raised but not investigated
- It was not clear to some participants how they should be learning and what their role was
- The problem of dealing with a bad culture was raised, but was not explored
- There was incomplete attention given to tasks in small groups
- The facilitator felt hostility, but could not confront that, what it meant, and how it might be related to helping the participants learn
- There was not enough time to review at the end what this all meant for people as managers in practice

What could be done differently?

- The **balance** was wrong; there was too much emotionally charged engagement and not enough opportunity for structured reflection and review
- The **contrast** was too striking; the contrast between the initial discussion with the characters, then seeing them both lose their temper in action, and then trying to quiz them afterwards

CONCLUDING CASE STUDY (cont'd)

■ **Direction**; people were led through this experience according to the theatrical model, of conflict between characters providing a parallel universe that they could observe. That direction was clear. The other aspect of direction though, of where they were going with their discussions as a group, was not clear to some

■ **Economy**; in one sense the message was clear: managing equal opportunities involves dealing with complex and emotional situations where perceptions and behaviours matter as much as the letter of policy. In another sense the message was lost in extraneous discussions of what certain words meant, what the actual policies were

■ **Emphasis**; the emphasis was meant to be on people's behaviour and the impact of that on others. But the emphasis taken by the men was a moral one; Philip had behaved wrongly, and Angela had been wrong to lose her temper with him. The emphasis taken by the women was about culture; that culture determines people's behaviour, and changing culture is important. Understanding that if a work culture supports problematic behaviour then the culture itself is problematic and needs to be challenged is a fair objective, but was not the area that was meant to be emphasised

■ **Rhythm**; there was great rhythm in the theatre itself. There was a lack of rhythm in the broader learning experience; it stopped and started, got revved up then suddenly the brakes went on, it went smoothly for a while then stuttered

■ **Unity**; the event was well received, it seemed, by at least some people. In that sense it can be claimed that a degree of unity existed. In principle the form (theatre) and the content (management training on equal opportunities) and the goals (encourage insights into people's own behaviours) are in a positive relationship. In practice, though, unity depends on what happens in delivery, and that depends on the facilitation on the day.

In conclusion, some of the improvements needed hinge on the quality of facilitation; better facilitation, for example, would involve responding to hostility (Why are people hostile? What is happening here and how do I deal with it?) to keep a safe learning environment. Another example would be, were there real differences between the men and women in their perceptions of what mattered about this incident? If so, how can that be raised and reflected upon?

Part of this hinges on structure; there was a lot of activity, not enough time to go into detail on matters being raised, and not enough time for review at the end. The rhythm, economy, direction, emphasis and balance of the theatre, which was clearly extremely well done, were not matched by rhythm, economy, direction, emphasis and balance overall.

The actors involved appreciated that things had not gone as planned, and had not worked as well as previous events. Reflecting on these 'mistakes' is the source of new learning to improve the use of these kinds of method, to attain the great benefits they may bring.

REFERENCES

Bentley, T. (1994) *Facilitation*, London, McGraw-Hill.

Berry, M. (1993) 'Changing perspectives on facilitation skills development', *Journal of European Industrial Training*, Vol. 17 No. 3.

Clark, R. (2001) 'All the world's a stage in training management', *Glasgow Herald*, 12 April.

Eitington, J. (1984) *The Winning Trainer*, Houston, Gulf Publishing.

Ford, D. (1999) *Bottom Line Training*, Houston, Gulf Publishing.

Forsyth, P. (1992) *Running an Effective Training Session*, London, Gower.

Honey, P. and Mumford, A. (1982) *Manual of Learning Styles*, London, P. Honey.

IDS (1998) *Employee Development Initiatives*, IDS Study 649.

Kolb, D. (1984) *Experiential Learning*, Englewood Cliffs, Prentice-Hall.

Leigh, D. (1991) *A Practical Approach to Group Training*, London, Kogan Page.

Mager, R. (2000) *What Every Manager Should Know About Training*, Chalford, Management Books.

Megginson, D. and Pedler, M. (1992) *Self-Development: A Facilitator's Guide*, London, McGraw-Hill.

Pickard, J. (2000) 'Best supportive actors', *People Management*, Vol. 6, No. 5.

Rogers, C. (1969) *Freedom to Learn*, Columbus, Charles E Merrill.

Wilson, I. (2001) 'Dummy runs that end in death', *Glasgow Herald*, 2 April.

chapter five

Reviewing: Evaluating L&D

Learning outcomes

- Describe and explore specific methodologies in use in L&D evaluation
- Design and construct valid and reliable ways of evaluating L&D experiences
- Describe and analyse the main themes and challenges of evaluation as a general management process
- Relate these themes and challenges to the particular context of evaluating the L&D process
- Critically evaluate the use of cost-benefit analysis in the L&D evaluation context

FRAMEWORK CASE STUDY: BRISTOL ROYAL INFIRMARY

In January 1995 nine members of the medical staff at Bristol Royal Infirmary (BRI) met to discuss the heart operation procedure about to be used on 18 month old Joshua Loveday. They were meeting because of concerns about success rates with such heart operations at BRI in general since they had been introduced some ten years earlier, and the performance of the surgeon who would do this one in particular, Janardan Dhasmana. An anaesthetist at this meeting, Stephen Bolsin, urged doctors not to go ahead with the operation. He had been voicing concerns for some time, along with other colleagues. But he was outvoted and the operation went ahead. Joshua died that day on the operating table. These events set in train a review of performance that would eventually lead to the wholesale reform of performance management for surgeons in the NHS.

It had all begun in the mid 1980s, when a new 'arterial switch' heart operation for babies with heart problems was introduced. As is often the case death rates during the operation were initially high at all hospitals in the UK, as doctors and operating teams became expert in the procedure through practice. In particular, as they become practised they became quicker. This was significant for survival rates, as the longer people were on the support machinery needed to allow operations on their hearts the less likely they were to survive operations. By 1995 the early problems with performance should no longer have been an issue; the procedure was well developed, and surgeons had learned to complete it quickly and successfully. Death rates had reduced significantly; but not at BRI.

At BRI death rates remained high. This had not gone unnoticed. Reviews of performance were evident. There were several people who had concerns, and raised them. A later inquiry would conclude that in fact there were too many people and bodies involved in reviewing the performance of surgeons, but this had the net effect of significant problems being missed. The high death rates persisted, the surgeons at BRI claimed, because they were still on a 'learning curve'. Their powerful positions on the wards and in management meant that no one was able to question them effectively, to pursue an evaluation of their level of performance. Indeed a 'poisoned atmosphere' between management, surgeons and other staff meant that the people who raised concerns were either ignored or threatened. Stephen Bolsin, who consistently raised concerns and was instrumental in finally confronting these problems, was so affected by this that he eventually left and emigrated to Australia.

Concerns mounted, among managers at BRI and parents of children requiring the operation. As they sought to understand what was going on they were given confusing and unclear information. They were, in effect, being kept in the dark. What a later inquiry referred to as the 'delusions' of the leading surgeon at BRI in this field, James Wisheart, led to the suppression of internal criticism. He was also at this time the hospital's medical director. It was concluded in a subsequent inquiry that he misled the Trust board about the results being achieved. The surgeons involved were therefore able to spend years dismissing concerns about their work.

Eventually the concerns of a local GP led to this denial and resistance to evaluation being breached, and a proper evaluation was organised and done. There was a General Medical Council (GMC) inquiry, and a ruling against the BRI surgeons. Wisheart was struck off the medical register and Dhasmana was banned from operating for three years. Following that GMC review, Kennedy undertook a public inquiry into these events. The outcomes were general proposals for reforming the NHS (Kennedy 2001). The main aim of the proposals was to ensure that surgeons will face more scrutiny in the future, to ensure that their work is up to standard. This incident was not just about the failings at BRI, but an extreme example of a common problem and failings in the NHS as a whole: a 'club culture' among surgeons, which resisted and avoided proper evaluation of their performance. In 2002 the UK Government responded to that report, and introduced new means and systems to ensure that the review of surgeons' performance was open and clear.

INTRODUCTION

Having observed, planned and acted, the final phase of the L&D process is to review. Review provides an opportunity to complete the performance management process. Review is most often discussed in terms of evaluation. Evaluation is defined as the activity of determining the merit, worth or value of things. The BRI scandal illustrates some common problems that can arise when evaluating the merit, worth and value of the performance of people at work who are meant to have learned and be able to perform to the expected and desired standard. In the BRI case the surgeons were taken to be competent in general, but with the new procedure they were meant to have mastered there was an issue with their actual performance; they had not climbed the learning curve.

Evaluation is also then the final link in the chain of the L&D process, the phase when the L&D process is completed. Determining the value of L&D requires some

Figure 5.1   *Schematic overview of L&D evaluation*

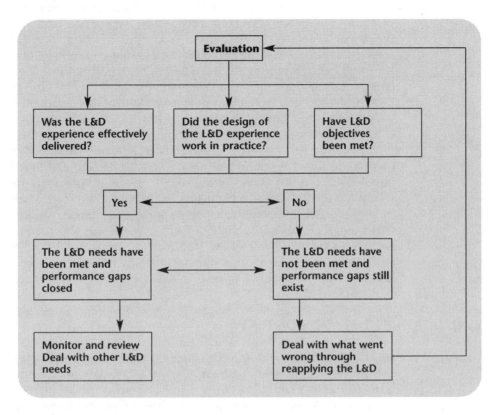

form of measurement and judgement to be made of the achievement of objectives, to confirm that the L&D objective that was initially defined has been met and that therefore performance will be as expected and desired. It also involves evaluating the delivery of the L&D experience and the planning and design process (see Figure 5.1). Have the specific objectives been met? Did the L&D happen according to plan? Was that the right plan? These all seem straightforward matters, and depending on the facts the L&D may be either judged a success or the L&D process may have to be re-run in order to deal with any shortfalls or continuing gaps.

Yet evaluation is often seen as the weakest link in the whole L&D process. It is the step most likely to be neglected or underdone. It is therefore the most likely source of failure in L&D at work having an impact on performance. To complete an L&D experience in itself is no guarantor of a gap being closed. Without knowing whether the previous phases of the L&D process have been successful the final outcome, the end to which this is all a means, improved performance may not be secured.

The evaluation phase within the L&D process has been seen as a difficult and challenging aspect of the L&D process. It was an established, and much lamented, fact that many organisations failed to evaluate their L&D. One survey (MSC 1989) found that 85 per cent of organisations failed to evaluate training. Another survey three years later found that while 98 per cent of organisations had specified training budgets only 25 per cent had specific targets for their L&D; the question was how, without targets, could L&D possibly be being evaluated properly?

Findings such as these sparked a keen interest in addressing the problems of the evaluation of L&D. The main outcome of this, encompassing as it did a wide range of concerns, was to argue that the evaluation of L&D in the context of meeting business needs was the key failing of the L&D process in practice. To put that right became the central focus; and the Investors in People (IiP) standard, for example, was developed in the early 1990s with this objective uppermost in mind. The analysis of problems with evaluation being the main flaw in L&D at work, and subsequent action to remedy that, appear to have had some impact. An IPD (1999) survey found that at least 75 per cent of organisations now have L&D activities designed to support business objectives, providing a framework in which L&D evaluation is at least possible.

The significance of properly evaluating L&D at work is now better appreciated. Where effective performance is dependent on L&D, and that means in most jobs and occupations that it is possible to think of, evaluating L&D and how far people have travelled the 'learning curve' during L&D, is the front line of scrutiny and accountability. But the BRI case also highlights that there are still many challenges inherent in evaluation; many factors can impede a full and proper evaluation. These often reflect aspects of relations of politics and power inside organisations. As has been emphasised for each phase of the L&D process, review is not just about using tools and techniques alone that can determine how effectively the L&D process is managed; it is also about working in a broader management and political context.

EVALUATION IN THE L&D CONTEXT

In the L&D context evaluation is an umbrella term, one that includes a range of activities with various purposes under its canopy. It includes obtaining information from learners; how they rate the L&D experience, and how much they feel they have learned or developed. It includes obtaining information about learners; testing learners to judge the extent of their cognitive capacities, their capabilities and their behaviours. It includes reviewing whether the right objectives have been set, and if the overall benefits warrant the costs that have been incurred. These various activities all seek to address the same question: was the L&D that was identified as needed, planned, designed and delivered done well and worth doing? In the evaluation of L&D at work basic methods have been formulated and in use since the 1950s (Hamblin 1974, Kirkpatrick 1975, 1996). Some 50 years later these same methods are still around and in use today, and provide reference points which still structure L&D evaluation in theory and in practice. The main method is one which defines and explores set levels of evaluation for L&D at work (see Figure 5.2).

In dealing with these different levels of evaluation a balance is sought between, on the one hand, collecting sufficient information, and on the other, managing the reduction of that information to a meaningful figure (Box 5.1). Most time in L&D at work is spent on identifying needs, planning, designing activities and delivering them; the time for evaluation, and the kind of methods commonly in use, do not generate large amounts of information. However, those who are being evaluated, whether they are learners on a course or the trainers who have provided the L&D, can argue that they are not being fairly evaluated. The use of simple tests and surveys for evaluation is only able to justify a distinction between a 'pass-fail' mark or a 'good-bad' course. That is a limited form of conclusion to draw. The alternative, to collect more information, may seem attractive, but is also problematic. If more information was to be collected on the activities delivered, on the outcomes achieved, the costs and the benefits, this could serve only to divert limited resources towards an L&D process phase that can

Figure 5.2   *Levels of L&D evaluation*

Evaluation level	Focus and concerns
Reactions	What are the learners' reactions to the L&D they have experienced; was the learning experience helpful and useful in their estimation? Generally involves post course or intervention feedback to the developers
Learning intervention	To what extent have the objectives of the L&D been met? What have the learners learned? Can involve tests and assessments of knowledge, skill and abilities
Performance	To what extent has the performance gap been closed? This is generally seen in the extent to which learning is or is not transferred to the workplace or is manifest in improved performance
Organisational	What have the costs and benefits of the L&D been? Is it confirmed that the L&D has provided value for money?
Ultimate value	What are the overall tangible and intangible outcomes of having provided L&D? Are staff more committed, are they more flexible? Is the organisation better placed to realise its strategy, to compete successfully?

Box 5.1

Quantitative information

Quantitative information provides data about facts that are measurable in the immediate period after L&D experiences. Other assessments of cognitive capacity, capability and behavioural change can be more difficult to collect and analyse.

Results	Facts
Cost savings	Doing more and/or better cheaply; unit costs, overheads
Time savings	Doing more and/or better quickly; order response, overtime
Work habits	Output of work; doing more; productivity, new accounts, absenteeism, rules violations
New skills	Quality of work; doing better; defects, accidents, presence and frequency of use
Work climate	Turnover, grievances, commitment, satisfaction
Initiative	New ideas, accomplishments

Source: Phillips (1991)

seem to have little visible impact on performance. And, no matter how much information is collected, it still has to be reduced to a kernel of judgement.

Phillips (1991) also outlines the 'myths' that can impede the proper evaluation of L&D (see Figure 5.3). He and Newby (1992) provide an overview of various tools and techniques of L&D evaluation (Figure 5.4) consistent with such evaluation being 'scientific'.

This kind of analysis of myths and promotion of tools and techniques reflect a common mind set. This is that it is good economic sense to evaluate L&D in these ways. It reflects trends in measuring and quantifying activities in management. It is

Figure 5.3 *Myths about evaluating L&D*

- The results of training cannot be measured
- It is unclear what information to collect
- If the return on investment (ROI) cannot be calculated it's useless to evaluate L&D
- Measurement only works in production and finance
- If the Chief Executive Officer (CEO) does not require it, why bother?
- There are too many variables affecting behaviour change
- It will only lead to criticism
- The trainers have a proven track record, so no need to evaluate further
- Measuring progress towards objectives is enough
- Evaluation costs too much to do

Source: Phillips (1991)

Figure 5.4 *L&D evaluation techniques*

- Questionnaires
- Interviews
- Critical incident review
- Repertory grid
- Reactionnaires
- Written tests
- Practical tests
- Behaviour analysis
- Cost benefit analysis

Source: Newby (1992)

necessary for the approval of L&D budgets, particularly where there is pressure from the top to make a 'clear' value adding contribution. There is, in modern organisations, more information about performance available to help complete such analyses. Overall it reflects well on the professionalism of L&D practitioners.

Yet this mind set and the activities it warrants may be misleading. This is because there are often difficulties with either identifying or getting agreement on standards, and there are inherent problems with the reductionism inbuilt in L&D evaluation using these tools and techniques. The difficulty of evaluation is not just confined to the technical problem of defining standards; it can also be perceived as a political and potentially threatening process. It provides one of the instances where the abstract idea of a balance of power in organisations is made concrete.

On one side are those with the power equivalent to the auditor's, who are acting like 'investigative journalists'. These are people concerned with seeing that others are held to account for their L&D and their performance. That may mean trainers evaluating learners, or other managers evaluating the L&D function, or regulators evaluating the organisation. On the other side are those who may perceive these evaluators as being ill informed and illegitimate judges. Thus learners contest the evaluations about capacities, capabilities and behaviours being made by trainers. Trainers contest the evaluations of their L&D provision by other managers. And organisations contest the negative evaluations of their L&D provisions by regulators. Often this simply takes the form of characterising these evaluations as the work and conclusions of 'outsiders'.

Depending on the balance of power between the parties to the evaluation, who the insiders and the outsiders are, evaluation may offer a lever for properly achieving and implementing change, or provide a front for change to be resisted. For if L&D is a means to an end, improving performance, the things that are entailed in improving performance may threaten some interests while being for the general good. In the former case an evaluation of L&D can act to reinforce change by legitimising new capacities, capabilities and behaviours among those who have changed, and by isolating those who have not changed as representing a problem. In the latter case negative evaluations of L&D can undermine the legitimisation of the new capacities, capabilities and behaviours being sought, and offer those opposed to the performance improvements being sought a way of undermining the whole strategy, by arguing that the L&D was ineffective, unsatisfactory, too costly, and so on.

So the apparently straightforward process of collecting information to evaluate the quality of L&D and its contribution to improving performance can then be fraught with difficulty. It is then either suppressed, not done well or becomes an area where a continuation of unhealthy power relations disturbs all the parties involved. The problems with performance in the BRI heart operation scandal illustrate what can happen when this happens to the extent that review and evaluation have broken down entirely. These problems of review and evaluation exist then across all areas of management and work, and the general issues are relevant to all aspects of organisational life.

These points are made to suggest that the apparent conversion from non-evaluation of L&D to robust evaluation in the context of business needs to be explored more critically. The tensions involved in evaluation have to be appreciated if effective evaluation is to be achieved. With L&D it is the specific methods and challenges of evaluating L&D in the context of performance management in work organisations that are the focal concerns. These are partly attributable to a desire to avoid evaluation, as there are costs and risks for those being evaluated. But they are also attributable to the fact that there are inherent challenges in evaluation. It is to an analysis of these general problems that attention must turn first.

EVALUATION IN GENERAL

Evaluation in L&D is often defined narrowly as the process of measuring the extent to which objectives have been achieved. However, evaluation involves more than accumulating and presenting facts about cognitive capacities, capabilities and behaviours to make judgements about the extent to which L&D objectives have or have not been achieved. It is about relating data to standards. This is where the complications arise, as it is often challenging, and sometimes fiendishly difficult, to identify and then use such objective standards to evaluate performance gaps, and therefore to evaluate learning related to closing those performance gaps. Objective standards seem to offer and provide a means of determining what has really been of value. Determining objective standards may mean specifying 'set business objectives', but then the question is raised, what is the objective standard for defining these? Is it to be defined in terms of return on investment (ROI) (Flynn 1998), or is it to be defined in terms of some other conception of expectations about what L&D can achieve, other ways of defining 'results' or 'outcomes'? Cost-benefit analysis (CBA) has been proposed as a means of structuring the evaluation of L&D. Of course the 'costs' are known in advance; the 'benefits' may be estimated, but cannot be determined in advance. In a business and management context the common sense this approach makes is evident; every other activity is subject to such evaluation, so why not L&D? Yet the argument against attempting such kinds of evaluation is also strong (see Box 5.2).

Scriven (1991) describes an evolution of systems of evaluation in general. Whether the focus of evaluation is the impact of a social policy, plans for developing a city, the effect of an initiative in economic development, or the evaluation of an L&D experience, there are common elements involved in evaluation. One is that most areas that are subject to formal evaluation have ways of evaluating results whose origins are in initial ideas and constructs about how to evaluate a particular field; whether that be social policy, town planning, economic development or L&D at work. These will then evolve through various stages up to a point at which a well evolved and robust system of evaluation for any particular field is established (see Figure 5.5).

Attaining a mature and well evolved system for evaluation matters, argues Scriven,

Box 5.2

The tyranny of numbers: measure or trust?

Boyle (2000) cites a definition of cost-benefit analysis as

a procedure by which the higher is reduced to the level of the lower, and the priceless is given a price. It can never therefore serve to clarify the situation and lead to an enlightened decision. All it can do is lead to self deception and the deception of others.

Boyle argues that the concern should be with analysing the qualitative benefits, the 'higher' things, but this gets driven out by concerns with the quantification of benefits. A parallel example is that of education. A concern with quantification has meant that education has become preoccupied with exam results alone, and the number crunching of pass rates preoccupies the compilers of league tables. But is it not the quality of development provided for a wide range of pupils that really matters, something which is not easy to quantify?

This measurement obsession, Boyle argues, is not rational or sensible; it is actually about standardisation and control as a response to a lack of trust among the people involved in a task. Some people insist on measuring other people every step of the way because the more strictly people are watched, they believe, the better they will behave.

Boyle argues that there is a mistaken belief here; the belief that it is possible through number crunching to attain perfect, objective, non-political decisions. It is possible, in short, to take out human prejudice and error. But he argues that this is a 'hopeless dream'. Indeed it is precisely the cut and thrust of prejudice and error that fires and keeps stoked up interest, creativity, and action. A fixation with quantification embroils people in a paralysis of analysis.

Instead of pursuing 'psuedo-scientific' precision, the impression of dealing objectively with things, people should measure less. Instead of analysing L&D costs and benefits why not trust L&D professionals to identify needs, design activities and deliver them professionally?

The argument is compelling, and attractive. Yet the BRI example illustrates one reason why the trend is to try to measure rather than to trust.

Source: Boyle (2000)

Figure 5.5   *Phases of evolution of evaluation*

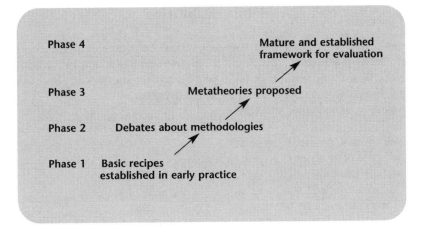

Source: Scriven (1991)

Figure 5.6   *The functions of evaluation*

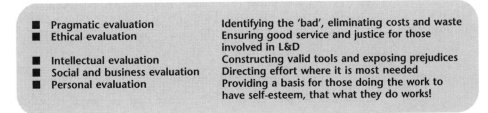

because without it the functions of evaluation cannot be properly realised (see Figure 5.6). The evaluation of L&D at work is trapped in a dilemma. On the one hand in L&D there is a premium on evaluation, given the interest in and practice of learning and development throughout human history. On the other hand the evaluation of L&D at work is arguably still at a primitive stage of debate, with the development of metatheories at best.

EVALUATING THE EVALUATION OF L&D

Scriven's stages of the evolution of and aspects of evaluation functions apply well to the specific field of L&D. The underlying questions here are, at which stage of evolution is the evaluation of L&D currently, and to what extent does the evaluation of L&D fulfil all the functions? The first phase of an evolution of evaluation is to formulate 'rubrics', basic and primitive models to guide prescriptions of what evaluation should, in practice, involve (see Boxes 5.3 and 5.4).

Developing such rubrics, headings that give instructions about what to do, is though only the first stage of evolution. While they may provide for a set of tools, such as the typical end of training course 'happy sheet', rationales for standard tests, models of how to analyse training costs and so on, these are only a basic and not very sophisticated means for evaluation.

Box 5.3

Practicability

Whether evaluating reactions, learning, knowledge transfer or ultimate costs and benefits, instruments need to be practicable; they should be easy to administer, not be burdensome. They should be simple and brief and economical, taking into account the costs of design, developing or purchasing, and the time to use them and analyse the data.

Determining what instruments to use:

- How will the data be used?
- How will data be analysed?
- Who will use the data?
- What facts are needed?
- Should the instrument be tested?
- Is there a standard instrument?
- What are the consequences of errors?

The next stage required is to evolve methodologies of evaluation. Methodologies of evaluation seek to define principles for the investigation and analysis of an area of practice. These tend to bring at least some aspects of the basic rubrics and prescriptions into question. This is because different methodologies will manifest and express different beliefs about what is important about the area in question and therefore what evaluation should involve.

In the area of L&D, Talbot (1992) argued that the 'levels of evaluation' model had not provided organisations with a means for attaining robust evaluations. Organisations using these methods often still did not know what they were getting for their money. In part this was because at least some of these aspects of the evaluation recipe were being ignored or done unprofessionally. L&D was still seen as essentially 'an act of faith', as its outcomes cannot be properly evaluated. It was not easy to properly identify L&D costs and benefits. And, in the final analysis, no one really cared; it was not a big issue. To move on from this situation of paying only lip service to the recipe he suggested there are two paths, reflecting a choice in methodology. He argued that there were both quasi-scientific beliefs and humanistic beliefs which could lead to different methodologies of L&D evaluation.

One methodology, embodying principles reflecting a way of exploring the world, is the 'quasi-scientific' path of developing hard measures which evaluate L&D objectively, as it were 'from the outside'; these usually require schemes for analysing return on investment (ROI) and costs-benefits.

Phillips (*op cit*) expands upon this quasi scientific methodology. Phillips' conclusion is to make the methodology of evaluation 'results oriented', with methods that reflect that. Courses should be results oriented and investment in them can be measured by financial returns, with CEO and line manager involvement and concern. The ultimate level of evaluation is to compare the financial benefits with the costs of the L&D. Phillips concludes that L&D should be managed in organisations by converting training departments to 'profit centres' to ensure that they are contributing effectively to the organisation.

Box 5.4

Evaluation instruments

Questionnaires

Questionnaires are the most common evaluation tool at the level of 'reactions'. They are easy to design, develop and administer. They are familiar to most people, and provide data that can be summarised easily.

1 Determine the information needed
2 Select question type:
   open ended
   checklist
   two way question
   multiple choice
   ranking scales
3 Develop the questions
4 Test the questions for understanding
5 Develop the completed questionnaire
6 Prepare a data summary sheet

Tests

Pre-course and post-course tests are used to evaluate the 'learning' level; to evaluate changes in knowledge, skill or ability. Tests can be classified in a number of ways. The two main ones are by media and by design:

Media

■ Written, paper and pencil tests
■ Simulations or actual performance
■ Computer based tests

Design

■ Essays and exams; the most common in formal education
■ Objective tests; specific and precise answers in relation to programme objectives
■ Norm referenced tests; compare participants with each other or other groups, rather than attainment of objectives
■ Criterion referenced tests; an objective test with a predetermined cut-off score for a minimum standard
■ Performance tests; to exhibit a skill either manual, verbal or analytical

Other instruments

Interviews; to secure data not available through other means, and probe to uncover stories useful for evaluation

Focus groups; if other quantitative methods are not adequate, to get at judgements about 'quality'

Observations; before, during or after an L&D event. Observers need to be prepared and trained, be systematic, know how to interpret and report what they see, and their influence should be minimised. Use behaviour checklists, coded records, video recording or delayed report

For Talbot the alternative methodology to this is the 'humanistic' one; to attempt better subjective evaluations of L&D, as it were, 'from the inside'. This requires involving learners in the evaluation process rather than subjecting them and their learning to the evaluations of others through the use of quantitative measures. This makes sense because the problems with attempting to foresee and calculate returns, in advance of actually investing in L&D, are intractable. No amount of ROI analysis can determine whether it is or is not right to invest in L&D at work, and indeed it can detract from focussing on what can be done to establish and improve L&D contributions to performance. Rather than organisations converting training departments into profit centres it is in fact organisations as a whole that need to be 'converted' into being 'learning organisations' where 'soft skills' and continuous development as much as specific investment in 'results' are valued. L&D is to be an integral part of working life, not confined to what happens in a separate activity called 'training' managed by a few training professionals in the organisation. If that is the case then its results cannot be separately and discretely measured; it is an organic part of the whole. To decide on the basis of results that it was not worth doing would be like deciding on the basis of a bad blood pressure count that the heart was not working, so it should be cut out to allow the rest of the body to work better.

As a specific example of the relevance of this humanistic methodology of evaluation Talbot provides the illustration of providing for and evaluating interpersonal skills training. L&D on interpersonal skills will often entail interventions with variable content; the 'same' course on communication, handling conflict, or whatever, will be experienced differently by different groups. This is because each course will evolve differently and flexibly as it is experienced. There is also great resistance from learners to formal assessment in areas such as interpersonal skills; people may want to be given feedback, but in no proper sense do they want to be 'tested' and judged on their interpersonal skills. Quantified evaluation of such L&D is then neither possible nor desirable. Talbot suggests that the best that can be done is some form of 'joint evaluation', with collaboration between the learners and the trainers to explore what has been learned and what might remain to be done.

So debates about methodologies of evaluation in L&D reveal different perspectives on the subject, suggesting that it is at a low stage of evolution; it is not an advanced and established system. For Scriven getting through this stage is both possible and necessary if the next stage is to be attained. This next phase involves investigating and developing what Scriven calls 'metatheories'. Debates about and rivalries between different methodologies of evaluation are often the first signs that there are more fundamental differences in theories about the field under review. For effective evaluation to be achievable requires that these theoretical matters and rivalries be clarified.

Scriven's use of the term 'metatheories' implies that there may be many different theories, where theories are defined as answers to questions about how and why things are as they are, but these can be clustered together into a few general metatheories, where 'meta' denotes 'higher order'. It is these higher order theories that can be seen to offer or provide coherent and comprehensive explanations of the subject. In some ways the idea of higher order theories in L&D is easy to apply; they may be taken to be those of the constituent human science disciplines in use in HRM. When developing or drawing upon metatheories to evaluate L&D and its value, the higher order theories of economics, psychology and sociology provide the frameworks for investigating and explaining what is of value and merit (see Box 5.5 as regards psychology). In L&D the current state of play is that these metatheories all have a role; psychological theories shape individual evaluations, sociological theories shape social policy evaluations and economic theories inform cost-benefit evaluation.

Box 5.5

Psychology and the characteristics of effective evaluation instruments

Effective evaluation instruments for learning experiences need to be, in the constructs of psychology, both valid and reliable. A valid instrument measures what it claims to measure. Validity is defined with respect to four aspects, here illustrated with reference to a student taking an exam:

Content validity; does the instrument represent the content of the learning? The evaluation instrument should test on a sample of what has been covered. All key items should be covered, with no imbalance. For example, does an exam cover all of the course, with an equal weighting for equal parts of the material covered?

Construct validity; does the instrument represent the construct it purports to measure? In this case, is the exam answer a reflection of all the abilities, skills, or knowledge in performance of the student? These are generally defined and defended by citing expert opinion or correlation with other constructs. For example here, do answers actually measure the real differences in people's capacities?

Concurrent validity; does the instrument agree with the results of other similar instruments at approximately the same time? If assignments or other tests are done, do they provide the same results as the exam? Are results in the other exams a person is taking consistent with results in the exam in question?

Predictive validity; does the instrument help predict future behaviours and performance? For example, does performance in the exam predict anything about that person's abilities in professional practice?

A reliable instrument is one that gives consistent measures. There are various sources of error with reliability in any instrument:

- fluctuations in the alertness of the participants
- variations in conditions of administering
- random effects cause by participant motivation
- the length of the instrument
- differences in interpreting the results of the instrument

For example, learners often complete post-course evaluation questionnaires, or 'happy sheets'. Are these reliable instruments for evaluating that course? Each of the factors above can create errors, leading to an inaccurate evaluation, whether that be favourable or unfavourable. With some learners focussed on the course and others thinking about getting home quickly, with some evaluations completed there and then and others taken away and perhaps never returned, with some learners who did not care about the course and others who cared deeply, the results of such happy sheets can be unreliable. And even if not, when trainers pore over them thereafter, they can interpret what has been measured and said selectively. Some may see them as just a 'beauty' contest ranking, and take some pride in rationalising away any bad evaluations as representing the learners' inadequacies in failing to engage with a 'complex and difficult' subject.

One conclusion is that there is some interplay among different kinds of theory in L&D evaluation. This is healthy and productive, as there is both a rivalry between and synthesis of interdisciplinary theories which makes the evaluation of L&D robust and balanced. An alternative way of characterising the state and nature of theories in L&D is given by Stewart (1999). He takes issue with adopting an unproblematic view of evaluating L&D by drawing upon such human science theories. Even though they differ in their backgrounds he sees them as sharing a core philosophy, that he calls 'realism'; they are all 'realists'. Realists are all equally implicated in the same mistake, of wanting to be seen as the best at objectifying aspects of evaluation. But, he argues, all these areas of theory in the human sciences are compromised because they themselves embody and reflect limited and biased views about people and social reality. The current state of theorising about how and why to evaluate L&D is diverted into disputes between one form of realism and the others; there is a distracting battle for hegemony among these theories. At best the situation is one of a 'Mexican stand-off', a paralysis where each group of theorists has the other in their sights, and no one from either psychology, sociology or economics can or will fire any shots.

A Mexican stand-off implies that a situation exists in which, among several people, everyone is capable of harming the others, and is exposed to being harmed by them; they are paralysed by being unable to act, as if they do they will be harmed. There is then an impasse at the level of theory in the evaluation of L&D. This implies that the final and highest phase of the evolution of evaluation is far from being achieved at the moment in L&D. For Scriven the mature phase is of an evaluation system with which it is possible to scientifically practicable to deal with primary value claims. If this is true, and if such an evaluation system is required to validate claims about what is in fact meritorious and actually valuable in a scientific and rigorous way, then the conclusion is that the evaluation of L&D is far from being the robust activity that many would like it to be. Until there is an agreed metatheory or paradigm within which people concerned with evaluating L&D can work and communicate, the prospects for improving the evaluation of L&D are poor.

'Paradigms' can be, and frequently are, challenged. Whether they are defended, reformed or replaced can alter the way that valid evaluation is seen and practised. In L&D there is no agreed paradigm at the moment. Stewart, as mentioned before, takes issue with what he argues is the dominant 'realist' paradigm; but even this is largely subscribed to by practitioners alone, and it is not agreed upon by academics, as his critique and alternative conceptions illustrate. It is arguable that a 'paradigm' of any kind, whether of this quasi-scientific or other variety, may never be established (se Box 5.6). If that is so then the evaluation of L&D will remain beset by the inadequacies of basic recipes and be subject to cycles of debate and rivalries without progress.

Take for example the use of various methods to support management development (MD) (see Box 5.7). The view of one longstanding and eminent academic in the particular area of MD (Pickard 2001) is that:

> There's no human endeavour about which someone hasn't said, 'We can make management development out of that' . . . walking on hot coals, outdoor training, role plays, business games . . . management development has been a major growth industry in the (last) 30 years . . . but the extraordinary thing is that there is no proof that any of it works.

One recent survey (Staunton and Giles 2001) reinforced this, finding that more than 80 per cent of organisations had yet to build frameworks to gauge the impact of MD on their businesses. There is a lack of clarity on what they are trying to do with their

Box 5.6

The never ending search for results

Mazlish (1998) characterises all the human sciences as 'uncertain sciences'. The pursuit of predictive and certain scientific knowledge to solve problems that seemed to be promised has not been fulfilled; not in regard to individual behaviour, or social relations, or economic development. Mazlish concludes that:

> Common sense tells us that a result emerges from people's passionate and political actions, not from predictive scientific knowledge. Many, if not most, problems are too delicate and disturbing to the actors involved to resolve clearly and rationally, even if a solution is available.
>
> An example might be the allocation of resources, where the attempt to impose a rational plan often leads to a violent conflict of interests or to an unacceptable authoritarianism . . . what solves social problems is social interaction . . . rather than a science that pretends to deal with social interaction. Actions, in turn, constitute a never ending sequence of solutions that create new problems.

If in general what solves problems is social interaction, and people taking actions that in their turn create new problems that others have to solve, then why should L&D be any different?

Rather than seeking a rational science of L&D evaluation, the realities of people's passions for or against L&D are what will determine what happens, what the results are.

Source: Mazlish (1998)

Box 5.7

Management development

Professional performers, including actors, artists, musicians, storytellers and comedians are helping firms in their training and development. The Jongleurs Comedy Club runs a one day course on presentation skills and teamworking, coaching people to write their own stand up routines.

Steps Role Play, established in 1992, produces drama based training programmes and interactive theatre productions. One event was based on 'storytelling'; this involved actors recounting how Caesar's and Cleopatra's warring destroyed the library at Alexandria unintentionally. By analysing the characters, their decisions and outcomes, those taking part are meant to learn about thinking and planning and the importance of contingency plans.

These arts based learning experiences are about using different parts of the brain. They are reflecting concerns with conventional areas, like teamwork, and newer concerns such as 'emotional intelligence' and creativity. They also reflect a challenge to conventional 'macho' views of management.

Source: Pollock (2000)

management talent. If this is true for the most heavily invested in and high profile area of L&D practice, MD, what about all the others?

CONCLUSION

Review and evaluation are the last phase which has to be managed to complete the whole L&D process. This phase has been seen as problematic in L&D at work. Recent improvements seem evident, but debates are still very much alive. In practice there are common rubrics, levels of evaluation, relating evaluation to the different aspects of the L&D process itself, to learners and the resolution of performance gaps. But the possibility of producing scientifically valid analysis of primary value claims about L&D, the ideal for evaluation that Scriven suggests, is still elusive. Analysing what was done well and what was worth doing is still beyond the reach of 'science'.

So while L&D evaluation is at least now done more widely than ever before it is stuck at the most basic level possible, with the prevalence and preference in L&D for using the basic recipes of levels of evaluation. One conclusion is that there is a need to engage with and deal with debates about methodologies and theories to progress beyond these conventional prescriptions. On the other hand is a conclusion that these debates, taking shape around the pursuit of either quantitative or qualitative measures, of the dominance of either psychology, sociology or economics, are the problem not the solution.

Whichever view is adopted it can be agreed that the possibility of effective evaluation of L&D, in terms of meeting all the functions of evaluation that Scriven listed, is problematic. In the end the formulas and techniques for evaluation of L&D have to balance the demands of scientific rigour with those of professional practice, and the theoretical goals of 'truth seeking' with the practical goals of 'pragmatic management'. To apply only the standards of scientific rigour and truth seeking to the evaluation of L&D would be to invest so much in evaluation that there would be little time for action. To accept only the standards of professional practice and pragmatic management would be to leave the evaluation stage of L&D, acknowledged as a critical phase and a weakest link, as a less sophisticated and robust element of the L&D process.

CONCLUDING CASE STUDIES

When to use cost-benefit or cause and effect analysis

In each of the following examples, identify:

(a) whether you would or would not use cost-benefit analysis (CBA) and
(b) if you were to use CBA analysis, what would be involved or
(c) if you were not to use CBA analysis, what else you would evaluate and how

1. A manufacturer of office and school supplies, with products ranging from paper clips to binders and computer related supplies intends providing training for new hires to its production lines
2. A company with 7000 employees intends spending a multi-million amount on a programme to put staff on a one week course on the company's new desktop environment

3   A group of managers is to be trained on a course about communication skills, to help cross-functional teams better communicate and work with each other

4   A photocopier manufacturer aims to shift to multifunctional products, where their copiers are no longer just copiers but also scanners, printers and fax machines, and their dealers need to be retrained

Analysis of cases

The idea of ROI is of an absolute number, a neat package that shows the exact value returned for an exact value invested in training. This is a seductive idea. Calculating the ROI of training can be simple and objective, or complex and involving more subjective judgements. Sometimes not worth the effort, sometimes it is seen as the Holy Grail for many involved in L&D. It seems that everybody wants it, many people have theories on how to find it, and some are willing to go to great lengths to do so.

The first thing to consider is then 'Is it worth doing?' Before embarking on any ROI quest, you should first estimate the ROI for calculating your ROI. Will it be worth the time and money you'll spend? The answer depends more on the type of training that is planned than on the cost as such. The ideal type of training suited for calculating ROI is one-time training on a specific skill; for example in **Case 1**, or in teaching customer-service staff the latest computer program. This is a discrete module in which few other factors will affect the outcome, and in which the outcome can readily be tested in a before-and-after scenario. This is the easiest and most clear-cut way to calculate an ROI.

In other circumstances, such as in **Case 3**, although L&D potentially will have a greater effect on the company, its effects are more difficult to quantify. It's hard to do a before-and-after test on leadership skills, and other factors will come to play in managers' performance.

Industries like manufacturing also have the easiest time doing ROI analysis. In **Case 1**, the manufacturer of office and school supplies, they tracked the effect of training on new production hires. After training, most new hires were able to produce vinyl binders at a 5 to 10 per cent higher rate than tenured operators. As a result of that finding, the company began re-certifying operators on an annual basis to retain that production level.

How is it done?

1   To measure ROI start by isolating the impact of training as much as possible. To do this it is necessary to have a control group. Train one group several months ahead of another, to have a control group to test against. Alternatively, narrowly focus the training so that a before-and-after comparison can be made.

2   Then decide the impact the training should have. If learning a computer program should shorten each customer service inquiry, then attach a cost to that extra productivity.

3   The bottom line is: calculate the productivity effect. For instance, will each customer service person be able to handle ten more phone calls a day? Calculate the money associated with that, say that each phone call represents £6 of the employee's time. Get a final value, for example that 20 employees each save an average of £60 a day; therefore £1200 per day, multiplied by 280 annual days. Divide that by the cost of the training. The result is the ROI.

In **Case 2** there was a two-year training effort of the workforce. They also sought an ROI figure, but based on testing employees on their skill sets before training, immediately after training, and 60 to 90 days after training. This provided some sort of objective measurement. The pre-training tests asked employees to perform tasks and answer questions surrounding software, Internet, e-mail and spreadsheet capabilities. These had an average 22 per cent of items answered correctly. Directly after the training, employees answered 84 per cent correctly; and 90 days after the training, 93 per cent of items were correct.

It often isn't quite this simple. In more complicated scenarios the focus is best placed on value and results, rather than a number based ROI. Once you move away from an objective 'x more bolts sold' scenario into more vague managerial skills, there is a need to use more sub-jective judgments to determine the effectiveness of the training. This involves making very strong assumptions which can be difficult to defend. Yet in other areas of management, like advertis-ing expenditure or internal auditing practices, these kinds of assumptions are also made, and are not usually challenged; it is worth spending on advertising, it is worth spending on inter-nal auditing.

An alternative to calculating return on investment is to measure return on expectations instead. In this kind of approach, those who are involved decide exactly what they expect to achieve from the L&D. This set of expectations becomes the baseline for determining success. Months after the L&D is complete, the stakeholders review their agreed-upon expectations. They then decide if the results are in line.

This approach allows for more anecdotal analysis. For example with **Case 3**, where a group of managers completed a communications training course, stakeholders can discuss the ways they feel communication has or has not improved. This provides a more realistic picture than if HR were forced to place a convoluted financial figure on the value of improved communica-tions. It is softer but it's not false rigour. Before the L&D was complete, the teams constructed mission statements, ground rules, and team and individual roles. The teams also had six dis-tinct performance measures that were expected to improve. It appears that now people are meeting on a regular basis, and using the skills and plans introduced in the training. People are communicating and getting issues addressed, prioritised and categorised. The division was able to articulate improvements it wanted from L&D, and now is busy tracking those improvements.

If you choose such an expectations based approach keep a tight focus. Name specific behav-iours that are expected to change. That allows for a more direct cause and effect. Rather than saying, 'I want my people to manage time better', say, 'I want 95 per cent of deadlines in my department to be met'. You can compare before-and-after percentages to see if the L&D is effective. This offers a chance of having a closer relationship between L&D and change; you can't make it absolute, but you can come much closer.

In **Case 4**, the company made a conscious decision to focus on the value of L&D rather than the ROI of L&D. This is because L&D was seen as an investment, and all investments have risks associated with them. The company could not find a direct correlation between costs and helping their dealers move toward the 21st century. The company has been able to double its market share, although it doesn't credit L&D alone with that success. Rather, the company treats L&D as one key piece in an overall business strategy.

In conclusion, given the pressures around to quantify and speak the language of finance in organisations, it can be a challenge to wean companies from an ROI obsession in the field of L&D. But those demands aren't as much for an ROI as they are for trainers to take more accountability and for L&D to be more applicable to jobs. Meeting these demands by showing some form of cause and effect for L&D will often be enough. For instance, when training for salespeople in relationship-building and negotiation it can be difficult to quantify an ROI, but

CONCLUDING CASE STUDIES (cont'd)

tracking whether sales and customer approval ratings have risen, and whether the salespeople can decrease the marketing expenses of their customer programmes, would be a sign that they can close a deal without granting too many concessions, but still achieving a 'win-win'.

The fewer hard-and-fast ROI numbers there are to work with, the more anecdotal information will be needed. Anecdotal evidence can be a useful tool; so survey customers, external or internal, and survey the L&D participants themselves. Trainers can use evaluation to align with line managers, and have them be advocates. The person on the line is going to see the change, and it's building the relationship with the line managers that's going to give trainers credibility, and give them the support they need. When people are arguing the need to have an ROI, it is right to argue a version of 'No, I don't agree. Line managers will vouch for the changes'.

So if L&D lends itself to a simple calculation of ROI, doing so gives trainers more credibility as a business partner. But if the training is too abstract to support an ROI, time and money would be better spent elsewhere. When all is said and done, ROI is a means by which to measure the value of L&D. There are other ways, returns on expectations, ROI thresholds and anecdotal information, to evaluate L&D success.

Worked example

A course is planned that will cost £30,000 to design, develop and run. It will have a useful life of three years. During the three years it is expected to produce £60,000 savings. Is it worth doing?

1 *Cost-benefit ratio*

$$\text{Value of 1 or above} = \text{a positive return}$$
$$<1 = \text{a loss}$$

$$\frac{\text{Benefits}}{\text{Costs}} = \text{cost-benefit ratio} = \frac{£60,000}{£30,000} = 2$$

2 *Return on investment (ROI)*
   Measures the anticipated profitability, a standard measure for performance.

$$\text{Average ROI} = \frac{\text{Pretax earnings}}{\text{Average investment (capital expenditure)}}$$

Savings are £20,000 per year (over three years). Investment is based on using the 'average book value', as the costs are spread over a period of time where the investment has depreciated (with some of its value written off, here taken to be half the initial costs of £30,000).

$$\text{For ED} \frac{\text{All benefits}}{\text{Cost of analysis, development, delivery and evaluation}} = \frac{£20,000}{£15,000} = 133\%$$

3 *Payback period*

$$\text{Payback period} = \frac{\text{Total investment}}{\text{Annual savings}} = \frac{£30,000}{£20,000} = 1.5 \text{ years}$$

Source: Cases and analysis based on examples given in Flynn (1998)

REFERENCES

Boyle, D. (2000) *The Tyranny of Numbers: Why Counting Can't Make Us Happy*, London, Harper Collins.

Flynn, G. (1998) The nuts and bolts of valuing training', *Workforce*, Vol. 77, No. 11.

Hamblin, A. (1974) *Evaluation and Control of Training*, London, McGraw-Hill.

IPD (1999) *Training and Development in Britain*, IPD.

Kennedy, I. (2001) *Learning From Bristol: The Report of the Public Inquiry Into Children's Heart Surgery at the Bristol Royal Infirmary 1984–1995*, Bristol, Bristol Royal Infirmary.

Kirkpatrick, D. (ed.) (1975) *Evaluating Training Programs: The Four Levels*, New York, Berett-Koehler.

Kirkpatrick, D. (ed.) (1996) *Evaluating Training Programs*, Alexandria, VA, American Society for Training and Development.

Mazlish, B. (1998) *The Uncertain Sciences*, New Haven, Yale University Press.

MSC (1989) *Training in Britain*, Manpower Services Commission.

Newby, T. (1992) *Training Evaluation Handbook*, London, Gower.

Phillips, J. (1991) *Handbook of Training Evaluation and Measurement Methods*, Houston, Gulf Publishing.

Pickard, J. (2001) 'Test of faith', *People Management*, Vol. 7, No. 4.

Pollock, L. (2000) 'That's infotainment', *People Management*, Vol. 6, No. 25.

Scriven, M. (1991) *Evaluation Thesaurus*, London, Sage.

Staunton, M. and Giles, K. (2001) 'Age of Enlightenment', *People Management*, Vol. 7, No. 15.

Stewart, J. (1999) *Employee Development Practice*, London, Financial Times Management.

Talbot, C. (1992) 'Evaluation and validation: a mixed approach', *Journal of European Industrial Training*, Vol. 16, No. 5.

part two

Practices

A comprehensive review of each and every method involved in L&D practice could be provided; that would give breadth, but little depth. Alternatively a series of themes could be provided, to structure the discussion of L&D practice in contemporary organisations. The approach taken here is to describe and review a representative range of practices. This allows for coverage of contemporary content, what is done in practice. It also allows for an exploration of themes, what questions and issues arise in contemporary organisations in practice. These are not the only areas of practice involved in L&D at work. They are areas which can be emphasised to provide an introduction to contemporary practice. The four areas of practice covered in Chapters 6 to 9 respectively are:

Organisational L&D Strategies	Organisations can and do use different strategies, different kinds of policy for achieving major goals, in managing L&D. These are described and analysed.
L&D partnerships	An important feature of L&D for many organisations is making partnerships with institutions and people outside the organisation.
The Investors in People Standard	The IiP standard has been a major feature of the L&D landscape for around ten years. What it involves, and the issues raised, are of great interest and significance.
Information and communication technologies	The evolution of e-learning, and the impact this is having on L&D practice, provide some of the greatest challenges facing L&D at work now and in the future.

This part of the book aims to give a balanced review of what is involved in practice, and illustrate how practices can be analysed to explore their strengths and weaknesses.

Organisational L&D Strategies

FRAMEWORK CASE STUDY: CAPITALAIRPORT

CapitalAirport is a large and busy airport in a country that has become increasingly dependent on air travel. It serves the nation's capital and is run by a State controlled company. In the last five years there has been a virtual doubling of passenger numbers and a big increase in freight as well. Staffing has not increased at the same rate however, and there is a strain on existing resources. Senior managers see some key problems. Managers are concerned that many staff are not going out of their way to help customers; customer service does not seem to be a high priority. Increasing competition with services offered by other travel companies, both ferry and train, is a factor. Customer surveys present a reasonably positive picture, but with a near monopoly people cannot vote with their feet. But the real threat is of privatisation if poor service is not improved. The company wants to provide a quality service for passengers and other customers but is not making any significant investments in training. It is known that some workers feel themselves undervalued, and at best a 'necessary evil'. For example the airport police service feel this; yet they are the biggest employee group in the organisation and play a big day to day operational role. There is conflict between the police service and the operations department. Management feels this whole situation needs changing.

The L&D strategy

It is decided that an L&D strategy aimed at improving handling of increased levels of service has to be set up. Three key activities are organised. First consultants are hired to run a course on 'the human factor'. This off-site company wide course involves getting employees to think about their careers, life/work balance, and also includes role playing for dealing with customer service problems. Then, following this, new customer service teams are introduced, based on quality circle principles to look at continuous improvement. Despite initial successes with these teams, relations in them deteriorate; two years on they have ceased to function. Finally there is another training programme; an event called 'the winning factor'. This is a one day, organisation wide event. It is run at a nearby hotel. It consists of a film presentation on dealing with customers, a workshop on identifying competitors and how well they deliver customer service, a play performed by airport staff, a question and answer session with the chief executive, and awards given at a ceremony to 'outstanding employees'.

Managers and employees have strong views about this last aspect of the training, and it fails to have any positive impact. They think it treats managers and staff like fools, insulting their intelligence. The people responsible for organising and running the programme are seen as two faced, saying one thing and doing another. Some express very strong views, that the event has been fraudulent and a disgrace. This reflects general discontent.

The reasons that the managers and staff have been so irritated and provoked by this aspect of the training are many layered. The key point seems to be that the message being promoted is that all employees are 'winners', heroically undertaking a grandiose piece of work, for which they should be loudly applauded. All employees are winners, they are all heroes; or they could all be winners, they could all be heroes.

This is an idealised view that bears no resemblance to their day to day reality, which is routine, hard work. Even on the training day itself only a few actually received awards. In fact employees struggle to meet customer needs. They are involved in exhausting and difficult interchanges with customers who project their anxieties and frustrations onto staff. They see themselves as being far from winners in any sense, and cannot see any sense in which they might be winners in the future. Even the airport firemen, the most likely 'heroes', are struck by the incongruity of the idea of being 'winners'. Much of their time is spent in extreme boredom waiting for things to happen. What is so irksome is that the whole idea of the L&D strategy denies the reality of their day to day work. It seems that managers do not want to know about, and therefore do not care about, the employees. The managers cannot acknowledge the realities of stress and boredom that characterise the employees' work. The L&D strategy of instilling in everyone the thought that they are 'winners' is at best deluded and at worst dishonest.

Source: Stein (2000)

INTRODUCTION

The preceding chapters have outlined the core elements of observation, planning, design and review as they are managed as a means to the end of improved performance through L&D at work. The 'winners' case demonstrates all these elements of the L&D process in practice. It is not the absence of a phase or step in the L&D process that explains the failure of the L&D in this case; it is the way that all these phases were put together in a strategy for L&D which was a problem.

An L&D strategy is a policy for action to achieve major L&D at work goals. It will embody beliefs about L&D, result in a preference for a certain kind of system for L&D, and lead to the manipulation of different levers to achieve L&D. Just as organisational strategies, plans and policies for achieving major goals can vary, so can L&D strategies. Policies for achieving L&D at work, while embodying the same elements of the L&D process, can take different forms in practice. An L&D strategy may exist in the form of a training plan that contains the following elements:

- a statement of policy; what are the key L&D themes and priorities?
- an outline of the training budget; what are the planned levels of income and expenditure on L&D?
- an operational plan; providing timescales, and schedules of resources
- an allocation of responsibilities; who is responsible for doing what?
- integration with and reference to associated systems, such as appraisal and career development

The discipline of compiling such a training plan can be an annual focus for discussions about performance issues, gaps and the design of new L&D initiatives. But such training plans are not in themselves all there is to L&D strategy. They are just pieces of paper. What matters is how they embody different beliefs about L&D, different conclusions about what is strategically important, and how they depend on different levers for implementing L&D at work (see Figure 6.1). A contrast between sets of possible beliefs, aspects of systems and levers illustrates the range within which L&D strategies can be developed. One side is defined as the 'conservational' strategy and the other as a 'transformative' strategy. The conservational strategy reflects doing what has been done as commonplace in the past, while the transformative end reflects different and changing aspirations.

Such a framework of establishing a range within which different practices can exist by modelling ideal contrasts (see Box 6.1) is often used in HRM. Such analytical frameworks are popular because identifying such polarities, and expanding upon them, is meant to provide a means of developing a more elaborate but truthful picture of practice than can be gained from simply being told what 'best practice' is and analysing deviations from best practice as the source of problems in practice. The source of

---

Box 6.1

Dichotomies and analysis

The most common method of obtaining the truth in Western cultures is to set up an adversarial match between rival explanations. The competing theories of the human sciences, the judicial process of prosecution and defence, and the mass media's presentation of contrasting views of news events to provide 'balance' all represent this structure for exploring the truth. In the end one of these theories, views of guilt or accounts of the news are deemed to be true, and the other deemed false.

But the dichotomy being presented here between conservational and transformative strategies is not of that kind; there is no rivalry to determine the truth of L&D at work as being either conventional or new. Rather what is being explored is a range of possibilities. The dichotomies between 'soft' and 'hard' HRM, or between 'conventional personnel management' and 'strategic HRM', are better examples. It is not that one of these is true and the other false, but that they represent ends of a continuum; and within those parameters many combinations are possible.

Figure 6.1   *L&D strategies: parameters and differences*

Parameters for L&D strategies	
Conservational strategies	Transformative strategies
Beliefs and assumptions	
'Sheep-dip' and 'injections'	Lifelong learning
Company takes responsibility	Individuals take responsibility
Specialists know best	Managers know best
Basic training is enough	Innovate and change
Education is better than training	Parity of esteem
Systems	
No strategic concerns; do basics in induction, H&S and job related training. A fragmented approach to other HR	Integrate with strategy and processes, eg rewards
Other HRM functions take priority (harmony in relations, flexibility in resourcing)	L&D is the key to adapting to economic and social change
Link strategy to individual performance objectives that can be appraised	Promote organisational learning
Defend L&D against 'short-termism', cuts	Extend the role of L&D
Management development	Development for all
Key levers	
Managers have a minimal role	Managers have a major role; instructors, coaches, mentors
Individual instruction	Learning partnerships
Group instruction	Action/experiential learning
Classroom facilitation	Corporate universities, EDAP schemes
Recruit using formal qualifications	Define and refer to competency
Traditional internal/external programmes	New vocational or new in-company programmes

Source: parameters based on a framework created by Storey (1992) problems in L&D practice is more likely to be found in the management of a coherent L&D strategy than in the failure of any one technique or phase of the L&D process.

There is an argument against analysing L&D strategies in these terms, which is that is it is overly reductionist, and simplifies too much the analysis needed to develop a holistic understanding of patterns of L&D at work in practice. Notwithstanding these reservations the point is that there will be a range and patterns of organisational practice that can be usefully described and reviewed in regard to these parameters and boundaries that helps to capture and discuss variation in patterns in practice.

Take, for example, the 'winners' case. This does not represent either conservational L&D or transformative L&D; it can be seen to involve elements of different parts of the beliefs, systems aspects and levers involved in L&D strategy. The 'winners' case describes an organisation trying to use an L&D strategy to improve customer service levels. This seems to reflect the business oriented L&D philosophy. Improving customer service is seen to be a need identified through reviewing the business, in the context of a threat from privatisation. It also reflects elements of managing L&D through systematic training, that is by using professional trainers and consultants to provide formal training events. The development and use of 'quality circle' teams also reflects some concern with the continuous development of staff, but this failed to take. The main problems seem to be that while the aim was clear the L&D means adopted to attain it, from the observations made about needs to the events delivered to staff, were mistaken. The L&D strategy, to run some training courses, embodied management assumptions and desires rather than an honest review of work and people.

An alternative strategy for this organisation would be to manage the L&D process of observing, planning, acting and reviewing using other beliefs, systems and levers. They would then have better identified the kinds of problems and needs which later reviews of the failed L&D highlighted; about the emotional content of jobs and about the realities of work. These might have then led to L&D events that were not considered an 'insult to the intelligence', but which actually helped improve cognitive capacities, capabilities and behaviours. They would also have shown some need for reviewing other aspects of management and organisation, and not just the use of training as a magic bullet to solve a host of related problems.

So the L&D strategy in this case was designed and implemented reflecting beliefs, systems and levers that led to failure. There was insufficient diagnosis of the work and organisation of the airport. This would have helped identify problem areas, like the pressure on the airport police. Management did not understand the social psychology of the workforce, where the use of the 'winners' concept was counterproductive. They were trying to impose an idea on people rather than learning with them and from their experience. This chapter explores the kinds of variation in L&D strategy found in practice, reflecting different beliefs, systems and levers. It provides an elaboration of the kinds of strategies that can exist between the parameters of the conservational and the transformative beliefs, systems and levers. Such an analysis of practice adds another dimension, in addition to the model of the L&D process, in describing and analysing the challenges of managing L&D at work (see Figure 6.2).

L&D STRATEGIES

The core elements of the L&D process provide the tasks that have to be undertaken in L&D: assessing needs, planning and designing L&D, acting to professionally deliver L&D, and evaluating L&D. But there is no single, universal way of practising and man-

Figure 6.2   *L&D strategies and the L&D process*

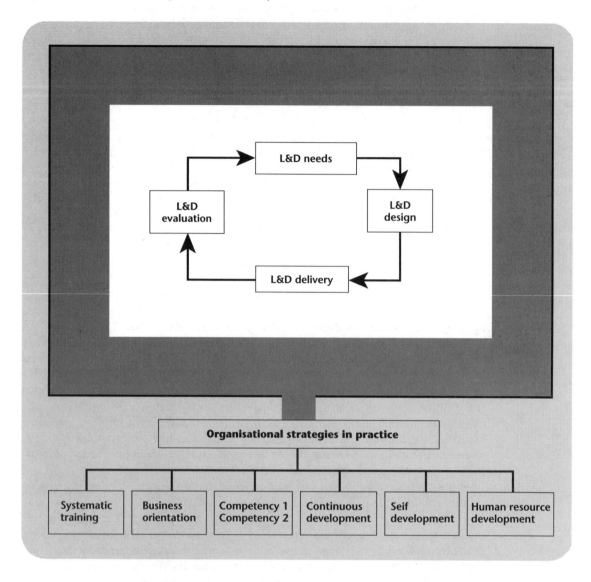

aging L&D in business and management. It is evident from studies of L&D practice that what happens inside organisations can be described and analysed in regard to these phases of a common process, but what precisely happens varies greatly (IDS 1996). There are different ways that these core elements of the L&D process can be managed and organised.

Within this variation it is possible to discern different patterns of practice. These different patterns of practice will be described and reviewed here as different L&D strategies, different kinds of policy for achieving major L&D goals. These plans and policies for achieving major goals are relatively coherent sums of different beliefs, systems and levers.

Box 6.2

Organisational L&D strategies

L&D strategy	Representative beliefs, systems and levers
Systematic training	Training courses
Business orientation	National Training Awards
Competency 1	Mapping behaviours and abilities
Competency 2	Accreditation
Continuous development	Experiential learning
Self development	Personal development plans
Human resource development	Integrated HR policies and plans

The several different strategies that can be defined (see Box 6.2) can be analysed in an evolutionary, chronological sequence. The impetus for the development of a new form of strategy has been disenchantment with prevailing and dominant 'prescriptions' for L&D, and the problems they seemed to create with the quality and quantity of L&D in organisations. A crisis with the existing strategy, usually insufficient attention to and investment in L&D, and concerns with its quality, prompt fresh thinking. There is an element of truth to that. These several different strategies also reflect broader changes in performance, work and organisation.

Discussions about L&D strategies are either explicitly or implicitly about beliefs, systems and levers. Where HRM professionals are 'on the back foot', reacting and responding to performance management demands with insufficient effect, the beliefs, systems and levers they have come into question. It's not that organisations do not want effective L&D, and do not properly concern themselves with the L&D process; it is that what they believe, and elect to do to organise and manage L&D become part of the problem, not part of the solution to performance management gaps. There are arguments from all corners about the merits of each of these L&D strategies; there is no single dominant, validated L&D strategy from among these various contenders. They are to be interpreted not so much as rivals, but as different perspectives on what is involved in effective L&D to achieve major goals in business and management. They have varying implications as to what to observe, what to plan in detail, what to do, and what to review when managing L&D at work.

Systematic training

The systematic training (ST) framework is the earliest L&D strategy to be identified and discussed. It is best characterised as being a strategy where the L&D process is being managed systematically by professionals whose specific job is to handle L&D. This will include the formal assessment of needs by an L&D 'expert'. It moves on to the planning and organisation of formal on-job training and off-job training courses by L&D experts. Off-job courses may be run either inside the organisation or by outside providers, but in either case the emphasis is on professional trainers and developers taking the leading role. Such courses are designed and delivered by training specialists. Such training is formally evaluated by professionals or experts; it

involves tests, is often recognised or accredited, and leads to the award of some recognised qualification.

Critiques of the systematic training model have been that it is associated with the
bureaucratic use of formal training programmes, particularly off-job training programmes. The professionals and experts may be professionals and experts in L&D in
general, but they are not best placed to identify needs, deliver and evaluate. The
emphasis on specialists designing/implementing training programmes and evaluating
these programmes means that the whole L&D process is 'owned and controlled' by
specialist trainers, and this is seen to be a source of potential problems.

This systematic framework had its origins in a period when the major problem was
perceived to be that clearly identified skills shortages existed which required large scale
interventions to address them. But there was a lack of commitment among employers to training as an investment. To attain the levels of L&D desired meant being more
systematic, and that required specialists exploring needs and organising courses. But
because this was not properly grounded in the specific performance needs of actual
businesses, teams and individuals, it more often meant spending on generic courses
and initiatives. It was L&D detached from the business; a lot might be going on, but
it was not necessarily directed towards the right ends.

Business orientation

Dissatisfaction with the systematic training strategy had always been voiced (Allen
1994) and the need to adopt other kinds of L&D strategy was highlighted (Schlesinger
1996a, 1996b). There were discussions of problems with the 'transfer of training',
as effective learning in a classroom did not result in improved performance in practice. In addition there were complaints about the costs of such 'sheep dip' training,
where everyone had to have their period of immersion in training, and the bureaucracy that entailed. Alternatives were sought which provided different ways of
observing and planning for L&D. The business orientation (BO) strategy was one
outcome. What is meant by the business orientation strategy is best exemplified in
the UK by the structure of the 'National Training Awards' framework (see Figure 6.3).
In addition to an emphasis on performance management in the context of business
objectives there is a greater emphasis on managerial involvement and performance
review.

Such a 'business oriented' system, dealing with the concerns being expressed about
the weaknesses of systematic training, seemed rational and logical, indeed to be
'common sense'. But it is, nonetheless, an expression of a particular way of perceiving and managing the L&D at work process which is partial and in some respects
limited (Rainbird 2000). Some would argue (Coleman and Keep 2001) that this way
of thinking about the L&D process has become part of the problem, not part of the
solution. They argue that the business oriented strategy is essentially a 'British' way
of thinking about L&D. It reflects more about the balance of power among stakeholders in employment in the UK, in favour of employers rather than a partnership
with employee representatives, than it does a valid L&D strategy. Other countries con-
ceive of L&D strategy in different ways because there is greater partnership between
employers, employees and government. They are less business oriented and take more
account of other interests in what kinds of L&D should be provided. In the UK business oriented debates about L&D tend to 'decontextualise' skills, that is to discuss them
only with reference to the existing workplaces within which they will be deployed.
Concerns then involve 'looking back' into the education system, where skills for work

Figure 6.3   *National Training Awards as part of the business oriented strategy*

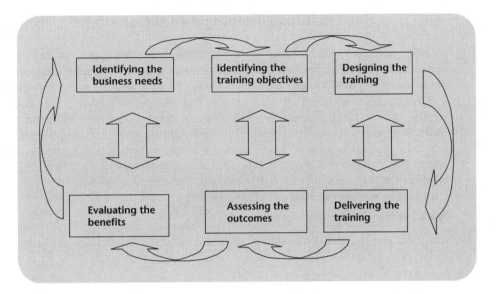

are meant to be developed; if there are skills problems then there must be problems in these education systems. The conclusion is to change education systems to accommodate employer needs for skills. But this is a questionable argument (Coleman and Keep *op cit*):

> Elsewhere in the developed world it is much commoner to integrate issues about skill formation with issues concerned with how those skills then get used. In these circumstances, issues such as work organisation, job design, industrial relations and co-determination issues, as well as other aspects of formal and informal people management systems, form a natural part of discussions about how skills are created and then used and renewed.

So discussions of L&D do not have to take place in a vacuum which results in a spotlight being shone only on educational reform. Such critics also argue that the links between L&D, citizenship and life outside work are often weakly articulated in the UK (Coleman and Keep *op cit*):

> Token mention may be made of education for adult life, but, in contrast to the Scandinavian countries, and their development of the notion of the learning society, the reality is that education and training to enhance citizenship, voluntary activities, parenthood, or political, social and cultural life, has limited resonance here.

The conclusion is then that, as a result, in the UK the 'work' or business related learning theme is too dominant. This is particularly relevant when observing and thinking about adults whose jobs demand limited skills, for whom other sources of motivation to engage/re-engage with opportunities for learning might be more fruitful than an agenda dominated by the business oriented determination of needs.

Box 6.3

National Training Award case study

A catering company won an award for demonstrating that the organisation had invested time and resources in a comprehensive training programme to achieve a business objective of retaining skilled employees. The company employs around 23,000 people providing catering for over 1 million people every day. They need to retain their skilled chefs and be competitive in a price sensitive market. Many organisations had cut costs and de-skilled chefs. This had demoralised them. They sought to equip them with more skills to raise morale and team spirit. They used a modern apprenticeship system, and evaluated this by looking at their success in regional and international culinary competitions. Their sales have since increased, and 85 per cent of the staff who had the training are still with the company. The company has benefited, but so have the staff, as they receive recognition for their efforts.

Source: NTA Award Winners, http://www.empnto.co.uk

Continuous development

While the evolution of and critique of business oriented L&D strategies were centre stage other developments were taking place. One was the definition of and concern with continuous development. A basic definition of continuous development is that it involves L&D that occurs in informal and unstructured ways in everyday settings as much as it involves formal and structured L&D in special learning environments (IDS, *op cit*, p 1):

> In the 'state of the art' employers' training has moved from sending staff on ad hoc courses to a process of continuous development . . . equipping employees with new skills becomes an ongoing process.

One implication is that this places an emphasis on individuals and their managers organising ongoing development in the course of normal work, and utilising options like coaching, mentoring rather than drawing upon the help of professional trainers. If development is an ongoing process then observations about L&D needs are an integral part of work, and planning for meeting those needs should be integrated with work. If this is so then it is limiting to depend upon sending staff on courses now and then to achieve development; delivery must be integrated with work as well. What this has meant in practice has been the growth of new kinds of L&D strategy. The growth of 'corporate universities', for example, (see Box 6.4) is a manifestation of how continuous development can impact on L&D strategy (Stumpf 1998, Kotte 1999). Meiser (1998), reporting on the top 100 corporate universities throughout the world, claims that achieving continuous development is cited as the main reason for them being set up. Corporate universities are concerned with the development of the organisation as a whole over time rather than just developing the skills and knowledge of individuals. However, these kinds of apparently new institutional management of L&D at work can be interpreted as old style systematic training being 're-branded', not a step change or strategic change in L&D (Arnone 1998).

> ## Box 6.4
>
> ### Corporate universities
>
> Employers are setting up 'corporate universities'. These take a variety of forms. Some may be little more than revamped training departments, while others represent ambitions to coordinate learning and share knowledge across organisations in 'continuous development'. They are using the terminology of academia to describe and raise the status of corporate training and development.
>
> A bank was considering setting up a 'corporate university', and undertook a study into its feasibility. It was felt that this would help galvanise the disparate training and development activities into a coherent programme. A corporate university would have to include all training and development platforms, including a significant use of technology. To measure the success of this they wanted to move away from metrics based on 'training days' delivered. A corporate university was a way of re-branding training and development activities. These were (based on budget spend):
>
> | Media usage | | Share of budget | |
> |---|---|---|---|
> | CBT | 42% | Line trainers | 24% |
> | Courses | 26% | External providers | 23% |
> | Multimedia | 12% | In house training | 16% |
> | Distance learning | 8% | Travel | 11% |
> | Books | 7% | Accommodation | 10% |
> | Video | 5% | Training centres | 10% |
> | | | Materials | 6% |
>
> From the first instance in the UK of Unipart in 1993 there are now around 200 in the UK. The uses of technology in learning and the 'war for talent' are cited as factors. As companies cannot award their own qualifications corporate universities often still link up with 'real' universities. The companies are more involved in L&D design and delivery, with the academics providing assessment. These relationships provide revenues for universities. But there are tensions. These are between the performance driven learning imperatives of corporations and the independence of thought and critical thinking required in academic communities. In the future will undergraduate and postgraduate programmes come to be influenced by organisations and their ways of providing L&D? Would standards increase or decrease if there was more corporate influence in this way? And will a reliance on these partnerships for revenue lead to problems of viability for universities, given the uncertainties of business development, where mergers or business failures might eliminate these sources of revenue?
>
> Background source: Aitken (2001)

Human resource development (HRD)

The term HRD is being increasingly used within companies and within research on L&D at work. The term has long been in use in North America (Rothwell and Kazanas 1994), where HRD is synonymous with what is here being called L&D at work. In the UK, HRD can mean something more specific. Moorby (1991: p 6–7) in defining HRD argued that:

> The human resource development [HRD] function can be regarded as encompassing what is often described as training and development, the field of motivation and reward . . . job description and job evaluation, management and/or career development . . . and the whole question of career management, recruitment and assessment . . . at the organisation level there are other aspects that need to be included for completeness. These are change management and organisation development.

Thus HRD can be distinguished from other L&D strategies by its explicit concern to better integrate L&D with other aspects of HRM and management. This integration may be 'horizontal' integration, with other HRM systems, such as career development, recruitment, rewards and performance appraisal systems. It may also be 'vertical' integration; linking L&D to strategic management and organisation development. Ideally, for proponents of pure HRD, it should mean both; the management of L&D at work is integral with the management of work and the business as a whole, it is not a separate service function. All the debates and concerns that have been raised about strategic HRM in general (Mabey *et al* 1998) apply here to L&D in particular. The idea of HRD promises a great deal, and is seductive; but whether there is evidence of organisational examples of this being delivered is questionable. Indeed the 'rhetoric' involved is arguably being used to cover changes which are far removed from the espoused aims; instead of better valuing the human resource, such re-inventions can mask the greater exploitation of people.

Both the concept of continuous development and that of HRD are now frequently in use, but some would see them as being only stepping stones onto the grander concepts of 'knowledge management' and 'organisational learning', which provide the contemporary focus for learning in and at work.

Competency 1: Behaviours

Boyatzis (1982) defined competency as being the capabilities of superior performers. The promise was that L&D strategies concerned with going beyond what was required in order to *do things well* and to move on to *doing things better and doing better things* could be based on mapping and developing such competence. Many organisations have subsequently sought to develop their own 'maps' of competency. Competency based L&D systems were to help bind a set of initiatives together with a set of managerial and workforce behaviours which would lead to some future desirable state. These were also often meant to provide a coherent framework for the integration of various HRM processes and initiatives as well as being the focus for L&D strategy.

A recent report (Miller *et al* 2001) raises concerns about these competency frameworks. Problems with competency frameworks were identified in organisations (see Table 6.1). Almost all organisations reported problems with terminology, and many reported problems with understanding the concepts involved. The survey suggested that their popularity as a tool for linking to other HRM systems was waning, with limited use of the competency frameworks in appraisal and development, and even some decline in their use for pay purposes. In addition there are concerns about the possible 'cloning' aspects of using competency profiles; that they undermined the promotion of diversity by establishing a single standardised model of the ideal performer. The concern is that competency profiles are based on modelling 'acceptable' individuals rather than a range of possible kinds; thus competency profiles may reflect exist-

Table 6.1 *Problems reported by users in developing, introducing or implementing competency based L&D*

Problem	% reporting
Language/terminology used	65%
Employees' understanding of the concepts	65%
Line managers' understanding of the concepts	62%
Assessment of individuals' competencies	60%
Resources required; time, cost, other resources	54%
Developing the definitions for the competencies	48%
Getting employees' and managers' commitment to the use of competencies	47%
Keeping the competencies relevant	45%
Relating the competencies to the corporate culture	44%
Complexity of the competency framework, including the paperwork involved	42%
Incorporating emotional intelligence concepts	25%
The attitude of trade unions to competencies	10%
Other	5%

Source: Miller *et al* (2001)

ing successful types, setting a pattern for future recruitment. This may impede the achievement of workforce diversity goals.

Competency 2: Functional analysis and vocational qualifications

There has also been much effort put into the identification of standardised competencies for occupations. Competency is defined in this sense as the things that people need to be able to do in order to be effective in employment. These maps of competency are based on establishing universal maps for occupations, and the accreditation of individual competency through demonstrating possession of these sets of competencies. From these National Vocational Qualifications, and Scottish Vocational Qualifications (N/SVQs) have been established. An L&D strategy can then be based on using these specific job-related standards of achievement and certification. These qualifications have an impact where they shape L&D for employees wanting qualifications in a particular job or wanting specific training in vocational areas. Since their introduction in 1987 over 3.2. million N/SVQ awards have been made (LMQR 2001). It is estimated that 3.1 million people hold one of these qualifications. In autumn 2000 there were 946,000 people studying towards N/SVQs. The majority of these were employees in work.

This framework also has an impact on other aspects of L&D. General National Vocational Qualifications (GNVQs) are designed for studying within a broad occupational area, like 'business', or 'health and social care'. GNVQs are available at foundation, intermediate and advanced levels, which are now called Vocational A-levels. GNVQs are unit-based qualifications, and do not involve an end of programme examination. In order to complete each unit, students have to prove that they can do a number of tasks, often by completing projects. Students have to take responsibility for planning their own learning. They are expected to organise activities either alone or as part of a group, and contact employers and other people in the community.

Table 6.2　　*Vocational qualifications*

Occupational group	GNVQs GSVQs	NVQs SVQs	Other* VQs
Management and admin	5	13	2
Professional	0	6	3
Associate professional	30	5	19
Clerical and secretarial	39	24	56
Craft and related	4	23	11
Personal and protective services	22	19	2
Sales	0	4	0
Plant and machine ops	0	3	1
Miscellaneous	0	3	5

* Other VQ awards made by City & Guilds, Edexcel and OCR
Source: LMQR (2001)

There have been over 577,000 awards of GNVQs/GSVQs since they were introduced in 1992 (see Table 6.2).

In 1999/2000 nearly all people who obtained a level 2 qualification aged 16 and a level 3 qualification aged 16–18 did so by the academic GSCE and GCE A level routes. Nearly all people who achieve a level 2 qualification aged 17 and over or a level 3 qualification aged 19 and over did so by the vocational route.

Self development

While investment in structures for competency based L&D was proceeding apace a quite different basis for L&D strategy was being evolved; the self development basis. In theory self development can encompass many streams of L&D. Two axioms inform the self development perspective and system in practice. First is that any L&D is a good thing as it involves embracing the new, and changing capabilities and behaviours. Second is that the L&D which has the most potency to achieve change is that chosen and specified by the learners themselves. The first axiom leads to the practice of employee development and assistance programmes (EDAPs) (Hamblett and Holden 2000). The second axiom leads to the learner being given the central responsibility for managing the whole L&D process; this is often centred on establishing personal development plans (PDPs) in practice. Illustrative issues that arise in this L&D strategy are that ambitions that involve L&D have to be fired and drive development, that people need 'space' to grow through L&D at work, and that managing how people learn from their own mistakes in the course of this is critical (Stickland 1996).

Antonacopoulou (2000) studied the use of self development in three retail banks, analysing the difficulties in applying these kinds of principles of self development in practice. There are tensions and contradictions that can accompany such L&D strategies based on choice and self direction among individuals. Development of the whole person, willing and indeed determined to commit to actions on their own part for their own reasons, is the essence of the system. But this is of benefit to the organisation; it enhances individual confidence and abilities that can be directly integrated with better work performance. Development 'of self' and development 'by self' go together and are unified in the workplace. Changing organisations need changing people, and self development is the way to support and achieve this. While mutual benefits can be seen, the process is still one that requires much negotiation; the organisation is dependent on individuals growing and changing but the individual is also dependent on the organisation supporting their growth and change. Balance and synthesis between these interests and priorities are far from easy to manage; but the problems of this are the issues that HRM practitioners need to confront and deal with.

Organisational cultures and attitudes of top managers affect how initiatives take shape and have effect. If an organisation does not allow mistakes, does not welcome ambition and does not create 'space' to grow then self development cannot take root. If people are blamed when things go wrong, if there is no scope for promotion, and if there is no empathy with concepts of personal growth in the workplace then self development will fail, even though as a way of managing L&D it might have seemed attractive. Equally there are problems here for the individual, not just the organisation. If individuals neither wish to follow, or actively resist the self development philosophy, then as a basis for L&D it will fail and L&D will fail. Learners often rely on the organisation to manage development for them; they may have neither the interest, the will, nor the skills to handle self development. They could be developed so that they had the ability and the inclination; but the suspicion is often that this is a way to put the burden for development onto the individual, and for the organisation to avoid responsibility. Employees may then resist self development based L&D.

CONCLUSIONS

While there is a core and common L&D process there is great variety in L&D practice. To explore how and why L&D is done well, or how and why there are problems with L&D, the kinds of strategies for L&D at work need to be discussed. One basis for exploring L&D strategies is to define system parameters for L&D at work; aspects of beliefs, aspects of strategy and levers for implementing L&D at work. Using these parameters helps to establish boundaries of theory; with conservational beliefs, systems and levers at one end and transformative beliefs, systems and levers at the other.

Within these 'ideal' boundaries several versions of L&D strategies, different policies for achieving the main goals of L&D at work, can be identified in practice. These involve different beliefs, systems and levers for putting together the parts of the L&D process (see Figure 6.4) to provide L&D at work. Each has strengths and weaknesses. For example, systematic training as an L&D strategy is based on a system that includes professionals and experts conducting a thorough analysis of needs, job analysis and performance appraisal processes. Other elements of this strategy have to be consistent with this. The kinds of problem that may exist with this type of strategy are that in practice this kind and degree of thorough and complete analysis are not done. It is too time consuming and complex. In that case other aspects of the system will not support the strategy.

There are no merits that make one kind of organisational L&D strategy better than another; each deals with aspects of the contemporary L&D agenda. Alternatively the problem may be that multiple strategies are in use in an organisation, with subsequent conflicts between systems being the source of problems. Multiple strategies may be in use because the organisation aspires to be systematic in L&D, to be business oriented

Figure 6.4   *L&D strategies and L&D process concerns*

Strategy	L&D process concerns			
	Observe needs	Plan objectives	Act/ deliver	Review/ evaluate
Systematic training	Organisation, job and individual analysis	Identify and close performance gaps	Formal courses and trainers	Take up of training, learning transfer, learner reactions
Business orientation	Strategic aims and needs impact	Focus on key business aims, eg IiP	Involving line managers	Growth and development
Competency 1	Lists of behaviours/ values	Competency required	Appraisal, assessment centres	Gains in competency areas
Competency 2	SNVQ models of occupations	Clarity on abilities in the employment	In work or in education	Attainment of qualifications
Continuous development	Ongoing; daily, weekly yearly, lifetime	Continuous improvement	In the course of work organisation	Is this a good climate for learning?
Self development	Personal reflections	Personal and customised objectives	Variable; up to the individual	Have I developed?
Human resource development	Fit with and integrate with other systems development	Connections; attract, retain, career	Select, train, career, reward	HRM generally

in L&D, and to be innovative in L&D all at the same time. If this is so, then the problems for practice are often of managing these multiple strategies, of addressing all these different aspects of managing and organising L&D. Dealing with all these aspects of L&D strategy in a balanced way presents the challenge in practice.

Organisations may also use different L&D strategies to deal with different groups; for example, employees' L&D may be managed through systematic training strategy, while managers' L&D will be managed through an HRD strategy. Describing several different L&D strategies in this way is possible and valid, but it too has weaknesses and disadvantages. While these different L&D strategies are discussed in the literature, and are evidently in use in practice to some extent in many organisations, as surveys and case studies show, it is possible to discern overlaps among them.

The concluding case study to this chapter offers an example of some recent research on L&D at work which attempts to provide a modern perspective on these matters of L&D strategy.

New learning for new work

Question

Read the following brief account of a recent report that proposed a new way of thinking about what L&D strategies at work should involve. Which version of L&D strategy, as defined in this chapter, does this way of thinking about 'new learning for new work' seem to reflect? Think about what the major goal is seen to be, and what the principal plans and policies are that follow from that.

Figure 6.5   *A paradigm for learning at work*

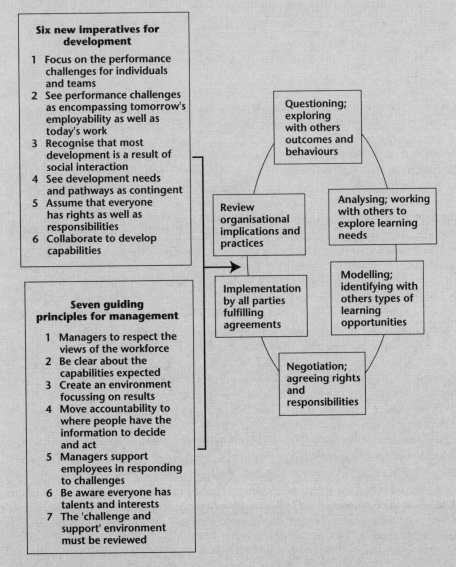

Six new imperatives for development

1 Focus on the performance challenges for individuals and teams
2 See performance challenges as encompassing tomorrow's employability as well as today's work
3 Recognise that most development is a result of social interaction
4 See development needs and pathways as contingent
5 Assume that everyone has rights as well as responsibilities
6 Collaborate to develop capabilities

Seven guiding principles for management

1 Managers to respect the views of the workforce
2 Be clear about the capabilities expected
3 Create an environment focussing on results
4 Move accountability to where people have the information to decide and act
5 Managers support employees in responding to challenges
6 Be aware everyone has talents and interests
7 The 'challenge and support' environment must be reviewed

Questioning; exploring with others outcomes and behaviours

Analysing; working with others to explore learning needs

Review organisational implications and practices

Modelling; identifying with others types of learning opportunities

Implementation by all parties fulfilling agreements

Negotiation; agreeing rights and responsibilities

Source: Fonda and Guile (1999)

CONCLUDING CASE STUDY (cont'd)

Case

A consortium of groups interested in L&D at work produced a report 'New Learning for New Work' (Fonda and Guile 1999) that proposed changes in the way that L&D at work is managed. The issue was not improving one or other element of the L&D process; the whole system of L&D at work needed to be rethought and transformed to meet increasing performance expectations. This rethinking should reflect current organisational realities rather than past best practice. For example, people are not expected any more to 'do what they are told to do'; they are all individually responsible for adding value through continuously improving their own performance as empowered employees. The report's authors conclude that a new 'map' of what L&D at work involves is needed. They provide one (see Figure 6.5) based on three elements: new imperatives for development, new principles for management as a whole, and therefore a new paradigm for L&D at work.

Analysis

Fonda and Guile's model illustrates how broader ideas about management and organisation shape and inform how learning at work is seen. It does so by making explicit their own assumptions about partnerships at work; about partnerships of commitment rather than 'command and control' systems of management; about the partnership between rights and responsibilities in organisations as social institutions; and about how HRM professionals have to act as a strategic partner, not in an administrative role. Their view of learning at work is intended to be consistent with these different aspects of partnership. That is the major goal, and plans and policies must then make sense in relation to achieving this.

The beliefs are about seeing learning as a 'joint venture' between managers and staff. The levers are those relevant to the role of HR professionals being focussed on supplying the advice and services needed to assure that these joint ventures, learning partnerships between managers and staff, work. These components of the model lead to a conclusion that learning at work depends on successful 'joint ventures' between managers and staff, not the design of one day training courses. In place of a reliance on courses and qualifications there should be an ability to manage learning as a collaborative and engaging part of work.

In this respect it seems far removed from the systematic training strategy, and more in harmony with continuous development and HRD forms of L&D strategy. But the model does, nonetheless, contain a version of the systematic training cycle as well; albeit modified, as the National Training Awards were, to reflect a business orientation.

The issue then is, what kinds of elements need to be managed if a system is to be developed that enables such a strategy to be implemented? What is it that organisations would have to do differently with L&D in comparison with what they do at the moment? And what about the possible tensions between getting 'results' and 'respecting' people, between what is referred to as 'challenge' and 'support'? Does that challenge involve potentially removing people from their jobs, which may impede the 'partnership' being sought; and should that support include rewarding L&D as a good thing in itself, which again may cause systems problems? Stating imperatives and principles is not the end of the search for an effective L&D strategy; it is only the beginning. Implementing strategy, so that there is systems support rather than systems

CONCLUDING CASE STUDY (cont'd)

blocking of the achievement of the goal, is the issue. Often changing one element of a system leads to unintended consequences which create new problems elsewhere. Implementing a new L&D strategy can create problems elsewhere; or problems elsewhere can impede the realisation of a new L&D strategy.

REFERENCES

Aitken, G. (2001) *Corporate Universities: A Case Study*, unpublished MSc dissertation, Strathclyde University.

Allen, R. (1994) 'The need for diversity in corporate training: one size doesn't really fit', *Industrial and Commercial Training*, Vol. 26, No. 10.

Antonacopoulou, A. (2000) 'Employee development through self-development in three retail banks', *Personnel Review*, Vol. 29, No. 4.

Arnone, M. (1998) 'Corporate universities: a viewpoint on the challenges and best practices', *Career Development International*, Vol. 3, No. 5.

Boyatzis, R. (1982) *The Competent Manager: A Model for Effective Performance*, New York, Wiley.

Coleman, S. and Keep, E. (2001) *Background Literature Review for PIU Project on Workforce Development*, SKOPE-url.

Fonda, N. and Guile, D. (1999) 'Joint learning ventures', *People Management*, Vol. 5, No. 6.

Hamblett, J. and Holden, R. (2000) 'Employee-led development: another piece of left luggage?', *Personnel Review*, Vol. 29, No. 4.

IDS (1996) *Training Strategies*, IDS Study 608.

Kotte, J. (1999) 'Corporate universities; lessons in building a world class workforce', *Personnel Psychology*, Vol. 52, No. 2.

LMQR (2001) 'Vocational qualifications 1999/2000', *Labour Market Quarterly Report*, August.

Mabey, C., Salaman, G. and Storey, J. (1998) *Human Resource Management: A Strategic Introduction*, London, Blackwell.

Meiser, J.C. (1998) '*Corporate Universities: Lessons in Building a World Class Workforce*', New York, McGraw-Hill.

Miller, L., Rankin, N. and Neathey, F. (2001) *Competency Frameworks in Organisations*, Chartered Institute of Personnel and Development.

Moorby, E. (1991) *How to Succeed in Employee Development*, London, McGraw-Hill.

Rainbird, H. (2000) *Training in the Workplace: Critical Perspectives on Learning at Work*, London, Macmillan (now Palgrave Macmillan).

Rothwell, W.J. and Kazanas, H.C. (1994) *Human Resource Development: A Strategic Approach*, Amherst, Mass., HRD Press.

Schlesinger, E. (1996a) 'Why learning is not a cycle 1: discovering a pattern', *Industrial and Commercial Training*, Vol. 28, No. 2.

Schlesinger, E. (1996b) 'Why learning is not a cycle 2: developing a pattern', *Industrial and Commercial Training*, Vol. 28, No. 5.

Stein, M. (2000) ' "Winners" training and its troubles', *Personnel Review*, Vol. 29, No. 4.

Stickland, R. (1996) 'Self development in a business organisation', *Journal of Managerial Psychology*, Vol. 11, No. 7.

Storey, J. (1992) *Developments in the Management of Human Resources*, Oxford, Blackwell.

Stumpf, S. (1998) 'Corporate universities of the future', *Career Development International*, Vol. 3, No. 5.

chapter seven

L&D Partnerships

Learning outcomes

- Analyse the market for L&D at work
- Identify different kinds of providers of L&D products and services
- Describe the ways in which work organisations develop partnerships with these providers to manage L&D
- Critically evaluate the issues involved in using external consultants for L&D

FRAMEWORK CASE STUDIES: PARTNERSHIPS

Jim attended a one day 'sources of stress' workshop, delivered in his own organisation but by an external consultant. The issue of stress had not been dealt with before in his organisation. The organisation selected an external provider to do this, a specialist trainer in the area who was also medically qualified. They gave a professional presentation on stress and its impact on people and organisations. They then used creative exercises in relaxation techniques to develop skills for dealing with stress. Jim got personal insights into stress and its organisational impact, and was both more aware of a lot of issues afterwards and able to manage them. No trainer in the organisation would have been as good as this external expert.

In an organisation where there was a concern with communication among staff, the organisation elected to send its staff to an external training event provided by a specialist group, 'Peak Performance Speakers International'. They provided a three day course on themes related to motivation, belief systems, building rapport and communication. There was a mixture of theory and practical exercises throughout, and the training was fun but also thought provoking, and personally useful. It helped people to deal with personal and work relationship problems and to focus on what matters. There was also a good reading list provided at the course, with things to be investigated further afterwards if people wanted.

When dealing with team building many organisations elect to send teams from their workplace on a course provided by a reputable provider of team building courses and exercises. But for one organisation this failed. The trainer on the course had not had any briefing on the issues facing the particular group of people who attended the course. They just delivered a 'standard course', which was not tailored to the group's needs. This did more harm than good, as the L&D failed, in the words of one participant 'miserably', to meet great expectations on the part of the team members. They left the training feeling things had been made worse rather than better.

Finally, many organisations need and seek training in information technology (IT) applications, and do deals with specialist providers of IT training. One organisation had a deal with a training provider for courses on Microsoft Excel, at various levels of ability. It sent some staff on the 'intermediate level' course. This course was taught by a specialist tutor, who certainly knew their stuff. But it was far too easy for some of the staff on it, and they were not covering anything they did not already know. These people should probably have gone to the advanced course. However, they did not know what was involved in the courses beforehand, and just went to what they had been told to go to.

INTRODUCTION

Sending people out of the organisation or getting partners into the organisation as part of L&D activities are an integral element of L&D at work practice for many organisations. It has become such a prevalent and important part of L&D at work that the issues involved deserve a distinctive treatment (Carter 2000, Williams 2000). Two of the examples cited above illustrate why such partnerships are a useful and productive way to manage L&D. This does not mean, however, that L&D in practice can be neglected within the organisation. As the other two of the stories cited above illustrate the scope for things to go wrong if L&D practice is not managed is considerable. Partnerships with L&D providers still involve people in the organisation in managing the L&D process. Most clearly this involves identifying L&D needs, and the organisation may also be expected to manage evaluation. The partners' focus may just be on design and delivery. Alternatively it could be that a partner is required for the whole of the L&D process; to observe, plan, act and review along with people inside the organisation.

Partnerships may be with a range of people and providers, from individual consultants through to large institutions such as universities. The practice of L&D cannot be understood without exploring this market for L&D, and what is entailed in operating in that market (Baxter 1998). For partnerships cover both a large volume of L&D activity, and are central to some of the most important L&D projects that organisations will pursue (Stumpf and Longman 2000).

THE MARKET FOR L&D AT WORK

The market for L&D at work is a part of two bigger markets. One is the market for management consultancy, and the other is the market for HRM provision and services. Looking first at the general management consultancy market, the Management Consultants Association (MCA), which represents the major UK consultancy firms, defines consultancy as:

> The rendering of independent advice and assistance about management issues. This typically includes identifying and investigating problems and/or opportunities, recommending appropriate action and helping to implement those recommendations.

Consultants are experts playing a role as an external advisor to organisations based on their experience and expertise (MaCallan 1997, Massey and Walker 1999). Consultants can be hired for many reasons. These reasons may be strategic, connected with the organisation's plans and policy for achieving major goals; a client might want

---

Box 7.1

Consultants

Accountancy based consultancies; these are the big players, huge organisations with thousands of partners spread around the globe.

IT companies; IT based consultants include IBM, EDS, Unisys, Sema, Cap Gemini, ICL, CMG and Logica.

US based consultancies; they are usually in the strategy, marketing and business transformation sector.

Small to medium sized consultancies; in the UK firms such as PA Consulting Group and Hay Management Consultants, and also a number of smaller accountancy based firms.

Actuarial firms; these firms' primary business is in employee benefits, pensions and remuneration, to which have been added human resources and organisational change consultancy.

Business schools; most business schools have people within their staff who act as consultants. Some institutions actively promote themselves as centres of consultancy.

Small consultancies; There are also a large number of small consultancies. They often have no more than ten staff. They may have split off from a larger consultancy or they may be partners who have had their own consultancy.

Sole practitioners; there are tens of thousands of sole practitioners. In all, there may be around 40,000 sole practitioners in the UK alone.

Source: Baxter (1998)

---

help in putting in a new financial system, or they might want advice on redesigning the organisation. The reasons may be narrower and more specific; a client might require an external review of its pay structures or recruitment policies, or they might need help in product design and marketing. One common perception is that buying in consultants means that a company has inadequate management. In principle consultants are valued because they are external resources who can bring in knowledge of best practice (Kubr 1996). The consulting industry can be broken down into several kinds of private sector suppliers (see Box 7.1).

As traditional consultancy firms have prospered and grown other kinds of business have started to offer consultancy services too. Advertising agencies and design firms offer consultancy, as do IT companies and law firms. Many specialist management consultancies started up as numerous redundant executives set up on their own as consultants. Today the consultancy industry is seen to be both huge and amorphous. All these kinds of company can become partners in providing L&D at work in the course of their work with organisations. Management consultancy can also be analysed by looking at its market sectors and those who provide consultancy.

The second market is the HRM consultancy market (Table 7.1); this includes services and provision in HR planning, recruitment, reward, training, development, appraisal, career development, leadership and communication. It interfaces and overlaps with two other segments of the consultancy market: corporate communications and organisation development.

Table 7.1   *Market sectors for consultancy*

Sector	Share of market %
Information technology (IT)	38
Corporate strategy and OD	18
Production and services management	12
Financial and administrative systems	12
Project management	7
Human resources	6
Economic and environmental studies	3
Marketing and corporate communications	3

Source: Baxter (1998)

The market can also be analysed by identifying the kinds of organisations that use consultants. The importance of the financial services sector has been rising each year. Consultancy earnings from the energy and water industries increased dramatically in the 1990s as these industries were subject to much public interest both as takeover targets and as public service providers. Public sector work as a proportion of total consultancy revenues declined during the 1990s. In part this was because the public sector was now much smaller than it used to be, and in part also due to the fact that the major privatisations in the UK are over.

So the market for consultancy involves various kinds of providers, offering a range of different kinds of services including HR related and L&D services, working with diverse kinds of organisations.

THE PROCESS

There are various models of how good consultants should work (Steinberg 1989, Kaarst-Brown 1999). They are generally variations on the theme of consultants providing help as partners without taking over. Good consultancy is about being able to give the right advice, in the right way, to the right person at the right time. To do this consultants need to keep abreast of trends, anticipate changes, offer useful advice, and be able to discuss costs and benefits, measurable and tangible. Consultancy is supposed to operate with professional standards and principles (Phillips 1993, Ashford 1999). They should be independent in a number of respects (see Box 7.2) to ensure that they are objective, drawing on experience and research.

The outcomes of such independent help are diverse; they can work to restore previous levels of performance, to attain a new standard, to identify new opportunities, to enhance learning or to manage change. The roles consultants adopt to achieve this can be informational, providing contacts/connections, giving expert opinion, or providing diagnosis and actions.

Consultancies are dependent for revenues on obtaining business through contracting with companies and organisations. Some other training organisations also obtain revenues from grants associated with Government funded training schemes (Tables 7.2 and 7.3). Determining how much employers spend on training, the size of the market, is a challenge, both in theory and in practice (Ryan 1991). Any estimates must be treated with caution and qualification. Many use an accounting rather than

---

Box 7.2

Independent partners

- Technical independence — Not tied to one kind of solution
- Financial independence — Not dependent on 'getting results' to earn fees
- Administratively independent — Not part of the organisation
- Politically independent — Not tied to any power grouping in the organisation
- Emotionally independent — Not emotionally involved with the organisation or its people

---

Table 7.2 *Private sector expenditure on formal training (£bn), 1993–1998*

Year	1993	1994	1995	1996	1997	1998
Expenditure	12.0	12.4	13.2	14.0	15.0	16.0

Source: Baxter (1998)

Table 7.3 *Expenditure by the UK Department for Education and Employment and OFSTED (£m), 1998/1999*

Category	Expenditure
Total expenditure	14,023
Expenditure on employment and training programmes of which:	3,311
'Welfare to Work' programme	951
Work based training for young people	741
Work based training for adults	340
European Social Fund	308

an economic definition of spending on L&D. An accounting definition looks only at the direct and indirect costs associated with L&D. An economic definition would seek to also include factors such as the 'opportunity costs'; that is, to include an estimate of the costs of what has been foregone in order to involve someone in L&D. Another issue here is only counting formal training in assessments of spending, excluding the costs of informal training or other performance support related to L&D.

Whether the figures that emerge represent an accurate picture of employer commitment to L&D or underspending on L&D is equally still open to debate. Ryan (*op cit*) concludes that it is both possible to argue that employers spend significant amounts on training and that there is scope for them to do more. This is where comparative benchmarks come in, as no absolute criteria can exist. Moreover Ryan concludes that what the money is spent on, rather than how much is spent, should actually be the primary concern.

PARTNERS IN TRAINING

Organisations have always involved consultants in their L&D activities as they can provide support for performance systems improvement through advice or support for change. Partners may be able to better identify needs, to plan and design L&D, or to deliver a programme of L&D. A more recent factor influencing the use of partners is that, while many companies have developed and retained their own in-house training function, a number have cut back their own internally managed provision in recent years. Consequently, a growing number of organisations have to choose an external training provider when dealing with L&D demands.

The main reasons cited for selecting an outside provider (see Table 7.4) are to obtain the best training available and because the required training cannot be supplied in-house. Factors of quality and capacity combine to lead organisations into partnerships. Other factors influencing the specific choice of partner include the training facilities available and the quality of the L&D design. A dedicated L&D company is likely to have broad experience in designing different courses for the various needs of different clients. An in-house training department is unlikely to have this breadth of knowledge and experience.

Table 7.5 shows that training managers play a significant role in the selection of trainers. Between 1997 and 1998, the proportion of training managers with responsibility for selecting the L&D provider increased from 31 per cent to 51 per cent, reflecting a shift in responsibility away from the personnel/HRM function towards the L&D function. While external partnerships may be required for design and delivery, companies still need internal L&D departments and L&D professionals with a knowledge of training suppliers.

Despite this apparent shift towards using external L&D resources there are a number of factors which continue to make in-house L&D both attractive and economic. The Industrial Society suggests that three factors play a crucial role in persuading companies to carry out their own training rather than using partners. One factor is price, and in many cases external providers are too expensive. Another factor for many organisations is the need to tailor the training to their own needs; they did not want 'off the shelf' training from an external provider. The number of people being trained

Table 7.4 *Reasons for selecting external training providers (%), 1998*

Reason	%
Quality of trainers	48
Facilities: venue, no distractions, etc	43
Quality of training design	38
Accreditation	35
Ability to tailor to client's needs	27
Number of people to be trained	26
Quality of support materials	22
Price	11
Better evaluation	6
Corporate policy	5
Other	15

Source: Industrial Society (1998a)

Table 7.5   *Personnel responsible for selecting training providers (%), 1997 and 1998*

Post held	1997	1998
Training manager	31	51
Personnel/HRM director	21	21
Personnel/HRM manager	28	18
Personnel/HRM training officer	19	18
Training director	13	17
Line manager	15	15
Personnel/training administrator	3	4

Source: Industrial Society (1998b)

Table 7.6   *Factors influencing the choice of training provider (%), 1997 and 1998*

Factor	1997	1998
Feedback from trainees	58	57
Personnel recommendation from internal colleagues	46	47
Personal experience of trainers' courses	45	46
Personnel recommendation from external contact	37	41
Reputation of individual trainers	36	35
Tendering process	14	21
Approved list of providers	11	11

Source: Industrial Society (1998b)

was also an important consideration for a substantial number of companies; the larger the number, the more likely the company is to opt for internal training, in order to control costs.

Table 7.6 provides data on the factors which influence the choice of L&D provider where one is to be employed. It highlights the importance of personal knowledge and recommendation. This can be feedback from trainees, recommendation from internal colleagues or external contacts, or previous personal experience. It seems that experience of an individual trainer is often more important than a training company's reputation (Stumpf and Longman 2000).

Table 7.7 shows the qualities which are considered important when selecting an external LD provider. Being able to tailor a course to a company's needs is of paramount importance. Quality and perceived value for money are also seen to be important. Less important are price differences between one training company and another, and a training company's image and professionalism.

Another factor affecting the choice of training is venue. Partners can be brought into the company's own premises, or go to a trainer's premises or some other location. Table 7.8 shows that the most popular choice in practice is to use a private sector trainer working on-site, followed by an educational institution working off-site, then a professional association/institute or a non-profit making training body working off-site. For on-site training the private sector comes out top, but equipment

Table 7.7   *Qualities sought when selecting an external training provider (%), 1997 and 1998*

Quality	1997	1998
Ability to deliver tailored training	76	77
Reputation for quality	47	49
Perceived value for money	44	44
Experience of training provider in your industry/sector	31	35
Price	39	34
Image/professionalism	26	30
Accreditation of course	9	10
Ability to evaluate training	10	10
Locally based	11	5
Ability to provide other training/support	6	4

Source: The Industrial Society (1998b)

Table 7.8   *External providers of training: % of organisations using each type and % working on-site, 1998*

Type of training provider	Overall	On-site
Private sector trainers/providers	78	74
University/college/other FE body	68	28
Professional association/institute	55	24
Non-profit making training body	48	20
Equipment supplier	33	48
Training and Enterprise Council/ Local Enterprise Council	24	21
Informal employer's network/club	10	15

Source: Industrial Society (1998a)

suppliers are also widely used for on-site work. The 'equipment suppliers' are generally IT companies or providers of computer related systems on which staff are being trained.

IN THE L&D MARKET

Marketplaces exist for selling L&D products and services, and the activity there is an indication of who is in the market. These marketplaces are trade fairs. One main UK trade fair is the annual Human Resource Development Exhibition organised by the CIPD in conjunction with its national training and development conference during April. In 2001 this event was attended by over 7000 potential buyers of products and services, where they met up to 300 exhibitors. The exhibitors ranged from training providers, open learning providers, and interactive learning providers to individuals selling leadership courses or sales and marketing training.

Independent training organisations are arguably the most important type of L&D provider. They can be public companies, private limited companies or, occasionally, charities. Most employ from 50 to 100 people, making them small businesses. Most of their trainers they will employ full time, though some training companies rely heavily on contract staff.

Colleges of further education and business schools are also important. Colleges of further education provide vocational training, while business schools offer general management training with an academic input, which is mainly for managers and executives. Information technology (IT) companies are expanding rapidly in the L&D market. L&D has become a natural additional service to their traditional products. Providing L&D can also help to increase their customer base. The L&D market is also served by a large number of sole practitioners. These sole practitioners have often developed their skills at a larger management consultancy, training organisation or business school, and then gone independent. They may have worked as a training manager with a specific company, designing and managing training courses in-house. Some may have started up on their own when their former employer decided to outsource provision of all company training needs. A number will work for their former employers as L&D consultants.

Partnerships with these kinds of organisations and individuals will involve either bringing consultants into the organisation, or sending staff out to events or courses; or a combination of both. The issues and tensions of managing this effectively are about assuring the quality of the person coming in or the external provider. Good consultants give value for money, and care about the working relationships they have with clients. Partnership is a way of working, not an opportunity to 'dump' things on consultants, and abdicate responsibility because a consultant has been paid to manage an aspect of L&D. If that approach is taken disappointment is almost inevitable. Before using a partner, an organisation should be clear about why they are using consultants, what they want the consultant to do, how that will be managed, and then be effective in choosing the right person or company (see Box 7.3).

The initial practical focus for partnership is writing a consultancy brief, detailing the outcomes wanted, the scale and scope of a project, and being very clear about what is needed in a submission. Selecting a consultant from a written submission to a brief means it has to tell the client what they need to know about the consultants. In addition the client has to be confident that they feel they can work with the consultants, and that other key stakeholders feel the same. It needs to be appreciated that good consultants work in a high risk environment, and have to be commercially focussed. They seek good relationships as a partner with the client, to earn their fees and their living. The key to effective partnerships in this context is to begin with a clear brief.

What is required to work with the consultants will vary depending on the project. If they are to be used to provide one off courses, then once the format is agreed they can be left to get on with it. If they are to be involved in a larger scale project then regular meetings, and perhaps some kind of project steering group will be appropriate. Maintaining a good partnership over a longer term project will be more challenging, as challenges and issues may arise in the course of the project. The conclusion to any partnership should be an evaluation that mirrors the usual evaluation of L&D. What were people's reactions, what learning has occurred, what improvements in performance are there, and what have the costs and benefits been?

Box 7.3

Questions to ask when using L&D partners

■ **Why?**   Are partners needed because of:
           the scale of a project?
           a lack of resources?
           a need for objectivity?
           a need for credibility?
           a lack of confidence among internal staff?
■ **What?** What are the outcomes being sought?
           How you will these be identified and measured?
           Agree outcomes with all the key stakeholders, including the consultants
■ **How?**   Consider in detail what the project is likely to involve
           Be prepared to consider ideas and options the consultants have
           Keep in mind the implications of any options for budgets and other resources
           Be realistic about expectations
■ **Who?**   Know the L&D consultancy market, and test it by asking for tenders
           Be clear about what you want in a consultant
           Consider the stakeholder relationships
           Be clear about the skills a consultant can offer; they are not all things to all people

---

CONCLUSION

Much L&D at work is provided for by external suppliers coming into an organisation, or staff going out of the organisation. This approach to L&D has always been used, but seems to be increasing for various reasons. Effectively managing L&D then means effectively managing partnerships. The nature of the market for L&D services and products is ever evolving, but the main sectors and providers are fairly well established. Being able to research and access them as needed is an integral part of modern L&D at work. In developing relationships the building of positive partnerships should be the key. That means a high degree of clarity about what is wanted, and skills to ensure that the right partners are selected.

Organisations are in part dependent on what the market offers. The effectiveness of market forces as a driver of improvements in the provision of and quality of L&D remains an area that will concern many stakeholders: work organisations as buyers, providers as sellers, and the Government as they seek to evolve better L&D at work provision over the years ahead. Changes in Government policy, trends in outsourcing HRM work, and the merging of organisations in the consulting and HRM sectors will all provide impetus for change in the L&D at work market. New forms of, or areas for, partnership may emerge and evolve.

CONCLUDING CASE STUDY

Working in partnership with consultants

Below is an outline of a situation where a company is seeking to develop a partnership with an external provider for a programme of management development.

Read the brief on the company's background and the tender they have put out. Then answer the following questions:

1 Is the current level of information given enough, or what else do you need to know in order to put a tender together?
2 How will you find out?
3 What impression do you want to make on the organisation? How will you achieve this?
4 What 'ball park' daily fee rate would you consider reasonable? How did you arrive at this figure?
5 What, in general terms, would you expect to provide for this fee?
6 What kind of relationship would you seek to build with the client? How would you go about doing this?

The company background

The hard-pressed human resource development directorate of a large water utility has raised the need for management development in the company. Since separation from the public sector several years ago, the authority has found it hard to develop its own businesslike and managerial culture. Many of the new staff have come in from the private sector and find the level of management skills in the organisation disappointing. A staff opinion survey has confirmed this view. The chief executive has, somewhat reluctantly, agreed to the idea of running a management development programme for managers at all levels. The HRD manager is assuming that:

■ managers need to develop people management skills (Personnel are tired of dealing with grievances, and some cases have led to employment tribunals)
■ managers need to get better at coaching staff and delegating responsibility
■ leadership is lacking and needs to be encouraged
■ change in the organisation is constant

The HRD manager has decided to go out to tender for the delivery of a programme that will achieve these outcomes (see the tender document on the following pages). The invitation to tender process should produce a list of potential providers who have made the shortlist because of submitting an outline proposal scoping their broad approach to the project, their experience of working on projects of this nature and scale, and their range of fees for such work.

Consultancy brief

As an established management and training consultancy you want to respond in writing to the tender. Your market intelligence tells you that it is from the potential client's hard-pressed human resource development directorate, and that since separation from the local authority several years ago the organisation has found it hard to develop its own businesslike and managerial culture. You know that a number of staff have come in from the private sector and find the level of management skills disappointing. You also know that the chief executive is not the kind to use training to develop managers, and you are surprised to see the tender invitation.

CONCLUDING CASE STUDY (cont'd)

THE WATER AUTHORITY (TWA) INVITATION TO TENDER

Introduction

Tenders are invited for the development and delivery of a comprehensive management development programme (MDP) for TWA. The principal aim of the programme is to provide all existing and new managers with the competencies expected of a successful manager. The key target group will be staff with direct people management responsibilities, around 140 managers, plus the 16 senior managers.

The programme

The provider will be expected to carry out research work to gain the necessary understanding of the organisation and its culture in order to ensure successful tailoring of the programme.

The structure of the programme will take into account company culture, programme coordination, learning styles, development needs and so forth. The programme should also have regard to the appropriate mix and emphasis of course elements according to the seniority of the target group.

The delivery methods should be highly interactive, participative, demanding and very challenging.

The MDP is expected to have a major impact on all staff. It will be a teambuilding exercise for the whole organisation. Staff participating in the programme will be able to build closer and trusting working relationships with their colleagues. The programme will also support the creation of a shared vision for the future to which all are committed.

Contract period

The contract will be for one year. It is anticipated that subsequent contracts will be awarded on an annual basis.

Tendering process

Proposals, outlining expressions of interest, approaches and fees, should be supplied.

Acknowledgement

Case study outline by Carol Pease, 2002

REFERENCES

Ashford, M. (1999) *Con Tricks: The Shadowy World of Management Consultancy and How to Make It Work For You*, New York, Simon & Schuster.

Baxter, J. (ed.) (1998) *Keynote Training Report*, Seventh edition, Keynote.

Carter, C. (2000) 'Keepers of the knowledge capital: legislating for the new millennium', *Management Decision*, Vol. 38, No. 3.

Industrial Society (1998a) *Training Trends*, May/June, The Industrial Society.

Industrial Society (1998b) *Training Trends*, July/August, The Industrial Society.

Kaarst-Brown, L.O. (1999) 'Five symbolic roles of the external consultant – integrating change, power and symbolism', *Journal of Organizational Change Management*, Vol. 12, No. 6.

Kubr, M. (ed.) (1996) *Management Consulting: A Guide to the Profession*, Geneva, International Labour Organization.

MaCallan, M. (1997) 'The company doctors: good, now say aaah', *Scotland in Business*, June.

Massey, C. and Walker, R. (1999) 'Aiming for organisational learning: consultants as agents of change', *The Learning Organization*, Vol. 6, No. 1.

Phillips, J. (1993) 'Evaluating outside resources', in *A Handbook of Training Evaluation and Measurement Methods*, Houston, Gulf Publishing.

Ryan, P. (1991) 'How much do employers spend on training? An assessment of the 'Training in Britain' estimates', *Human Resource Management Journal*, Vol. 1, No. 4.

Steinberg, D. (1989) *Interprofessional Consultation*, London, Blackwell.

Stumpf, S. and Longman, R. (2000) 'The ultimate consultant: building long-term, exceptional value client relationships', *Career Development International*, Vol. 5, No. 3.

Williams, T. (2000) 'Networking as a way of gaining business for training consultants', *Industrial & Commercial Training*, Vol. 32, No. 5.

chapter eight

The Investors in People Standard

Learning outcomes

- Describe the Investors in People (IiP) standard
- Outline what is involved in organisations being accredited as an IiP
- Explain the reasons for the development of the IiP standard and accreditation process
- Critically evaluate the evolution of IiP and the current situation with IiP in the UK
- Identify and evaluate the strength and weaknesses of the IiP standard

FRAMEWORK CASE STUDY: SOLUNA TRAVEL

Around 20,000 organisations in the UK are recognised as being Investors in People (IiP), and over 34 per cent of the UK workforce work in IiP accredited organisations (Johnson *et al* 2000). One example is Soluna Travel, an independent retail travel agency with several branches in the South Yorkshire area.

In the 1990s the large organisations that dominate in this industry sector were adding hundreds of high street travel agencies to their stock. Many independent travel agents, unable to compete, were going out of business. The head of Soluna Travel, Barbara Neale, saw this coming; she decided they would have to be smarter and work harder. This could be done by investing in L&D at work. She started with herself; going on a leadership course. She then focussed on two areas. First was increasing employee motivation and commitment by decentralising decision making, which required a new appraisal scheme. Second was developing a training programme that fitted with their marketing strategy. That marketing strategy involved focussing on niche markets, for example expensive cruises.

Staff undertook several cruise training courses, and also visited ships to familiarise themselves with them. All staff undertook accredited training given by the Passenger and Shipping Association for Retail Agents (PASRA). They did this as they wanted to gain a £250,000 turnover in cruises in two years; they achieved it in one year. Soluna Travel is now seen as a major player in this market.

This has encouraged them to move into other areas of quality holiday provision: golf holidays and long haul tailor made holidays. Developing a specialism through L&D is the way ahead. With this background in place Soluna applied to be accredited as an Investor in People (IiP). They achieved the standard, and their practices are seen as an exemplar of the value of L&D, embodied in IiP principles, in a small business.
Source: Johnson *et al* (2000)

INTRODUCTION

Instead of enforcing regulations requiring the provision of L&D at work, the philosophy of promoting best practice is the strategy adopted in the UK. IiP is the quality standard for L&D at work which is central to this strategy. It was developed in the UK to help organisations to develop their business through developing their people, by a task force in the early 1990s. It was the main element of a national strategy to improve L&D by involving employers themselves in improving L&D (Alberga *et al* 1997).

The task force that designed the IiP standard looked at successful businesses and explored why they were successful. They concluded that successful organisations took care to develop their employees effectively. A view that an acute skills shortage was hampering the UK's ability to be a truly competitive player in the world economy was commonplace. According to one report, the UK was ranked 23rd out of 44 world economies in its ability to provide a skilled workforce to employers (King 1995). When future competitiveness success would increasingly be dependent on employers actively developing their people's skills and potential, the UK was lagging behind.

The aim then was to establish a standard of good practice which would enable organisations to improve the quality and effectiveness of their L&D at work practices (Down and Smith 1998). The IiP standard links people development to strategy, organisational goals and performance (Mason 1994); in these respects it is a mix of the systematic, the business oriented and continuous development L&D strategies outlined in Chapter 6.

In Soluna Travel, where L&D in specialist holidays provided a competitive edge for a small organisation competing with large multiple chains, accreditation as an IiP was straightforward. They were, it seems, already doing the kinds of things the IiP standard was established to promote. To become accredited did not apparently involve substantial or significant change in policy or practice for them. It did provide recognition and some further support in evolving L&D for an organisation already committed to L&D at work. The example can be cited as evidence that the rationale of IiP does work, and that striving to be an IiP is indeed a valid way to help develop businesses.

The IiP standard was 'developed by business for business'. This was meant to ensure that the standard would link L&D to achieving organisational goals, rather than being a wish-list of what 'outsiders' thought businesses ought to be doing. Such an approach was entirely consistent with the era of its origin, where 'employer-led' initiatives were the foundation of National Vocational Education and Training (NVET) in general. This was the era where the 'business oriented' L&D philosophy was paramount, with the strengths and weaknesses of that system. The standard was developed with the backing of most of the UK's major business organisations, including the Confederation of British Industry (CBI), the Trades Union Congress (TUC), the Institute of Directors (IoD), the Chartered Institute of Personnel and Development (CIPD) and all the

Table 8.1   *IiP target and actual attainments,*
England 2001

Organisation size (employees)	IiP 2001 target	IiP 2001 actual
<50	10,000	2,334
>50	45%	19%
>200	70%	34%

Source: National Advisory Council for Education and Training Targets

major political parties (IiP UK, 2000). Yet it was still very much part of an overall Government strategy, supported by the then Department of Employment. Consistent with the characteristics of the British institutional and economic context, it was part of a market-led, voluntarist strategy. There was to be no requirement for organisations to be accredited as IiP, as there is with other areas of standards in HRM such as health and safety at work.

One other aspect of the IiP approach to note is that the rationale was that a single standard would be suitable for all sizes and sectors of organisation (MacVicar and Brown 1994, Daniel 1997, Hill and Stewart 1999). According to the developers and those who promote IiP it is suitable for all sizes and sectors of industry. The headline figures of 20,000 accredited organisations and 34 per cent of the UK workforce in IiP organisations since it was established seem to suggest that this initiative has been a success. But when the attainment of targets for IiP recognition is looked at, however, the picture is not so good (see Table 8.1).

Why these targets have not been attained requires an analysis of organisations' motivations, the standard itself, and the process of being accredited. The motivation for obtaining IiP accreditation will vary from organisation to organisation. For some it is an opportunity to review current policies and practices against a recognised standard, receiving recognition for their good practice. For others it provides a structured way to improve the effectiveness of basic L&D activities, offering an opportunity to improve on what is being done. For others it can provide a framework for introducing a strategy and plan of action for L&D at work, where that has not yet been properly thought through.

Organisations tend to be motivated to obtain accreditation to get both tangible and intangible benefits. They want the kudos and status of being accredited. That may help attract and retain staff, and attract business. Organisations also seek benefits from being accredited as an IiP in terms of lower staff turnover, higher morale, greater motivation, ownership and understanding of the organisation, higher calibre recruits, better communications and higher productivity. These are certainly the kinds of practical benefits emphasised by those who promote IiP (see Box 8.1).

Table 8.2, which compares average UK companies with IiP accredited companies, appears to validate the claims for tangible benefits, certainly for private sector organisations.

With benefits like these associated with accreditation as an IiP it seems surprising that the initiative has not yet reached the targets set. Why would organisations fail to take advantage of such a good thing? The gap between targets and achievements has raised questions about the standard itself, and its role in NVET policy overall. For some IiP is clearly a necessary and sensible promotion of L&D at work, but for others

Box 8.1

Benefits of accreditation as an IiP

■ **Improved earnings, productivity and profitability**
Skilled and motivated people work harder and better. Productivity will improve, extra effort will be made to close sales, and a positive impact will be seen on the bottom line.

■ **Reduced costs and wastage**
Skilled and motivated people constantly examine their work to contribute to reducing costs and wastage.

■ **Enhanced quality**
Investing in people significantly improves the results of quality programmes. IiP adds considerable value to BS 5750, ISO 9000 and other total quality initiatives.

■ **Improved motivation**
Through greater involvement, personal development and recognition of achievement, motivation is improved. This leads to higher morale, improved retention rates, reduced absenteeism, readier acceptance of change and identification with the organisation beyond the confines of the job.

■ **Customer satisfaction**
IiP is central to helping employees become customer focussed, thus enabling the organisation to effectively meet customer needs at a profit.

■ **Public recognition**
IiP status brings public recognition for real achievements measured against a rigorous national standard. Being an IiP helps to attract the best quality job applicants. It may also provide a reason for customers to choose specific goods and services.

■ **Competitive advantage**
Through improved performance, IiP organisations develop a competitive edge.

Table 8.2   IiP benefits

Area of benefit	Average company	IiP accredited company	Gain
Rate of return on capital	9.21%	16.27%	77%
Pre-tax profit margin	2.54%	6.91%	172%
Average salary	£12,590	£14,195	13%
Turnover/sales per employee	£64,912	£86,625	33%
Profit per employee	£1,815	£3,198	76%

Source: National Advisory Council on Education and Training Targets

it has involved little more than an 'Increase in Paperwork' for those who are already doing L&D well and want to be 'badged'.

There have also been questions about the amount of 'investing' that has been done in the promotion of the IiP standard itself, with concerns about the resources devoted to its promotion among organisations and the quality of assessment and help that are given through the process of accreditation. The lack of integration in the standard with other HRM elements that concern organisations, and competition with other benchmarking tools, like more general quality standards which are of interest to many organisations, have also been discussed as problems for promoting the standard. Most critically, the lack of interest and uptake among small/medium sized firms, where productivity and L&D issues have long been acknowledged, have raised doubts about the design and development of the IiP standard.

In 1998, after consultation with organisations, stakeholders and individuals, the standard was redesigned and revamped. This was done, IiP UK claim, to take into account what their customers now required. The changes were needed for the standard to stay relevant and credible, to provide greater flexibility in its use, and to make the standard more suitable for smaller organisations. The redesigned standard was given the 'stamp of the New Labour Government' and was relaunched in April 2000.

The changes included:

- An 'outcomes' based standard; accreditation was to be less concerned with evaluating what L&D organisations were doing and more concerned with what outcomes they attained from L&D
- Equal opportunity issues in L&D at work were to be a more prominent and explicit concern
- The paperwork previously required to be accredited was reduced or even not required; assessors will seek out materials themselves
- Flexibility is built into the process of accreditation; it is not the same for every kind of organisation
- Measures on subjective matters, the 'soft side' like motivation, are now seen as important, not just objective measures of the use of, for example, appraisal

Further developments are planned to continue evolving the IiP standard. These include 'stretch modules' for organisations who want them, providing additional areas of assessment in areas like recruitment and selection. Partnerships with other quality programmes are also being explored. Plans also include exporting the IiP standard, with projects in countries such as Belgium, Australia, Chile, Sweden, New Zealand, Bermuda, and Malaysia. That IiP might become an export from a country with a record that many see as having inadequate L&D at work is a testament to the efforts put into designing the standard.

THE IiP STANDARD

The framework of the revised standard consists of four principles, present in both the old and new standards (see Box 8.2).

The changes to the original standard include a reduction in the number of indicators associated with these principles. Organisations are now required to show evidence of IiP standards in these four areas in 12 rather than in 23 categories, resulting in a reduction or deletion of paperwork and a simplification of the language used in the standard. The language is 'plain and simple', not jargon or 'HR speak'. The 12 indicators supporting the four key principles are given in Box 8.3.

The rationale behind the need for the change in the standard was to ensure that the standard was more accessible to a wide range of organisations, especially smaller firms who may not have internal HR expertise of their own. IiP UK also felt that they must retain the challenge for those companies already recognised.

Box 8.2

IiP principles

1 **Commitment**
Public commitment by top management to training and developing people as a core means of achieving organisational objectives

2 **Planning**
Planning to review training and development needs in the context of the business

3 **Action**
Assuring relevant steps are taken to meet training and development needs

4 **Evaluation**
Measuring outcomes of training and development for individuals and the organisation

Box 8.3

IiP indicators

Commitment

1 The organisation is committed to supporting the development of its people
2 People are encouraged to improve their own and other people's performance
3 People believe their contribution to the organisation is recognised
4 The organisation is committed to ensuring equality of opportunity in the development of its people

Planning

5 The organisation has a plan with clear aims and objectives which are understood by everyone
6 The development of people is in line with the organisation's aims and objectives
7 People understand how they contribute to achieving the organisation's aims and objectives

Action

8 Managers are effective in supporting the development of people
9 People learn and develop effectively

Evaluation

10 The development of people improves the performance of the organisation, teams and individuals
11 People understand the impact of the development of people on the performance of the organisation, teams and individuals
12 The organisation gets better at developing its people

Box 8.4

IiP costs

The average unit cost for delivery of an Investors in People recognition by a TEC/LEC* (from the commitment stage) was an estimated £6058 in 1999–2000. The mean unit costs of the other elements of the IiP process are estimated as £951 for pre-Investors support; £507 for post-recognition support; and £2689 of overheads per recognition per year. This amounts to a total average annual unit cost of £10,205 for the delivery of the whole IiP process for an organisation.

The proportion of income recovered through charges by TECs for the commitment to recognition stage varies substantially, ranging from 100 per cent to less than 6 per cent; some organisations will cover these costs, while others will not. This is an indication of the difference in the extent to which TECs approach the promotion and delivery of IiP. The average net unit cost of support from commitment to recognition is estimated at £4216.

The average costs of delivering Investors in People to employers of different sizes are estimated at:

£4300 for small firms (10–49 employees)
£5400 for medium sized firms (50–199 employees)
£5250 for larger firms (200 or more employees)

The variance around this mean is considerable, with some TEC/LECs estimating that the costs of supporting small employers is higher than those needed on average for medium to large employers.

* TEC Training and Enterprise Council; LEC Local Enterprise Council

Source: Dodd *et al* (2001)

The process still works as was initially envisaged when IiP was set up. First a company must commit to becoming an IiP. This requires exploring, internally and with others, how the company needs/wants to develop. A gap analysis is then undertaken, to identify where there is a match or gap between the organisation and the IiP standard. In order to achieve the standard an organisation must have a business plan which incorporates a training plan, and mechanisms by which to evaluate the training and development which takes place. Actions may be required to close those gaps. The organisation is then externally assessed by IiP. This whole process takes on average 18 months. Organisations are then reviewed regularly within three years.

The costs involved in accrediting organisations as IiP are shown in Box 8.4. Dodd *et al* (2001) conclude that characteristics other than size are felt to have at least an equal impact on the level of support required. The employers' 'baseline position', the extent to which the principles of IiP are in place before they get involved with IiP, and capacity to manage change, are the critical factors. The way in which TEC/LEC IiP advisors work with employers to support them to recognition varies, and subsidy and charging policies also vary considerably. In most TEC areas small to medium size enterprises (SMEs), schools and the voluntary sector pay few or no costs. Overall, IiP support can be characterised as belonging to one of three models (Dodd *et al*, *op cit*):

- free 'unlimited' assistance: mostly free services and 'hands-on' support given to help achieve the standard. Investors advisors' time is given free
- costed assistance: mostly free TEC support given to a costed ceiling and employers are aware of the value of any services received
- charged services: some charges made for most elements of support including IiP advisors' time

Their research also suggested that there was some 'deadweight' associated with the delivery of IiP, in that around 30 per cent of employers would have made the changes they needed to make to become IiP accredited without any TEC/LEC support. However, the vast majority of employers say they value all of the elements of support offered to help achieve IiP status.

Queries have been raised about the revised IiP standard, to add to the concerns expressed about the original standard. While it is too early to cite research for these, the most common seem to be as follows.

The new 'commitment' definition is seen to be clear and concise, but:

- What percentage of staff are to be assessed, and how representative are they of what is typical in the organisation?
- Should assessors do random interviews with staff?
- Is 'commitment' to L&D really continuous, or just present in the period before accreditation?

'Actions' are now more broadly defined in the revised standard, but:

- Are these definitions now too broad, vague, and general?
- Are they open to a degree of interpretation, and therefore misinterpretation?
- Is it too easy to embellish the evidence?
- Why is there no definition of 'development'?
- Why is there such a great emphasis on obtaining formal qualifications?

The revised process has also been criticised. Will this different process of accreditation make a difference to those on the 'shopfloor', and influence their perceptions of the value of IiP? In organisations where the motivation seems to be to get another 'badge', staff perceptions can be quite cynical. There is not enough flexibility. It is still a 'one size fits all' model, from the very small to the very large. And the possibility of flexibility in terms of levels of IiP, perhaps based on a 'star rating' system, differentiating quality on a scale rather than making an all or nothing judgement, has been overlooked.

Armstrong (2000) provides a good example of an upbeat evaluation of the original IiP standard, through the success story for IiP in the form of Disaster Restoration Limited (DRL), who used the standard to structure themselves to maximum effect, enhance the company's strengths and improve the areas of organisational weakness. DRL noted that the 'pitfalls were few and far between' with the small exceptions of the time consuming requirement of the portfolio for accreditation and the difficulties in understanding some of the 'communicators' which have since been revamped through the new standard. IiP has helped DRL secure the recognition they sought amongst potential clients, which has inevitably had benefits for prosperity and growth prospects.

But others (Mahony 2000) report that few employers believe that IiP status helps to boost profits or income. Companies agreed that IiP had improved training and the link between training and business needs, but they did not believe that this had affected profits. All those with IiP status said that achieving it had brought some benefit but the standard, which was developed to improve business performance, was failing to do so. Statistics showed that 81 per cent of businesses surveyed hought IiP resulted in closer links between training and business needs, 52 per cent mentioned positive publicity, and 40 per cent agreed that it had boosted staff morale.

IiP UK counter this by arguing that that the IiP standard is a tried and tested flexible framework that helps companies succeed and compete through improved people performance. Research among accredited organisations showed that 80 per cent have increased customer satisfaction and that 70 per cent have improved their competitive edge and productivity (Create 1999). Research among employees within recognised organisation showed that 94 per cent are satisfied in their jobs, versus 37 per cent in the businesses lacking the standard (Planet Research 1998).

Although the overarching view is that the original IiP standard was a successful initiative (Hillage and Moralee 1996), and the revised standard is a useful evolution, there remain difficulties. It is not a panacea and does not guarantee improved organisational performance, particularly for SMEs. Hill and Stewart (*op cit*) note that 'there is much evidence to suggest that SMEs do not train and develop their workforce and, where training does occur, it is more likely to be informal, reactive and aimed at the solution of immediate problems rather than long-term development initiatives'. L&D in small and medium sized enterprises is critical to the success of the UK economy, but SMEs frequently do not have the L&D expertise, infrastructure and general resource which larger organisations enjoy. This then presents a potential barrier to L&D in SMEs and to SMEs themselves.

Research indicates that resistance to IiP focusses on issues involving time, money and resource, fear of unnecessary formality and bureaucracy, lack of clarity about the essential nature of IiP, and confusion and uncertainty about the value of IiP to a small organisation.

Ram (2000) argues that the experience of IiP in action had seldom been investigated, but that there is now an emergence of quantifiable data in the form of large-scale surveys. However, now that the standard has changed these data are outdated. Even so, he argues that there are two assumptions with IiP that are largely untested. The first is that there are definable standards of 'best practice' to base a standard on; it is not clear that is so, as the various L&D strategies and options available discussed in Chapter 6 illustrate. The second is that there is a causal link between HR practices and organisational performance; such causality is difficult to establish.

Based on research within three companies at different stages of the IiP recognition process, Ram concludes that the most effective motivation for engagement with IiP was the influence of key customers. Employers tended to be sceptical regarding the alleged benefits of IiP, but were worried about diminishing work from customers if they were seen not to be adhering to the standard. In other words the badge was important for retaining and attracting customers. Employees also stated that employers appeared to avoid and compromise the substance of the initiative when IiP procedures were often compiled in a 'minimalist fashion' in order to 'limit their impact on the nature of the workplace'.

Ram argues that the types of firms committing to IiP appear to be initially uncon-
vinced of its contribution to business performance and think that the standard will
have little impact on their organisation. For others IiP may be irrelevant or inappropriate, for example, small professional service firms, where deployment of knowledge
and educational credentials are an essential personal asset, and where informal
approaches to communication and a cultural resistance to being managed influence
the daily running of the business. Ram goes on to conclude that IiP may be viewed
as little more than an administrative requirement for marketing purposes, rather than
an important contributor to organisational performance.

Down and Smith (*op cit*) conclude that the evidence suggests that the organisations
currently achieving IiP recognition are those with 'least to change and the least to
gain'. They contend that, because the initiative is voluntary, the organisations with
most to gain from IiP are less likely to take up the standard. Many of the organisations they surveyed already had the procedures and controls in place to gain IiP. The
reasons these organisations were accredited are twofold. The first is that the TEC/LEC
delivery networks were 'cherry picking' organisations that were going to achieve the
standard easily. Second, that organisations were more attracted to IiP if it was relatively easy to obtain. IiP was merely 'encapsulating what organisations were already
doing rather than introducing any new substantial element in training'. Down and
Smith conclude that significant measurable business benefits can result from the IiP
process but organisations do not usually quantify them or recognise them as business
benefits. They comment that present research has failed to quantify the benefit as
there seems to be a lack of interest among organisations in doing so and that their
motivation for embarking on the process does not include achieving such quantifiable benefits. Down and Smith suggest that Government policy in this area would
benefit from the introduction of greater incentives to any organisation that is currently unlikely to adopt the standard.

CONCLUSION

The revised and revamped IiP standard has yet to have time to be implemented and
then evaluated. The claims that the original standard was effective clearly had to be
modified, because of concerns among those who were accredited and those who were
reluctant to get involved with IiP. To review the standard and 'continuously improve'
it is of course quite sensible and laudable. But whether the review really got to grips
with criticisms of the standard and its contribution to improving L&D in the UK
remains to be seen.

IiP is likely to remain a centrepiece of NVET policy, as the core of a voluntarist strategy for encouraging employers to adopt good practice and improve their L&D. Further
changes are planned; widening the scope of the standard and liaison with other
standards in business might suggest that a 'merger' of standards, including L&D and
employment concerns, is likely. For some it is not the content of the standard, but
the extent to which L&D at work can be motivated entirely through 'encouragement'
that is the key issue. Research investigating IiP as a means of encouraging improvements in L&D, and through that business development, will continue to keep the sta-
tisticians busy. Whether that can convince and persuade employers who are currently
outside the system to come into the fold is another matter altogether.

HospitalityCo and IiP

Read and analyse the following case study of a company which has been accredited as an IiP.

■ Why did the company commit to IiP?
■ Compare and contrast responses from subsections of the population regarding the perceived benefits derived from IiP.
  – What benefits have the organisation and directors derived from IiP?
  – What benefits have employees and managers derived from IiP?
■ What have been the major costs of IiP and has it been an effective investment for the company?
■ Should the company seek IiP status for its new units?

Company background: HospitalityCo

The HospitalityCo Group is a family run SME, comprised of a number of hotels, public houses and restaurants in one local area. The company has been established since 1990 and has grown from one unit to seven units, to a turnover of approximately £3 million per annum, with 136 members of staff. The company's first unit, the Hotel (1), was recognised as an Investor in People (IiP) in February 1997 through the original standard. Since then HospitalityCo has gone on to be successfully reassessed as a three-unit company, including Hotel (2) and Bar (1), in relation to the new IiP standard. More growth and expansion have taken place since this, and the company now encompasses seven units in total, four of which have not yet been assessed as Investors in People.

The units which have successfully achieved the standard vary a great deal in size and characteristics. Hotel (1) is a 15-bedroom hotel and restaurant, which also has three bars, one nightclub and two function suites. It has 53 employees and a below average rate of staff turnover in comparison to the industry as a whole. Their main revenue is acquired from 'wet sales' due to very busy and successful bars within Hotel (1).

Hotel (2) has five bedrooms, 38 staff, and acquires the majority of its revenue from restaurant business. It also has two function rooms and a public bar. Again, staff turnover is low but only three of the original Hotel (2) staff remain since the hotel was taken over by the current owners. Finally, there is Bar (1) that consists of a lounge bar and small public bar. It has 13 employees, twelve of whom have been with the pub for over ten years.

Non IiP accredited units have been purchased. These include Hotel (3), Bar (2) and Bar (3), and an Italian restaurant. These units at present have less than ten employees each and will continue to employ approximately the same number in the near future. The exception to this is Hotel (3), which should eventually operate with the same type of facilities as Hotel (1) and as a result require approximately the same numbers of staff.

Internal research was carried out in the three IiP accredited units to assess the costs and benefits of IiP within HospitalityCo Group, and to allow the directors to make an informed decision as to whether the company should continue to use IiP in their new units. The research started with interviews with directors.

The directors

Both directors were made aware of the IiP standard through the national press and other companies' headed notepaper and literature. The managing director stated:

I liked the quality mark and the fact that we were about to improve our HR practice and that this was a recognised standard and a method of appraisal and communicating far better to your staff. Also it structured you into creating goals and targets and being a lot more open about how you operate your business with your people.

Director-perceived benefits included team working, improved training systems, improved management systems and procedures, staff relationships, ownership and understanding of the organisation, improved communication, increased customer satisfaction, better productivity and profitability and improved recruitment and retention. The directors believed their evaluation of these factors was a result partly of opinion and partly measurable data and agreed that there would always be difficulties in attempting to measure such intangibles. They concluded that challenges with evaluation did not lower their opinion of IiP.

The directors stated that IiP is a 'tool in the toolbox' to help organisations 'achieve a higher standard of service and people' that would be of use to an 'unstructured' organisation in order to 'lead them in the right direction'. Other benefits included access to external sources in the form of training consultants and organisations. Recognition also proved useful when dealing with external bodies including 'licensing authorities, the police and banks'. Overall the directors agreed that the initiative had been successful but felt that it had not brought all the benefits boasted of by IiP UK.

The directors could show a number of costs resulting from the process. The TEC offered a trainer or consultant to aid in the movement towards the standard and some assistance with assessment fees. One director felt the company would 'probably not' have gone for recognition if they had not been offered this assistance. The other director felt they might still have taken on the standard but in hindsight would not make the same decision. Both agreed that the investment had been 'quite effective'.

They outlined other costs:

We had to invest in somebody's time to get it all packaged together.
It does take a lot of two people's time for quite a while.
Assessment fees, consultation fees, all the things you had to do for the assessment . . . it was very expensive. All the meetings – we put a cost of about £20,000 against it. The ongoing training that you must carry out if you are committed to the IiP culture etc.

The managing director agreed that there had been a great deal of training costs but 'we would probably have done the training anyway'. When questioned regarding the ongoing costs of assessment for each unit one director thought that a 'cost is always a problem for reassessment and recognition but it probably galvanises that we keep on the line'.

Both directors believed that the company was naturally travelling down an employee training and development route but that IiP gave them the structure and discipline to arrive at their destination at a faster rate:

We were going that way, it just helped us . . . it was quite an easy process to get into . . . the exact Investors in People way of doing things.

CONCLUDING CASE STUDY (cont'd)

When asked if the company would have moved towards and achieved the same systems, practices and procedures without the aid of IiP recognition the directors felt they would have but it would have been a slower process:

It speeded up the process, which has been a major benefit of it.

With regard to the general usefulness the directors felt that you could pay lip service to the standard and still achieve recognition:

It's a tick box exercise in many respects . . . you could get absolutely nothing out of it if you really want that. Tick all the boxes and be reviewed by the IiP people and have the status without any effectual benefit to the system of the business.

When asked if IiP could create a culture which is beneficial to the organisation both directors agreed that the standard could help to create a culture but would not be responsible in itself for that creation. Their opinion is that it is 'one tool in the toolbox'.

The directors mentioned an 'opening team' to aid in the transference of culture. With regard to processes and procedures they felt they therefore 'got installed very quickly and very easily' with the assistance of IiP.

Both quotes below summarise the general opinion of the HospitalityCo directors to the IiP standard:

I have a far better understanding of it now right enough; I'm comfortable with the principles behind it. Where we come from though, we're comfortable with it . . . the principles behind it align very closely with our own principles and we're not really that bothered anymore about getting it because of the things we do anyway. But whether we do it or not again, well, it all depends on the financial help to be honest. If the assistance wasn't there we might not bother.

Possibly we would do it again. To not have it – it would have a negative impact in some shape or form but it wouldn't break the business.

When asked what they thought their employees' opinion would be of IiP the response from each director was similar:

I think they'd be slightly sceptical. I think over the last wee while we've lost the focus of it a tad. They don't have as good a perception . . . their perception or opinion isn't as good as I would like it to be. Let me put it that way. But we're living in the real world here and life goes on, business goes on. You're not going to get everyone going 'oh yeah, IiP, its great!' I'm a dishwasher and they've trained me how to do x, y and z this week. That's the pipe dream I think and I think in terms of other organisations and successful ones – I can name you an organisation in the area, HotelCo, they do it to perfection but their profit levels are terrible.

I think they would say, 'yes I've learned a bit more about the business . . . a situation to sit down with your manager on a one to one and discuss your performance and progress and strengths and weaknesses within the business. They'd say its quite good – they're never going to say its whoopee doo, brilliant, all that. And there's probably been a bigger focus on training things for them.

CONCLUDING CASE STUDY (cont'd)

The managers

The managers of each unit gave the following reasons why they felt the company committed to IiP:

> To enhance the culture of the workforce and improve performance.
> To enable us to offer a better service, happy staff, satisfied customers and hopefully more profit.
> To standardise procedures and to improve company image.
> To be recognised as a company who value their employees as much as their customers.
> Improved profile and to improve training and customer service.
> To improve working standards and training within a fast growing company.

The managers all seemed to focus on improvement and standardisation of the business which could be said to mirror in some ways the reasons that the managing director gave for committing the company to IiP.

When managers were asked what costs they had encountered with regard to the IiP process they appeared not to have experienced many. Only two of the ten managers noted any costs, which included:

> Time required by everyone to attend appraisals and training sessions.
> Can be a burden especially in the hospitality industry.
> Loss of time for paperwork etc.

The benefits managers reported are given in Figure 8.1.

Most managers drew their evaluation of IiP from opinion and many stated they would have a higher opinion of the standard if they could determine its measurable benefits. The managers also highlighted a number of benefits in the structure IiP provides:

> It gives structured communication.
> Yes, I am more aware of employees' need for knowledge and information and the thirst for further training.
> Offers guidance in handling staff.
> Appraisals have helped with training and communication.
> Yes, because it gives you guidelines on how to evaluate people and recognise training needs.
> It gives you a clearer view of people's strengths and weaknesses and to identify training needs.
> It made me a better communicator with the staff.

All managers were also asked if they felt IiP would be useful for the transference of culture from an established company to a new venture. Nearly all managers agreed it would. Reasons given included:

> Systems to transfer procedures are useful.
> It would help greatly as a training plan could be implemented quicker and more effectively.

CONCLUDING CASE STUDY (cont'd)

Figure 8.1   *Manager view of benefits of IiP*

A   My efficiency and the way I work has improved
B   Management team working has improved
C   I have more opportunities for career development
D   Training has a greater benefit to me
E   Management team communication has improved
F   My motivation has increased
G   I am more willing to be trained
H   I know more about the business
I   I feel more committed to the business
J   I have improved skills and competence
K   I an more flexible

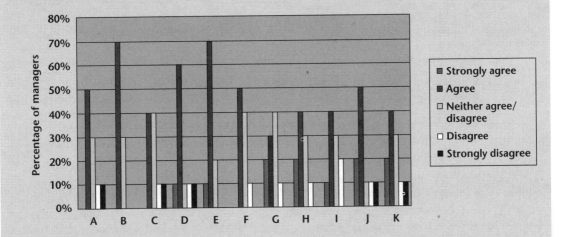

Obviously it is easier to install good working practice when it has been established in a good working unit.
Because procedures, practices, structure can be transferred across.

The staff

The staff were surveyed. Table 8.3 shows the results of an employee questionnaire in the three IiP accredited units.

Case answers and analysis

Why did the company commit to the IiP standard?

The first objective was to investigate why the organisation committed to the Investors in People standard. The research found that the directors had a previous awareness of the IiP logo from various sources including company letterheads, literature and newspaper articles, and felt that it

CONCLUDING CASE STUDY (cont'd)

Table 8.3   *Staff opinion of IiP benefits*

Question asked	Hotel (1) 56 staff Agree	Hotel (2) 42 staff Agree	Bar (1) 13 staff Agree
Staff efficiency has improved	76%	93%	67%
Customers are more satisfied	62%	80%	75%
Team working has improved	85%	93%	66%
Our image is better	85%	93%	92%
The way we work has improved	84%	100%	83%
Communication has improved	92%	80%	58%
Training has a greater benefit	92%	73%	67%
Our work procedures and systems have improved	92%	80%	75%
I have more opportunities for career development	54%	67%	8%
My motivation has increased	62%	80%	42%
I am more willing to be trained	61%	87%	75%
I know more about the business	76%	93%	58%
I feel more committed to the business	69%	73%	17%
I have improved skills and competence	77%	80%	50%
I am more flexible	53%	73%	50%
Other staff are staying longer with the company	53%	80%	50%
People are not off work as much as they used to be	53%	73%	42%

would be advantageous to the company. Apparently IiP had a number of characteristics which appealed to the directors including a structure for communication, performance review and the establishment of goals and targets. One director noted that they had been approached by their local TEC regarding the standard. This could suggest that the company had been 'cherry-picked'; however the company only consisted of one unit at that time and it was noted that the company had originally dropped the process as it was presently not suitable. It would appear then that the TEC would have no substantial reason to 'cherry-pick' Hotel (1) at that time.

Managers of the company gave similar reasons as to why they felt the directors had committed to the IiP standard. These included improved performance, image, increased profit, improved work standards, procedures and training systems. All managers seemed to focus on the standardisation and improvement of the business through recognition. There appeared to be a heavy emphasis on the 'image' of IiP and its logo or badge. Quotes noted contained reference to recognition, profile and image.

The perceived benefits of Investors in People

The second objective was to investigate the overall opinion of IiP and its benefits within the subsections of the organisation, which include staff, managers and directors. Overall the staff agreed that improvements had been made as a result of IiP. Agreement was high with regard to improved image, efficiency, work methods, communication and training among others. However agreement was lower regarding opportunities for career development, increased motivation, commitment, flexibility, retention and absenteeism.

Reasons for this could be varied. The hospitality industry is known for being a 'gap filler' for people before they more on to a 'real job'. There is a high percentage of part time staff and students employed by HospitalityCo who may not consider the hospitality trade as a career path. This is reiterated through the results of the bi-annual survey where low percentages from both Hotel (1) and Hotel (2) were reported regarding opportunities for promotion. Also retention and absenteeism may not be an issue that most employees are concerned with. The lower percentage of agreement with regard to motivation, commitment and flexibility may be of concern as they are promoted as direct benefits of IiP. Reasons for perceptions of IiP as being less favourable in Bar (1) may be due to its small size.

The managers were also asked their opinion of IiP and the benefits they had gained from it as managers. Again, differences in agreement can be seen with regard to efficiency, motivation, willingness to be trained and knowledge about the business. It may be understandable that staff now have a greater increase in knowledge than managers who would previously have been better informed. These differences highlight a higher opinion present among staff regarding IiP and its benefits. When asked if and how IiP had helped them as a manager, positive answers involved better and more structured communication, the ability to identify training needs and guidance in handling staff. Thirty per cent of managers however felt that IiP had not helped them at all as managers.

The directors, when discussing the benefits of IiP, also raised the issue of structure. They felt it was a successful 'tool in the toolbox' to lead unstructured organisations in the right direction. Both directors, however, agreed that IiP did not dramatically alter their financial performance, increase their competitive edge or improve their product quality. In other words they would question the standard's ability to deliver bottom line results.

All members of the HospitalityCo Group agreed that customer satisfaction was higher as a benefit of IiP and the directors, although they did not find any substantial improvement in competitive edge, agreed that productivity had improved. Overall the directors could highlight progress in a number of ways but were unsure as to the actual financial improvements. The type of evaluation which is carried out within the company may have a direct impact on this. Eighty per cent of managers drew their evaluation of IiP from opinion whereas the directors said their evaluation was as a result of a combination of opinion and measurable data. The managing director noted that they did not have the time to fully evaluate financial implications of IiP. Possibly a better evaluation of financial progress could be made if the results were measurable. Sixty per cent of managers stated that they would have a higher opinion of the standard if they could determine its measurable benefits whereas the directors felt there would always be difficulties in attempting to measure intangibles. They concluded that these challenges did not lower their opinion of IiP.

In summary both staff and directors appeared to have a higher opinion of the standard than managers. The perceived benefits appeared to vary and the directors were not convinced that IiP can show bottom line improvements. They felt the initiative has been successful but had not brought about all the benefits that IiP stated that it could.

Major costs of Investors in People and the effectiveness of investment

There was a lack of awareness of these factors among managers with only 20 per cent having acknowledged any costs. These were 'loss of time for paperwork' and 'time' for appraisals and training sessions. It was noted that this is an especially difficult burden in the hospitality sector. Contrary to this the directors could highlight a number of costs of the process. These included the assessment fees, consultation fees, training, time for meetings and preparation for assessment.

This may show a lack of communication between managers and directors or simply the lack of strategic thinking amongst managers. They could highlight the costs that affected their time but not focus on or highlight organisational costs. This may be a product of weak questionnaire design where respondents were not prompted regarding what would be considered to be a cost and whether the question was regarding organisational costs or management costs.

As noted the local TEC gave the organisation assistance by reimbursing the cost of consultation fees and by partial aid with assessment costs. One director stated that they would not have gone for recognition if they had not received this financial help while the other, when discussing costs, said in hindsight they probably would not make the same decision to go down the IiP route. It was agreed that training costs were high but that the training would have been carried out regardless if it was required for business effectiveness and that costs are always a problem when considering recognition and reassessment, but that this in itself would encourage the organisation to toe the line.

In summary the costs are high to commit and be recognised as an IiP, and in hindsight the directors would probably not make the same decision again. They accepted the cost of training, as they would have embarked on this whether they committed to the standard or not, but still felt that IiP gave them a structure to achieve higher standards over a shorter period of time. It begs the question as to whether gaining a 'structure' was worth the costs of recognition. If the training will be carried out regardless why face the costs of constant reassessment when the organisation now has the required structure in place? Is it cost effective to pay assessment fees to provide an incentive to maintain standards or does the recognition or 'badge' carry more weight than most would like to admit? Regardless of the costs both directors felt the investment had been 'quite effective'.

The relevance of Investors in People to HospitalityCo units

HospitalityCo Group has a number of units and the three businesses where research was carried out differed in both size and characteristics. Both directors felt the IiP initiative had been successful for their particular business and would be successful for others depending on size of the organisation. Both agreed that smaller business would have difficulties with the standard. They considered themselves not to be a small business and noted that previously, when the company had consisted of only one unit, the standard had not been right for them.

Bar (1) public house results were significantly different from both other units, which were hotels and restaurants. As previously noted Bar (1) had only 13 members of staff compared to 56 and 42 at Hotel (1) and Hotel (2) respectively. The findings show that Bar (1) had a significantly lower level of agreement compared to both hotels with regard to staff efficiency, team working, communication, the benefit of training, motivation, knowledge of the business, commitment to the business, the improvement of skills and competence, absenteeism and opportunities for career development.

The research concluded that this is a direct result of the size and characteristics of Bar (1). Due to the size and length of service of the staff, efficiency, team working, communication, motivation, business knowledge and skills level were not issues for the unit. As the staff had been carrying out their roles for more than ten years it was not surprising that they might feel there is little scope for career development within Bar (1). In summary IiP was probably given little scope to improve this business. However Bar (1) staff agreed that customer satisfaction had increased, the way they work had improved, staff were more willing to be trained and the company image had improved. Again IiP could have improved structure, staff might have access to training opportunities and image had improved.

Staff at Bar (1) might be more willing to be trained because they had access to opportunities the previous owner could not afford to provide. If Bar (1) had been a single unit it is doubtful whether time and resources would be available to train to a high level. However, the economics of HospitalityCo allows Bar (1) staff to attend company wide training courses provided for all staff and this way a smaller unit can enjoy the benefits of a larger organisation.

This then raises the point that, if HospitalityCo continues to expand and buy new smaller premises, will IiP be relevant to them or only to their larger units? Would there be a difference between TUPE transfers where staff have long lengths of service, and new acquisitions where systems are set up and staff are recruited from the beginning of the new venture? Is IiP useful for growth and expansion or are these determined by the size and characteristics of each new unit?

Investors in People and its usefulness for expansion and growth

Both directors felt that the company was naturally travelling down an employee training and development route but that IiP gave them the structure and discipline to arrive at their destination at a faster rate. Without the IiP standard the process would have been much slower. This structure and discipline could be considered very useful for the expansion and growth of the business, with the successful culture being implemented in each new unit. IiP UK also state that the standard can help companies manage the process of change, which could be invaluable in growth stages.

The issue of lip service was also discussed. If the standard was achieved in this manner its usefulness for expansion and growth would diminish. Both directors and many managers acknowledged that you could pay lip service to the standard and still achieve recognition. It was considered a 'tick box' exercise by some, where you could 'get nothing out of it' if that was your goal. In this case IiP encapsulated what the organisation planned to do but allowed them to achieve their targets in a shorter time period. Both directors admitted that they would have reached the same stage in training and development at some stage in organisational growth.

With regard to the standard's ability to create a culture which is beneficial to the organisation, the response was very positive. Both directors believed that IiP could help create a culture which was positive to the organisation and that it was a useful 'tool in the toolbox'. IiP's use for transference of culture was also highly rated. All managers agreed to some extent that IiP is beneficial to the creation of a culture.

As mentioned in the previous section, economies of scale for training costs and resources are a benefit of larger organisations. Growth and expansion would be aided by the presence of training resources, systems and procedures that could be rolled out to each new unit. In summary, the bigger you get the easier it is to extend your successful processes to other premises, bearing in mind that each individual unit had unique characteristics which may render elements of IiP irrelevant.

REFERENCES

Alberga, T., Tyson, S. and Parsons, D. (1997) 'An evaluation of the Investors in People standard', *Human Resource Management Journal*, Vol. 7, No. 2.

Armstrong, B. (2000) 'Small company "champions" IiP: disaster restoration firm finds training pays off', *Industrial and Commercial Training*, Vol. 32, No. 4.

Create (1999) 'Building capability for the 21st century', on IiP UK (2001) *Investors in People Fast Facts*, http://www.IiPuk.co.uk

Daniel, M. (1997) 'In-house evaluation against the Investors in People standard: some pointers for self-regulation in higher education', *Quality Assurance in Education*, Vol. 5, No. 4.

Dodd, M., Cutter, J., Rodger, J., Shaw, N., Owens, J., Cowen G. and Lawless, M. (2001) *Research On the Costs of Investors in People and Related Activities*, DfES Brief No. 274.

Down, S. and Smith, D. (1998) 'Investors in People: the search for measurable benefits', *Personnel Review*, Vol. 27, No. 2.

Hill, R. and Stewart, J. (1999) 'Investors in People in small organisations: learning to stay the course?', *Journal of European Industrial Training*, Vol. 23, No. 6.

Hillage, J. and Moralee, J. (1996) *The Return On Investors*, IES, Brighton.

IiP UK (2000/1) http://www.IiPuk.co.uk

Johnson, S., Campbell, M., Devins, D., Gold, J. and Hamblett, J. (2000) *Learning Pays: The Bottom Line*, NACETT.

King, S. (1995) 'IiP, the skills gap and business performance', *Management Development Review*, Vol. 8, No. 5.

MacVicar, A. and Brown, G. (1994) 'Investors in People at The Moat House International, Glasgow', *International Journal of Contemporary Hospitality Management*, Vol. 6, No. 6.

Mahony, C. (2000) 'Firms fail to see how IiP boosts profits', *People Management*, Vol. 6, No. 16.

Mason, D. (1994) 'Investors in People: journey to continuous development', *Health Manpower Management*, Vol. 20, No. 2.

Planet Research (1998) 'Satisfaction at work', on IiP UK (2001) *Investors in People Fast Facts*, http://www.IiPuk.co.uk

Ram. M. (2000) 'Investors in People: small firms case study evidence from the business service sector', *Personnel Review*, Vol. 29, No. 1.

chapter nine

Information and Communication Technologies

Learning outcomes

- Describe a range of information and communication technologies (ICT) in use in L&D at work
- Discuss the strengths and weaknesses of contemporary uses of ICT in L&D
- Analyse the cost, quality, and speed features of ICT in L&D
- Evaluate the challenges faced in making greater and more frequent use of ICT in L&D

FRAMEWORK CASE STUDY: ICT IN PURCHASING

A large pharmaceuticals organisation was going through a period of major change, introducing new ways of working. The purchasing function in the organisation, which bought supplies and materials, was to be changed. It was to shift from having 'do it all' purchasing units based on each of the several sites that the company had, to being organised in units dealing with discrete categories of expenditure for all sites. This purchasing function involved 500 people in 41 different countries. Making better decisions and savings was the goal for the company as a whole. The business objective for the purchasing function was to take the function to being 'best in class'. To do this required more than new technical skills as a result of the reorganisation, it also needed the development of core competencies in these new ways of working. Without such L&D and retraining the organisation faced a mass exodus of staff, and thus a recruitment need and then L&D.

The first step to using the retraining option was to develop a competency framework for an organisation where several layers of management had been stripped out, and therefore many people's jobs had changed. This also required a clear career map showing how individuals could progress in different roles: the roles of buyers, budget holders and senior managers. In doing this, technical competencies such as negotiating skills and financial analysis had priority.

The organisation used courses, on the job development and 'development zones'. These last involved the use of self contained multimedia modules. They also used

Internet based materials. They developed an online career and development planning tool. It enabled staff to identify their own competency requirements and gaps. There were then links to development activity suggestions, from courses to self study modules. This was a flexible way of providing L&D across the globe for all their staff. However they faced problems with:

- different technology infrastructures in different parts of the company
- variations in bandwidth capacity in different countries, causing problems with accessing Internet materials
- variations in levels of computer literacy among staff
- building in effective L&D; existing instruction material could not just be transferred online, interaction had to be built in
- costs; it took around 300 hours of development to create one hour of content, at a developers' fee of £100 an hour. This meant a cost of £30,000 for one hour's learning material

Source: Finn (2000)

INTRODUCTION

In his analysis of the 'digital economy' Tapscott (1995) identifies L&D at work as a key area of change. The net effects of developments in information and communication technologies (ICT) on L&D are seen to be of an order that would mean that new media could transform learning. The use of ICT would make learning more enjoyable, more self-directed and more realistic, resulting in higher retention rates than past media and learning processes. But the use of ICT, new media, and Internet based and multimedia training is far from being the norm. A recent survey (George and Cooper 2001) found that, in the UK, only 19 per cent of organisations used any kind of ICT for L&D. Even then the survey suggests that those with access to these technologies would use paper based versions of learning materials where they could, as they were easier to use or provided more detail. The much heralded advent of 'e-learning' as the new nexus of L&D at work seems as distant now as it ever has been. In part this is because the case for more effective L&D using these new media is far from clear, and the cost-benefit analysis of their potential is also ambiguous (see Box 9.1).

When the University for Industry (UfI) was established by the UK Government, as a 'clearing house' for providing technology based training (TBT) learning packages, over 700 organisations submitted samples of their work for inclusion as resources. No more than a quarter of these were deemed to have achieved UfI quality standards for good materials at first assessment by a panel of experts (Seabrook and Rushby 2000). The main reason for this seemed to be the lure of using presentational spin rather than informed learning design, relying on glossy presentation rather than basing design of L&D materials on an analysis of learning.

A BRIEF HISTORY OF L&D TECHNOLOGIES

Learning, for most of human history, was not mediated by any technology, that is by systems of communication which required the use of equipment and resources. It was about a direct social relationship between master and apprentice. The 'expert-learner' nexus was based on direct communication between these people, in the context of

Box 9.1

Learning technologies costing model

Research and development	Staff time, reports and reviews, administration, research activities, displacement costs, briefing meetings
Initial investment (non recurring)	Building or refurbishment, electrical work and cabling, furniture, fittings, hardware and peripherals
Initial investment (recurring)	Replacements for hardware, software, insurance, staff training, TBT development, support staff, admin support, telephone charges
Operation and support	Hardware, software, peripherals, security, rentals, materials, staff and evaluations
Disposal and salvage	Sale of hardware, disposal cost, retraining

Source: Hunt and Clarke (1997)

work experience on actual tasks. There were no 'learning technologies' as such; there were the technologies of work, the mysteries of a craft, which were learned through experience. Working and learning were interconnected. The development of publishing, and then the classroom, provided the first technology that mediated learning and work; learning from and with books, in groups with formal teachers in a classroom. The value of this system of technology in delivering mass education, training and instruction was evident. But the cost was that learning and working were no longer interconnected, as the social context for learning changed from work to institutions of learning. The technologies and systems of learning that evolved in these institutions of learning were largely based around providing more effective instruction. An evolution of kinds has been evident; from the blackboard to the whiteboard, from the spoken lecture to the use of LCD projectors, and from the rote memorising of core texts to the use of learning projects involving Internet research. This system of technology, instruction in a classroom, still represents the core image of learning for many if not most people.

Dissatisfaction and operational problems with using standard text and classroom based instruction techniques among educationalists and trainers have been perceived and experienced since the inception of this system of learning. These have motivated an interest in the use of other technologies to support learning in education and in L&D at work. As and when new technologies arise their application to support L&D is often avidly explored. The first modern technology to offer something apparently new and different for learning was film. This was a medium able to provide structured and stimulating communication, enabling consistent messages and instruction to be delivered economically to huge numbers of people in locations throughout the world. The US military were pioneers in this field, before and during WW2, in developing and using the army training film; they used film for L&D that spanned instructions on weapons maintenance to the promotion of personal hygiene. Thereafter commercial film providers evolved, concerned mainly with provision of learning materials for schools. The modern L&D at work industry of video based, or CD\DVD based, learning materials continues this tradition started by film.

Next in line came the development of broadcasting, with radio and television. As radio and television became a mainstream feature of people's lives their educational as well as entertainment applications were explored. In the UK the system of pubic control of broadcasting, with the establishment of the British Broadcasting Corporation, explicitly incorporated a mission to educate. Radio and TV broadcasts were cheaper and quicker to produce than film based productions, and could be communicated to vast audiences simultaneously. In the educational context there were visions of the eradication of teachers, and their replacement with the 'teacher on a screen'. These visions failed to materialise. In the UK the most sophisticated incarnation of this vision was the development of the Open University (OU) in the 1960s. The OU continues to provide much programming, often with higher production values than in the early days. But the impact of broadcasting was not as the visionaries had thought. There was not enough money for making good educational programmes or the staff to make them. And programme makers did not know how to do 'learning' programmes well when they did make them, producing material that was too often too boring, with no scope for interaction or feedback. Teachers in classrooms, and trainers in training facilities, were safe.

Then came the development of computers, and the promise of computer based training (CBT). This offered the promise of interactivity (Galbreath 1992), getting beyond the problems of the passive learner by enabling involvement and participation (Hill and Francis 1999). With the development of powerful personal computers (PCs) the prospects seemed even better. The use of multimedia, of text, graphics, animation, film and audio mixed together to provide information and enable interaction, was heralded as a way to 'turbo charge' learning. But in practice there were technical problems, as there were different kinds of platform and operating system. And the material that was created was, in the view of many, deadly dull; with content just like textbooks, and interaction that was restricted to unstimulating 'drill and practice' processes. More critical was the problem of content stability. Content stability refers to the extent to which material dates; high content stability material does not change quickly, low content stability material has a short shelf life. CBT cost a lot to develop, but often its content was rendered obsolete quickly. This fact alone curtailed interest and investments, regardless of the technical and quality problems. It was only any good as a medium in circumstances where many people needed instructing in a short time in something with a short shelf life.

With the use of film, broadcasting and CBT there has been an apparent cycle of fad and failure. Expectations are raised of a revolution, but then there are problems with poor design and inadequate materials, leading to frustration and criticism of the media, and the abandonment of the technology as an agent of transformational change in L&D at work. The current question is whether the growth of e-learning will replicate this cycle of fad and failure (Sadler-Smith *et al* 2000), or whether this medium will be different, with a genuine and high impact transformation of L&D at work (Sloman 2001, Stevens 1996). For some the uptake of e-learning through the characteristic ICT simply replicates the benefits and problem of distance learning systems. As distance learning has been used for a long time there is no transformational change with e-learning. For others the use of ICT and e-learning is a genuine step change in the management of L&D. This is because it goes beyond the delivery of instruction to the handling of information (Stevens and Stevens 1995) as the core of the L&D process (see Figure 9.1 and Box 9.2).

Figure 9.1   *Conventional media and e-learning*

L&D through conventional media: Instruction	L&D through handling of information: e-learning
Based on a diagnosis of user needs	Based on people searching for knowledge in the course of their work
Purpose and direction of learning defined by instructional designers	Purpose and direction of learning defined by users as they experience problems in work
Focussed on a defined learning outcome	Focussed on providing contents that can be accessed in varying combinations
Sequenced for optimum memory retention	Sequenced for optimum reference in the 'here and now', then can be forgotten
Contains presentations, practice, feedback and assessment relating to learning set outcomes	Centred on effective presentation of many kinds of information relevant to performance

Source: Rosenberg (2001)

Box 9.2

Cisco Systems

The world of business is 'now less like an ocean cruise than it is like white water rafting', and learning has to adapt to that. For Cisco part of this is its frequent and regular takeover and purchase of new firms as it expands. In buying firms it inherits training needs, particularly for sales staff in the purchased companies.

With 10,000 sales staff in 150 countries, taking them out of the field to train them is costed at £16 million a week. They decided to transfer all that they could online.

This was difficult and expensive, even for an organisation that makes the equipment that enables the Internet. But they have halved the delivery costs of training and moved 80 per cent of sales and technology training online. On the day Cisco buys a new firm the sales team can be trained immediately. Their training for engineers is delivered online. The classroom is not eliminated, but it is shrinking.

Source: Hammond (2001)

INFORMATION AND COMMUNICATION TECHNOLOGIES (ICT)

The umbrella term ICT includes a range of technologies (TfT 2001). The technologies include:

- computer and multimedia software
- the Internet and company Intranets, including their use for computer conferencing
- video and audio tapes
- television and radio broadcasting
- telecommunications
- satellite communications
- videoconferencing
- virtual reality

Technology based training may be used as a self-study resource, with or without tutorial support and/or mentoring, for small groups or as part of a larger course or training event. Learners may study at a single CBT workstation in the workplace, in a learning centre, on the premises of an external training provider, or at home, if they have the right equipment. Organisations are increasingly delivering CBT via networks, Intranets and the Internet, but these do impose some limitations.

A technology based approach may entail a significant investment. Decisions on hardware will depend on the software applications that will be used. For some applications, a standard PC will be sufficient; for others a higher specification multimedia PC will be essential. A wide range of 'off the shelf' software is available for CBT L&D. Buying an off the shelf package, if a suitable one exists, will normally be much cheaper than commissioning new material.

Rosenberg defines e-learning as 'the use of Internet technologies to deliver a broad array of solutions that enhance knowledge and performance' (2000, p 28). It is network based and therefore capable of instant updating, unlike other CBT platforms. It is delivered using a computer and standard Internet technology. E-learning involves a broad view of L&D at work, not just an interest in conventional training and instruction. See Box 9.3.

An emphasis on this kind of e-learning is valid, but it is also narrow. Much recent and current growth has been in the development of 'learning centres', not in network systems as such.

Learning centres

To date the most visible and popular use of ICT has been through developing learning centres rather than network based systems (DfEE 1997, Scott 1997). Learning centres are physical spaces devoted to providing resources for learning in organisations, usually with PCs which have Intranet and Internet access. The benefits are:

- a good learning environment; away from the workplace
- a secure place for often expensive materials
- a focal point for providing learner support
- provides a physical presence, for image and marketing
- can use existing standard hardware

Box 9.3

E-learning facts

Organisations	Almost all organisations have access to PCs
	66% have an Intranet
	27% have dedicated PCs for training
	Less than 10% of training budget is spent on e-learning (of those who are aware of costs)
	57% of organisations using e-learning buy in products
	45% search the web
	41% develop in house products
Learners	Formal use of e-learning by 91% of staff in the last year; 45% rate it highly
	Informal use of e-learning by 95% (surfing the web); 58% rate it highly
	96% of e-learning users want better support for it

The main problems with e-learning are wasting time on searches, computers crashing, poor quality of materials and gimmicky websites

Source: Campaign for Learning (2000)

The process of developing a learning centre involves various steps: researching what will be supplied in the centre, planning the administration of the centre, and marketing it on launch and thereafter. Retaining some of the social aspects of learning on courses can be important in the success of a learning centre (see Box 9.4).

Computer based training (CBT)

Computer based training (CBT) is the delivery of learning through computer based training or multimedia, typically as self-paced open learning. CBT offers all the advantages of flexible and open learning. This includes consistent presentation of material, the flexibility for the learner to work at his/her own pace, and the opportunity for the learner to study at a convenient place and time.

There are specific advantages of CBT over paper based open learning. These include interactivity, which can improve motivation and retention, immediate feedback to completed question and practice exercises, and the greater realism which results from including graphics, photographs, sound and moving images in simulations. There are also disadvantages of CBT compared to paper based open learning. These include the need for a power supply and specialist equipment, equipment that is not easily portable, and learning material that is more costly to prepare. The relative costs of technology based and paper based open learning depend upon a number of factors. In general, CBT has higher origination costs, lower production and packaging costs and higher delivery costs.

CBT systems simulate work tasks, apparatus, systems, processes to support learning. They may involve the development of large scale business systems, modelling, how something works, replicating an operation or decision making exercises. The ben-

---

Box 9.4

The need for social contact

A study of a large banking group, the TSB, which had opened up 450 learning centres, showed variations in their usage. Some were clearly more used than others. The most popular centres had facilitators who provided a welcoming face for learners. Learners liked to be left on their own to study, but to talk afterwards. They liked to have pre- and post-course discussions.

At Plymouth College 40 rural outreach centres were opened, for access to flexible training. The quality of tutoring was important, providing a point of personal contact; as was interaction with fellow students. For some students 'It was a way of getting out and meeting other people, and it was nice to have a gossip and a coffee – a real social gathering'.

Source: Hills and Francis (1999)

Box 9.5

Developing CBT

Training needs analysis	What training is needed; is CBT appropriate?
Training specification	Synopsis, delivery platform, screen design, measures
Training plan	Schedule of modules, project plan
Detailed task analysis	All skills and knowledge for standards
Define content	Teaching points and information
Write storyboard	Interactive units, passed to programmer
Code in authoring system	Actual programming
Validate	Content accuracy, teaching effectiveness, operational reliability, field test
Produce complete pack	CBT and associated materials
Publish	Market/sell

Source: TfT Briefing No. 5, Version 1.1 (2001)

---

efits of such simulations are of practice in a safe environment, being able to measure learning as it occurs, and being able to control situations to various degrees of difficulty. They are popular as they can substitute for on job training, and actively involve the trainee in the learning.

There have now been over three decades of experience in design and development of learning materials for CBT. Despite guidelines for doing this (see Box 9.5) there have been many problems experienced. These are:

■ The content was not good; courses had not been revised and updated to take into account changes in policy and procedures
■ Exercises were not 'authentic'; people did not believe the steps they completed were realistic, and simulations were not believable
■ They were great looking, but awful to use

Figure 9.2   *Producing good CBT*

- Use expert modelling and stories in developing the materials
- Ensure authenticity in relation to jobs
- Write meaningful objectives to structure material development
- Use the power of simulations; immersions that test what people have learned
- Allow learners to learn from mistakes; allow safe failures
- Provide robust coaching and feedback
- Re-use after learning; build in search capabilities
- Do not just 'shovel' material over onto multimedia; if design is not considered it will not work

- Users were at the mercy of rapid changes in technology, making their technical platforms redundant
- CBT learning packages were useless after the initial use, because they were not searchable
- Learning was not being reinforced
- There was no support for it within the organisation; CBT was not really cared about
- It went against people's views of what training should involve, what 'real' training should be
- It was plain boring
- It was just 'shovelware'; delivering old material in virtually the same way, just moving the delivery to CBT or the web

To build better CBT, whether it will be accessed through networks or through other modes of delivery, then requires that these lessons from experience be learned and acted upon (see Figure 9.2 and Box 9.6).

Networked options: e-learning

It is the use of the Internet and Intranets which has most caught the imagination (see Boxes 9.7 and 9.8). The Internet is a global web of computers interconnected with each other. It enables three functions relevant to and important for effective L&D. It enables communication; one to one, one to many, many to one. It enables the search for resources. It enables the publication of resources. Intranets are internal networks within organisations using web browsers and web protocols (IRS 1998). Because they are internal networks they are faster than the Internet. They are also more secure than the Internet, and provide a controlled environment for communication, accessing resources and publishing resources. Intranets can also be more assured of the standardised software/plugins required to access web pages.

Rosenberg (*op cit*) is clear that these systems not only enable new approaches to instruction; they open up new possibilities with the provision of information to support performance improvement and knowledge management as well.

Box 9.6

Learning styles and computer based training (CBT)

Analytic verbalisers; like bit by bit structure with headings and paragraphs, have good verbal memory

Analytic imagers; like bit by bit structure with diagrams and illustrations, have a good picture memory

Holist verbalisers; like overviews and then explorations, with a preference for text

Holist imagers; like overviews and then explorations, with a preference for diagrams and illustrations

For CBT	Against
Fun; mimics games	Less than inspiring systems
Multimedia presentation	Mainly text based
Self control order of presentation	Pre-structured
Choose activities	Required activities
Pace self	Being on your own
Able to monitor and assess on your own	Celebrate success with other people
Use of simulations (experience)	Quality of 'realism'
Links to tutors or groups	Limited feedback
Access Internet	Not available

Source: Adapted from Riding (1996)

Box 9.7

The national grid for learning (NGfL)

The NGfL is a network of interconnected websites and education services based on the Internet. It provides content to support teaching, learning and administration in schools, colleges, universities, libraries, the workplace and home. It structures learning and teaching materials, and the Learning Resources Index (LRI) can be searched.

The aim is to train teachers and students to be ICT literate and use the NGfL, as well as connecting all institutions up and using the system for administration too. It is funded by Government and some private sector funding, and managed by the British Educational Communications and Technology Agency (BECTA).

Source: http://www.ngfl.gov.uk

Box 9.8

BankCo

BankCo has over 20,000 employees in 650 branches. They wanted a learning platform that was flexible, consistent, scaleable and accommodated different learning styles. In developing a network based strategy they knew there were potential problems with competing for bandwidth on existing networks; so they developed a parallel network.

Now in each branch there is at least one dedicated PC for training, and access to the Intranet. In the head office all PCs access the Intranet. The Intranet has superseded CBT, and all previous CBT is now integrated with the Intranet.

They have developed over 100 hours of learning content, developed by both internal training staff and a consultancy.

They also use a satellite based interactive classroom (virtual classroom). This uses the organisation's own broadcasting studio in their head office. A trainer in the studio carries out training sessions viewed on PCs in the branches. Trainees can respond with messages and interact. They have their own business TV network. One hour every Wednesday morning there is a broadcast for training purposes with items broadcast to branches.

They are now experimenting with interactive multimedia, using video, graphics, audio and text to simulate situations encountered in the branch; real life video of customers coming in with queries, which staff have to deal with; given data and situations, they need to make the right moves in situations of varying difficulty. Responses are monitored and recorded.

Videoconferencing

Videoconferencing has been seen as the least used and understood technology. Videoconferencing involves people in various locations being linked by a visual, audio and information channel carried through cable. It may occur with people using one to one connections over the Internet, or using special videoconferencing facilities. One problem has been that the hardware for this is very expensive; it has therefore only been used by large companies. However providers of videoconferencing facilities now exist, and can hire time out to anyone. As with other aspects of technology operational standards are evolving, and some of the problems of the technology are being overcome. For some there is a lack of potential as it is seen as just a poor 'face to face' substitute, rather than being seen as a source of innovative learning experiences. In the aftermath of events like the September 11th attacks on the USA, with the impact on air travel that they had, the prospects for videoconferencing tools to be more used and to improve seem good. Whether that then means that L&D applications will also evolve remains to be seen. It does highlight how the uptake of technologies reflects a whole host of factors that are not directly concerned with learning.

Virtual reality learning

Virtual reality learning involves people experiencing a 'fully immersive' environment. The classical example is that of the flight simulator, used to train and test pilots. In these the pilots are exposed to simulations of flights which are fully immersive because they are in a model of a cockpit, with the plane responding to their actions. The logic of this is obvious; the costs of errors using the 'real environment' are so high that the

---

Box 9.9

Learning with the Sims?

One reservation people have is about the relevance of such technologies for studying human science based subjects, or those that involve 'soft skills', such as HRM and management. The development of simulations of people seems an impossible task.

Yet there is a game on the market which attempts to do this, called 'The Sims'. People can be created, given personalities, given jobs and roles, and then set up in families and communities. Whether they thrive or not depends on how well they have been set up as characters, and how carefully their experiences are monitored and adapted as the families and communities evolve. Neglecting people can lead them to decline.

The point of The Sims is to provide entertainment, not to learn about people; but the scope for L&D about people raises the possibility of modelling people for other circumstances. Why not present managers with virtual models of groups and teams and ask them to develop that team? Why not develop a virtual model of the people in the organisation, and 'play' with that to see what happens if certain scenarios are envisaged – such as new teams being built or certain people being promoted?

The Sims is a Maxis product; details at http://thesims.ea.com/us/

---

costs of developing simulators make sense. The advantages are the possibilities of controlling complex tasks, to provide situated learning and monitor learners closely as they learn. Fully immersive simulations and environments have been developed and used for many purposes. Entertainment is probably number one, with architectural design, sales and prototyping functions also important applications of virtual reality technologies. Learning environments have been low down the priority list for the application of virtual reality simulations, perhaps with the exception of the military, though the scope for the evolution of learning environments can be glimpsed (see Box 9.9).

Performance support uses of ICT

One of the options that ICT makes possible is to help people do something better, faster, cheaper without having to learn it completely and fully in the conventional way. For some roles and tasks full and formal training is a necessity, and cognitive capacities and capabilities need to be internalised and kept up to date; for example doctors and pilots. For other roles and tasks this may not be the case; people can become 'expert' through finding and using information rather than being formally instructed and trained. For example, all new managers in an organisation do not need to know all the HRM policies immediately in order to perform well. Performance support provides the means for more efficiently supporting L&D as and when it is needed (Stevens and Stevens *op cit*), in the course of accomplishing tasks, without having to learn chapter and verse. Equivalents to job aids enabled by ICT can be classified as either external aids to work or extrinsic aids to a computer packages. External aids are those where there is a need to stop work to get support from job aids and documents, or help desks. Extrinsic aids take various forms that can be accessed while work continues: software help, wizards, or cue cards that are provided as part of a computer package.

Box 9.10

Organisational resources

- Course catalogue
- Registration system
- Up front competency assessment
- Launch and track
- Assessments

- Library of materials
- Point to knowledge resources
- Provide reports
- Support knowledge communities
- Integrate with other systems

THE ORGANISATIONAL CONTEXT

For organisations to make use of ICT in L&D they need reliable access to technologies and partnership with IT professionals inside or outside the organisation. They should aim to create a learning portal, a single point of access that serves as a gateway to a variety of resources (see Box 9.10). They also need to establish a learning management system (LMS) to manage e-learning; for example, recording who is learning what.

The uptake of ICT also involves a challenge to the organisation's learning culture; the beliefs and values that people have about learning, and what makes for effective learning. Organisations need to get beyond lip service about learning being a valued part of what people do, rather than seeing it really as a waste of time. This means overcoming the perception that learning and work are different.

All this raises the need for 'champions' of ICT in L&D among senior management. But it is argued that often what happens is that ICT in L&D projects are assigned to people who 'don't have a clue'. They are given verbal support but no money. This happens because senior managers are not involved, there is a belief that L&D is really a remedial activity, and managers see access to the Internet as potentially disruptive to work and performance. Success will come where there is a sound business case, and there are success stories. It requires a process of educating and coaching managers to change perceptions and to 'work the politics' in favour of ICT in L&D. That presents communication as an integral part of changing to ICT in L&D, more than just investing in the ICT. To achieve such change is an exercise in change management; overcoming resistance to change, establishing the skills and abilities to engage in e-learning, and providing resources. Box 9.11 provides the background for doing this.

Reviewing ICT, the advantages are all the advantages of flexible/open learning: of consistency, and flexibility of place and time. In addition there are the benefits of interactivity, immediate feedback, and high realism. Training time, it is claimed, is reduced by 26 per cent, excluding the gains from reduced need for travel to locations of L&D. Direct costs are dramatically reduced: premises, travel, course fees. See Box 9.12. It is more enjoyable than paper based alternatives. Checking progress is easy, as is practising in safety.

Box 9.11

Business concerns and e-learning

Cost   *What will it cost and how can that be managed? Savings create higher profits or resources*
               for investment
             What will training cost to get or develop?
             E-learning is more efficient; conveys information quicker. Costs more on development,
               saves on the delivery, particularly opportunity costs

Quality   *Are we meeting customer expectations?*
             Reactions; proper surveys built in
             Learning; use for feedback not assessment
             Performance
             Results; for the business, intellectual capital

Service   *Do we respond to needs?*
             Access and availability (24 hours a day, 7 days a week)
             Tailored to individuals

Speed   *How fast can we change strategy, bring in a new product, respond to customers? These*
               are the key criteria
             To get up and running
             To reach everyone
             To be altered as the need arises

Source: Rosenberg (2001)

Exercise 9.1   Redesigning for ICT

How could the course you are currently doing be redesigned using these elements of ICT:

- a learning centre?
- Internet/Intranet?
- CBT?
- Videoconferencing?
- Virtual reality immersions?

The problems with all these kinds of ICT based learning are all the disadvantages of flexible/open learning: individual isolation, motivational problems, the quality of help and support. And the use of ICT is not right for all kinds of learning and L&D. It is seen as the best option in certain circumstances. These are when:

- learners are dispersed
- difficult to assemble at same time
- blocks of time are hard to schedule
- a computer related task is involved
- consistent messages are absolutely essential
- systematic test marking is required
- instructors are in short supply

Box 9.12

Cost comparisons

To train 200 employees per year

Multimedia		In house course	
4 hours per week average		2 day course for 12–14 at a time	
	£		£
Develop	379		757
Courseware	4,171		–
Running	10,514		37,203
Total	15,064		37,960
Average	75		190
per employee			

Box 9.13

Evaluation of ICT in L&D

Reactions   Learners are positive about using ICT

Learning   The use of ICT makes no significant difference? (Mogey 1998)

Costs   Lower costs at volume; so big organisations can use it, the smaller cannot

Transfer   If it is IT learning itself the learning transfer to performance is high; if it is other kinds of learning, transfer is still an issue

Ultimate   Organisations need to be on the wave or be left behind? It is becoming the norm to at least 'blend' e-learning into L&D at work, if not to rely on it entirely

---

There are also problems presented by the changing roles which the use of ICT in L&D raises. Trainers become purchasers/developers/facilitators of hardware and software. Providers have to shift to be online and producing multimedia materials, which takes a great investment. Government is concerned with infrastructure development, for example the National Grid for Learning and the University for Industry. Users too have to change; to being learners live at the screenface. And, once again, managers are taken out of the L&D loop. See Boxes 9.13 and 9.14.

EVOLVING DELIVERY TECHNOLOGIES

The further evolution of delivery technologies will impact on the design and delivery of e-learning (Spectrum 2000). Until recently distance learning and e-learning services had been available either via dial-up access to the Internet or broadcast TV. Though the Internet is the obvious choice for hosting interactive digital courseware, dial-up access is slow

---

Box 9.14

An evolution

		Concern
Entry level	Convert some existing provisions to CBT or purchase CBT	Experiment
Stage 2	Develop a learning resource centre and HR web site	Unify
Stage 3	Develop network provisions and/or make use of 'e-partnerships' for up to 25 per cent of L&D needs	Expand
Stage 4	Full integration of all elements of development between learners and managers mediated by ICT (from entry to evaluation)	L&D integrate
Stage 5	Electronic performance management; integration with other information and HR systems (appraisal, career development)	Business integration

---

and available only to those with a PC. Networks are currently being developed which will give Internet access to students and teachers at all schools, colleges and universities. Nevertheless, the majority of the population still does not have Internet access from the home. Some 24 per cent of homes had Internet access in the UK in 1999, limited in comparison with the USA which had 37% of households online.

There are other options, with intriguing implications for how L&D at work could evolve. Most organisations have a TV set, but these to date have only provided access to broadcast educational programming and limited analogue interactive educational services. Only limited numbers of educational programmes are available and no interactivity is possible without cable or satellite. The development of cable modems, digital subscriber line (DSL) technologies, and broadband wireless technologies could provide simpler and cheaper access devices. Meanwhile the quality and reliability of Internet access will evolve. Broadband technologies will provide much faster download times and facilitate new services such as CD quality video and audio applications that simply cannot be supported by dial-up connections.

Whilst DSL and cable modems will make Internet access much easier and permit video streaming from the Internet, interactive digital TV is currently much more efficient at delivering applications which depend for their impact on moving pictures. Digital transmission allows extra channel capacity, which enables operators not only to expand the number of channels, but also to extend the range of services offered.

Interactive TV rather than computer based learning may be the future. It appeals more to most people, as it is nearly 'always on' and is more user friendly and visually appealing than the Internet. It also appeals to people who are uncomfortable dealing with a text based medium, who have literacy problems. Web TV technologies can allow access to the wider Internet through URLs embedded into programming. Web-enhanced L&D applications could include links from learning materials to in-depth back-up information. As technology evolves and bandwidth increases the nature of this interactivity will develop further.

Technological developments with mobile phones may also have a role to play. While the current second generation networks are seen as limited, the use of wireless data applications is meant to change this. The technology is meant to make the wireless interface to the Internet more user friendly, and with transmission speed increases. A Wireless Application Protocol (WAP) microbrowser embedded into a phone will filter and display Internet text information on a mobile screen in a readable format. In addition to this improved interface other potential enhancements are being highlighted. The third generation of mobile telecommunications is meant to bring mobile networks closer to the capabilities of fixed networks. They could provide mobile users with full interactive multimedia capabilities and make full video streaming possible, allowing people to watch 'broadcast' materials on their handset. All of these may provide new means to give instant performance support L&D to people in all kinds of work situations. However, the evolution of technologies in themselves is not enough; users have to be able to integrate these tools into their learning. The shortcomings of putting multimedia on a screen on a mobile phone may restrict the kinds of material and functions that this form of technology can be used for. Mobile phones may be popular for brief text messaging, but will not fit in with more substantial learning needs.

CONCLUSION

The promise of greater access to and potential cost savings in L&D through using ICT generates a lot of hype. But gnarly issues about platforms, technologies, and organisational realities in using e-learning present challenges. Rosenberg rightly counsels care in an era of apparently unbridled enthusiasm for e-learning. He emphasises that the classic 4 'Cs' still matter: culture, champions, communication, and change management, if the potential of e-learning is to be realised.

At present most organisations do not use ICT for L&D, or have an e-learning strategy; some have websites, use courseware and other e-learning artefacts. This perhaps reflects three important factors:

1   Internet technology may be the key to a profound revolution in learning, but technology is just a tool
2   There is an enduring and important role for classroom instruction; to think otherwise is misguided
3   Learning is a continuous process, not a series of events; it is not just formally organised provisions and training

In order to leverage the potential of e-learning an overall business and people centred strategy is needed. Deployment of e-learning is absolutely dependent on this. This is a message reinforced in all areas.

Many questions are raised (see Box 9.15). If ICT in L&D is to flourish then who develops the infrastructure and the content – special institutions, organisations of L&D providers? Is it infrastructure driven, so that because the delivery mode exists and it can be done and must it be done – e-this, e-that, e-everything? Are there maturing systems with clear standards, for both hardware and software?

The uptake of new ICT provides an opportunity to rethink and redesign learning experiences, with conventional problems such as access, flexibility, quality, and cost resolved. But this may be still be a false dawn. It is still the quality of basic needs analysis, design, delivery and evaluation that matters. Equally the management of implementation matters as much, if not more, than the new medium itself. Retaining the benefits of the 'old ways' of learning in groups and in personal relations is still important, hence the concern with 'blended' leaning, where e-learning offers something in addition to conventional media and methods rather than a substitute.

Box 9.15

Claims and issues

Claims	Issues
New multimedia are relevant everywhere	Limited to some kinds of instruction
Lower costs	Higher initial costs
Greater access and volume	People switch off
More effective learning	No difference
Replicates situated learning	Can't replace situated learning

CONCLUDING CASE STUDY

Does e-learning work?

A company providing IT services worldwide with an annual turnover of some £170m has sites in the UK, mainland Europe and the Asia Pacific regions. Naturally, it is difficult to train such a widely dispersed group of people, and some 80 per cent of staff are at clients' sites at any one time, which adds to the challenge. They work in a number of industrial sectors, including defence, finance, government, commerce and telecommunications. Staff who work in each of these sectors need different IT skills. They undertake customer specific projects and assignments, so the skills they need to learn depend on what their clients want them to do. The company's income comes from its fee-earning staff; so if they are off the job undergoing training, they are not earning.

In recent years it has made increased used of technology based training (TBT) to train its 2500 IT professionals around the world. Originally it had a library of IT professional TBT products available via its Intranet. More recently it has moved to a bespoke, online learning solution. For one practitioner involved in this, after 15 years developing TBT products, writing authoring systems and managing projects, trying to implement what others had developed was 'different'.

Transferable and up-to-date skills are crucial, and there are issues of staff recruitment, expectations and retention, along with key performance indicators and staff utilisation rates. Moreover, it is difficult to plan training on the basis of which of the company's bids for work will be successful. It is also difficult to second guess both the future requirements and the technologies that will be successful. There is also the prevailing mentality of 'start yesterday, deliver tomorrow' and the perennial problem of utilisation rates and conflicting resource demands. All this means that it is difficult for the company to deliver training in a 'traditional' way.

Where traditional, instructor-led training is involved, travel and accommodation costs are inevitable. Despite the company having its own training centres, the cost base for these is increasing. Then again, if it publishes a public schedule for courses, it is always unsure that the dates will coincide with staff availability to go on the courses. And if it makes the courses 'closed', it cannot be sure that sufficient numbers of staff will be released to allow the courses to run.

This prompted the company to use TBT, delivered via discs and CD-ROMs. It solved many problems but it proved to be a logistics nightmare. The company had a large number of widely varying courses. There were 'licence issues'. For example, it found that the staff passed copies of the discs to their clients and friends. Some copies were lost. There was no tracking of usage and no evaluation of the training undertaken, in terms of whether the course was suitable for the student; whether or not the student completed the course, and what learning actually took place. And costs kept escalating.

The company found that many people who were using this TBT material felt isolated. The material offered little actual 'learning' and there was no way of measuring the return on investment. On the positive side, the TBT material was available whenever a member of staff was not required to be 'fee-earning'. It offered just-in-case and just-in-time training and could be studied at home. This was important because some staff did not like having to learn at the same screen where they worked all day.

Then along came Intranet-delivered TBT. This coincided with both an upgrade of the company's network and the globalisation of the company. Learning materials became available on the company Intranet. Users merely had to download them and 'play'.

The learning materials were semi-integrated with the company's knowledge base and other training resources, including classroom delivered training. It solved many of the problems the company had had with stand-alone TBT materials. However, the downside of this included technical difficulties with the installation of and access to the materials – and there was still no real evaluation of the resulting learning.

The company then switched to an Internet-based, externally hosted system. This meant that the learning materials were accessible from anywhere in the world. In addition, this system made it easier to add or remove courses; tailor course paths, and also monitor and track usage. Since some 80 per cent of the staff did not go to the office, when the learning materials were placed on the corporate Intranet, they had to go in to the office to download the material and take it away. Now, these people could access the material from anywhere that had an Internet connection. The added value from this arrangement was that the host had the same technical partners as the company. The company could take part in online seminars and briefings with them, and have automatic access to white papers as and when these were published; it not only used leading edge technology to train staff, but also to understand these technologies in its work with its own clients.

The company has removed the isolation of the learner through making chatrooms available and instigating a '24–7' online mentoring service. This online mentoring service, an extra cost, encouraged people to work at home in the evening, because they knew that, if they had a question, someone was available to give them the answers they needed.

One case study involved disseminating Java skills among the workforce. It was undertaken to bring staff to a base level of skill with regard to Java. The company could not deliver all the training via e-learning but, having completed the e-learning element of the training, the trainees attended a five day 'boot camp'. This reduced, by ten days, the amount of time taken to train people in Java skills compared with the 'traditional', classroom based approach.

The company used to allow people access to all of the online library but found that they only 'tasted' a great many programmes and did not complete any. Now, it allowed 'tasters', but they had to request access to the library and be authorised to do so. This also added an element of cost control to the process and helped to ensure that, by incurring a cost to access the library, people would value the training materials. The advantages of the current Internet-

CONCLUDING CASE STUDY (cont'd)

based system included access to mentoring, white papers, chatrooms and so on. They also included the reduced costs of both the system itself and the related technical support. Moreover, they could change the content of the learning materials easily and rapidly. Access to the courses was now truly flexible: from anywhere at anytime.

The disadvantages included loss of control over access to the material held on the Internet. In fact, this material was heavily password protected, especially for those administrators who accessed the system to examine student records. In addition, there were security and firewall problems, especially for those staff who logged on to the materials from their clients' sites. Many of these firewalls allowed the user to get into the materials but not to download them, that is, bring them back through the client's firewall.

In addition, the company had no control over downtime and the costs of online access, and it paid the telephone bill for those who accessed the learning materials.

From its experiences the company now knew that the system must be easy to log on to and use. It needed to have an easy to use and stable administration system. There was also a need for flexibility in the contract with the service provider, along with a well-worded service level agreement that allowed for escalation of the service.

For example, the company agreed a group of courses with the system's hosts but, after three months, realised that some of these courses were unpopular and unused, and wanted to substitute other courses for these. Yet their contract did not allow them to do this. In addition, the host was not keen to include courses developed by other producers on the system. But, in order to provide the most effective learning materials for staff, the company did want to include other courses on the system, and had a learning management system in place that would cope with this.

A recent cost-benefit analysis by the company, comparing classroom-delivered training with e-learning, concluded that in order to get the same amount of classroom-delivered training as was currently delivered via e-learning, the company would need a budget of over £2m. The e-learning system, containing 195 modules and being used by some 1000 users, with access to 24–7 mentoring and so on, was nearing the end of the first year of a three year contract valued at £0.5m over the three years.

Source: Little (2001) 'The eLearning Network': http://www.elearningnetwork.org/

REFERENCES

Campaign for Learning (2000) *Attitudes to e-learning: A National Survey*, London, Southgate Publishers.

DfEE (1997) *Learning Centres: A Guide*, DfEE.

Finn, W. (2000) 'Procure-all', *People Management*, Vol. 6, No. 5.

Galbreath, J. (1992) 'The educational buzzword of the 1990's: multimedia, or is it hypermedia, or interactive multimedia, or . . . ?' *Educational Technology*, April.

George, A. and Cooper, S. (2001) *Employers' Use and Awareness of Vocational Learning Approaches*, DfEE.

Hammond, D. (2001) 'Reality bytes', *People Management*, Vol. 7, No. 2.

Hills, H. and Francis, P. (1999) 'Interaction learning', *People Management*, Vol. 5, No. 14.

Hunt, M. and Clarke, A. (1997) *A Guide to the Cost Effectiveness of Technology-Based Training*, DfEE.

IRS (1998) 'Intranets: delivering just-in-time training', *Employee Development Bulletin*, No. 103.

Mogey, N. (ed.) (1998) *Learning Technology Dissemination Initiative: Evaluation Studies*, LTDI.

Riding, R. (1996) *Learning Styles and Technology Based Training*, DfEE.

Rosenberg, J. (ed.) (2001) *E-learning: Strategies for Delivering Knowledge in the Digitial Age*, San Francisco, McGraw-Hill.

Sadler-Smith, E., Down, S. and Lean, J. (2000) 'Modern learning methods: rhetoric and reality', *Personnel Review*, Vol. 29, No. 4.

Scott., A (1997) *Learning Centres: A Step-by-step Guide to Planning, Managing and Evaluating an Organizational Resource Centre*, London, Kogan Page.

Seabrook, J. and Rushby, N. (2000) 'An unhappy medium', *People Management*, Vol. 6, No. 17.

Sloman, M. (2001) *The E-Learning Revolution*, London, CIPD.

Spectrum (2000) *Issues in the Delivery of Technology-Based Learning*, Glasgow Development Agency.

Stevens, G. H. and Stevens, E. F. (1995) *Electronic Performance Support Tools*. Englewood Cliffs, NJ, Educational Technology Publications.

Stevens, L (1996) 'The Intranet: your newest training tool?', *Personnel Journal*, July.

Tapscott, D. (1995) *The Digital Economy: Promise and Peril In the Age of Networked Intelligence*, London, McGraw-Hill.

TfT (2001) Technologies for Training website, http://www.tft.co.uk/

part three

Perspectives

Perspectives are different points of view. There are different points of view from which L&D at work can be explored. What is seen to be important about L&D at work depends on the point of view being adopted. To get a complete view of a subject it is useful to look at it from different points of view. In much of HRM, for example, a common version of this is to consider both the employer and employee perspectives on a matter; and by seeing things from these different perspectives come to a balanced view on a question of policy or practice. In the case of L&D at work there are three major points of view which are currently the source of much discussion and debate:

Principles and Problems	L&D in theory, as a subject that is studied by human scientists, and the conclusions derived from these about L&D at work
Policy in National Vocational Education and Training (NVET)	Government has both an economic and social policy agenda which involves engaging with the promotion of L&D at work
The Knowledge Management (KM) Perspective	The rise to prominence of the concept of KM has involved both emphasising the importance of L&D at work and challenging conceptions of what L&D at work is all about

These are addressed in Chapters 10 to 12 respectively. The aim is that the concerns of each perspective, and what they have to offer as ways of making sense of L&D at work, are understood. Familiarity with the debates and discussions involved within these different perspectives is to be expected among students of L&D at work.

chapter ten

Principles and Problems: L&D in Theory

Learning outcomes

- Define principles and problems in L&D at work using theories of learning
- Discuss the relevance of wisdom, psychological, sociological and economic theories as perspectives on L&D at work
- Critically evaluate the role that theories of learning play in the design and management of L&D practices
- Critically evaluate practices in assessing learning needs, designing learning environments and evaluating learning outcomes using theories

FRAMEWORK CASE STUDY: LEARNING — THE MUSICAL

Is there a connection between music and effective L&D at work? This may seem to be a curious connection to explore in the context of improving performance at work. But, in theory, there are a number of possible connections between music and effective L&D. It is, indeed, a subject on which conferences are being held. These conferences discuss and review research which claims to show a connection between the use of music and L&D. The research seems to show that 'music can make you smarter'. If it is a fact that music can help make people smarter, how might this be demonstrated and explained? Various kinds of social scientists, and others, are now researching this; exploring concepts of how music and effective brain function can be correlated.

The role of music in supporting L&D is being envisaged in a number of ways. Music is envisaged as affecting the brain in various ways that can support effective cognition and therefore support learning. For example there is a hypothesised 'Mozart effect'. This is an inclusive term to describe the positive, transformative and uplifting power of certain kinds of music on a listener's mind and body. This is something that those who listen to music while studying may already appreciate. But could these kinds of musical effects be systematically used to enhance L&D?

In addition to such cognitive aspects of the effects of music there is also the emotional power of music, the role of the 'tingle factor'. The use of music to influence the emotions is a commonplace in film, where a soundtrack is used to manipulate the audience's emotions, to elicit or to heighten emotions. Could the same process be used to support better learning? It can, according to research, apparently help with supporting and stimulating creative thinking among children in the pre-five and primary school age group. Music can be used to soothe, or to enliven and animate parts of the brain associated with effective learning. In adults it can also have similar effects; apparently helping with relaxation, and stimulating the right hand side of the brain. Split brain theory suggests that the right hand side of the brain is the zone that is involved in, for example, creative thinking; awakening this part of the brain can help people achieve creativity. There is possible value in using music to enable improved concentration, imagination, and expression, which are all factors that can either help establish receptivity to L&D or help some kinds of L&D directly.

These contemporary ideas about music are all prefigured in the earlier work and theorising of an educationalist, Lozanov (Meier 2000). He was a pioneer in the use of music to support accelerated learning, who introduced and experimented with music in the classroom. He believed that, and wanted to prove that, music can increase learner effectiveness exponentially. This was possible, he believed, because music changes the whole mind-set of the learner while s/he works at tasks involved in learning. It calms the whole organism, exciting and therefore opening up people's peripheral capacities, and mobilising emotions which help ensure that information is committed to long-term memory. The claims were not only that the use of music could enhance learning ability, it could also improve physical and psychological health. So the theory has been around for some decades now, and has recently had a new lease of life.

This may all be very well for the learning and emotional development of five year olds, but does it really apply to and matter in the hard headed world of contemporary L&D in work organisations? There is some evidence that it seems to. Composers and jazz musicians have been invited to give presentations and talks in companies, and at conferences on leadership and teamwork. The metaphor of organisations being like groups who make music is the ostensible reason for this; but the popularity of the music itself, and its affects on those attending such events, seem an important factor as well.

More broadly there is a new concern with understanding how to help people 'learn how to learn'. People should be given hints and tips about learning in order to be motivated and confident as learners. This is one reason why conferences such as those discussing the role of music, exploring ideas about improving learning by understanding how the brain, learning and memory work, are so popular. These 'brain based' perspectives on how to learn have led to investigating the use of music. But can research into such a topic ever prove the theory that there are such connections? Or will such research only ever represent a 'quasi scientific' justification of beliefs, giving people false hope about being able to use such techniques to make learning more effective?

INTRODUCTION

If it seems that music can help L&D, which is the case according to some social scientists, then in what ways could music be used to support L&D? The answer to that question will depend on the theory being advanced, about how and why music can help learning. Such theories are not certain and validated explanations of the truth; they are possibilities with which to try and make sense of the facts. One theory would be that music activates parts of the brain that are often left dormant in typical learning environments, such as the typical classroom. So music should be used when these otherwise dormant parts of the brain are required; for example, when creative think-ing is wanted or needed as part of the learning experience. Another theory might be that music helps people relax and concentrate; it should then be used selectively to create a relaxed atmosphere. Yet another theory would be that certain kinds of music are useful for helping process information into long term memory; music should there-fore be used where there is a concern with processing a lot of information, as happens for example during a presentation. So depending on the theory adopted the uses of music in practice would be quite different.

Which theory is correct? The answer to that, from a scientific perspective, depends on research to check and prove a connection between the use of music and increases in the rate or effectiveness of learning. The example of the connections between music and mind, in brief, illustrate how theory comes to matter and why it is important. The assumption being made here is that theories are sets of ideas formulated in the course of reasoning about causal relationships, and checking out facts to determine if such relationships exist. But this definition raises a new question; what field of 'fact' is L&D at work concerned with? Entwistle *et al* (1992, p 3) noted that

> When adults from a wide range of ages and educational backgrounds are asked to explain what they understand by 'learning' a series of contrasting conceptions is found which can be seen as a hierarchy, increasing in both sophistication and complexity.

The concept of learning does not mean one thing at all times to all people; it means different things to different people at different times. The kinds of things, and the kinds of relationships they may or may not have, that are the subject of learning theory can therefore vary greatly depending on what exactly is being meant by 'learn-ing'. The hierarchy of meanings Entwistle *et al* found is given in Figure 10.1. It ranges from learning meaning 'increasing one's knowledge' to learning meaning 'changing as a person'. These are placed by Entwistle *et al* on a continuum; from surface to deep learning.

Learning theories are then to be defined as sets of ideas formulated by reasoning about the facts involved in a range of experiences, from 'increasing knowledge' to

Figure 10.1   *A hierarchy of learning*

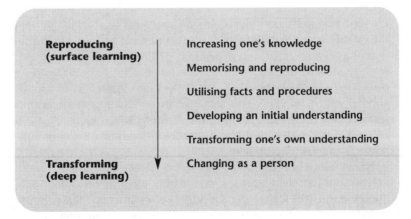

Source: Adapted from Entwistle *et al* (1992)

Box 10.1

Is 'surface learning' the main problem?

Marchese talks about the central fact being that surface learning rather than deep learning appears to be the norm in many L&D interventions, at work and elsewhere.

Surface learning is defined as the superficial packing of the short term memory; it is learning which is transient and fades away. Deep learning is real assimilation and change; it is transformative and permanent. Many learning experiences seem to achieve surface learning, not deep learning.

Explaining why this should be so, and reasoning about how to support effective deep learning, is a holy grail for learning theory. Practitioners in L&D at work will be concerned that this impedes getting results. Human scientists would want to focus upon research into the design and delivery of L&D interventions. For some the starting point would be the extent to which practices were consistent with principles suggested by various psychological theories. For others problems with surface learning in L&D might be due to problems in the social context of relationships and institutions involved in learning. They might want to explore what makes learners dysfunctional and only achieve surface learning. For others the problem might be seen as an integral part of the operation of market forces, and how these were stimulating or failing to provide support for deep learning and effective L&D.

Source: Marchese (2000)

'changing as a person.' Such theories can then be tested and evaluated, with the 'good' theories being used to shape and inform practice and the 'bad' theories being rejected (see Box 10.1).

There are four main sources of theory which provide perspectives on the principles and problems of L&D at work. Each of these can provide insights into the how and the why of effective L&D at work. They are wisdom, psychology, sociology, and economics. We now take each of these in turn.

THE WISDOM LITERATURE

The first perspective on principles and problems is provided by theory derived from the experience of practitioners. Such theories can be found in the 'wisdom literature' that practitioners write and disseminate. HRM as a whole is replete with wisdom literature; work written by and for practitioners. This literature encompasses work concerned with texts on 'how to do it' to the latest bestsellers of management gurus and popular writers on L&D. This source of theory is a highly popular, but a problematic resource as a means of exploring the facts of L&D at work. This is because the theories and prescriptions found in the wisdom literature are not, usually, based on robust research and valid argumentation.

Nonetheless reflections on personal experience that result in prescriptions for good practice can provide useful and stimulating learning for others. Reading the wisdom literature is useful for getting checklists of 'what to do'. But it is also possible to read it and analyse and evaluate the theories that are being used. Being able to evaluate the theories in use in the wisdom literature provides one way of critically evaluating the strengths and weaknesses of what is being prescribed. Mager (2000) provides a good illustration of a writer providing a practitioner's wisdom about the field of L&D. His text is aimed at managers involved in L&D rather than being for specialist trainers or student learners. He is critical of much training as 'a fraud' or 'an extravagance', which managers have rightly been sceptical about in the past. He is claiming to explain how and why L&D at work works from personal wisdom based on experience.

He argues that effective L&D can provide performance improvements through instructions in skill, and help develop employee self-efficacy; but it is up to managers to provide the opportunity and support which translate instruction in skills into improved performance. There are often other, non-training means to the same end. What Mager is arguing is actually a version of the theory of behaviourism, the 'behaviourists' ABC' discussed in Chapter 4. This is an interpretation of L&D derived from formal theories in psychology. He agrees that knowing learning theory will not make a person a good instructor. But he still concludes that it is important to be able to describe the relevant characteristics of adult learners and know the key principles of supporting effective learning.

Both these aspects of theory, theories of how adults learn best and general principles for supporting learning, are presented by Mager as simply being commonsense guides. They are not based on citing studies or evidence; they come from knowing 'reality' and being experienced. The implication, sometimes expressed explicitly, is that it is theorising that gets in the way of good practice. What is required is a better prescriptive account of the best practice, not the mess of theorising.

The strength of this perspective on L&D at work, and the theory it involves, is that those who have experience are often the best placed to explain and discuss what works and what does not work. The weakness of the wisdom literature is that the research base is not rigorously collated or presented. Taken further, those who seek to argue that they are being atheoretical, focussing on providing ideas about 'getting results' in practice rather than debating the academic merits of competing ideas, are misleading. Such texts may often be written without reference to facts derived from research and studies on learning, but they do involve the use of theories. It is not their concern to evaluate different theories, but rather prescribe the 'best way', and so the focus is on 'getting results' rather than the validity of the theories involved. The wisdom literature tends to suggest that problems with learning at work are a consequence of ill prepared and unprofessional trainers and managers. Reflecting on the experience of trainers and others this stream provides admonitions, recipes, tips and techniques for supporting effective learning.

PSYCHOLOGY

L&D at work has long been a subject for applied psychology, with the facts and the associated theories of the psychological literature providing a perspective on the principles and problems of L&D at work. It is indeed this stream of theorising which is often taken to be, and presented as, the most relevant for L&D. This stream contains theories from the various schools of psychology. These provide different explanations of the principles and problems in learning given depending on the perspective adopted (see Boxes 10.2 and 10.3). The main fields of theory are those derived from the behaviourist and cognitive perspectives. For behaviourists the principles and problems of L&D at work are the principles and problems of conditioning and reinforcing desirable behaviours. For those adopting a cognitive perspective the principles and

---

Box 10.2

Are self illusions good for you?

Psychology seeks to explore the characteristics of individuals which make for effective learning. One assumption is that 'normal', healthy and happy people are those who have a realistic understanding of who they are, what they are capable of, and what will happen in the future. People who lack this may be considered either unwell or egocentric.

But some argue that the facts show that the healthiest and happiest people are those who have unrealistically positive illusions about their own good qualities, their control of chance events, and their future prospects.

People will be better learners if they

- see themselves as happier, healthier, luckier, more virtuous and more skilled than others
- think of their own qualities as being rare or unique and their flaws as being common and unimportant
- think their future will be better than their past, being optimists rather than sober realists
- indulge in 'magical thinking', believing in an ability to control events and people

Source: Gamon and Bragdon (1998)

---

problems of L&D at work are those of information processing. Learning fails if it is not constructed to best fit with people's natural learning styles and to harness people's natural learning abilities.

The perspective provided by 'psychological theory' is increasingly diverse, ranging from the classics of the early pioneers of psychology to the frontiers of cognitive science and neuroscience. The continuing relevance of 'classical' theories, for example modified and updated behaviourism, attests to the robustness of the research and theorising that they were based on as early human sciences. Whether the newer fields of cognitive science and neuroscience oriented 'brain based' theory fare as well over time remains to be seen. Much research is being conducted, but the collection of the facts is currently mainly related to investigating and defeating diseases of the brain.

Cognitive science seems the most productive. Cognitive science is

the interdisciplinary scientific study of mind. Its practice and knowledge derive from those of the primary contributing disciplines, which are computer science, linguistics, neuroscience, psychology, cognitive neuropsychology, and philosophy . . . cognitive scientists aim to construct causal accounts by linking three levels . . . the behavioural level . . . the cognitive level . . . and the biological level (Green *et al* 1996, p 5).

To understand L&D is to engage with an analysis of the brain and mind (see Box 10.4). The rationale of cognitive science is that the human brain, the seat of learning, can best be understood in terms of the use of representational structures in the brain and the computational procedures that operate on those structures. The brain is a machine for creating and using representational structures in the form of logical propositions, rules, concepts, images, and analogies. It uses procedures on these such as deduction, search, matching, rotating and retrieval. The cells of the brain, the neurones, embody these representations and enable such computation.

Box 10.3

Fruit flies and memory enhancement

Repetition is the mother of all learning because our brains must undergo a physical change in order to form a long-term memory: neurons have to grow new connections to one another to create a structural basis for whatever it is people remember. Memory construction takes work. But what if you could swallow a little pill that gave you a photographic memory, and the ability to form long-term memories instantly?

Researchers at Cold Spring Harbor Laboratory are researching a protein that helps nerve cells in the brain store memories. A sudden increase in the activity levels of the protein sends the memory-making process into overdrive and allows neurons to make long-lasting storage structures immediately, without the slow work of repetition.

Researchers first discovered the importance of this memory protein while working with fruit flies. They created two new, genetically altered strains of fruit fly: one with extremely high levels of memory protein and one with almost none of it. Then they conditioned the flies by placing them in tubes and blowing in scented air currents. One scent was like smelly shoes, the other smelled like liquorice and was accompanied by a small electric shock. A fly that is zapped every time it smells liquorice should eventually build a set of neural connections that says, 'Avoid liquorice!'. The question is: how much repetition does it take for that long-term memory to form?

Researchers tested the flies by placing them in the middle of a double-ended tube and blowing smelly shoe scent in one end and liquorice scent in the other. Flies with normal levels of the memory protein needed to be zapped ten times before they stopped moving toward the liquorice scent. The flies with an overabundance of memory protein formed long-term memory instantly. After only one trial, they knew to avoid liquorice the rest of their lives. Tully points out that these flies haven't gotten smarter – they'll never solve quadratic equations. Extra memory protein simply accelerates the pace of memorisation by eliminating the need for repetition. Researchers suspect that the memory protein is a sort of construction crew foreman in the brain that turns on the genes neurons need to grow new connections, a process that normally occurs bit by bit with repetition.

The pharmaceutical challenge is to find a compact chemical that can infiltrate neurons, stimulate an over-production of the protein, and thereby give the human brain a hurry-up, neural-connection construction crew. This pop-a-pill enhancement is expected to last only a few hours before memory protein levels return to normal, but while levels are up, people would be like the one-zap flies, with supercharged memory-making.

Great news? Perhaps the reason evolution made repetition the mother of learning is that repetition ensures that you remember only what you try to remember. With these pills the minutiae that once flitted lightly through your short-term memory will lodge in your brain forever, like it or not.

Source: Weed (2000)

One weakness of the analogy of the brain with computing is that the brain cannot be seen as being a computational machine in the common sense that most people would use, acting as a serial processor of information in bits at a time, albeit so quickly that it seems as if complex processes are being handled all at once. The brain is more like a parallel processor; doing many things simultaneously. But critics of cognitive

Box 10.4

What is the brain like?

Cognitive archaeology involves exploring what was going on in the minds of early humans, using the evidence of artefacts. The critical point is exploring the change from being hunter-gatherers to producing the sudden burst of art, technology and religion that occurred around 30,000 years ago. The archaeological record shows an increase in brain size, but it is not just about the brain getting bigger. Different models of how the brain evolved are possible.

1 The brain is like a sponge, ready to soak up information; some sponges are better than others. But minds can compare and combine; sponges cannot compare and combine.
2 The brain is like a computer; it takes data, runs programs, and provides outputs. The same program is running all the time, a general purpose learning program. Different minds are like different specifications of computer, with varying speeds, capacities, and software.
3 The brain is like a Swiss Army knife; it has a central system (the case) and several independent special tools (the blades) that can be used for various purposes. These 'tools' are present at birth, built into the brain, and are opened out for use in the course of experience. For example language has to be learned, and interpersonal psychological abilities have to be stimulated through the use of cunning and deception to build alliances and friendships.

These different models can be used to explain the development of the mind in historical terms, and as a process that is reprised in the development from child to adult.

1 First the sponge, the general purpose intelligence; the 'soaking up' phase of learning among children
2 Then the 'computer', a core general intelligence in central control and using several modules during development into adulthood
3 Finally the Swiss Army knife, the use of 'specialised' tools in the right context by experienced mature adults

Source: Mithen (1996)

science have questioned the whole notion that the human mind, consciousness and sentience, can be explained and mapped in terms of the representation and computation functions of the brain. They argue that cognitive science neglects the role of emotion in human consciousness (Thagard 1996), making the functioning of the brain, and therefore the learning associated with it, something cold and calculating. Cognitive science disregards the 'messiness' of human consciousness, and the ways in which what people think and feel is always enacted in social contexts. Indeed Mithen (1996) argues that the origins of the human lie in the demands being made on social intelligence because of living in large groups; an increase in brain size and the development of mind enabled cunning and alliances, deceptions and friendships to be managed consciously. These were the foundations of the modern mind.

One way in which thinking and theorising about the brain and its properties can be discussed to accommodate such concerns is to view cognitive functions, including learning, in the context of evolution. This involves drawing upon explanations of the brain and its properties couched in terms of evolutionary psychology. Evolutionary psychology proposes that people's propensities and abilities, including the ability to learn, evolved to solve the problems of our hunter-gatherer ancestors. This approach allows for a role for emotion in such an analysis, an area previously excluded from thinking about learning.

This is important as thinking about emotional intelligence (EI), discussed in Chapter 2, suggests that the emotions are the executive governors of the brain and mind; that reason is the slave of the passions. While there are many diverse theories of emotion (Strongman 1996), the interest here is with cognitive accounts (Pinker 1997, Le Doux 1996) of how the mind works. These combine the two big theories, the computational theory of the functioning of the mind and brain and an evolutionary theory of the behaviour of the species, to provide an account of why for many aspects of human behaviour emotion features so prominently.

The capacity to scan and view brain activity, a fairly recent capacity, has opened up the exploration of brain structure and function. The brain is viewed as a precision instrument that allows people to use information to solve the problems presented by their lifestyle; it is this cognition machine which underpins human success at the top of the evolutionary ladder. The human brain is certainly large in comparison with that of all other animals. It is not just bigger; specific areas of the brain are seen to be highly developed and specialised for specific cognitive tasks, but seem to act in unison on even the simplest of tasks.

Exploiting information to sustain the 'camping trip that never ended' was the challenge of the lifestyle of all our original ancestor foragers. Early humans could use the fast and effective processing of information to outsmart competitors who might endanger them, and to work out how to exploit nature for their own ends. This meant that human populations could grow and prosper.

The heart of the analysis is the importance and value of information in the first instance, and therefore the value of developing symbol systems to capture and use information. Pinker suggests that the value of information is that life involves making a choice among gambles for each and every move a person makes. The more and the better the information people have, the less the risk they will have to take. If this is true it is then worth 'paying' for information, and being able to handle symbols and meaning which enable quick and complex information processing, to lessen these risks and reduce the gamble. The benefits for the organism outweigh the costs.

The costs of this information processing capacity for the organism are the resources needed for developing and maintaining the sense system it requires, and the need to learn symbol systems: the resources required for the brain and consciousness. These costs are varied and considerable. They include females having to cope with lengthy pregnancies, and the risks of giving birth to babies who have large skulls. They also include the young being exposed to a prolonged period of dependency in development through to maturity and competence.

The mechanics of data representation in people's heads take the form of visual, phonological, and grammatical data transformed into what Pinker calls 'mentalese', or modes of inscription in the neural networks of the brain. Neural networks act to enable cognition based on set symbols being manipulated by basic rules and procedures.

The empiricist model of the brain asserts that culture determines what is imprinted on the 'blank slate' of the brain; thus upbringing is powerful and irreversible in forming the mind. This kind of computational theory asserts rather that there is 'hard wiring' in the brain, selected for through evolution, for obtaining and handling information. The brain is not an empty slate. It is from people's evolution of stereoscopic

---

Box 10.5

Brain friendly learning

- The brain is 'plastic' across the lifespan; people are naturally able to learn and re-learn
- Learning is achieved best with all five senses engaged
- Learning takes time, as it involves a balance of input and accommodation/assimilation (reflecting on feedback) and output (practice)
- Emotional well being is essential for learning; high challenge stimulates learning, but high anxiety impedes it

---

vision, bipedal walking, which freed the hands for using tools, group living, hunting that required coalitions and reciprocity among the group, that this hard wiring was formed. The view that the brain is formed pre-wired, that it is not a blank slate, is a classic rationalist view. In the contemporary human environment, with the lifestyle challenges and risks it involves, these original hard wired elements of the human brain, determining its functions and structures, remain the same. Only the 'goals' of intelligent behaviour and the context are now different. From the viewpoint of evolution theory it is still implied that the brain and mind, and the use of learning in their operations, are ultimately to be judged in terms of how they help in the survival and replication of the species.

For Pinker the point is that these analyses of hard wiring lead to the conclusion that 'the emotions are mechanisms that set the brain's highest level goals' (Pinker *op cit*, p 373). Exploring emotions, scientifically, as drives to deploy the intellect in pursuit of certain goals, brackets any judgements about whether they are 'good' or 'bad'. They have the function of keeping people in tune with their environment and the risks and opportunities it presents, at all times. Most evidently this is seen to be true at critical points of fight, flight and reproduction. In a scientific sense their function is to help people secure the cooperation of others in all these contexts while pursuing their individual interests and goals. In the L&D at work context the kinds of conclusions that are derived from these kinds of analyses are given in Box 10.5.

SOCIOLOGY

The prevalence of psychological theory can eclipse the existence and amount of social theory related to and relevant to understanding L&D at work. This is surprising, given that the 'natural' way in which L&D at work has been organised for most of human history has been in the form of apprenticeships. The key features of apprenticeship are that it involves an individual in an established system that in turn involves the learner totally in learning from a master and mentor. The L&D process is to totally immerse the learner in the domain of learning, for a master to structure and supervise their learning constantly, then to require them to make their own way as their own masters. The fact that learning has been, and still very much is, 'situated' in such social contexts (Brown *et al* 1989, Brown and Duguid 1991, Lave and Wenger 1991) provides a role for social theory and theorising to investigate how and why L&D at work is successful or fails.

Even though it seemed that apprenticeships had been largely displaced by formal and universal schooling and education, occupational development and much of L&D still occur in the workplace (Garger 1999, Hager 1999). The L&D that happens outside the classroom and formal learning involves learning from and learning about the 'tacit knowledge' of communities of practice. Tacit knowledge is the knowledge that experts have which enables them to achieve their performance, but which is not codified and highly articulated; you won't find it in textbooks. Communities of practice are networks of people in an occupation or an organisation who are consciously sharing and supporting each other's learning through experience. Entry to such communities of practice and the learning that it can provide is neither easy nor automatic. It involves 'rites of entry', to attain a status of belonging at the equivalent of an 'apprenticeship' level. This enables what has been termed 'legitimate peripheral participation'; in other words, a learner has earned the right to be among practitioners and learn from them. For many students getting work placements is a form of legitimate peripheral participation. Once a person is a member of such a community of practice they need to be alert to the way that learning is shared; situated learning is managed through personal relationships, and people telling and sharing stories. It is this rather than reading textbooks which is the key to L&D at work.

The principles and problems of L&D are therefore bound up with social relationships and the institutions of learning, formal and informal. Reading every textbook and learning from them will not produce as good a performer as will being nurtured within a community of practice. Being nurtured within a community of practice is either the main path to capability, or is a necessary complement to formal learning elsewhere.

Adopting a social theory perspective on L&D can lead to some illuminating insights. Recent research (Frosh *et al* 2001) claims to show that a strict playground code on 'what it is to be masculine' is being blamed for teenage boys' (those aged 11–14) under-achievement at school. Rather than concentrating on school work boys feel they have to focus on performing well at sports, wearing the right designer labels and avoiding close friendships. To fail to conform is to risk being bullied or labelled as 'gay'. This applies to both State and public schools. However, in State schools working hard was 'unmasculine', while challenging authority was a key to popularity; in public schools this was not so, and attitudes to academic success were different. A classic study in this tradition which challenges some of the assumptions being made in these kinds of analyses is Willis's (1977) study of boys 'learning to labour'. These working class boys were labelled as troublemakers, as they had explicitly rejected participation in formal education at the secondary school level (see Box 10.6). He studied this situation of apparently dysfunctional behaviour, with the boys alienated from education, and argued that their behaviour was in fact functional. Given the way their future was most likely to unfold, far from rebelling 'against the system' they could be seen as colluding in making themselves part of the next generation of workers.

The social studies stream highlights that which is often missing from much of the wisdom and psychological literature on L&D. This is that people are always in a social situation. They are either immersed in social relations that they may find amenable or that they may be alienated from, or involved in or excluded from 'communities of practice' that enable access to superior performers. The principles and problems of L&D are of having effective relationships in formal learning settings or within those communities of practice, whether they be found in work or within special education and training institutions. The quality of access to and relationships within a 'com-

Box 10.6

Learning to labour

Paul Willis observed the lives of a group of rebellious working-class boys in an industrial city in England in the 1970s. He followed them from their 'hi-jinks' in and out of the classroom during their last year of high school, to their first year of working-class jobs on the factory floor. He argued that the material reality for them was that better jobs as a result of success in education did not exist for most of them, even if they conformed to the middle-class values espoused by their teachers. To conform with those values, and the expectations of working at learning they involved, were also contrary to their working-class values, and the boys' search for autonomy as they grew up. The net effect was that they were alienated from education, and the careers that opened up. They were more enticed by the allure of being 'temporary rebels', consistent with their core values of alienation from authority as an external power, and consistent with their desire to be autonomous, not under the control of authority. The end result is that they reproduced themselves as the next generation 'stuck' in the working class, as they failed in education and their brief autonomy as free agents was ended by becoming employed and settling down.

The research conclusion raises disturbing questions about the failures of schools, which people believe are agents of social mobility. It seems they in fact serve to perpetuate the divisions of wealth and opportunity, reproducing patterns of poverty in Western countries rather than overcoming them.

The relevance is in thinking through the problems other kinds of learners may encounter in L&D at work. Such insightful research from the perspective of social theory may help illuminate why, despite the best intentions, the promotion and provision of L&D fail to have an impact among some people or groups.

munity of practice' can determine how effective learning will be. To be excluded from these communities of practice is to be excluded from effective L&D. To be part of a thriving community of practice is to be accessing the best L&D possible.

ECONOMICS

According to the economic perspective, the facts and theories of L&D at work are investigated within a context of broader economic and political economy facts and theories. There is, for example, the fact that there are shortfalls in training provision resulting in skills shortages. Too many people want to be managers, and not enough people want to be train drivers; so any managerial job in a train operating company receives many applicants, but there are not enough staff to actually run the trains. Problems in market relations exist, and need to be theorised about. Such skill shortages represent a form of market failure. How these market failures can be addressed by governments, firms and individuals, equally in some part, will depend on the theoretical position adopted. There is often a primary concern with the policy implications, with an argument for interventions by governments, to help make training 'pay' (see Box 10.7). For firms the conceptual and theoretical concerns increasingly involve discussing 'intellectual capital' (see Box 10.8).

Box 10.7

Does training pay?

One analysis of the current state of knowledge on the economic benefits of training identified major gaps in our knowledge of this issue. The economic benefits are threefold:

- to the individual in terms of higher wages and better job prospects
- to the firm in terms of increased productivity and profitability
- to the economy as a whole in terms of higher economic growth and other benefits to society as a whole

There is a lack of data and evidence to back up claims that training 'pays', from an economists' perspective, in any of these respects.

The most important major gap in the literature is that little is known about the cost side of the training equation. Information on the benefits of training is merely the first step in terms of calculating the overall private (and social) return from training investment. The research community need to obtain better measures of training. For instance, data need to differentiate more effectively between the different types of employer provided training.

'The primary research objective should be to say something considerably more than "training pays". One needs to be able to inform individuals, firms and policy-makers as to which types of training yield what level of private and social returns'.

Source: Machin and Vignoles (2001)

Chapman (1993) argues that L&D at work has received little attention from economists. There are different economic approaches to analysing L&D at work that could be better explored as the bases for policy. The first is the market failure approach, explaining shortfalls in training provision and highlighting several areas of fact. The facts are that the UK lags behind other countries in its provisions, for example, in the proportion of young people participating. There has been an increase in some forms of training; job related in the 1980s, but there is a bias to academic achievement not vocational training, as shown for example by HE expansion. Large numbers receive no training, or only for low level qualifications.

This happens because at existing costs individuals cannot afford training they would otherwise undertake. There is also the free rider problem; firms fail to train as they fear poaching. There are contract restrictions; employers and employees ideally need continual re-contracting to reflect changes in value, but this works against advantages of fixed wages. Market failure as a consequence of these explains the dominant fact, the under provision of training. It implies that interventions in markets will be the remedy, and cooperation among various stakeholders is required for such a remedy.

Another framework is human capital theory, developed in the 1960s. This argues that individuals are wealth maximisers who calculate the value of different training options. In this context training is either general and portable or specific and non-transferable. In general training there is an increase in trainees' marginal productivity, by the same amount for any firm. This benefits workers (through higher earnings), so it should be paid for by workers. With specific training there is a productivity

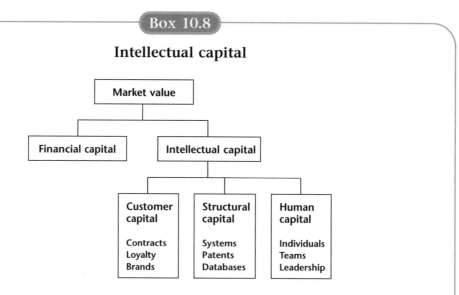

Box 10.8

Intellectual capital

New models of enterprises and how they create value raise the concept of 'intellectual capital'. Instead of seeking to define value in terms of short term profits, and seeking to define gaps between balance sheet values and market valuation, there is a concern with the 'intangible assets'. Traditional accounting systems are challenged to find ways of describing ands valuing intellectual capital as an asset of the organisation. Increasing intellectual capital, through learning, rather than cost cutting or the introduction of new technologies, becomes a strategic imperative. The growth of intellectual capital, in theory, depends upon ED in practice.

Source: Mayo (2000)

increase, of use only to the host firm; the firm acquires the gains from training, so it should meet the costs. The fact is that earnings follow a lifecycle pattern, rising to a maximum and declining. This is because wages are determined by human capital, which depends upon education, training and job experience, as attainment in these leads to higher productivity. Individuals with higher skill levels may be rewarded with higher wages in recognition of their superior productivity. So human capital acquisition, training and education are investment decisions. In the 1960s this purported to explain why there was such a spectacular recovery of post WW2 defeated nations; it was human capital that was the significant factor, not physical capital. It also explained the Third World trap; they needed human capital aid, not physical aid. It also explained lifecycles of earnings: low for the young, increasing, then a decline.

The implication was that certain 'externalities' impeded the operation of a rational system. Individuals could not get the resources to increase their human capital; capital markets do not give credit for training. And inter-firm factors applied as well; using the prisoners' dilemma model and game theory, both should invest in training to increase human capital, but both fear doing so, and therefore pursue sub-optimal strategies, both losing out.

The institutional school sees differences in L&D being explained by the emphasis on external or internal labour market forces; L&D will be carried out within the firm where recruitment is limited to certain ports of entry. For occupational labour markets wages are set by market supply and demand, so wages will be equalised across firms due to mobility. But once hired the internal labour market becomes paramount; progress to different skill levels, and inter-firm differences in this respect, mean that wages vary, reducing mobility. Firms seek to buy in cheap at certain levels, to develop specific skills through learning by doing, then to protect their internal market against poaching.

THEORETICAL PERSPECTIVES: CONCERNS AND APPLICATIONS

Taking into account aspects of all these different ideas about the principles and problems of L&D at work, there are implications for L&D at work (Billington 2000, Boud and Garrick 1999) which are well established (see Figure 10.2), as are the methods suggested for dealing with these concerns (see Figure 10.3).

Trying to promote L&D at work without understanding these principles and problems is likely to impede adult learning; to create fear of failure and other anxieties, and to promote surface rather than deep learning. These perspectives can all offer something to enable effective adult learning, as they use methods consistent with the principles needed to engage with people and achieve deep learning. These learning theories can be of use for exploring and explaining all aspects of L&D at work, from helping in standard knowledge development based on insights from 'brain friendly learning' to helping the management of the change of the whole person in the occu-

Figure 10.2   *Principles in adult learning*

- Need independence and choice
- Need intrinsic motivators and curiosity
- Need feedback with time for reflection
- Need active involvement in real world tasks
- Concerned with higher order abilities (such as critical thinking, problem-solving)
- Concern with high challenge-low threat environments
- Concern with practice and reinforcement

Figure 10.3   *Methods for supporting adult learning*

- Collaborative learning
- Cooperative learning
- Problem based learning
- Case method teaching
- Peer based methods
- Research based learning
- Portfolio systems

pational and performance context. They can inform the design of learning systems and interventions. They can provide perspectives on issues of motivation and environment, how to diagnose problems to get results, and how to analyse problems with learning transfer. These theories are all ways of exploring how people learn that can be related to better manage learning, either by informing the work of specialists supporting learning, or by providing insights for learners into what they can do to 'learn how to learn'.

CONCLUSIONS

How and why L&D at work works in principle or faces problems provide the spur and questions which lead people to propose and explore theories of L&D. Why are some people failing to learn when they seem to have the capability? Is it the organisation and quality of learning materials? Or is it something to do with failures in the relationships of learning that are being depended upon? Or is it related to the value of what is being learnt being out of synchronisation with what is required vocationally?

Time and again practitioners find something that works, and want to be able to repeat that; so they try to define what it was that worked. Researchers from various social sciences are drawn to research L&D at work, and attempt to apply their theories to exploring topics in L&D at work. The wisdom literature, the psychology literature, the sociology literature and the economics literature all offer something. In a context of change the importance of the accuracy and validity of theories is evident. The exemplary case of this is found in the uptake of e-learning, and the use of information and communication technologies (ICT) to support L&D, as discussed in Chapter 9. There is no doubt that problems in using e-learning and ICT have arisen because of inadequate or incorrect theorising about learning.

Learning about theories of L&D is not then about memorising guides to what to do in each and every situation. Insights from psychology, from sociology and economics can help, as can wisdom theories. But these are themselves only sources for developing an independent and critical intelligence, so that 'facts' can be spotted and interpreted as L&D cases and themes are encountered and analysed. This matters for practitioners who are designing L&D interventions that draw upon appropriate learning methods, with an understanding of their strengths and weaknesses. It matters for managers when diagnosing problems with implementing L&D systems in organisations. And it matters for Government and others when it is necessary to critically evaluate the application of innovative solutions to L&D demands, such as introducing e-learning. The role of good theories of L&D is to be able to provide a perspective from which to critically evaluate in an organised and informed way the facts of learning that arise for analysis (see Box 10.9).

Box 10.9

Theory needs research

Human sciences are invested in because theory is needed to inform practice; there is nothing as useful as a good theory. In L&D research there are various users, influencers and partners who shape what research is done.

This research may be quantitative research, based on exploring labour market information and surveys. It may be qualitative research, in the form of analysis of case studies. It may be research undertaken in the pursuit of problem-solving, and work in partnerships.

There are a number of 'investment gatekeepers', the funding councils who distribute money: research trusts, the Government, and others like the CIPD. The DfES for example manages some key surveys:

- Labour Force Survey (quarterly)
- Skill Needs in Britain (annual)
- Labour Market and Skill Trends (annual)

Source: http://www.dfee.gov.uk/datasphere/lists.cfm

An example of a research council funded project is the Skills, Knowledge and Organisational Performance (SKOPE) project. This is a project to model the interaction of competitive advantage and skills. It aims to advise on implementing competition and skills strategies. It will review the supply-demand for skills and knowledge, and advise on policy and institutions for high skill strategies.

Source: http://www.economics.ox.ac.uk/SKOPE

CONCLUDING CASE STUDY

Learning styles

In planning the design and development of L&D experiences it has long been argued that learning styles should also be understood and accommodated. Learning styles were discussed in Chapter 4. They are defined as different personal preferences for processing. In theory they provide an automatic way of responding to information and situations, favourably or unfavourably. Various ways of characterising learning styles exist (see Figures 10.4 and 10.5).

People all have the same basic perception systems and brains, but yet they can perceive and process information in very different ways. The learning styles theory implies that how much individuals learn has more to do with whether the L&D experience suits their particular style of learning than whether or not they are 'smart'. The concept of learning styles is derived from the classification of psychological types. Learning styles theory is based on research demonstrating that, as the result of heredity, upbringing, and current environmental demands, different individuals have a tendency to perceive and process information differently.

Traditional schooling and instruction tend to favour one style: that which is suited to the abstract, perceiving and reflective processing of information. Other kinds of learning are not reflected in a curriculum design that favours reading books, an instruction method requiring

CONCLUDING CASE STUDY (cont'd)

Figure 10.4 *Learning styles version 1*

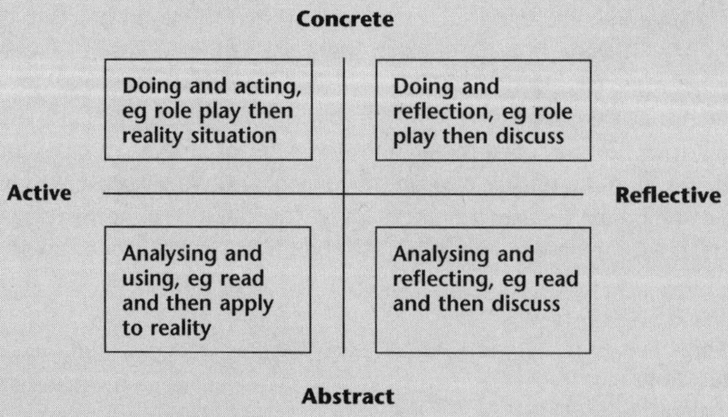

Concrete

| Doing and acting, eg role play then reality situation | Doing and reflection, eg role play then discuss |

Active ———————————————————————— **Reflective**

| Analysing and using, eg read and then apply to reality | Analysing and reflecting, eg read and then discuss |

Abstract

Concrete perceivers prefer to learn from direct experience, by doing, acting, sensing, and feeling
Abstract perceivers prefer to learn from analysis, observation, and thinking
Active processors prefer to learn from making sense of an experience by immediately using the new information
Reflective processors prefer to learn from having an experience then reflecting on and thinking about it

Figure 10.5 *Learning styles version 2*

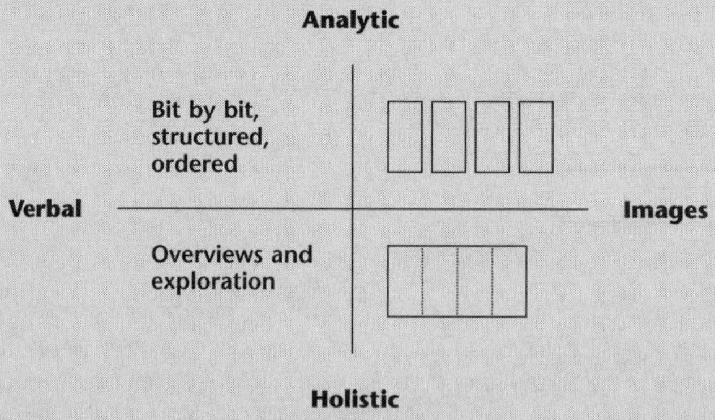

Analytic

| Bit by bit, structured, ordered | ☐☐☐☐ |

Verbal ———————————————————————— **Images**

| Overviews and exploration | ☐☐☐ |

Holistic

Analytic verbalisers like to learn from a bit by bit structure with headings and paragraphs, having a good verbal memory
Analytic imagers like to learn from a bit by bit structure with diagrams and illustrations, having a good picture memory
Holist verbalisers like to learn from overviews and then explorations, with a preference for textual and verbal communication
Holist imagers like to learn from overviews and then explorations, with a preference for diagrams and illustrations

people to sit in classes, and assessment which tests people through written exams. In L&D the implication is that there is a need to take into account other styles, that use intuition, feeling, sensing, and imagination, in addition to the traditional skills of analysis, reason, and sequential problem solving in learning experiences. Designing L&D events to suit all learning styles means

CONCLUDING CASE STUDY (cont'd)

using various combinations of experience and practice, reflection and time to think, conceptualisation and time to debate, and experimentation. Employing a variety of assessment techniques is also a necessary element of this.

Exercise 10.1   Learning styles

Review a recent learning experience you have had and map it against each of the models of learning styles in Figures 10.4 and 10.5.

Was the design of the event one that accommodated all the learning styles of version 1, or did it favour one style in contrast with the others?

Was the event one that would have suited a specific kind of learning style from version 2?

Points of reflection

The ideal is to design L&D which covers all these aspects of learning style, otherwise the design of L&D will favour one form of learning at the expense of others. But to attain that ideal requires:

- defining learning styles and their characteristics; yet there are various models and this is not as straightforward or 'scientific' as it might at first seem
- assessing learners through self tests so that they are aware of their own learning style
- using structures and modes of presentation associated with each, for example presenting graphic overviews as well as 'chunks of text'
- including activities appropriate for each style: graphic presentations, handouts, chances to try things in practice

Further information

http://www.learningbuzz.com/

REFERENCES

Billington, D. (2000) 'Seven characteristics of highly effective adult learning programs', http://www.newhorizons.org/article-billington1.html

Boud, D. and Garrick, J. (1999) *Understanding Learning At Work*, London, Routledge.

Brown, J.S., Collins, A. and Duguid, P. (1989) 'Situated cognition and the culture of learning', *Education Researcher*, Vol. 18, No. 1.

Brown, J. and Duguid, P. (1991) 'Organizational learning and communities-of-practice: towards a unified view of working, learning, and innovation', http://www.parc.xerox.com/ops/members/brown/papers/orglearning.html

Chapman, P. (1993) *The Economics of Training*, London, Harvester Wheatsheaf.

Entwistle, N., Thompson, S., and Tait, H. (1992) *Guidelines for Promoting Effective Learning in Higher Education*, Centre for Research on Learning and Instruction.

Frosh, S., Phoenix, A., and Pattman, R. (2001) *Young Masculinities: Understanding Boys in Contemporary Society*, London, Palgrave (now Palgrave Macmillan).

Gamon, D. and Bragdon, A. (1998) *Building Mental Muscle*, South Yarmouth, BrainWaves Books.

Garger, E. (1999) 'Goodbye training, hello learning', *Workforce*, Vol. 78, No. 11.

Hager, P. (1999) 'Finding a good theory of workplace learning', in Boud, D. and Garrick, J. (eds) *Understanding Learning At Work*, London, Routledge.

Lave, J. and Wenger, E. (1991) *Situated Learning: Legitimate Peripheral Participation*, Cambridge, Cambridge University Press.

Le Doux, J. (1996) *The Emotional Brain*, London, Weidenfeld and Nicolson.

Machin, S. and Vignoles, A. (2001) *The Economic Benefits of Training to the Individual, the Firm and the Economy: The Key Issues*, Centre for the Economics of Education, London School of Economics.

Mager, R. (2000) *What Every Manager Should Know About Training*, Chalford, Management Books.

Mayo, A. (2000) 'The role of employee development in the growth of intellectual capital', *Personnel Review*, Vol. 29. No. 4.

Marchese, T. (2000) 'The new conversations about learning',
http://www.newhorizons.org/lrnbus_marchese.html

Meier, D. (2000) *The Accelerated Learning Handbook*, New York, McGraw-Hill.

Mithen, S. (1996) *The Prehistory of Mind*, London, Thames and Hudson.

Pinker, S. (1997) *How the Mind Works*, London, Penguin.

Strongman, K. (1996) *The Psychology of Emotion: Theories of Emotion in Perspective*, Chichester, Wiley.

Thagard, P. (1996) *Mind: Introduction to Cognitive Science*, Cambridge, MA, MIT Press.

Weed, W. (2000) 'How about a little Viagra for your memory?', *Discover*, June.

Willis, P. (1977) *Learning to Labour*, London, Collier Macmillan.

chapter eleven

Policy in National Vocational Education and Training (NVET)

Learning outcomes

- Describe and analyse the aims and goals of National Vocational Education and Training (NVET) policy
- Discuss the historical and political context for current NVET policy in the UK
- Analyse the politics of 'voluntarism' and its impact on NVET in the UK
- Critically evaluate the evolution of NVET policy and practice in the UK

FRAMEWORK CASE STUDY: GETTING BEYOND BLAME

Show me a skilled individual, a skilled company, or a skilled country and I will show you an individual, a company or a country that has a chance to be successful. Show me an unskilled individual, company or country and I will show you a failure in the 21st century. In the economy ahead, there is only one source of sustainable competitive advantage: skills. Everything else is available to everyone on a more or less equal access basis.

Thurow (1994, p. 52).

National Vocational Education and Training (NVET) policy is the means by which Government seeks to support, through working with other stakeholders, the development of skilled individuals, skilled companies and a skilled country. The UK, currently the world's fourth biggest economy, acknowledges the challenges facing it in these respects. Figure 11.1 presents some key data about individuals.

The record at the company level is equally criticised. At a recent conference on the 'Future of Learning at Work' (Cooper 2001) a variety of research and advisory groups concerned with NVET in the UK who attended were unanimous. They were unanimous in condemning virtually every aspect of vocational and in-company training in the UK. At the country level, involving key planks in producing lifelong learning (see Box 11.1) and a skilled workforce in the country, around the same time the Office of Standards in Education (Ofsted) claimed that their research showed schools were not committed to vocational learning reforms; they used vocational learning schemes only

Figure 11.1   *Key data about individuals*

40%	of adults do not have intermediate levels of skill (craft to associate professional). It is arguably this level of skill that matters most in modern economies
30%	of young people fail to reach basic skill levels by age 19. Clearly this reflects not just a failure in itself, but also an alienation and disengagement from learning that has many consequences
20%	of adults are functionally illiterate and have poor numeracy. Such a level of problem here speaks for itself

Source: DfEE (2000a)

Box 11.1

UK lifelong learning policies

National Curriculum Review
Technology in Education
Work related learning for 14–16 year olds
Education Action Zones
National Record of Achievement
New Start
Family learning projects
GNVQ design and development
Key skills
University for Industry (UfI)
Individual learning accounts
Centres of excellence in IT
EC: LEONARDO DA VINCI
EU Education programme: SOCRATES

Investing in young people
Work based training
Learning card
Careers guidance
Employment Zones
Lifelong learning
SNVQs
HE and employment
National training organisations
National childcare strategy
Skills Task Force
New Deal
CEDEFOP study visits

to keep low achievers occupied. The Training Standards Council (TSC), who monitor the schemes that governments fund but which are delivered by training providers of companies, branded some State funded work based training schemes as 'disgraceful'.

INTRODUCTION

A 'low skills equilibrium' or 'trap' has been identified for some time as a problem in the UK (Esland 1991, Finegold and Soskice 1988). But while the economy boomed and employment soared in the 1990s such a state of affairs, though much criticised (NCE 1993), did not seem that dire. It seemed enough that targets for lifelong learning were set (see Table 11.1) and that overall sufficient progress was being made towards achieving them.

Table 11.1   UK national education and training targets

Target area	Targets (by 2002)	Current
11 year olds	80% reaching literacy standards	71%
	75% reaching numeracy standards	69%
16 year olds	50% with 5 higher grade GCSEs	48%
	95% with at least 1 GCSE	94%
Young people	85% of 19 year olds with a level 2 qualification	75%
	60% of 21 year olds with a level 3 qualification	53%
Adults	50% with a level 3 qualification	46%
	28% with a level 4 qualification	27%
	7% reduction in non-learners	Not known
Organisations	45% of medium sized or large organisations recognised as IiP	26%
	10,000 small organisations recognised as IiP	4,098

Source: NACETT (2000)

But as the 21st century dawned, and with it threats of an economic downturn impacting on existing companies and jobs, the modesty of these targets as drivers for the scale and kind of change that are needed seemed exposed. And the complex system of schemes that has evolved to achieve them seems not only increasingly inadequate, but also to be impeding the achievement of goals. Trying to break away from the acknowledged problems of multiple agencies dealing with the same issues makes it look like people are rearranging the deckchairs on the *Titanic*.

Analysis of culpability in creating this state of affairs identifies all the usual suspects. Some blame those in the education system, for failing to change to providing quality vocational learning experiences (Cooper *op cit*). Others blame successive Governments for not having effective policies, because they have resolved to remain 'voluntarist' (see Box 11.2). That is, they encourage employers and employees in L&D, but do not seek to intervene directly on the 'demand' side. That would require some form of regulation, promoting and increasing levels of investment among employers in L&D. Government has sought rather to influence the 'supply side' by increasing provision of L&D. Others blame employers, for depending on competitive strategies that require only poorly qualified people, and investing in management and professional development rather than more general workforce development. Others blame everyone equally, arguing that all these main stakeholders, education, Government and employers, are all complicit in a 'national culture' that has failed to promote learning.

There is no shortage of people or agencies to blame for these apparently chronic and now acute inadequacies in NVET. Reform and change of NVET require a firm and honest assessment of what has been going wrong before it can be put right. What matters most is getting beyond blame for the existing state of affairs, to ensure that past weaknesses do not come to impede future success. That is the key role of the politics of L&D, and the future evolution of NVET.

NVET POLICY AND PROGRAMMES

National Vocational Education and Training (NVET) policies and programmes can have a major role in effective L&D in organisations. NVET policies and programmes are developed by Government, in partnership with other agencies and stakeholders,

Box 11.2

What does voluntarism mean?
The case of learning representatives

Unions were, at their inception in the 19th century, concerned with learning; with opportunity through improvement and education. In the 1960s and 1970s they were involved in the tripartite approach to training, working with employers and Government to improve investment in training. Then came the 'wilderness years' when unions were sidelined in general by the UK Government and employers, and became occupied with issues other than learning and training at work. With the return of a Labour Government in 1997, and a recognition that learning is again a crucial issue, that has now changed.

The Trades Union Congress (TUC) has established a network of over 2000 learning representatives. They have been giving people advice about training, and about funds for accessing training. The Government is now considering seeking to use these learning reps as part of its strategy to improve on basic skills, by giving them statutory recognition in the workplace. They would have time and facilities to advise and consult with employees, training providers and employers on learning concerns of employees in the workplace.

Employers are resisting this, arguing that it is further regulation of business which is unnecessary and a burden. They do not want training to become a subject of collective bargaining. The Government is seeking to influence those organisations that do not train, but using the leverage of legislation and trade unions is not the way to do it. They also query whether the concern with problems of literacy and numeracy among the low skilled and low paid is the correct focus for all this in any event.

This all puts into sharp relief the apparent lack of partnership and trust in partnership between stakeholders in employment. Suspicions about 'where it will all lead to' lead to opposition to the basic concept of giving learning representatives a statutory role, which is in any event a minor change compared with integrating training into collective bargaining and consultation systems.

Source: Rana (2001)

---

to support the development of a knowledgeable, capable, and committed workforce. The scope and kinds of initiatives that fall under the NVET umbrella are always changing; indeed for some critics that is part of the problem (CPPBB 1997). However, for the UK, the goal stays the same even with changes of government and of environment and the means of achieving the goal. They aim to ensure that the necessary skills base for effective economic performance exists, so that skills shortages are avoided and opportunities for economic development can be taken.

Concerns about NVET in the UK have been voiced for decades (NCE *op cit*, Mayhew and Keep 1999). These concerns expressed a need to better use L&D to deal with the changing economic environment, involving the effects of globalisation, technological innovation, and a continuing high pace of change. There were also concerns about the changing workforce. As changes in the composition of the workforce, the types of work available, and career structures and patterns, were experienced there was a need for L&D to evolve as well. And there were concerns about a changing society, where an apparent growing polarisation between those 'getting on' and those 'going nowhere', the rich and poor, was manifest in polarised lifestyles, expectations and

> ### Box 11.3
>
> ## The PIU project aims
>
> ■ To fit workforce development into a strategic framework, which is shared by the key stake-holders and grounded in a rigorous and hard-headed analysis of the issues
> This implies that past NVET policy has not been based on hard-headed analysis of the issues, and has not been shared by key stakeholders. The levers of research and the politics of stakeholder partnerships are therefore important
> ■ To ensure Government policy is genuinely strategic; not, as has so often been the case in the past, piecemeal, tactical, disjointed and low impact
> If being piecemeal and disjointed means low impact, then being genuinely strategic means having a greater impact. Strategy is about plans and policy for major goals; however it seems that what matters here is institutional reform, not goal change
> ■ To ensure the analysis of the issues leads to real improvements in workforce development 'on the ground'
> This is in contrast with improvements in the abstract, that produce better looking or sound-ing policy; improvements 'on the ground' means with real people, and real companies
> ■ To engage fully with the different Government Departments with a stake in workforce devel-opment – not just DfES but also DTI which is responsible for most of Government's deal-ings with business, and the Treasury which leads on fiscal and other matters
>
> This is a Cabinet Office review, so the focal concern with improving relations within Govern-ment, to create 'joined up Government' in this area, is logical.

attitudes (Hutton 1997). In combination these factors were driving major concerns about L&D at work in all industrialised countries. Such an environment once more focussed attention on the need to develop the workforce, both to be able to compete effectively in the new environment, and to be able to take advantage of the increas-ing opportunities arising from globalisation and technological innovation.

One initiative to review and relaunch NVET in the UK has been instituted by the Performance and Innovation Unit (PIU), a project management group at the heart of Government in the UK Cabinet Office, discussed in Chapter 1, which has been tasked with a 'workforce development project' (see Box 11.3).

The PIU brief acknowledges that in the past in the UK workforce development has not been grounded in rigorous and hard-headed analysis of the issues, nor genuinely strategic, nor had an impact 'on the ground', nor engaged all relevant Government Departments. The project was set up to change this by first providing a thorough analysis of the workforce development problem and its causes, covering the full range of demand and supply-side factors that determine investment in workforce develop-ment. Then it would examine what has worked well, what works less well and what gaps remain in provision. This would allow the development of policy options based on the aspirations and capabilities of the main stakeholders. The focus would then be developing a coherent strategy that draws together all the key initiatives and actors involved in workforce development.

So L&D at work is central to two major UK Government agendas: the UK's pro-ductivity performance agenda, and the employability and social inclusion or social justice agenda. This is because, 'on the whole' the available evidence suggests there is a positive link between L&D and private benefits for individuals and firms, and social benefits for the economy and society at large.

On some indicators the UK performs well in terms of L&D at work. It has high labour force participation rates, high rates of participation in higher education and high levels of expenditure on L&D at work, comparable with or better than other developed countries. But on many other indicators it does not look good: learning is not central to the business culture of many firms, there are significant inequalities in access to L&D at work as less well qualified individuals are less likely to receive development, and the smaller a firm the less likely it is to invest in L&D. In addition much L&D tends to be job-specific, and the volume of L&D (as opposed to numbers of people participating in L&D) has stagnated in recent years. And institutional weaknesses have resulted in few businesses participating in training networks, which promote workforce development, or accessing and using supportive Government structures.

These problems are all implicated in the UK's productivity problem. The quality of the UK labour force, as measured by the skill mix, compares unfavourably with other countries. Problems exist in both the current stock of people in the workforce and those entering the workforce. The National Skills Task Force concluded that an underdeveloped workforce produces less, works harder and longer for the same pay and attracts less capital investment. Statistics seem to bear this out (DfEE 2000a); for example, output per head is 40 per cent higher in the US, 20 per cent higher in France and 10 per cent higher in Germany than in the UK. For Government all these L&D concerns are not isolated and distinct; they need to be addressed in the wider context of Government and business strategies towards innovation, IT policies and so on.

There is evidence to show that L&D can contribute to enhanced productivity. School reforms have been put in place to support better L&D. But such reforms take time to impact on the quality of those entering the workplace. Equally there is a lot of evidence about the potential contribution of L&D to employability and social inclusion. More L&D means higher earnings. But, at present, the distribution of L&D in the UK tends to reinforce social exclusion. There is a link between skill levels and deprivation. Particular groups, for example the disabled and certain ethnic minorities, are disproportionately likely to have low skills. Such low skills on entering the labour market are correlated with poor employment prospects. The low skilled are more likely not to receive L&D opportunities that might help to overcome their disadvantage. The L&D rich get richer and the L&D poor get poorer. How did the UK get into this position, and are the kinds of issues being explored by the PIU going to be enough to generate change?

The background

The reasons that such a problematic state of affairs with L&D exists, and has existed for some time in the UK, reflect three kinds of argument (see Box 11.4).

Notwithstanding the good intentions of those now involved with the PIU and other exercises in NVET in the UK, a 'skills revolution' has been sought for some time but the UK still lags behind. It lags behind in producing a skilled and educated workforce, particularly with young people. It lags behind in changing the view that academic education has higher prestige than vocational training. It lags behind in that employers and the State are stuck in an uneasy dance on these matters; who takes the

Box 11.4

Three arguments about problems with L&D

■ **The economic development argument**; the premises are that L&D provisions will match the demands of economic practices, and economic practices in the UK involve low skills. Therefore there is ineffective L&D because employment as a whole, and skills and performance within that, in the UK are trapped in a 'low skills equilibrium'. It does not make economic sense for people to be investing in L&D when organisational strategies and individual career success do not require it.

■ **The flawed NVET system argument**; the premises are that a coherent NVET system has to be constructed by Government, but that in the UK there is no coherent NVET system. Therefore the assessment of needs, design and delivery of NVET are bound to be flawed. While NVET is a key part of the political agenda, the system that emerges, of agencies, initiatives and policies, only provides inconsistent and confusing, poor quality and provider driven NVET.

■ **The social factors argument**; the premises are that L&D provisions can only have an impact if people are motivated to and in a position to participate in L&D, but in the UK many people are neither motivated nor able to participate. Therefore the NVET system fails above all else because it encounters the challenges of social exclusion, where the vulnerable and disadvantaged are alienated from and will not engage with learning. Until NVET policy deals effectively with social inclusion issues as much as economic development concerns it will always be hampered and obstructed. Providing opportunity has to be an engine of policy.

lead, and who pays? It lags behind as there is congestion within the field of local economic development; there is confusion, overlap, duplication and even active competition between the many agencies involved. These arguments have been long debated (Shackleton 1992, Steedman 1993) and they are now generally collated into one argument; the premise is that all these factors matter, and that on all these factors the UK is deficient. The conclusion is that all these factors matter equally and need to be addressed (DfEE 2000b).

To understand the current situation the historical background to NVET policy and practice needs to be explored. The point of reviewing this history is arguable. One view is the optimistic view, that those who do not understand history are condemned to repeat it; analysing history informs intelligent analysis. On the other hand is the pessimistic view, that the only thing we learn from history is that we do not learn from history; the same patterns are repeated no matter how much historical insight exists. The approach taken here is to briefly review the distant, the recent and the immediate history of L&D. The distant past which influences recent concerns needs to be analysed. Recent concerns with change and unemployment have shaped the system substantially, and influenced what happened in the 1990s, where a complex web woven of programs and agencies was created.

The distant past

There is an image, part factual and part mythical, of a pre-industrial 'golden era' when L&D was an organic part of the lives of working people, in an agricultural and home based crafts economy. Learning was something that happened within families or within guilds. Capabilities and knowledge, and behaviour as well, were shaped within these close, personal environments. There were no schools or colleges, no exams or qualifications, no government departments or agencies. Colleges, the few that there were, were institutes linked to the mediaeval powers, either royal or religious, for the development of clerics through scholarship associated with the 'classical' disciplines. People learned to be farmers, or cloth makers, or tanners, or smiths, or bakers, or masons, or fishers, as a 'natural' and integral part of their lifestyle.

In the broadest sweep of history, with the rise of industrialisation and the development of capitalism, this era ended. Indeed this approach to L&D had to be radically transformed as part of industrialisation and the rise of capitalism. The reasons why and the effects of this are many, but two in particular matter most for understanding the subsequent history and current state of L&D in the UK. First is to do with the requirements of efficiency in mechanised production in the factory systems and the large scale bureaucracies and 'clerical factories' required for business and government. Adam Smith famously gave the example of the pin maker. Where in the past a single person would complete all stages of pin making, using various skills, a division of labour among several people was proposed as being much more efficient. Each person would complete only one stage; concentrating on this alone enabled them to be much more productive. So several people now made one pin in a 'production line' process rather than several people all making their own whole pins.

Because this was much more efficient it took less people in total to make the same number of pins. This was a shift from a system based upon individuals completing all stages of a process, with all the L&D that required and the skills it involved, to a system based upon a division of labour with little requirement for L&D of the individual. It was a shift that killed stone dead the requirement for the complex development of independent and multi-skilled working and gave birth to the world of employment in unskilled 'production line' type environments. But the accompanying social upheaval, involving the destruction of small town and country jobs and ways of life with the shift to urban and factory environments, had greater and well documented consequences. As unemployment, poverty, health and safety, and crime provided more pressing issues for policy makers and campaigners, as people came to terms with the onset and evolution of industrialisation and capitalism, the question of L&D seemed marginal.

The decline and eradication of old systems of development and a lack of concern with L&D in policy were, however, offset by the other side of industrialisation and the development of capitalism. This was the drive to increase wealth through the creation of profit making firms which required and involved an increase in knowledge, the development of new skills and the establishment of new patterns of behaviour. An era where the quality of the workforce would matter as much as technological innovation, requiring greater investment in L&D, was born. This was the age when science and scientific research into materials, production processes, and engineering were complemented by the growth of institutions and industry in areas such as banking and finance. These pillars of industrialisation and capitalism required literate, numerate and knowledgeable professionals. They also required armies of literate, numerate and skilled clerical and administrative staff to push all the paper that had to be processed for the engineering innovations, the factories and the institutions to work. How were these people to be developed? The answer was to be investment in mass education, in the development of technical schools, the evolution of colleges and universities, and the development of L&D at work.

At the onset of industrialisation and capitalism there was then a tension between forces undermining and precluding investment in L&D and forces dramatically increasing the requirement of investment in L&D. The skills and knowledge involved in manufacturing cloth were made redundant, when all that was required was a 'hand' to mind a machine that did the work. But the skills and knowledge required to make the machines and manage the legal, financial and operational aspects of such manufacture were now in demand.

Through industrialisation the guild system for managing L&D, where L&D was the responsibility of independent masters in trades and professions, was superseded by the growth of large employers. But the issue of apprenticeships in the new major industries where crafts were practised, the factories and shipyards, the publishers and mines, became an interface where employers and trade unions came to contest their different interests. For trade unions controlling the time serving of apprentices was one way of guarding their existing members' interests, pay and conditions of work. For employers there was an interest in enforcing their control of work and changes to methods of work by challenging job demarcations and the kinds and levels of skill needed for jobs.

These kinds of tensions persisted throughout much of the 20th century. They formed the background to ongoing debates in economic and social policy, though major events tended to bring them into starker relief. The three primary events for the UK were WW1, when there was an influx of the unskilled into the labour market and into organisations. The problems with using such an unskilled workforce, or creating systems to develop one, were evident then; as was the opposition of trade unions to 'dilution', to using unskilled and untrained people to do the work of skilled craftsmen. Next there was the depression in the 1930s. The causes of this economic collapse were many, with mass unemployment as one of the greatest effects. To respond to this, and to provide some foundation for moving on to recovery, the issue of L&D was important. In this respect the era is remembered for the development of Government training centres, of intervention designed more to get people off the streets rather than fit any specific strategy for an L&D led economic recovery. Finally there was the period of WW2. Once again the need to draw upon an influx of new people into work organisations exposed labour market deficiencies, with many being unskilled. This period is most remembered for the influx of women into the workforce, proving their worth and value in a whole range of occupations they had never been considered suitable for before.

After each of these major events things returned to 'normal'; that is, with little concern for or investment in L&D to improve the skills of the labour force, or to consolidate new people in the workforce. But later, during the 1960s, concerns about the economic consequences of performance problems in industry as a result of skills shortages arose finally to real and sustained prominence in the UK. The solution to these was seen then to lie with intervening to make employers invest in L&D. The 1964 Industrial Training Act was passed by a Labour Government. This established a network of training boards for the main industries and sectors of employment in the UK. Their purpose was to promote investment in L&D by monitoring employers' spending on training, and raising a levy for investment in L&D.

Recent concerns: change and unemployment

In the 1970s the concern remained, but the institutional context changed; from a concern with the investments of employers in training to the role of Government in dealing with the unemployment which was accompanying the decline of traditional heavy industry. In 1973 an Employment and Training Act was passed. This had the practical effect of both reducing the levy on employers and of sidelining employers from a central role in dealing with L&D issues. Instead there was to be a Manpower Services Commission (MSC) as the central leading body dealing with training and unemployment concerns. Here are the origins of the proliferation of schemes and agencies which, over the next three decades, would be set up, expand and contract, be renamed and relaunched almost constantly. By 1981 the need to change the institutional context again was evident, and another Employment and Training Act was passed. This created Industry Training Organisations (ITOs), which were to be a new means of re-involving employers more in the analysis, design and delivery of training in the UK. Then in 1986 the National Council for Vocational Qualifications was set up. In the face of persistent criticisms of the quality and quantity of vocational education in the UK this body was to establish a coherent and comprehensive system of vocational qualifications.

The 1990s: complex web weaving

By the early 1990s reviews deemed much NVET activity to have been a failure. The new strategy was to give more emphasis to the role of ITOs, and to create new employer led bodies, Training and Enterprise Councils (TECs), in Scotland Local Enterprise Companies (LECs). Through the 1990s TECs/LECS were meant to provide business led, local leadership to organise and implement schemes to deal with skills deficiencies in local economies. To provide a national strategy for this a set of national targets was established by the National Advisory Council on Education and Training Targets (NACETT), in Scotland the Advisory Scottish Committee on Education and Training Targets (ASCETT). In addition a major new initiative was the development in 1993 of the Investors in People (IiP) standard. This standard was considered in detail in Chapter 8; it was meant to be a way of promoting best practice by assessing accrediting organisations through an external inspection. Participation in IiP was to be at the discretion of an employer, it was not to be compulsory or regulated like health and safety policy was.

Yet barriers to achieving goals still seemed to exist. There were further attempts at institutional reform to break these down. In 1996 the Department for Education and Employment (DfEE) was created, with the intention of ending the 'schism' in thinking and policy about training and education that had been enshrined in two separate departments dealing with each issue. In an illustration of the constant name changing occurring, this department is now known as the Department for Education and Skills (DfES). When in 1997 a Labour Government was elected, the first for 18 years, the opportunity for wholesale reform of the NVET system was possible again. They initially settled for 'refining the system', to be relevant to what they called the 'learning age' rather than undertaking wholesale change (IRS 1999). By the creation of a 'learning age' is meant the establishment of a culture where everyone recognises and takes responsibility for their own L&D. Work by the National Skills Task Force to provide research and evidence about NVET effectiveness was funded. A Learning and Skills Act was passed in 2000. Among other things this established Learning and Skills Councils (LSCs) to replace TECs (Rana 1999). There was also an investment of resources, and of hope, in the era of the Internet and the 'e' business boom; that the use of technologies could offer a new route to better NVET performance.

Stewart (1999) reviews this history as one demonstrating all the key flaws of a 'voluntarist' approach. Voluntarism does not mean abstaining; it means a policy of encouragement by the State but a dependence on others to fulfil expectations. In practice, when this fails to materialise, the Government set about constantly changing policy. Voluntarism also does not mean there is no State responsibility; the State role in education, and in responding to unemployment is evident. What it does mean is an evasion of leadership in a dual system, where both the State and employers are partners. There is an uneasy dance about who should do what, who should take the lead. Another aspect of voluntarism is that it appears to be neutral; taking no stance on where L&D investment should go, as that is a question for employers or their representatives. But in practice there has been a less than neutral policy, that undervalues skills development. The 'higher education' of professionals has always attracted more middle class angst, and therefore more political attention, in the UK than deficiencies in intermediate level development of skills, creating the 'Cinderella' sector of further education because of the low status of vocational education.

NVET policy has therefore been hamstrung by the rivalry between political philosophies, between 'laissez faire' opponents of State intervention and liberal proponents of a social agenda for L&D. This has been largely fought over interpretations of what 'voluntarism' should involve, rather than taking issue with voluntarism itself. For the laissez faire opponents of State intervention in L&D, NVET should happen 'naturally' in the interests of all as market forces drive investments and activities, and employers have a key role as they have the greatest knowledge of and interest in NVET. NVET activity should be left free to track labour market supply and demand dynamics; wherever earnings and employment are growing there will be NVET. Voluntarism is preferred to its alternatives. One is greater State intervention, that would involve greater taxing and spending. The other is a corporatist model, such as that found in Germany, which involves a degree of assumption of control and responsibility by employers for things that employers see that the State should rightly be concerned with. The conclusion is that there is no role for intervention through legislation on NVET, nor the establishment of individual 'rights' in matters of NVET.

Liberal proponents of voluntarism argue that the fact is that markets fail, for various reasons, to provide the necessary NVET. Instead of a natural evolution of NVET, and change in it being driven by change in labour markets, there are many failures; the skills required by employers are in shortage because the NVET system is not developing them. Interventions by Government are then needed to deal with these market failures, to shape and centrally allocate resources to the NVET system. Laissez faire voluntarism does not deliver sufficient NVET quantity or quality. Some employers train, some do not. Some programmes are good, some are bad. There is value in the State and employers working together through institutional developments such as SNVQs, IiP, and the National Training Awards.

Stewart's conclusion was that the UK was now, at last, seeing the development of a clear, coherent and comprehensive NVET system. The muddle of different kinds of voluntarism was not resolved, but the new system was well supported by employers, Government and institutions in a range of areas. The 'cultural' blocks were being overcome, though there were still reservations; S/NVQ takeup is still low, the performance of reformed institutions is still problematic, for example ITOs and LSCs, and the 'culture' is still one where the esteem and credibility of vocational qualifications are low and the importance of L&D in the worldview of many employers is also low.

Exercise 11.1   Does the UK need more legislation?

More State investment and intervention might mean, for example, legislation to make IiP compulsory, equivalent to the requirements on employers about health and safety, and an employer responsibility. Or, for example, a new form of levy, in effect a tax, to be centrally controlled and redistributed to high quality training facilities and centres (private or public sector) which employers can then use. Does the UK need more State intervention like this, or less State intervention?

The contemporary agenda: lifelong learning

The problem set in Exercise 11.1 is one which is currently exercising many experts in the area. As was indicated above the Labour Government elected in 2001 set up a task force to review workforce development. For, despite many decades of reports and surveys, it is apparently still not clear what the problem is or what its causes are. The focus on the role of Government is clear; whether this will mark the end of the voluntarist muddle or not remains to be seen. Certainly as a part of the Cabinet Office, at the centre of Government, the PIU is well placed to take the wider view that a project of this scope requires. It is a 'cross-boundary issue' and the PIU will work with key stakeholders inside and outside Government to reach its conclusions. The way this project is managed involves project teams including staff from several Government Departments, academics and people on secondment from the private sector. The approach is evidence based, outward-looking and focussed on outcomes.

The European agenda

The European Union has an interest in and influence on L&D and NVET policy. The political foundations of EU level government provide a means through which ends in both economic and social agendas can be attained. While a major focus in the past was on standards in employment, and associated matters of employee consultation and representation, the focus is now more firmly on learning. The European Commission (EU 2000) considered the direction of policy and action in the European Union. It concluded that Europe has indisputably moved into the 'knowledge age', with all that this will imply for cultural, economic and social life. Patterns of learning, living and working are changing. This means that individuals must adapt to change, and that established ways of doing things must change too.

The EU discusses these concerns under the umbrella of learning by talking about a move towards 'lifelong learning', as accompanying a successful transition to a knowledge based economy and society. The Commission defined lifelong learning, within an overall European Employment Strategy, as 'all purposeful learning activity, undertaken on an ongoing basis with the aim of improving knowledge, skills and competence'. Lifelong learning is no longer just one aspect of education and training; it must become the guiding principle for provision and participation across the full continuum of learning contexts. All those living in Europe, without exception, should have equal opportunities to adjust to the demands of social and economic change and to participate actively in the shaping of Europe's future. The implication is that Europe's education and training systems are at the heart of the coming changes. The Member States, the Council and the Commission within their areas of competence, need to identify coherent strategies and practical measures with a view to fostering lifelong learning for all.

A memorandum on lifelong learning was circulated. Its purpose was to launch a Europe-wide debate on a comprehensive strategy for implementing lifelong learning at individual and institutional levels, and in all spheres of public and private life. The implications of this fundamental change in perspectives and practices deserve and justify much debate. The Member States, who are responsible for their education and training systems, should lead the debate. The aim is to fix European guidelines and timetables for achieving specific agreed goals, establishing where appropriate indicators and benchmarks in order to compare best practice, and then regular monitoring, evaluation and review of progress. This decentralised approach will be applied in line with the principle of subsidiarity in which the Union, the Member States, the regional and local levels, as well as the social partners, will be actively involved, using variable forms of partnership.

The EU case for implementing lifelong learning is similar in some ways to the current UK concerns, but is different in other ways. The EU argues that promoting active citizenship and promoting employability are equally important and interrelated aims for lifelong learning. The UK context tends to emphasises competitiveness and organisational performance. Member States agree on the priority, but have been slow to take concerted action. They then argue that the scale of current economic and social change in Europe demands a fundamentally new approach to education and training. Lifelong learning is the common umbrella under which all kinds of teaching and learning should be united. Putting lifelong learning into practice demands that everyone work together effectively, both as individuals and in organisations. This is then analysed in terms of six key messages which offer a structured framework for an open debate on putting lifelong learning into practice, with priority areas for action. A comprehensive and coherent lifelong learning strategy for Europe has various aims (see Box 11.5).

A framework of partnership is needed to mobilise resources in favour of lifelong learning at all levels. The memorandum closes with examples of how European level actions can assist Member States to make progress. Working together to put lifelong learning into practice is required to build an inclusive society which offers equal

---

Box 11.5

Lifelong learning: European aims

- Guarantee universal and continuing access to learning for gaining and renewing the skills needed for sustained participation in the knowledge society
- Visibly raise levels of investment in human resources in order to place priority on Europe's most important asset – its people
- Develop effective teaching and learning methods and contexts for the continuum of lifelong and lifewide learning
- Significantly improve the ways in which learning participation and outcomes are understood and appreciated, particularly non-formal and informal learning
- Ensure that everyone can easily access good quality information and advice about learning opportunities throughout Europe and throughout their lives
- Provide lifelong learning opportunities as close to learners as possible, in their own communities and supported through ICT based facilities wherever appropriate

opportunities for access to quality learning throughout life to all people, and in which education and training provision is based first and foremost on the needs and demands of individuals. This in turn means a need to adjust the ways in which education and training are provided, and how paid working life is organised, so that people can participate in learning throughout their lives and can plan for themselves how they combine learning, working and family life. This, it is argued, will help to achieve higher overall levels of education and qualification in all sectors, to ensure high quality provision of education and training, and at the same time to ensure that people's knowledge and skills match the changing demands of jobs and occupations, workplace organisation and working methods. Ultimately it will encourage and equip people to participate more actively once more in all spheres of public life, especially in social and political life at all levels of the community, including at European level.

The key to success is argued to be the same at the European level as it is at the UK level: to build on a sense of shared responsibility for lifelong learning among all the key actors. These include the Member States, the European institutions, the social partners and enterprises, regional and local authorities, those who work in education and training, voluntary organisations, associations and groupings. The shared aim should be to build a Europe in which everyone has the opportunity to develop their potential to the full and to feel that they belong. This European agenda clearly emphasises the broader social and political aspects of better L&D at work.

CONCLUSION

Describing and analysing L&D from the perspective of NVET policy is not easy. In the present situation NVET appears as a mosaic of overlapping initiatives, an alphabet soup of acronyms (Golzen 2001), all subject to several different kinds of Government review, all evolved from an equally complex past. Exploring the historical context multiplies the initiatives and acronyms to be understood several times over. Yet the underlying facts are stark: the gaps in L&D in the UK from an economic and social policy perspective are glaring. They are longstanding and, despite many studies, initiatives and policy reviews, what is to be done is still not clear and agreed. Hence the latest PIU study into workforce development and the European Commission consultations on, and promotion of, lifelong learning.

Taking the long view, both looking back and looking ahead, there is a case for arguing that these kinds of problems with NVET are a symptom of the general problem, of the interaction of the key partners in contemporary political economies. Is it important to influence either Government policy or the practices of firms in free market capitalism? Neither alone can provide the L&D at work required, but those seeking to influence either, or indeed both, find it difficult to strike the right balance of partnerships. This was true of the industrialisation era, when nation states were pursuing national interests in conjunction with indigenous firms; and it seems to be true of the post industrial, service based era where regional alliances, such as the EU, seek to deal with the realities of governing a large region where international firms are operating as actors in an open global economy.

The UK's problems seem to reflect a set of circumstances where a commitment to a voluntarist philosophy has made the encouragement of investment in L&D a process bound up with endless institutional reform, hoping to hit the right mix by finally having 'sound' grounds for the right approach to involving individuals, employers and Government in an optimum way. The rationale for the PIU review is not original. But even with the PIU review there are evident tensions. On the one hand the brief is to provide 'a strategic, impartial and wide-ranging view' of workforce development and its role. But on the other they explicitly admit that they will seek to develop 'a strongly argued case for the benefits of workforce development, with clear links to productivity and economic performance'. There is a contradiction in that: they are assuming what they seek to prove, that investment in workforce development and skills is the answer. The point is that, no matter how strong the argument for L&D, other political and economic forces and factors exist.

The PIU will be seeking to make 'a step change to UK workforce development, bringing the UK up to best international standards in workforce development and so bringing about tangible and measurable improvements in productivity, competitiveness and opportunity'. Yet this is the goal that has always been pursued, and with some intensity, since at least the early 1970s. The point made in Chapter 5 about the 'tyranny of numbers', about how quantifying drives out analysis of what is important and replaces it with the futile analysis of what can be measured, is applicable here.

The kinds of issues that face such attempts to reform and reconstruct NVET policy for the 21st century in the UK can be understood by reviewing the concluding case study. This attempts to provide an analysis on a scale that relates the realities of NVET to the experience of what happens in a specific city.

CONCLUDING CASE STUDY

The learning city?

It is challenging to try and visualise and analyse themes and issues in NVET as a whole. In looking at the UK as a whole, for example, the PIU is drawing upon a specialist core team, an advisory panel, a panel of experts and a 'reality group'. And even then, for these most well informed people, it's confusing. One option is to bring the level of analysis down a step; to look at the example of a city and what happens in that city. The city discussed here is Glasgow, a regenerating metropolitan area which is trying to respond to the era of 'lifelong learning'. Reform to untangle the complex web of NVET policy and practice is a central concern.

Case study questions

The questions you should bear in mind as you review the case of Glasgow as a 'learning city' are:

1 Who are the main actors in NVET in this city, and what roles do they seem to have?
2 Is the NVET system being described here clear, coherent and comprehensive?
3 Does the net effect of the NVET activity going on convince you that the city is a 'learning city'?
4 What could be done to improve the NVET system in Glasgow?

Background

The context is one of a metropolitan area with a population of 518,000, of whom 318,000 live within the current city boundary. In this area there are 16,000 businesses, producing an output of £6.7 billion annually, with employment in them distributed by classification as shown in Tables 11.2, 11.3, 11.4 and 11.5. In addition to this distribution of employment Glasgow is a city with 30,000 self employed people and 95,000 students. The three universities in Glasgow manage £420 million of income, with 16 per cent of this from research grants. Strengths are in science and engineering.

Table 11.2   *Employment in Glasgow*

Sector	Number
Primary sector	5,665
Manufacturing	31,288
Construction	15,364
Services	259,862 (including call centres 10,000)
Total	312,179

Table 11.3   *Employment distribution in Glasgow*

Sector	%
Public administration	30.8
Banking, finance, insurance	22.1
Distribution, hotels, catering	20.3
Manufacturing	9.8
Transport and communication	5.5
Construction	5.2
Other services	5.1
Energy and water	1.0
Agriculture and fishing	0.1
Total	100.0

Table 11.4   *Structure of the workforce in Glasgow*

Category	%
Professional, managerial and administrative	34
Personal services, sales, drivers	
Industrial plant and machine operators	27
Clerical and secretarial	17
Engineering and construction (skilled)	11
Elementary occupations	11

CONCLUDING CASE STUDY (cont'd)

Table 11.5   *Additional figures for Glasgow*

Category	%
Workforce gender	48.4% Male
	51.6% Female
Unemployment	12.9% (ILO definition)
Long term unemployed (over 1 year)	29% of all unemployed
Qualifications	25% have no qualifications at all
	Only 30% of 21 year olds have
	level 3 or above

Source: SEG (2000)

The tangled web in a city: NVET schemes and agencies in Glasgow

In Glasgow, as in most of the UK, there are a range of national programmes available and running. These have varying objectives, different participant eligibility, and different sources of funding. The main ones are:

- Skillseekers
- New Deal
- Training For Work
- Training and Employment Grants Scheme
- European Structural Funds (Strathclyde European Partnership)

Glasgow also provides a number of local programmes with related objectives, participant eligibility, and funding. The main ones are:

- Glasgow: The Learning City
- Glasgow Employment Zone
- Glasgow Works

Each of these programmes is now outlined in turn.

Skillseekers

Skillseekers is a training programme for young people. All young people between 16 and 24 are able to participate, though priority is given to school leavers aged 16 to 18. Skillseekers is the national approach to training young people that represents a major investment and is the largest single initiative run by the agency Scottish Enterprise Glasgow in a partnership approach. It aims to equip young people with the skills, knowledge and capabilities for employment. The Government provides a direct contribution towards the cost of training young people. It is meant to help employers achieve more flexibility, efficiency and greater productivity through providing them with skilled people. People on the scheme are working towards the achievement of Vocational Qualifications (VQs) at Levels 1 to 3, depending on the young person's abilities and aspirations.

CONCLUDING CASE STUDY (cont'd)

New Deal

The New Deal was set up with the aim of getting people off benefits and into jobs. It would do this through providing access to jobs, training, further education and work experience. The New Deal is delivered by local partnerships of businesses, Local Enterprise Companies (LECs), local authorities, career service companies, job centres, voluntary organisations and training providers.

For young people the New Deal means entering 'the Gateway', a period of intense advice, guidance and support in helping them find a job. This will help participants in the search for work, and prepare them to obtain maximum benefit from New Deal. It is expected that many young people will move from the Gateway into a job. Otherwise they will then move on to a subsidised job with an employer, or work with the Environment Task Force, work in the voluntary sector, or full time education or training to obtain a recognised qualification. Employers are given a subsidy of £60 per week for up to six months for each full time New Deal employee. They also receive £750 towards the training costs of each person recruited. It is stipulated that the job must include a period of training equivalent to one day a week towards an approved qualification.

Training for Work

This scheme aims to provide companies with people who will satisfy their requirements. It is aimed at adults over the age of 25 who have been out of work for over six months. The Government provides unemployment benefit plus an additional £10 plus help with expenses. Employers may be expected to make a contribution towards the cost of the training. The training is provided by colleges, industrial bodies, employers and commercial training providers, either to national standards or to the standards and skill levels required by local employers. The scheme is open to all sectors of business within Glasgow city boundaries.

Training and Employment Grants Scheme (TEGS)

This aims to provide employment opportunities with training for long term unemployed people in specific areas of the city, and to address specific skill shortages among employers in those areas. It involves providing a subsidy to employers of up to 60 per cent of the wage costs of the employee for up to the first 26 weeks. TEGS also provides a training grant of 100 per cent for the first year. This can cover the costs of external training and also any in-house training. The scheme is open to businesses which recruit unemployed people resident in TEGS designated areas.

There are grant conditions. The number of employees recruited under the TEGS programme must not be more than 30 per cent of the employer's total workforce. New recruits should live within a TEGS postcode area and be aged 25–64 and registered unemployed for at least 26 weeks or returning to the labour market after a break. The training programme associated with the job involves around 200 hours of structured training. The employer must demonstrate that the proposed employee is additional to the existing workforce and that the job is full time and permanent.

CONCLUDING CASE STUDY (cont'd)

Strathclyde European Partnership (SEP)

SEP is an organisation which seeks to access European Structural Funds to complement private sector and public sector funding for training in the Glasgow area. This funding has some general objectives: to help regions needing most help generally; to help regions with urban or rural problems, and to improve people's skills. European aid may come in two forms: from the European Regional Development Fund (ERDF) or from the European Social Fund (ESF). Funding from the ERDF is given for creating or maintaining jobs, starting or growing businesses, developing sites and developing facilities. Funding from the ESF is provided for supporting training and learning, helping the long term unemployed, helping young people and helping those who are socially excluded.

An example of ERDF related help was the development of a log-in cybercafe, for young people to have access to technology and other services. This was meant to provide learning and a fun environment. The ERDF provided £67K. An example of ESF support is the initiative 'Glasgow Works'. This is a multi-agency partnership which in 1999 provided 500 intermediate labour market (ILM) places in 26 work projects. It required funding of £3.8 million.

Glasgow: the Learning City

Responding to lifelong learning is not restricted to the workplace and schemes for getting people into work. It is relevant to everyone at all stages of their lives. To address these aspects of being a 'learning city' developments in Glasgow relevant to ED include the 'University for Industry', Glasgow Telecolleges Network and the Glasgow Education Business Partnership.

The University for Industry (UfI) was established to encourage links between the worlds of work and education and to connect those who want to learn with the means of doing so. It is meant to stimulate the demand for lifelong learning amongst businesses and individuals. It will do this by promoting relevant, high quality and innovative learning, particularly through the use of information and communications technologies. The UfI activities will include:

- analysing the needs of the market and potential customers
- driving the demand for learning
- providing people with information, advice and guidance
- ensuring the availability of, and connecting customers to, high quality learning programmes
- commissioning new learning provision
- ensuring the quality of products and services

The Glasgow Telecolleges Network is an innovative high speed communications network dedicated to education and training. It connects the ten further education colleges in the Glasgow area, providing access to 80,000 users. It is designed to provide a coherent, user-friendly telematics based learning environment. It provides vocational training for SMEs. It is concerned to develop innovative programmes for delivery over the network, and extend learning opportunity to excluded groups. It is linked to the National Grid for Learning and University for Industry.

The Glasgow Education Business Partnership (GEBP) provides liaison between business and schools. It aims to help produce young people with the skills required to enable local companies to remain competitive. It seeks to do this through raising levels of achievement. Its

CONCLUDING CASE STUDY (cont'd)

priorities for the next five years are support for learning and teaching, support for enterprise education, support for transition to work and further learning, and support for lifelong learning and Glasgow as a learning city.

Glasgow Employment Zone

GEZ is another local initiative; it is Scotland's only Employment Zone, one of five such zones in the UK. The GEZ works through innovative partnership approaches aimed at getting the long term unemployed back into the jobs market. These include the already mentioned Glasgow Works, the Glasgow Learning Alliance and the Glasgow Adult Guidance Network.

It involves people aged 25 years and over who have been at least one year unemployed. It includes ex-offenders and other referrals, indirect benefits recipients (partners), people for whom English is not their first language, those involved in large scale redundancies, and returners to work. The programe is voluntary. It lasts up to 52 weeks and carries an additional weekly £15 training allowance for the person on it. It includes built-in specialist support, learning, training and work experience components. It also aims to provide help with becoming self-employed or getting into work.

Glasgow Works

Glasgow Works is a partnership between Scottish Enterprise Glasgow, Scottish Enterprise, Glasgow City Council, the Employment Service, the Scottish Trades Union Congress (STUC) and the private sector. Its goal is to bring together the people that need jobs and the jobs that need to be done. It aims to provide a stepping stone back to work for the long term unemployed. It also aims to create work in activities beneficial to the city and its people.

Everyone taking part pursues the same training and work package, which consists of the following:

- work on an individual project that pays the rate for the job
- related and vocational training, working towards a recognised qualification and other core skills-related training and assessment
- personal development and support to ensure continuous learning
- a strong emphasis on counselling, job search and aftercare, both within the project and through an additional Glasgow Works service
- a minimum of six months support after leaving the project

Glasgow Works is available to people who live within the Glasgow city boundary and who have been unemployed for one year or more. Certain projects are aimed at people who have been unemployed for at least two years. The majority of Glasgow Works projects are located in designated regeneration areas; on average 80 per cent of participants in the projects should also live in the area. It has been assessed as outstandingly effective in getting long term unemployed people back to work. The methods and success are being used to develop similar programmes throughout the UK.

CONCLUDING CASE STUDY (cont'd)

Case answers

1   Is the NVET system being described here clear, coherent and comprehensive?

This overview of one city demonstrates the scope and kinds of schemes and agencies involved in NVET in practice. Everyone agrees that, despite some outstanding successes such as Glasgow Works, it is a tangled web. It is not clear, and it is not that coherent to either learners or employers, though it is arguably comprehensive.

2   Who are the main actors in NVET, and what roles do they seem to have?

Local government	A major player in NVET
Central Government agencies	Determines policy
European Union	Supplies funding
Employers	Provide the employment context
Colleges	Meet local needs
Universities	
New agencies, eg UfI	

3   Does this review convince you that the city is a 'learning city'?

I would expect you to have mixed feelings about this. On the one hand there is a lot going on, but on the other hand the achievements are not there to justify the claim. It is still a city that needs to make the 'step change' rather than one which has made it. Glasgow shows strengths of some degree of coordinated interventions and partnerships, innovation, effective schemes, and dedicated people dealing with economic and social goals. It also shows the weaknesses of current structures of intervention and partnership. The continuing unease on Government's part about taxing to spend on interventions (when unemployment has gone below a million anyway) and employers' unease about the quality of initiatives and the effort involved in participation, can mean that the low skills equilibrium will persist.

The interaction of information problems (what needs to be done), practical problems (who does what) and evaluation problems (what works) reflects philosophical differences (and, of course, different ideas about who pays). I grow increasingly uneasy about the prominence of technological solutions; while acknowledging the potential benefits, there seems to be something of a 'fiddling while Rome burns' feel about this.

4   What might be done to reform the NVET system?

There is a range of possibilities. In fact there are developments, centred on the creation of new 'local economic forums'. These are new bodies with up to ten representatives who will take responsibility for shaking up the whole system and streamlining local economic services in Scotland. These can be reviewed and compared with your ideas. The spirit behind these new bodies is to emphasise action, getting things done, not to agonise over NVET strategy. Their aims are to:

■   streamline local economic services in Scotland; there is currently insufficient coordination leading to overlap, duplication and inefficiencies in the fields of cluttered business services, disjointed learning opportunities and underdeveloped trade and tourism services

CONCLUDING CASE STUDY (cont'd)

- get businesses properly engaged, leave the vested interests at the door, insist on early action and be willing to name and shame. For business time is money; plan the smarter engagement of business, with Chambers of Commerce leading
- membership of the forum: propose a tight core of around ten members from business, local authorities, local enterprise companies, the learning industry and tourism
- top priority tasks: streamline business development services, by setting targets on streamlining existing partnerships and cutting out duplication in service delivery
- early action: forums should assess 'what works' locally and be prepared to let the best locally lead
- new services: efficiency savings can be used to address gaps in existing service
- web based systems: can reach a wider customer base, better with a single door approach and online service delivery
- ministerial leadership and central support for the forums where necessary
- urgency: significant progress expected within the first year

REFERENCES

Cooper, C. (2001) 'Is education really to blame for the great British skills famine?', *People Management*, Vol. 7, No. 16.

CPPBB (1997) *Promoting Prosperity: A Business Agenda For Britain*, Commission on Public Policy and British Business, London, Vintage.

DfEE (2000a) *Skills for All: Research Report from the National Skills Task Force*, DfEE.

DfEE (2000b) *Opportunity for All: Skills for the New Economy*, DfEE.

Esland, G (1991) *Education, Training and Employment, Volumes 1 and 2*, London, Addison Wesley.

EU (2000) *A Memorandum on Lifelong Learning*, European Commission Staff Working Paper.

Finegold, D. and Soskice, D. (1988) 'The failure of training in Britain: analysis and prescription', *Oxford Review of Economic Policy*, Vol. 4, No. 3.

Golzen, G. (2001) ' Eastern premise', *People Management*, Vol. 7, No. 6.

Hutton, W. (1997) *The State to Come*, London, Vintage.

Mayhew, K. and Keep, E. (1999) 'Demand and supply', *People Management*, Vol. 5, No. 8.

IRS (1999) 'Learning comes of age: Labour's skills strategy two years on', *ED Bulletin*, No. 112.

NACETT (2000) *'Aiming Higher'*, NACETT.

NCE (1993) *Learning to Succeed: A Radical Look at Education Today and a Strategy for the Future*, National Commission on Education, London, Heinemann.

Rana, E. (1999) 'Recipe For succession', *People Management*, Vol. 5, No. 16.

Rana, E. (2001) 'Low skills, low interest', *People Management*, Vol. 7, No. 18.

SEG (2000) *Glasgow, The Learning City*, Scottish Enterprise Glasgow.

Shackleton, J.R. (1992) *Training Too Much? A Sceptical Look at the Economics of Skill Provision in the UK*, London, Institute of Economic Affairs.

Steedman, H. (1993) 'Do Work Force Skills Matter?', *British Journal Of Industrial Relations*, Vol. 31, No. 2.

Stewart, J. (1999) *Employee Development Practice*, London, Pitman.

Thurow, L. 1994 'New game, new rules, new strategies', *RSA Journal*, Vol. 142, No. 5454, November.

chapter twelve

The Knowledge Management Perspective

Learning outcomes

- Define and explore the concept of knowledge management (KM)
- Analyse the connections between KM, information systems and performance support
- Analyse the connections between KM and organisational learning (OL)
- Analyse the connections between KM and intellectual capital (IC)
- Critically evaluate the challenges and implications of KM as a way of thinking about the L&D process

FRAMEWORK CASE STUDY: THE REPS' BREAKFAST

Brown and Duguid (2000, 2002) studied the learning of customer service representatives (reps) who fixed Xerox photocopying machines. Customers who were having problems with their machines phoned a customer service centre; they notified a representative, and he or she then went out to the customer's site. The rep would diagnose the problem and follows instructions for fixing it, with the help of 'codes' generated by the machine which reported the machine's state, and supporting documentation which showed what those codes meant. In this system L&D in the course of work seems irrelevant; work is simply about the rep 'following the map' provided by the codes and documentation, and doing what it tells them to do.

But when what actually happened in practice was studied it turned out to look quite different. Reps often only succeeded by departing from what the codes suggested and what the manuals prescribed. They were using knowledge gained from other sources. That knowledge had been generated by reps having to explore and learn what was wrong with a machine, as the codes and documentation were not complete or infallible. Indeed if on many occasions they had followed the instructions they were being given from 'the book', they would have compounded customers' problems, by work being disrupted for longer, rather than solving problems quickly. For while reps had a formal 'map' to refer to, they often fell off it and found themselves without guidance. The generic codes reporting problems and the instructions for fixing that went with them were often inadequate. Large machines made up of multiple subsystems, with different ages, patterns of use and environments behave idiosyncratically, not predictably. Reps had had to learn for themselves, to create their own maps based on diagnosing and fixing problems with these idiosyncratic machines. And the researchers were surprised to find that these areas mapped by the reps were common knowledge; they all seemed to know what to do with particular idiosyncratic machines. How had reps learned what to do when they fell off the map?

They had learned at breakfast. At breakfast with their colleagues before starting their work, reps shared experiences and explored the problems of difficult machines. Reps who knew the peculiarities of each machine would swap stories about what they had done to fix those problems. These brief discussions over breakfast provided more L&D than hours of formal training. While eating, playing cards and gossiping they talked continuously; posing each other questions, offering solutions, discussing their work and telling stories. What might appear to be time-wasting behaviour was in fact keeping each other up to date about what they knew and what they had learned. From hearing about an individual's improvised solution to a tricky problem everyone else could learn. So even in this apparently 'independent' job, where the reps worked alone, and the work did not seem to require any continuous learning, there was a social network in use to support learning, and work and learning were interrelated.

INTRODUCTION

The case of the 'reps' breakfast' raises the subject of knowledge management (KM). The concept of KM has become a prominent context for thinking about and analysing L&D at work (Leonard-Barton 1995, Davenport and Prusak 1998, Scarborough and Swan 1999). The core idea of KM is that in many organisations the key to greater current and future performance is how well their knowledge workers can work in a knowledge based organisation in a knowledge economy (Bell 1974, Little *et al* 2002). See Box 12.1.

Organisations are conscious that they now have technologies and need to develop systems which can help them make the most of the knowledge that has been developed and is held by their workers. It is this intellectual capital upon which many organisations depend for their continued existence and success. Thus the problem is of capturing and codifying new knowledge from employee learning (see Figure 12.1),

Figure 12.1   *Phases of knowledge capture and conversion*

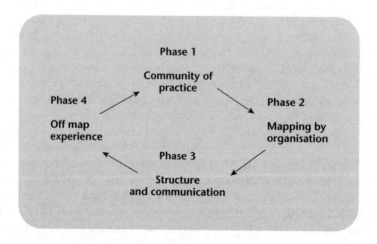

Box 12.1

The KM era

Commentators had for some time been analysing the extent to which the development of economies and firms in the 'post industrial' society (Bell 1974) were becoming knowledge based. The rapid rise of 'knowledge management' in the 1990s has been related to six factors:

- ■ wealth being demonstrably generated from knowledge and intangible assets; for example Microsoft, in 1996, was assessed as having 94 per cent of its market value of $119 billion based on intangible assets
- ■ the rediscovery of people as the locus of organisational knowledge; as organisations down-sized and made many redundant they soon found a need to re-hire them, as 'consultants', because they still needed their knowledge and know-how
- ■ accelerating change requiring continuous learning; the need to create, absorb and assimilate new knowledge, skills and behaviours
- ■ recognition of innovation as the key to competitiveness; innovation depends upon knowledge. This requires a high degree of risk, both in managing current knowledge to innovate and in seeking out the untypical
- ■ the importance of cross boundary knowledge transactions; a dependence on external sources of knowledge, and a need to access and absorb these
- ■ technology potentials and limits; information technology dominates at the moment, but it is knowledge not information that is meant to be the focus. But much knowledge cannot be caught and codified as information. The limits of information management present a need for knowledge management. Technologies used in communication remain a key part of this

Source: Quintas (2002)

---

where the concern is mapping and tapping the knowledge, capabilities and behaviours of employees as they go about their work.

In order to manage the capture and codification of new knowledge from employee learning a process of 'mapping' has to be managed. Phase 1 of this is that it needs to be acknowledged and recognised that communities of practice exist, where new knowledge, capabilities and behaviours are being learned by employees as they work. In phase 2 these knowledge, capabilities or behaviours are to be captured, or mapped. In phase 3 these mapped knowledge, capabilities or behaviours have to then be made available to all the others who may need and use them. But even with such updated learning and knowledge, new 'off map' experiences will then be encountered, once again leading the community of practice, the employees doing the work, to learn and generate new knowledge and skill.

Brown and Duguid (*op cit*) conclude that the kind of learning seen at the reps' breakfast, learning from each other through each others' 'practice' is universal, occurring in all organisations. The issue for managers is to convert this learning into structured information; to use it to expand the map they can provide for all employees to perform effectively. Thus the process of management as a whole can be configured to relate to capturing and using knowledge from communities of practice (see Figure 12.2).

Figure 12.2   *Management functions and knowledge mapping*

Management involves	**Communities of practice involve**
Specifying the way tasks are organised	Exploring the way tasks can be done
Establishing routine	Being spontaneous
Orchestrating work	Improvising at work
Assuming a predictable environment	Responding to a changing environment
Relying on explicit knowledge	Being driven by tacit knowledge
Making knowledge structured and linear	Seeing knowledge as web-like
Top down control of learning	Bottom up generation of learning
Imposing systems	Responding to invention

Figure 12.3   *Perspectives on KM*

Discipline	**Ontology**	**Contribution**	**Problematics**
Psychology	Human development	Cognition, learning styles	Defensive routines
Management science	Information processing	Knowledge, informating	Non-rational behaviour, information overload
Sociology	Social structures	Power, ideology	Conflicts, politics, actors and interests
Strategy	Competitiveness	Environment, experience	Alignments, pressures
Production management	Efficiency	Productivity, design	Measurements
Cultural anthropology	Meaning systems	Cultures, perspectives	Beliefs, hegemony, relativity

Source: adapted from Easterby-Smith (1997)

L&D is therefore not to be thought about by trainers or managers as 'filling up the empty vessels' of the brains of their workforce, but about the management and enhancement of the knowledge assets and intellectual capital (IC) of the workforce (Wilson 1996, McGinty Weston 1994). Many interpretations of KM exist, with different views of what it means reflecting different discipline bases. One recent text provides a review of the psychological, sociological, management science, economic, anthropological, political science and history perspectives as the constituent human sciences reviewing KM (Dierkes *et al* 2002). An article which provides a more concise review (see Figure 12.3) of these is found with Easterby-Smith (1997).

In this broad academic context KM provides an interface between all the disciplines. This is reinforced by the UK's research funding regime focussing upon KM as a distinctive area of research in business and management for research funding. In this sense KM provides a new and distinctive area of study for the human sciences.

And in the context of management concerns and disciplines, the fields of information management, strategic management, change management, HRM, and innovation management are all interfaces with KM. In this sense KM provides a potentially new way of thinking about L&D altogether, in contrast with the past major ways of situating L&D in a context of performance management seen from either a scientific management and 'content', or a human relations and 'process' perspective.

The importance of KM here, in management practice, is that some see organisations as only having a future if they can master knowledge generation and capture (Brown and Duguid *op cit*). The idea is that organisations must redefine themselves as 'communities of practice'. The concept of communities of practice is one that has been around in L&D for some time, and was reviewed in Chapter 10 in relation to L&D. But the argument now is that communities of practice are not only needed to help people learn their jobs and roles.

Exercise 12.1 Communities of practice

Think about an organisation you are familiar with. To what extent are there 'communities of practice' among employees which provide for the creation of new or different ways of working emerging from employee learning? Are there equivalents to the 'reps' breakfast' where employees share learning with each other but not with managers?

Organisations can only perform and achieve their objectives by better facilitating communities of practice. It is groups, not individuals, that create and share 'know-how' and sense making. There is always a collective knowledge base. Organisations can be seen then not as a unified, single community of practice, but as several overlapping and interdependent communities of practice. As models of KM develop, there seem to be three important currents of thinking:

- ■ the information systems (IS) perspective, which emphasises the capture, storage and retrieval of knowledge
- ■ the organisational learning (OL) perspective, which analyses how L&D in organisations is mediated, managed and contested in organisations as sociotechnical systems
- ■ the intellectual capital (IC) perspective, which emphasises the value of IC and the worth of knowledge as embodied in patents and strategic core competencies

The Brown and Duguid example of the photocopier engineers provides an example of each of these streams. The reps' learning needs to be captured and stored and more widely shared. But that is not as simple as just recording what they have learned and putting it on a website; for the reps have certain interests, as do others in the organisation, in retaining some power through having knowledge and getting returns from that. This turns the business of L&D on its head; rather than being about imparting cognitive capacities, capabilities and behaviours to staff, L&D involves learning from staff and sharing that learning.

THE INFORMATION SYSTEMS (IS) PERSPECTIVE

The IS perspective on capturing and codifying knowledge in organisations is analysed by Rosenberg (2001). He suggests a tripartite structure for L&D of instruction through training, performance support through information provisions, and KM. KM can be seen as the pinnacle of a hierarchy of IS and performance management concerns (see Figure 12.4), concerned with creating what he terms an 'intelligent enterprise'.

At level 1 the concern is with creating documents and reports which can be used to inform performance support. Conventional resources such as job aids have always existed at this level. What IS enables is an online resource in a central repository, that people can download. At level 2 people are contributing information and creating new knowledge. This is equivalent to the concern that Brown and Duguid have with mapping what communities of practice are learning. Again conventional activities such as suggestion schemes have always existed to tap knowledge; what IS enables is more extensive and quicker sharing of such knowledge. Finally at level 3 the business depends on the integration of enterprise resource planning (ERP) systems, where IS enabled systems monitor and analyse the performance of all aspects of the organisation's functioning. The organisation has the equivalent of a brain, embodied in the ERP system. In addition the expertise of people is embedded in the system. What people know is logged in the ERP systems, so as well as reporting on data they can allow access to ideas and analysis relevant to any issue. People in the organisation who develop new learning continue to log this, so the system grows organically. Thus KM issues and concerns in performance support range from a concern with better access to existing mapped knowledge, to the wider sharing of newly captured knowledge, to the attainment of enterprise wide OL capacities.

Figure 12.4 *The IS and performance support pyramid*

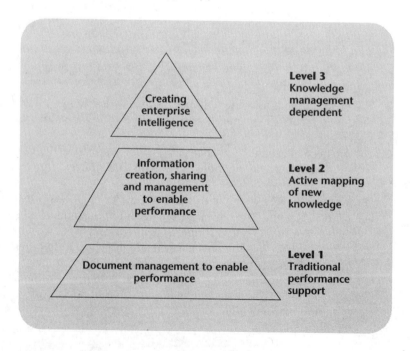

THE ORGANISATIONAL LEARNING (OL) PERSPECTIVE

Discussion of this aspect of L&D, both pre-dating and accompanying the IS perspective, was found in debates about what was involved in 'organisational learning' (OL). The themes and issues discussed here were diverse in their initial form (Senge 1990, Pedler *et al* 1991, Pedler and Burgoyne 1994) and are even more so now. The essence of the concept of OL was that the complex interactions which were involved in the operations of organisations as systems required L&D constantly in a host of ways. L&D was not a discrete function, restricted to trainers providing training. It was the lifeblood of the organisation as an organism.

OL was a focus for systems thinking, for exploring the complexes of connections and feedback loops in organisations, which govern and regulate performance. Performance cannot be magically improved by providing some training courses. There needed to be an exploration of the whole system, and the factors inhibiting or enabling the kinds and level of performance desired. Interventions involving L&D, working on cognitive capacities, capabilities and behaviours, cannot be properly conceived of or implemented without analysing these. Therefore a 'systemic' rather than a 'systematic' approach to KM and L&D is appropriate.

This leads, undeniably, to a different and more elaborate and sophisticated way of thinking about L&D at work. It is also potentially confusing. Having got used to thinking about L&D at work being something systematically done through the mechanisms of the L&D process mapped as a cycle of identifying needs, planning, delivering and evaluating, the tasks seemed to make sense; run training courses, provide on-job coaching or multimedia software packages. But with OL these kinds of activities are displaced by others: systems thinking, action research into problem-solving, trying to 'map and tap' the knowledge of the workforce. For many OL has meant seeking a substitute recipe of prescriptions, or a new 'toolkit', to help manage such systemic learning; learning that is needed as an integral and inherent part of the organisation going about its business. This is in spite of the authors of the varying concepts of OL stating the contrary; that what is involved is the application of a systemic perspective on organisation, not the adoption of a new toolkit for L&D.

There has been a long history of ideas and debate about the OL concept (Argyris and Schon 1974). An industry of 'interpretation' has grown up around the various models that have been proposed (Easterby-Smith *et al* 1997, Harvard Business Review 1998, de Geuss 1999). All that there are, however, are models; no-one claims to be able to point to a complete 'learning organisation'. No templates exist in the way that, for example, the Ford car production line became an exemplification of a certain kind of management and organisation practice. Proponents of OL constructs suggest that they can show 'glimpses', or suggest practices and tools. But the first generation prescriptions have not been up to helping achieve large scale reform.

Burgoyne (1999), one of the key developers of the concept, has acknowledged that the idea has not delivered on its full potential or lived up to aspirations. But he argues it is not an idea whose time has gone. Burgoyne suggests a range of frontiers to address, for example, that organisational politics, the roles of factions and interest groups, have to be better taken into account. New methods have to be developed, beyond conventional L&D methods such as team building and personal development. All these kinds of frontiers are indeed relevant. But at an introductory text level, to avoid becoming entangled in exploring the metaphysics of OL as an abstract and philosophical concept, a preoccupation with tangible and concrete concerns needs to be adopted. The current flux and debate that accompany discussion of KM incorporate

---

Box 12.2

Streams of thinking in OL

The ways in which OL capacities relate to the solution of major business problems have origins in three main streams of thinking:

Traditional organisational analysis

How can we describe the processes and problems of organisational design, structure, culture and development?

The organisational learning idea as another 'metaphor' of organisation; the organisation functions like a 'brain', to learn and regulate itself

Innovative L&D

How can the organisational/work environment be used to enable individual learning?

The organisational learning idea as an embodiment of 'continuous development' in the workplace

'New age' thinking

How can work and workplaces be made better environments for the 'whole person', consistent with the insights of alternatives to traditional Western cultural mores and values?

The organisational learning idea as 'transformations' of workplaces and environments for personal development

These streams of thinking have all had a part to play in generating an idea of OL, and are emphasised to different degrees in different models of what a 'learning organisation' should be.

---

and amplify the flux and debate that have existed in analysing OL (see Box 12.2). Rather than try to review that flux and debate here, the idea of OL is introduced in essence, as a way of thinking about solving major business problems.

Organisations have tangible and concrete business problems about OL in three areas:

1 identifying and dealing with problems while they are still small, minor problems
2 drawing on internal resources and 'tacit' knowledge
3 using systems thinking about snowballing and balancing feedback loops

OL can be seen to provide solutions for all of these tangible and concrete kinds of business problems. Where they are not managed effectively the results can be devastating (see Box 12.3). Some proponents of OL ideas claim that it is a revolutionary idea, identifying the 'learning company' as a new solution to a new 'era' in organisational design and development. Ultimately, it is argued, the learning organisation idea sets an agenda for L&D beyond performance improvements through either training or other forms of performance management support. But for the purposes of this analysis the OL concept is evolutionary; it builds on what has already been done.

First, identifying and dealing with small, minor, fragmented problems is the stuff of everyday organisational life. It is happening all the time in healthy organisations,

---

Box 12.3

Space shuttle *Challenger* disaster

One of the achievements which best illustrates the power of L&D has been the ability to explore space. It brings together the knowledge and skills of the world's foremost experts, the 'rocket scientists' and others, in projects of immense complexity and sophistication.

On January 28, 1986 seven US astronauts died when their shuttle, the *Challenger*, exploded 73 seconds after launch. It was the coldest day in history that a shuttle had been launched. The cause of the accident was the failure of the aft joint seal in the right solid rocket booster in these cold conditions. The boosters, the largest solid-fuel rockets ever used for manned space flight, are assembled in sections, with four fuel segments making up each motor. The O-ring seals are used in the joints between fuel segments to maintain internal pressure and prevent hot gas or flame from escaping in a catastrophic 'burn through'.

Yet, the night before, while the crew slept, engineers from NASA's Marshall Space Flight Centre in Huntsville and Morton Thiokol Inc., builder of the shuttle's giant solid-fuel booster rockets, had held an unscheduled teleconference to discuss the effects of the record cold weather on sensitive rubber O-ring seals in *Challenger's* booster rockets.

The context was that several previous attempts to launch had been aborted. Morton Thiokol engineers unanimously recommended another launch postponement because they feared the O-rings might not seal properly because of the cold weather. But NASA managers from Marshall, where the solid rocket programme is managed, strongly objected to the Morton Thiokol recommendation, claiming the engineers did not have enough data to support their concerns, despite a known history of past O-ring erosion during flight. This philosophy of 'prove it's not safe to fly' was a direct reversal of a long-standing NASA tradition of 'prove it's safe or we won't launch'.

Bowing to pressure from NASA, Morton Thiokol managers who originally voted with the engineers to delay launch, reversed the decision and sent a telefax to the Kennedy Space Centre approving blastoff. Word of the debate was never passed on to higher level NASA managers because the issue was taken to have been resolved.

---

so that people hardly even notice it. From afar the organisation appears a seamlessly efficient operation. Close up, in fact, the organisation is seen to be a hive of activity around large numbers of errors being noticed and dealt with.

Identifying and remedying small problems at source as a strategy for ensuring organisational effectiveness has been addressed primarily by the quality movement over the last 50 years. One way of summing up the whole quality movement is that it represents a desire to identify and eliminate all errors that can be eliminated, continuously improving systems and processes. The oft acknowledged barriers to the detection of small problems, all illustrated by the *Challenger* disaster, are often related to human communication failures:

■ managers claiming 'but nobody told us there was a problem'
■ employees claiming that 'nobody listened to us when we told them'
■ information was available and communicated, but was overshadowed by other concerns that took precedence

Second, there is the question of best using internal resources, the intelligence and knowledge of people inside the organisation. As the *Challenger* example shows, smart people, the smartest possible being the archetypal 'rocket scientists', can fail to be an effective resource. Argyris and Schon (*op cit*) had been concerned with the effectiveness of professionals in modern organisations. Professionals were meant to be the solution to many organisational problems; experts with the knowledge and skill to ensure organisational effectiveness. Indeed professionals' value to organisations was seen to lie in the way that they could help organisations to 'learn', and therefore be more effective. But there was a lot of discontent within professions themselves at the time, and a number of criticisms of their effectiveness within organisations. Doctors in hospitals, engineers in manufacturing or personnel managers in work organisations were often perceived as not being as effective as they could be. One source of this ineffectiveness was thought to lie in the education of professionals, suggesting a need to reform that education. However, Argyris and Schon argued that it was the climate within organisations themselves that hindered the use of professionals. There was little point simply reforming education of professionals; organisations needed to appreciate the ways in which they presented barriers to professionals using their knowledge and capabilities inside organisations.

It was in this context that Argyris and Schon came to outline and model two types of learning. First they modelled what they called 'single loop' learning; this occurs when an organisation detects errors in performance which will compromise the achievement of its pre-set goals. For example, productivity may not be high enough to meet an important order on time. The organisation will have to adopt a new strategy to meet its goals, organising extra shifts or increasing productivity. Identifying and correcting these kinds of 'error' is single loop learning. The organisation is acting, by analogy, like a heating system governed by a thermostat; as long as it acts to maintain the temperature set by the thermostat it is said to be 'single loop' learning. Many performance management systems are elaborations of this kind of learning; to set goals, to get feedback on them, and to then take corrective action to attain those objectives.

But there is also another form of learning. This occurs when an organisation can detect 'errors' in its overall master goals, and respond to those. The authors called this 'double loop' learning. Extending the thermostat analogy, it is the ability to determine that the pre-set temperature is wrong; that it is no good trying to run the system to meet that set temperature, as the thermostat setting, the goal itself, needs to changed. If the environment is too hot or too cold it needs a new thermostat setting to be set. Following the productivity example, there is little point increasing the productive capacity if either the market is declining or a new market is emerging in other products. What has to happen is that the overall goal needs to be reviewed, to look at new product development. Double loop learning does not supersede single loop learning; it complements it.

The problem with many organisations, and the problem for professionals in organisations, according to Argyris and Schon, is that they are not at all good at this double loop learning. They find it hard to question the appropriateness of the governing variables they have adopted, their key goals. Hence they will continue adopting new strategies to try to reach pre-set goals when what they actually need to do is question the goals themselves. Argyris and Schon went on to describe and analyse the ways in which organisations could be seen to be inhibiting professionals' contributions to double loop learning. They concluded that professionals' behaviour in organisations was characterised by what they called 'espoused theories' and 'theories in action'. An espoused theory is the explicit reasons given by people for their behaviour; a 'theory in action' is a description of the beliefs that actually underpin their behaviour, regardless of the 'espoused' reasons which are given. 'Theories in action' reflect what people 'really' think rather than what they say they think (see Figure 12.5).

The net effect is that professionals, and others, behave competitively and are mistrustful. They are then stuck in cycles of either compliance with goals they do not believe in, or find themselves pursuing goals that they know are no longer right but which they seem powerless to change. Even though people may be aware of impending disaster, they cannot use their own internal resources to break free and stop it happening. Individual awareness about these dynamics, and professional development to provide individuals who can manage to support double loop learning, people who can confront its challenges with what would now be called 'emotional intelligence', are the key to creating an environment that supports OL.

Figure 12.5 *Espoused behaviours, theories in action and organisational problems*

Aspect	Espoused behaviours	Theory in action	Problems because of the theory in action	Solution
When defining goals . . .	Collaborate with each other to set goals; review collectively as well	Act unilaterally, set own goals, or only with peers. If someone wants to change these goals that is a threat	An absence of commitment among various parties' goals. People are used to acting unilaterally	Maximise acting participatively, with commitment to common goals
When problem solving . . .	Adopt a win-win outlook; see problem solving as beneficial for all	I need to maximise winning and minimise losing in the course of problem solving	People seek to own and control problem solving, to assure winning and avoid 'losing'	Be able to manage problem solving which can explore failure without 'blame' cultures
The culture should be . . .	Everyone should speak up and be open	I need to minimise provoking others, and therefore eliciting negative feelings towards me	Protect yourself by keeping quiet, keeping things to yourself; do not take the risk of aggravating others	Maximise valid information/ options; people should be aware of and discuss feelings as well as ideas
Conflict should be handled . . .	Rationally; people in formal roles should interact rationally	Everyone else thinks like me; if I (secretly) protect them then they will not attack me	Conflicts do not come into the open. Behind closed door 'politics' arise, which in fact endlessly stoke up conflict	Surface and talk about dilemmas, and get 'politics' out from behind closed doors

Source: from Argyris and Schon (1974)

Finally, there is systems thinking (Cambridge University Press 2000). Systems thinking investigates the principles common to all complex entities by developing abstract models which can be used to describe them. Analysts emphasise that systems are open to, and interact with, their environments. Because of this they can acquire qualitatively new properties through emergence, resulting in continual learning. Rather than reducing an entity, for example the human body, to the properties of its parts or elements, the organs and cells, systems thinking focusses on the arrangement of and relations between the parts which connect them into a whole. The body works as more than the sum of its parts, under the influence of active learning. Socio-technical work organisations can be explored as examples of a system.

Being a system implies that something other than simple cause and effect relations are involved. Rather than A affecting B, there is the possibility that B may also be affecting A. From the mutual interaction of the parts of a system there arise characteristics which cannot be derived from the characteristics of any of the individual parts and one way causal relations between them. The phenomenon is synergy; the whole is greater than the sum of its parts.

There are multiple ways of characterising systems. Systems may be characterised as either closed or open. A closed system is one that does not need to interact with its environment to maintain its existence. Examples of such systems are atoms and molecules. Mechanical systems are closed systems. Open systems are organic, and they must interact with their environment in order to maintain their existence. People are open systems in that they must interact with their environment, for example in order to take in food and water. An open system will interact with its environment in a growing or in a balancing fashion.

There are two types of 'loop' that occur within systems, which mean they either grow or are balanced. First are reinforcing loops. A reinforcing loop is one in which the interactions are such that each action adds to the other; what happens to A adds to B and what happens to B adds to A. Any situation where action produces a result which promotes more of the same action is representative of a reinforcing loop. The 'snowballing' metaphor represents the reinforcing loop. Typical examples of 'snowballing' reinforcing loops are population growth or decline, uncontrolled nuclear reactions, or panic runs on banks in times of financial crisis. This is, for example, what happens in a savings account. The principal in the savings account interacts with an interest rate and the principal is increased. This reinforcing action happens regularly, depending on the period over which the institution computes the interest.

The other form of loop is the balancing loop. This is one in which an action attempts to bring two things to 'agreement'; what reduces A reduces B, and what reduces B also reduces A. As the system state gets closer to the desired state, the gap gets smaller and smaller between A and B, so the action adds less and less. Once the action has moved the current state to a point where it equals the desired state the gap is zero, and there is no more action. A typical example of a balancing loop is closing a gap in space by making a journey from location A to location B. The desired state is to be at B, the actual state is being at A; the further from A, the closer to B, the less action is required to get to the desired state. Another example is developing from being incapable (A) by trial and error (action) until competent (B). The more that the action, trial and error, reduces A the more also it reduces what is needed to get to B.

These effects of actions, leading to snowballing or balancing loops, can combine in numerous ways which result in all manner of typical situation characteristics that can be recognised in daily and organisational life; the escalations that run out of control and attractions to states of satisfying equilibrium. Sometimes snowballing is wanted, sometimes it is not. Sometimes equilibrium is wanted, sometimes it is a form of paralysis. The point of this systems perspective is that it opens up insights into the pitfalls of 'obvious solutions' to apparent problems. 'Obvious solutions' are those which may have a short term effect, may improve situations temporarily, but they make the situation worse in the long run: for example, safeguarding crops from insect infestations by using insecticides, dealing with crime by greater levels of imprisonment, or encouraging economic growth by investing in the 'new' economy rather than the old. These obvious solutions seem to work. But these actions occur within systems, with snowballing loops; using insecticides causes pollution which makes the land useless, or balancing loops as insects evolve immunity. Prisons become schools for criminals and fail to rehabilitate. Investment in the new economy peaks, the bubble bursts, and subsequently slows general economic growth or causes a recession. Where obvious solutions are seen to fail, seek to understand the apparent 'system' in operation, which has not been changed, or may even have been aggravated, by the intervention.

This is the approach of Senge (*op cit*). Situations in organisations exist where systems are in balance, are stable and persist, or they are reinforcing growth and escalation, or they set limits to success and can cause decline. Senge sees organisations as needing to develop a networking culture in which everyone engages in dialogue that questions their own assumptions, to expose and deal with these kinds of systems problem (see Box 12.4)

Systems thinking is synthetic, expansionist, and non-linear. It is synthetic and expansionist in defining problems in terms of clusters of variables, and the interac-

Box 12.4

Systems thinking and learning

One problem in the NHS was with patients who had suffered serious illness and been hospitalised for a long time. When they were discharged they tended to 'yo-yo' in and out of hospital. A group looked at the experience of a 'stroke team'. They talked to patients there. They found that they had difficulties adapting to home life after hospitalisation; lots of professionals visited them to help after discharge, up to 20 in two months in one instance, but they generally felt hopeless and helpless. The hospital trust concerned starting cross training, to reduce the number of visitors and provide continuity of care on discharge. Patients planned with their carers what they wanted to achieve. They were then supported in specific projects relevant to them, such as the patient who was helped to use a keyboard and pen so he could start work again. They then networked with others to share their new knowledge, rather than doing what they might otherwise have done, which was to write up their innovations as a report to be published. They repeated this networking until it eventually grew to the point where many people were convinced this was the strategy to adopt, and Government policy came to be concerned with changing intermediate care. So here the initial attention to detail, networking and sharing knowledge moved from looking at one stroke team and patient stories to changing systems and then to changing policy.

Source: Pickard (2000)

tions within and between them, not in terms of discrete variables. It is non-linear in envisaging both cyclical and mutual interactions among the elements of a system: the inputs, processes, outputs and feedback elements. The net effect is to argue that to solve problems requires a way to understand interconnections and interdependence, producing a set of interacting solution ideas simultaneously. In terms of management and organisation, L&D and performance, the key conclusions are that:

- human systems are 'open' systems; they involve internal and external relations with regulation. People and organisations can always be learning
- there are both wholes and constituents; individuals, groups, organisations, societies. Trying to change one part may not work, if the other parts of the system are not in favour
- there are always clusters of problems
- real problems are ill structured and ill defined; they are 'wicked'
- the subjects must be included in any study of a system
- there can only ever be tentative, incomplete solutions
- ethical issues matter in redesigning systems

There are many difficulties with using systems thinking in organisations. If problems cannot be reduced to a situation where piece by piece problem solving to remedy larger problems step by step is possible, then any, and all, problems are 'wicked'. To understand the whole it is necessary to understand every part. If there is a need to understand interconnections and interdependence, and produce interacting solution ideas simultaneously, then every inquiry is about systems change. Any inquiry is then 'boundless'. Practicability and pragmatism in management and organisation favour more analytical, reductionist, and linear-causal thinking.

THE INTELLECTUAL CAPITAL AND STRATEGIC MANAGEMENT PERSPECTIVE

The connections between KM and L&D come into more stark relief in the analysis of intellectual capital (IC) (Gratton 2000, Mayo 2000). IC concerns the ownership, control and use of knowledge. It is knowledge rather than natural resources or technologies which provides the basis for wealth creation and prosperity. This provides new accounting problems and challenges for organisations, as IC is intangible. IC ideas challenge the dominant, conventional, financial modes of thinking in organisations and societies about economic activity. What is clear is that people with IC have a market price, and as owners of the 'means of knowledge' rather than the 'means of production' they can walk away with their capital. There are lots of problems with renewing IC if people leave. Will investors invest in companies where the assets are invisible? The lessons of the e-business boom and crash, where investors rushed to invest in many IC related projects that went nowhere, were salutary; but they do not mean that the evolution of the 'new economy' has now been written off.

The evolution of IC ideas and practices presents challenges for organisations. These issues are centred on concerns about loose-tight control and empowerment, communication and creativity. There are also wider social issues raised, such as the prospects of creating a new underclass, those without capacities in or involvement with IC, requiring substantial education and development. Scenarios suggest a boom in employment for highly knowledgeable and skilled people and organisations, who will be dispersed and mobile throughout the globe, but with on the other hand further unemployment and urban decay trapping those who are excluded from a share in IC.

Is an era of wealth creation dependent on IC, on the management of tacit knowledge, then upon us? In some sectors this is evidently so; in software development and the biotechnology sectors for example. Yet even they depend upon physical infrastructures and explicit knowledge as much as the tacit knowledge of their employees. But is it relevant to all organisations? In some ways it can be seen to be so. The story of the postal worker who left, taking with him his own 'map' of how to do the delivery route quickly and efficiently, is an example of an unexpected sum of IC disappearing. It is one that applies to many other organisations. For all that the era of KM appears new, the underlying issue is still an old one: how to try and quantify intangibles to render them into the language of hard cash. The capture of experience and learning, of tacit knowledge, into wealth creation and prosperity is just a variation on the theme.

A contemporary application of IC as an element of general and strategic management is provided by Leonard-Barton (*op cit*). Her model is broad in its concerns, but quite straightforward. Leonard-Barton sees knowledge as being the core capability of organisations. This core capability of knowledge is found in four forms: it is embedded in physical systems and technologies, in managerial systems, in skills, and in values.

- Core capability in the form of knowledge may be in a physical form. It may be, for example, in a design a company has protected by patent. This is knowledge you can see and touch; it is tangible.
- Knowledge may also be embodied in managerial systems. It can be embodied in learned ways of doing things most effectively.
- Knowledge may also be embodied in the explicit skills bases and tacit knowledge of employees, the individual competencies which have been brought into the organisation or developed within it through experience.
- Finally, knowledge is to be found embodied as values. These may be explicit 'big' values, the company values; for example the values of a bureaucracy that emphasise following all guidelines rigorously, or the values of an entrepreneurial firm which emphasises a bias towards action. It may also be found in what Leonard-Barton terms 'little values', to do with the norms of behaviour in the workplace, or what others would call organisational culture.

Leonard-Barton's concern is to analyse how knowledge embodied in these forms can come to be the foundation for knowledge inhibiting activities. Knowledge inhibiting activities are experienced as limited problem-solving, an inability to innovate effectively, limited experimentation and the 'screening out' of new knowledge in organisations. These problems, in Leonard-Barton's terms, are caused by an over commitment to the current knowledge base and recipe, as it is embodied in existing physical forms, management systems, skills and values. Overcoming old recipes which act as inhibitors, to promote experimentation, problem-solving, innovation and the inclusion of new knowledge, is the practical focus.

The implication of this analysis of 'knowledge' management is to emphasise that inherited knowledge is everywhere in an organisation, embodied in many different forms. To change and renew knowledge may require new physical systems, new management systems, new skills or new values. It is necessary then to understand how to ensure and enhance changes in physical systems, management systems, skills and values in order to effectively manage knowledge and maintain a core capability. Values as a form of embodied and fixed knowledge provide the form that is most difficult to change and develop. The evolution of new physical forms, products or services, facilities or technologies, is inherent in market capitalism as companies seek success. The evolution of management systems over time is an aspect that most organisations are well aware of as needing development over time. The need for new skills is also a touchstone of current thinking. The problem is often with the issue of new values.

THE EVOLUTION OF L&D IN THE KM CONTEXT

It seems straightforward enough to look at the KM implications for L&D; learn from and with employees rather than ignoring or suppressing their learning. If it was as simple as that then KM would be no more than a re-invention of the kinds of activity that have been associated with staff suggestion schemes. But as this discussion shows there are a number of different dimensions and aspects of management as it is conventionally seen that are challenged by the concept of KM. And, in practice, managers have been criticised as being too concerned with using 're-engineering' processes to increase efficiency using past management principles, rather than embracing the principles of working with communities of practice to better capture L&D. This continuing concern with imposing structures for L&D at work stifles knowledge capture and L&D that emerges from that. On the other hand, for organisations, there are evident problems with defining managers' roles in terms of the principles consistent with encouraging KM, and having to cope with L&D constantly 'bubbling up' and leading to changes in working practices in an almost chaotic way. In organisations there is a tension between the principles of KM and general management. It is manifest as the dilemma of balancing the freedom of communities of practice to learn and change while maintaining the necessary elements of structure that can 'fix' and stabilise such learning so that it can be more widely circulated and implemented.

These tensions and conflicts to be faced in capturing and codifying learning from employees are, in part, a reflection of the argument that 'knowledge is power'. Knowledge capture and codification cannot be analysed in a vacuum; it is pursued in circumstances where different groups, with different interests, are in contest. In the L&D at work context those circumstances are about the structuring of, control of and returns from work.

But organisations that illustrate what this means, what such transformative significance KM involves in practice, are to date limited. They include a few high profile examples such as Skandia, Xerox, and 3M, along with the major management consultancies. These organisations seem to illustrate that the challenges are defining the nature of knowledge, and that its 'tacit' nature often presents a problem: how do these organisations capture the tacit knowledge that is in their employees' heads rather than being articulated and public?

The KM context has obvious implications for L&D (see Box 12.5); the need to have processes and structures to help people create new knowledge, share their understanding, and continuously improve themselves and the results of the enterprise. KM is not just a different way of framing L&D programmes or projects, but a different kind of management philosophy.

Box 12.5

KM and L&D

Traditional L&D	Knowledge management
Employees receive skills training, executives receive development	All employees receive learning support and lifelong development
Training goals are based on requests by users	Learning goals are based on strategy and users' needs
Primarily addresses immediate or short term needs	Focusses on core competencies and long term needs
Needs assessments are done by trainers or managers	Needs assessments are done jointly by individuals, managers and trainers
Is conducted locally or at an off-site classroom	Takes place at the workplace, job site, anywhere
Training is scheduled on a periodic basis	Education is given real time upon request
Approach is a delivery of knowledge	Approach is to design learning experiences as workplace interventions
Is instructor driven; programmes are designed by specialists	Is self directed; design process involves participants
Content is generalised, developed by specialists and often prescriptive	Content is specific and developed jointly; trainees determine content
Trainers develop and deliver content, trainees are recipients	Educators facilitate process and coach learners, who are joint developers

CONCLUSION

Since the early 1990s authors talked about only being able to provide 'glimpses' of KM, as it was an evolving concept. The question to ask is, what progress has been made since then? While there are prescriptions for changing the L&D process in the context of KM in general there are many unanswered questions. Research about how to foster and further invention and innovation, through supporting 'free practice' and communities of practice, is still needed.

Easterby-Smith *et al* (1999) provide a recent overview of key debates. They acknowledge that instead of progress there has been what many see as a spiralling into greater and greater complexity, and in some views obscurity. With that there has come increasing criticism of these concepts. Perhaps more than any other concepts in recent times the concepts of KM, based on ideas of IS, OL and IC, have baffled and bemused both academics and practitioners. The 'glimpses' have become even more vague due to problems with defining and modelling and providing empirical evidence for these concepts, despite a good decade of intensive interest.

For Easterby-Smith *et al* one problem in accounting for developments in theory and practice is that there are different streams involved in the debate, not necessarily speaking the same language at all. In addition they suggest there is a further problem with the distinctiveness and separateness of European and US approaches to these kinds of concepts. While this may all be true, it still does not explain why developments in theory and practice have proven so problematic; for these issues exist in many other areas of the human sciences. Why should the KM field be so problematic?

It seems as if developments like KM are still detached from developments in L&D practice, with more prosaic developments such as better systematic training systems, employee development and assistance programmes (EDAPs) and corporate universities being the focus, leaving the concepts of KM stranded in a swamp of organisational theory. Perhaps there is always too much 'bundled up' in these grand synthesising concepts, and the most productive way ahead in theory and practice is to stick to promoting smaller, more specific and more discrete developments in L&D practice.

CONCLUDING CASE STUDY

Marks and Spencer

Read the Marks and Spencer (M&S) case below, and then use the Leonard-Barton model of knowledge management (Figure 12.6) to explain why the company experienced problems and explore how it has managed to overcome them.

Company development

Marks & Spencer (M&S), founded in 1884, is one of the UK's leading retailers of clothing, foods, homeware and financial services. Serving 10 million customers a week in over 300 UK stores, the company also trades in 38 countries worldwide. It has a group turnover in excess of £8 billion. Despite being viewed as the UK's most successful retailer, problems emerged in 1998. Forecasts had been for decline, but the scale of the decline in the retailer's profits took the City by surprise, when it was announced that half-year profits had plunged by a quarter. M&S shares tumbled nine per cent.

As one of Britain's most successful companies it led the way for many decades; it had a recipe for success which others envied: the kinds of store they had and their product ranges, their employment policies and practices, skills developed and cultivated in all staff and managers, the promise of quality and service. Yet while others evolved M&S was being left behind.

In 2001 M&S was apparently moving back into a successful position after several years of poor performance. Mr Vandevelde, the new chief executive appointed in the aftermath of the late 1990s decline, put the improvements down to M&S's moves to refocus its all-important womenswear on classically-stylish ranges such as the Perfect Basics collection. The company's Per Una range, designed by former Next and Asda clothing guru George Davies, has also proved popular, with demand outstripping supply.

Figure 12.6 A model of knowledge management

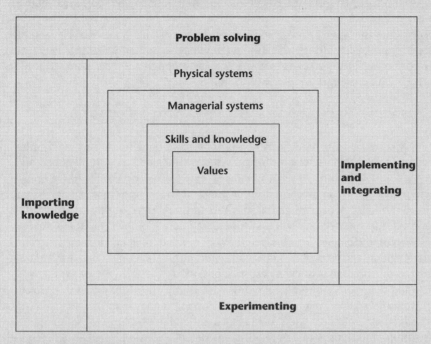

Source: Leonard-Barton (1995)

Mr Vandevelde, a Frenchman, said they had been caught by surprise. The success of Per Una by far exceeded their expectations. They were relatively cautious in building up their inventory; the roll-out was way above what any other retailer would have launched with any other product. He denied that the success of Per Una might lead to it cannibalising other M&S womenswear ranges.

Marks & Spencer has also joined the move to online trading, and has announced four alliances to offer electronic shopping over the Net, with Telewest Communications, Microsoft, BSkyB's subsidiary Open, and the BBC. The company has formed a three-year partnership with Microsoft's portal MSN that enables it to take a premier position on *msn shopping*, the relaunched channel. The retailer will also have a position on the *msn* UK homepage that will lead directly to M&S's shopping site.

The chain has also signed a three-year agreement with beeb.com, the shopping portal owned jointly by BBC Worldwide and ThLi Global Internet Managers, in which it will take an 'anchor tenancy'. The portal will have the option to include M&S products in the editorial reviews of its online consumer magazines. Readers will be able to buy M&S products displayed on the site, and M&S will have its logo 'prominently' displayed across the site, giving a direct link to the M&S website.

Marks & Spencer also has a five-year deal with Open, which is owned by BSkyB and British Telecommunications, under which it has agreed to sell its entire range, but will start with clothing and home products. The retailer has a three-year agreement with

Telewest to 'take a premier position' within Telewest's Active Digital interactive services. It will offer its full range, but will launch with 100–200 products from its fashion and sportswear, home, gift and flower ranges.

Marks & Spencer says that it will have over 3000 products available on its website, and all products available in store will also be available via the Internet and other digital channels. The company is also rolling out in-store kiosks that will enabler shoppers to order from its whole range rather than be limited by the size of a local store.

Reflections

It seemed that for M&S their core capabilities had become core rigidities. It had a recipe for success which others envied. This involved physical systems (the kinds of store they had and their product ranges). It involved managerial systems (they were renowned for their employment policies and practices). It also involved a set of skills and knowledge (carefully developed and cultivated in all staff and managers). And it involved core values (of quality and service).

In order to evolve, and not become stuck with outdated core 'rigidities', all these aspects needed to be reviewed and changed. This happen through problem solving, implementing and integrating, experimenting and importing knowledge. But in many organisations these activities are inhibited; the organisation is stuck in past solutions, won't change, will not experiment, and is insular, refusing to import knowledge. Progress comes from new approaches to problem solving, implementing new things, experimenting, and importing knowledge.

In this case the appointment of outsiders, in management and in clothing design, represents importing ideas. The partnerships with communications organisations represent experimentation. Problem solving, in the context of shortfalls between supply and demand, is an issue. The future now looks brighter again. As with many large companies which find the world changing around them, the shock of failure is needed to create the conditions in which resurgent KM becomes both possible and necessary.

Case sources:

Home page	*Then go to*
http://www.ananova.com	/news/story/sm_54437.html
http://www2.marksandspencer.com	/thecompany/
http://money.cnn.com	/1998/11/03/companies/marks/

REFERENCES

Argyris, C. and Schon, C. (1974) *Theory in Practice: Increasing Professional Effectiveness*, London, Jossey-Bass.

Bell, D. (1974) *The Coming of Post-industrial Society: A Venture in Social Forecasting*, London, Heinemann.

Brown, J. and Duguid, P. (2000) 'Balancing act: how to capture knowledge without killing it', *Harvard Business Review*, May-June.

Brown, J. and Duguid, P. (2002) 'Organizing knowledge', in Little, S. Quintas, P., Ray, T. (eds) (2002) *Managing Knowledge: An Essential Reader*, London, Sage.

Burgoyne, J. (1999) 'Design of the times', *People Management*, Vol. 5. No. 11.

Cambridge University Press (2000) *Cambridge Dictionary of Philosophy*, ed. R. Audi, Cambridge University Press.

Davenport, T. and Prusak, L. (1998) *Working Knowledge: How Organizations Manage What They Know*, Boston, MA, Harvard Business School Press.

de Geuss, A. (1999) *The Living Company: Growth, Learning and Longevity in Business*, London, Nicholas Brealey.

Dierkes, M., Berthoin Antal, A. and Child, J. (eds) (2001) *Handbook of Organizational Learning and Knowledge*, Oxford, Oxford University Press.

Easterby-Smith, M. (1997) 'Disciplines of organizational learning: contributions and critiques', *Human Relations*, Vol. 50, No. 9.

Easterby-Smith, M., Burgoyne, J. and Araujo, L. (1999) *Organizational Learning and the Learning Organization*, London, Sage.

Gratton, L. (2000) 'A real step change' *People Management*, Vol. 6, No. 6.

Harvard Business Review (1998) *On Knowledge Management*, Boston, MA, Havard Business School Press.

Leonard-Barton, D. (1995) *Wellsprings of Knowledge*, Boston, MA, Harvard Business School Press.

Little, S., Quintas, P. and Ray, T. (eds) (2002) *Managing Knowledge: An Essential Reader*, London, Sage.

Mayo, D. (2000) 'The role of employee development in the growth of intellectual capital', *Personnel Review*, Vol. 29, No. 4.

McGinty Weston, D. (1994) *Organizational Learning in Practice*, SRI Business Intelligence.

Pedler, M., Burgoyne, J. and Boydell, T. (1991) *The Learning Company: A Strategy for Sustainable Development*, London, New York, McGraw-Hill.

Pedler, M. and Burgoyne, J. (1994) *Towards the Learning Company: Concepts and Practices*, New York, McGraw-Hill.

Pickard, J. (2000) 'High mileage meditations', *People Management*, Vol. 6, No. 7.

Quintas, P. (2002) 'Managing knowledge in a new century', in Little, S., Quintas, P., and Ray, T. (eds), *Managing Knowledge: An Essential Reader*, London, Sage.

Rosenberg, M. (2001) *E-learning: Strategies for Delivering Knowledge in the Digital Age*, New York, McGraw-Hill.

Scarbrough, H. and Swan, J. (1999) *Knowledge Management: A Literature Review*, London, Institute of Personnel Management.

Senge, M. (1990) *The Fifth Discipline*, London, Doubleday.

Wilson, D. (1996) *Managing Knowledge*, Oxford, Butterworth-Heinemann.

Conclusion

Understanding different perspectives on L&D at work is a complement to both mastering the basic processes and implementing effectively a range of practices. The structure of this overview of L&D at work has been that all these aspects of L&D at work need to be appreciated if anything from the briefest episode of learning to the biggest Government investment in workforce development is to be described and analysed effectively.

The relevance of all these different aspects, processes, practices and perspectives is illustrated in this concluding section by exploring in Chapter 13 the use of formal mentoring. Formal mentoring has become a major tool in many organisations for a range of L&D purposes. It thus presents a contemporary example which can be explored in depth. The kind of analysis given here of formal mentoring can be applied to any other form of L&D at work.

Finally, some themes and issues about what the future may hold for L&D at work are given in Chapter 14. Whether an optimistic view of more and better L&D at work or a pessimistic view of less and worse L&D at work should be taken is the issue. There is a balance at the moment, between forces for more and better L&D and forces against this. If mistakes such as those made that led to the Ladbroke Grove disaster are to be learned from and reduced, it is not enough to just prescribe good practice and expect organisations to follow it. Awareness of the tensions and contests between these general forces is an important part of being able to intelligently discuss and explore L&D at work.

chapter thirteen

A Concluding Case: Mentoring

Learning outcomes

- Explore the use of mentoring as a process for L&D support at work
- Describe how mentoring practice reflects the social and economic context in which it is enacted
- Compare and contrast two perspectives on the conditions required for effective formal mentoring in the workplace
- Apply this analysis of process, practice and perspective to the design and development of formal mentoring schemes

FRAMEWORK CASE STUDY: WHAT DOES MENTORING MEAN?

Mentoring is a concept that embodies an archetypal developmental role, based on a partnership between a learner and a mentor. The associations of the concept of mentor are usually broad and varied; the roles of teachers, sponsors, guardian angels, advisers, counsellors, or 'gurus' have all been cited as instances of mentoring. One analyst concluded that:

> No word in use is adequate to convey the nature of the relationship . . . words such as 'counsellor' or 'guru' suggest the more subtle meanings, but they would have other connotations that would be misleading. The term 'mentor' is generally used in a much narrower sense, to mean teacher, adviser or sponsor. As we use the term, it means all these things and more.
> Levinson *et al* (1978, p 97)

What does the idea of a mentor mean to you? Write down what you think mentoring means, and give examples of it from your own experience. Who are mentors? What do they do? What is meant to be so useful about a mentor?

INTRODUCTION

This book has explored the varied elements of L&D at work, and its associated processes, practices and perspectives. This chapter aims to provide an opportunity to reflect upon and consolidate all that has been covered thus far. The different layers of the basic L&D process, elements of practice and perspectives, can all be applied through exploring and evaluating one central and now near ubiquitous practice: the use of mentoring at work. Exploring what is involved in the design and development of a formal mentoring scheme provides an ideal way to integrate and apply the material included in this book.

This is done here in three parts. First there is a review of process; the way this is done is through exploring the history of mentoring, as a learning partnership that has meant observing, planning, acting and reviewing different things at different times. Second there is an analysis of practice, with a case study of an organisation that has used mentoring and is considering the further and greater use of mentoring. Finally there is an outline of perspectives; the different perceptions of mentoring in practice as a method of establishing and enhancing cognitive capacities, capabilities and behaviours in modern organisations. The aim is to use the knowledge gained from the analysis of processes, practices and perspectives in Parts 1, 2 and 3, to produce proposals for an organisation's evolution of the use of mentoring.

THE MENTORING PROCESS: LESSONS FROM HISTORY

Mentoring is a process that seems to have always existed in some form throughout history. The classical roots of the idea in Western cultures lie in the cradle of civilisation, ancient Greece (Garvey 1994). The role of mentoring was also evident in the age of master-apprentice relationships in European cultures up to and beyond mediaeval times (Clutterbuck 1992). The more recent rebirth, or rebranding, of mentoring in modern history has been in the guise of 'humanistic' mentoring in the 1960s and 70s, concerned with the development of the 'whole person'. These all provide different accounts of what the mentoring process involves (Gibb and Megginson 1993). Each context provides a legacy that influences an understanding of mentoring. The meaning and form of contemporary formal mentoring in modern L&D reflect the legacy of these earlier contexts. Figure 13.1 provides an overview of these contexts. The aim is not to provide a history lesson for the sake of it; it is to illustrate that the mentoring process arises in and adapts to fit with specific social and economic contexts. The implications of this for developing an understanding of modern mentoring in work organisations and the future for mentoring in L&D are important.

Mentoring and classical mythology

The first conceptualisation of mentoring comes from the appearance of the eponymous Mentor, in Greek mythology and the story of Odysseus (Homer trans. 1946). Mentor was the name of the character who helped the son of the king Odysseus, Telemachus, to overcome adversity. The dramatic context in which Mentor helps Telemachus is one where his mother, the queen, is besieged by suitors in his father's absence; he is returning from wars elsewhere, though that journey is famously beset by many trials and tribulations. In the absence of the father Mentor is a *constant* companion and support to Telemachus, in circumstances where Telemachus initially has no strength to prevail against these suitors and their machinations to obtain his father's position of power. But in the course of the drama he develops from being a timid youth to becoming a self-confident and resourceful man, with the guidance of

Figure 13.1   *Mentoring in history: three defining contexts*

The context	Process and role	Process in context	L & D themes	L & D legacy
Classical mythology	Mentor as an archetype and symbol in the drama of the patriot-warrior	Heroes on quests and adventures The wise, the young, the villains	From timidity to resourcefulness Good vs evil	The role of wise 'counsel' The ascension to power
Craft guilds	Mentors as the lynchpins in the economics and society of small, independent businesses	Communities in emerging towns Masters-Apprentices	Craft regulation The community ethos	The role of masters The correlation with community
Humanistic psychology	Mentors supporting the development of the individual	Development throughout adulthood Counselling	Transitions in adulthood Helping 'processes'	Self-development issues for adults Human relations

Mentor. In the end Telemachus is reunited with his father, and they then both defeat the upstart suitors in battle.

The Mentor role itself can be read as an expression of a mythical archetype. An archetype is 'a primeval image, character or pattern that recurs in literature and thought consistently enough to be considered a universal concept' (Stewart 1992, p 16). Archetypes were developed in and transmitted through myths and stories. The classical myth of Odysseus is our original source for the archetype of the mentor, and therefore embodies a number of 'pure' and ideal aspects of it.

It is not necessary to have a had a classical education, or a grounding in mythology, to appreciate what this means. What is important is that mentoring is not a 'new' thing; it is indeed an archetypal concept that has been discussed for some considerable time. Other 'Mentor' like figures, wise and trusted counsellors, often appear in epic adventures and quest tales. This is because the hero of the adventures and quests is often a relatively naïve youth who requires the advice and support of a counsellor who will look after them. The popularity of two major movie series that involve naïve youths on epic quests, The 'Harry Potter' series and the 'Lord of the Rings' series, exemplify a continuing fascination with the dynamics of these archetypes and myths.

There is in the archetype a 'magical' and supernatural aspect to such Mentor like figures. This reflects the contemporary worldview of the original storytellers and their audiences, who believed in magic and the supernatural. But in essence the stories are all about how 'good' triumphs over 'evil', a basic and abiding storyline in all civilisations and cultures throughout time. The archetype of the mentor as the wise and trusted counsellor is only a part of the whole story; the central figure is the hero on the quest. Other important elements of the mythical context and original story from which ideas about mentors have been and are still derived can be highlighted.

The dramas of the Odyssey reflect the general values and culture of the time and people. For the Greeks of this period it has been said that the 'ideal man' was the patriot-warrior; and there can be no mistake that the process of mentoring is built around enabling male heroics. Certainly Odysseus was himself of this ideal mould, as his adventures attest. And the development of Telemachus is the development of a timid youth into a patriot-warrior. The culmination of the story is the youth's ability to engage in battle and win. Mentor does not supply the 'technical training' in fighting; he provides for the mental development of a warrior outlook, confidence in taking action and acting with valour. The 'Homeric ideals' of valour and physical fitness, the virtues of prudence, temperance, fortitude and obedience, were the background to the 'mentoring' process received by Telemachus in the drama.

Some might then associate the mentoring process with the development of outmoded and inappropriate patterns of 'male' behaviours, not appropriate in the contemporary world of work organisations. But setting aside such judgements about the historical context, mentoring in this archetypal form is for inexperienced youths involved in epic adventures or quests. Mentoring functions to help them achieve greatness in the face of adversity. The parallels with modern work organisations, and the support sought and needed by all kinds of people, whether male or female, to achieve 'greatness' through career success in the face of adversity, mean that the process still has relevance. Aspiring youths may need mentors because they are isolated from the normal sources of help; in Telemachus's case this was his male parent, but it could equally be the absence of any effective role model.

A more significant aspect of the story that does raise doubts about its use in the world of modern business is that both parties in the learning partnership and relationship are powerful people; but in fact the protégé is formally more powerful. The mentor as a counsellor is an advisor to the powerful, even a magical cipher for the gods. In the modern business context this is not usually true; it is more usual that the mentor is powerful and the learner is lacking in formal authority or influence.

This view of the mentoring process derived from an archetypal role is still important and resonant. It is no longer just a feature of the development of great heroes, though it is still that in some cases. It occurs in many similar, though more ordinary and everyday circumstances. Based on this myth the term 'mentoring' became a commonplace term for referring to the role that wise and powerful people can play in the lives of others who aspire to achieve greatness.

Mentoring and craft guilds

Clutterbuck (*op cit*), one of the UK's renowned researchers of mentoring, makes reference to the role of mentoring in another historical context, the master-apprentice relationships that were central to the guild system of mediaeval Europe. This historical era in the evolution of a process of mentoring is also replete with important insights and lessons for contemporary mentoring. This section explores, briefly, the development of guilds, the associated master-apprentice system, and the mentoring processes these involved.

Guilds were organisations of craftspeople that regulated employment in their sphere of work. They regulated who would be trained, how they would work, what they would be paid, what jobs they would get. All these and other matters were controlled by the guilds. In one sense they were the forerunners of both modern trade unions, and indeed of modern employing organisations. But the development of and ethos of guilds were an integral part of a distinctive context: an economy based on many independent 'small businesses' and a society imbued with Christian beliefs. Guilds were a form of 'community' rather than just devices for managing employment and its relations, and the mentoring process was shaped, above all, as a community relationship.

This reflects a culture where the guild was a 'confederation in societies for mutual help' (Brentano 1969, p xxiv). Brentano argues that the family is the archetype of the guild. This is so because its motivating spirit is 'solidarity'. Support is given to guild members according to their wants, not on the basis of any other criteria. Black sees the guild as an important species of community 'because in a precise way it harnessed certain communal values – brotherhood, friendship and mutual aid' (Black 1984, p xi).

Mackenney (1987) explains how, in the practical world, guilds for crafts became the chief source of organisation, initially having a role in the management of work but then also having a role in civic life more generally. Guilds were closed brotherhoods, regulating admission initially to work, but then also regulating the life of towns and communities. In both spheres they were preoccupied, above all, with maintaining standards. In work this was seen in a tightly controlled system where a master, part of the closed brotherhood, took on apprentices. Becoming an apprentice was the only route into work. These apprentices would then become journeymen. They could then, depending on ability and economic circumstances, become masters themselves, having demonstrated competence by producing their 'masterpiece'. Many, in practice, were restricted to being journeymen.

Craft guilds followed the general ethos of the broader guild movement, but applied it to the management of occupational groups. In this context craft guilds promoted sound workmanship, security for their members, fair returns for work, and they were concerned with the welfare of all their members. They helped to produce a cadre of skilled workers, disciplined and with high self-esteem. A central part of this was the control of apprenticeships. By regulating entry to occupations the guilds could control their field of work and the way it was organised. It is important to realise that apprenticeships in this context were quite different from more modern 'apprenticeships'. In the modern context an apprentice is employed to work with experienced and skilled people in a large modern enterprise, not to be part of the community of the occupation and their master's family. As Brentano notes:

The admission of an apprentice was an act of special solemnity, corresponding to the important legal consequences it involved. As it was the beginning of a kind of novitiate to citizenship . . . the apprentice was instructed as to his moral conduct and the trade . . . the apprentice became a member of the family of his master, who instructed him in his trade, and who, like a father, had to watch over his morals, as well as his work, during his apprenticeship. At the expiration of his apprenticeship the lad was received into the guild again with special forms and solemnities and became thereby a citizen of the town. (Brentano *op cit*, p cxxix)

In this context there is a form of mentoring process between the master and the apprentice. The process is both personal and professional, both very important and prolonged; it covers a period of major transition for the learner involved and is a significant role for the mentor. Brentano also emphasises the moral dimension of the role, its function in socialising the young person in the values of the occupation.

The decline of the guild system took with it this master-apprentice relationship and the mentoring process it incorporated. That decline can be explained by a number of factors. In short, the economic and social context changed and the system that had sustained these kinds of master-apprentice relationships declined. The guild and craft system became displaced by the factory system and formal mass education. Guilds became outmoded, essentially mediaeval institutions, left behind by changes ushering in a new era of economic expansion in the 16th century which marginalised the 'small business' masters. And with the development of the secular State, providing some of the benefits previously confined to guild members and closed brotherhoods, the guilds 'went to sleep' (Mackenney 1987, p 79).

The advent and development of mass education systems meant the end of an era when learning was dependent on mentoring processes between masters and apprentices. Apprenticeships were reformulated in the context of new industries and large employing organisations, but it was not the same kind of relationship anymore. Learning from masters had involved being in a close, long term, personally significant relationship. The learning of the 'mystery' of a trade was a personal business because it was part of a particular system: small scale enterprise where the occupation was a way of life central to the group working in it. Underlying these changes, though, there was a sea change in the relevance of the 'great idea' underlying guilds, the idea of association and solidarity.

For the modern mentoring process at work there are two key legacies from this era. The first is the abiding notion of the need to learn from master practitioners. In this context an important factor to note is the dependence of the learner on the master. The mentor is the central figure. Eventually the apprentice will become an equal to the master, and perhaps supersede the mentor's achievements. This is, ultimately, a process that involves a relationship that changes from one of the learner's dependence to one of their equality, then independence. Mentoring in the sense of a relationship with 'masters' survived in the systems of professional development that complemented formal learning in newer professional roles, such as in the law, engineering and medicine. For people to become professionally qualified they had to complete training in practice under the guidance of a practitioner in these fields. This principle is now more widely adopted in, for example, teaching nursing, careers advising and personnel management.

The second legacy is the connection between mentoring and a sense of 'community', the association of such processes and relationships with solidarity among groups of people. To this day, as Black (1984, p xi) notes:

> The notion of a tightly-knit, affective community is notoriously alluring to modern western man; we tend to associate it with an ideal past, and to see in its restoration a focus for our hopes for a better society.

Creating and tapping into relationships of solidarity and community are on the HRM agenda of many organisations. And one consequence of that is an interest in the mentoring process.

Mentoring and humanistic psychology

While guild based mentoring processes declined, the problems of living and working in economies and societies based on industrial production and market based capitalism would provide fertile ground for the seeds of a new incarnation of the mentoring process. These were the seeds of a humanistic perspective on human development, and the ground in which they were sown most fruitfully would be the modern work organisation. These first emerged in humanistic psychology throughout the 20th century, based on a scientific conception of people that complemented and critiqued the triumph of 'liberal individualism' in general, with its creed of freedom for the individual, and its North American version in particular, with its individualistic and achievement driven ethos. Here the themes and issues of the freedom of the individual to 'become all that they could become', and the need for effective human relations and personal development to ensure and enable that, became an important, indeed a preoccupying, subject.

Such humanistic psychology was also an application of the tradition of enlightened humanist thinking, which saw absolute importance in improving the condition of humankind and the promotion of living in tune with what were deemed to be 'positive' human values: being caring, compassionate, loving, respectful and tolerant. With the parents of individualism in psychology and an ethos of 'realising potential', the mentoring process was given a new birth, with humanistic psychology acting as the midwife.

Humanistic psychology has been described as a 'third force' in psychology (Dryden *et al* 1989), taking an optimistic view of human nature compared with the bleaker and 'pessimistic' views of psychoanalysts and the crude determinism of the classical behaviourists. Its goal is often related to the achievement of 'self-actualisation', a concept associated with Maslow and his ideas about the promotion of personal growth and the realisation of individual potential as the key to healthy adult development. In this form humanism is associated with thinkers like Rogers (1983), with the practical development of the widespread uptake of self-development in general (Megginson and Pedler 1993), and with the growth of what might be termed a 'therapy/counselling' culture.

Rather than seeing mentoring in the context of archetypal roles and heroic dramas, or in the context of a society and economy of guilds and brotherhoods, attention was to be focussed on the processes of psychosocial development of adults and 'everyman'. Rather than looking narrowly at the processes of learning, the mystery of a trade, attention was to be given to the more general 'mystery' and mastery of the down to earth dramas of human development in the context of modern work organisations and family. Levinson *et al* (*op cit*) are the exemplar of this stream of thinking, and important studies in mentoring, such as Kram's seminal work (Kram 1985) reflect this influence.

Levinson *et al* were interested in studying adult development, particularly what they called 'mid-life' stages and issues. The 'discovery' of problems in the mid-life period, what has become known as the 'mid-life crisis', for adults was a general issue in the USA at the time. Levinson *et al* saw the 'depth psychology' of Freud and Jung as the conceptual underpinning of their study. In particular they made much of the Jungian idea of 'individuation' as the factor influencing the process and course of adult development. Individuation is the process of 'becoming your own person', moving from dependence on others through to some realisation of an individual and autonomous identity as a person. This journey from dependence through individuation to being your own person was the journey of every human life. Problems encountered in adult development, of which there seemed to be many, were about failures to complete this process of individuation.

The key feature of individuation is making 'choices' at different stages; in particular, choices about occupation and marriage. Levinson *et al* were specifically concerned with the choices men make and then have to build upon; either living within them, enhancing them, or moving to make new choices at times of change and crisis. Within this context mentoring features strongly as a role that older men can play with younger men. In terms of the choices being made by the younger man they are to do with identifying and establishing their own personal 'dream'; the mentor is, most crucially, there to 'support and facilitate the realization of the Dream' (Levinson *et al*, p 98). In this context the process of 'mentoring is best understood as a form of love relationship' (*ibid*, p 100).

The functions of the mentoring process are for men in early adulthood who require a mentor, and men in late adulthood who can act as mentors. The context of this study is once again clearly 'male'; an undeniable aspect of the history of the mentoring process. It needs to be stressed again that the mentoring process applies to both genders; that the central concepts of dreams and individuation set the agenda, and these are as relevant to women as they are to men. For the development of boys into men individuation does not stop with becoming a recognised 'adult', by developing a career and becoming married. It goes beyond that to the process of ' becoming one's own man'. For the development of girls into women individuation did not stop either with attaining maturity and becoming a recognised adult, most usually in the form of becoming married and having a family. They too still had to go some way to 'become their own person'. As the economic and social context now clearly encompasses both men and women in the spheres of employment and family life, the kinds of individuation problems faced as choices are made, and crises with those are encountered, are more universal; and arguably more pressing if the level of debate about problems with life-work balance reflects levels of real problems in those regards.

In early adult life this process of individuation involves working through dependencies on others. Mentors are ambiguous figures in this respect; they are people on whom the young adult will depend, but whose primary role is to help the young adult overcome such dependencies. Combining the concept of individuation and the hypothesised stages of adult development as they saw it in the course of their research, Levinson *et al* arrive at a view of the mentoring process as a key, if highly problematic, resource for young men; and as a fulfilling role for older men. Thus the mentoring process is seen to be highly significant for both parties, crucial to effective adult development, through facilitating the continuing individuation of both parties. It is stressed that the mentoring process may be either difficult or highly problematic in its eventual outcomes for both parties. This is not a rosy view of a perfect, mutually beneficial partnership; it is a realistic appraisal of a partnership which like all partnerships can be fraught with difficulties and challenges.

Mentoring as a process makes good sense in this particular analytical framework, but it is also perceived as potentially hazardous and problematic. Some of these problems arise from the partial 'parental' impulse behind mentoring on the mentor's part. Other 'hazards' may arise from issues about power playing in such relationships, where dependencies exist but have to be renegotiated as the relationship evolves. Whatever judgement is made about the research and theorising of Levinson *et al* in particular, they represent a general articulation of the mentoring process that fits with a distinctive view. The mentor is, to use the term put at the heart of the humanistic approach, 'person-centred'.

Person-centred therapists are strongly anti-technical, anti-skill and anti-techniques. They prefer to talk about attitudes and behaviours, and creating growth-promoting clients. Their view of their clients is that they are intrinsically good, capable of directing their own destinies and capable of self-actualization. (Stewart 1992, p 199)

This edge to the mentoring process, being person-centred rather than being the giver of advice/wise counsel, assumes that for people to become happy they need, in terms that are now absolutely clichéd, 'to find themselves'. Cliché it may be; but in the modern environment of pressures at work and at home, problems with 'life-work' balance, and of uncertainties in terms of personal and career goals, such a need seems to be real, meaningful and pressing. The mentoring process is no longer about a wise figure giving counsel to heroes, or even necessarily a 'master' in any field developing an apprentice. The legacy of this view of the mentoring process is that, to the constellation of family, peers, formal educators and superiors is added the mentor as a person providing 'person-centered counselling' and a supporting role for adults.

MENTORING IN PRACTICE: INVESTMENTCO

The following case study gives an account of an organisation which is using formal mentoring in practice at the moment, and is planning to use more formal mentoring. InvestmentCo is a large provider of financial and banking services. It currently has two graduate programmes: one for the Investment Management ('front office') function, the other for the Investment Administration ('back office') function. An average of two trainees per year are recruited for each programme. Mentoring has been used in both areas for the last three years, although in different ways. The mentor who currently handles the back office graduates also collates feedback about and deals with their performance appraisals. The front office mentor, outside the line management and performance appraisal loop, deals specifically with issues around settling into the workplace and early career development. Graduates in the front office are also assigned a coach with responsibility for guiding workplace learning. The implicit objectives are to assist with transition from university and to maximise retention within the first two to three years of the graduates' careers.

A number of issues are impacting the success of this graduate mentoring. The objectives have not been communicated, leading to unclear expectations amongst both front and back office graduates. This has caused confusion between mentoring and performance management roles in the back office programme. Matching of mentors and learners has been an ad hoc process completed on the basis of staff availability, rather than suitability – this has led to mixed outcomes in terms of relationship sustainability. While a short workshop has been used to train mentors, limited further training and follow-up support have been provided. No formal evaluation of the mentoring arrangements has been carried out. Finally, little attention has been paid to the process for the mentoring relationships to end, causing some of the current arrangements to dissolve without guidance or intervention.

Scope for improvements

A planned or formal approach to mentoring is still regarded as appropriate for new graduate entrants. It demonstrates a commitment by the organisation to establish support structures to ease the transition into the workplace culture. The key priorities are a clearer statement of mentoring objectives and a review of the current matching process, moving back office mentors outside of the normal line relationship, and designing a proper evaluation process to assess outcomes and identify improvements. Greater clarity of objectives is required to enable clear contracting between mentors and learners over their respective roles. An evaluation process is required if the organisation wishes to assess actual outcomes and any evidence for learner 'insights' as a result of mentoring. After three years of the current arrangements producing mixed success in the front and back office, a more formal review of mentoring before the next graduates join would seem to be highly desirable.

Beyond the graduate programme

A review of needs within the organisation suggests three specific opportunities for extending the use of mentoring within the company:

Team leader development

A current in-house development programme is run in conjunction with the Institute of Management. This gives existing and aspiring team leaders accreditation towards a Certificate in Supervisory Management. The course is workshop and assignment based, requiring participants to gather evidence within the organisation. Delegates have often asked for additional 'offline' support to help them learn and develop. A new system of informal mentoring could enable course delegates to select other talented managers as role models for themselves, providing support for their skills and career development during and beyond the 12-month experience. As some of the course delegates have experience of formal mentoring on the graduate programme, they would be more confident in sourcing new informal mentoring relationships to further their development.

Women into leadership roles

There is the potential for mentoring to help women gain the confidence and opportunity to move into senior management roles. However, there are some concerns that formal mentoring may actually disadvantage women.

Although InvestmentCo has one senior female Global Equities manager, women are generally under-represented at higher levels within the organisation. Informal mentoring could have a role to play in assisting female middle managers or fund managers realise their full potential. Selection of their own mentors by female learners would maximise the chance of developing the openness, trust and 'natural chemistry' necessary for a productive mentoring relationship. In this way, mentoring could help unlock more of the talent within the organisation and improve female representation within the senior management team.

The 'old boy network' is seen as the strongest barrier to women's progression. Being a 'token woman' at the top puts immense pressure on the individual and the absence of an 'old girl network' as a support mechanism proves very difficult. Men still have more social power in the organisation and consequently women have become the 'outgroup' (Lahtinen and Wilson 1994). Therefore with these deep-rooted attitudes of male executives still inherent within the socialisation process, mentoring can be designed to target the glass ceiling, giving women the chance to gaze 'through the looking glass' to the men's world. So in the bid to climb up the executive ladder, can mentors really protect women from the complex array of discrimination and help them gain access to the 'ingroup' previously dominated by men?

To advance up the hierarchy women need to have a better insight into barriers, such as the male power networks. Thus if the mentor is male, they can provide women with information about the infamous 'old boy network' and develop their learning skills about how to cope with the political activity at the top. Equally given that most mentors are male due to the lack of women, this provides an opportunity for female managers to gain a better awareness of the executive environment. Mentoring also helps to establish contacts and uncover job opportunities that otherwise may not be possible. In this way the mentor reduces the learning curve for the protégé.

Peer mentoring is becoming a more widespread option within organisations as one of the natural forms of mentoring that may suit women more. Peer mentoring is a process where there is mutual involvement in encouraging and enhancing learning and development between two peers, where peers are people of similar hierarchical status or who perceive themselves as equals. Peers are more likely to share similar experiences and are the ideal sources of psychosocial support. Women's management styles tend to be more collaborative, hence the reason why peer mentoring might be a viable alternative.

However, there are naturally some weaknesses of peer mentoring. Women fundamentally need career-related help to advance in the male-dominated executive circles, which is not possible with peer mentoring. Formal peer mentoring could potentially have a negative outcome, as creating a recognised 'new girl network' might further segregate women.

Management development

There is scope to combine formal mentoring and guided learning in a development programme for middle managers. InvestmentCo will be designing and implementing a new management development programme for staff above the level of team leader. The benefits of assigning a coach or mentor to programme delegates have already been discussed as a possible option. As the objectives of the programme relate to the development of talent for future succession planning, it is proposed that a more formal system of mentoring would be appropriate.

The company could allocate senior managers as mentors, matching them to learners on the basis of underlying talent, learning needs and preferred working styles. As InvestmentCo begins to reorientate processes around expanding global opportunities, such mentoring relationships could provide a source of stability and reassurance during organisational change. Such 'strategic mentoring' could help promote the changing culture that will be necessary to manage operations in the UK, Hong Kong and other future locations.

PERSPECTIVES ON MODERN MENTORING IN WORK ORGANISATIONS

Reviewing the three historical eras that have contributed to the complex of meanings associated with mentoring, and the use of mentoring in practice in a case study organi-

---

Box 13.1

Mentoring process and mentoring perspectives

Analysing these modern factors in relation to the three historical legacies, the following issues about mentoring arise. Firstly, the new 'great' men, the heroes of business, are to be analysed as succeeding because of access to mentors. With the impeccable logic of the culture of 'aspiration' that produced this notion, the equation was simple. If current great men had been mentored then mentoring could produce other great men. The modern quest was the career in the large corporation; into the corporate labyrinth, with enemies, battles, and adventures ahead: the modern epic. An update on this is the quest for entrepreneuralism with a consequent concern for mentors to help develop entrepreneurs.

Secondly, the learning focus, the use of 'masters', has led to a concern with the role of practitioners in development. In general this is true in Britain of competence-based qualification systems, where assessors and verifiers of competence at work are the heart of the system. In particular it is true of the use of managers as 'developers' in the workplace.

Third, the 'person-centred' element is evident in the evolution of ideas about managers as counsellors, 'self-development' as a component of management development, and the common general guidance given to mentors to be non-directive in their dealings with protégés/mentees/learners. Clearly the whole notion of humanism and counselling has moved beyond the leisured and optimistic world of California in the 1950s and 60s. Many would argue that the view of 'self-actualisation' at the heart of that social context is outdated.

All of this might suggest that the prospects for mentoring are good. However, nagging and persistent questions about meaning, fact and value remain. Indeed some would argue that threat is aggravated by what has already happened, with pale versions of 'real' mentoring taken up half heartedly in many circumstances.

---

sation, a number of points emerge. Firstly, the mentoring process has always been incarnate in particular times and systems. Learning from history is not an academic exercise, it is vital to appreciate the fact that what is done now in the name of mentoring has been built upon these foundations. Secondly, the mentoring process varies, involving different things according to the system it is part of and its times. It adapts to fit with the needs and demands of the time and era, and in that case any core identity beyond a very vague essence, perhaps related to the mentoring process being a 'non-kin', substantial and significant relationship, is questionable. The mentoring process has been about counselling in the old sense, the wise advising the powerful. The mentoring process has been about masters helping apprentices to learn, in tight knit communities. And the mentoring process has been a force for realising the 'person-centred' and 'self-actualisation' philosophies of modern humanism (see Box 13.1).

In the present the following themes seem to be central to the use of mentoring in work organisations:

■ *Mentoring as part of a formal continuum of relationships or activities*

The need to define and describe mentoring as one role in a constellation related to a formal setting (education, work, and so on) continues to exercise most researchers and practitioners. The implication is that mentoring is a form of a broader role, suited to bridging, or bringing together, different domains. Differentiating mentoring as a form of a broader role is seen to be a useful way of defining and describing it. Describing the ways in which it might bridge gaps or provide a key role in certain situations is also much considered. The attempt to create generic models can be seen as an attempt to put some order into the otherwise apparently chaotic sets of roles associated with mentoring and mentoring like relationships.

■ *Defining the functions or 'skills' of mentoring*

Since Kram argued that two sets of functions were evident, career functions and psychosocial functions, most commentators have been keen to establish their own lists of functions or skills related to mentoring. Mentoring aided advancement up the hierarchy and contributed to feelings of self-worth inside and outside the organisation. Relationships which encompass all these functions are 'classical' mentoring relationships. Most relationships offer a subset of functions, with career functions prevalent.

Many lists of 'competencies' for mentoring now exist, with the strengths and weaknesses of competency lists in general much in evidence. These lists may be generic or they may relate to the different types of mentoring/sub-roles considered relevant.

■ *The development of mentoring 'systems' or 'cultures'*

The growth in Britain has definitely been in formal mentoring schemes, but that has not stopped a persistent questioning of the value of institutionalising mentoring in organisations. Clawson (1985) argued that 'career planners ought to worry more about the developmental quality of superior-subordinate relationships in the organisation than about mentoring relationships that are hard to define and harder yet to institutionalise' (p 38). It may, in theory, be more attractive to argue for broader organisational development (OD) initiatives. But in practice the development of a formal scheme is an essential first practical establishing step.

In the contemporary context of practice it is claimed that mentoring is more widely used in British companies than coaching and careers counselling. Mentoring is a central alliance in guiding workplace learning (Dymock 1999, Billett 2000). There are some caveats needed. One is that there are many definitions of mentoring, with all kinds of process and people being classed as mentor related when it is questionable if they are. In addition there are few valid and reliable data that suggest that mentoring 'works'. There are some studies (Gibb 1999, Garvey 1994) that have attempted to empirically explore mentoring in Britain through survey techniques and case study analysis. But these cannot be cited as proving that mentoring achieves the goals its proponents claim it can achieve, such as improved career management, better learning and the self-development of the 'whole' person.

Finally, it needs to be highlighted that there are different judgements made about the development of mentoring and its significance. The contrast between mentoring in different cultures, for example, bears some reflection. The origins of much of the discussion of mentoring in business and management lie in the US. This has been true of mentoring in general (Roche 1979), links to the 'systems' versus 'culture' issue (Clawson *op cit*, Zey 1991), and the field of equal opportunities (Shapiro *et al* 1978,

Thomas 1993). Questions arise about the relevance of mentoring to broader initiatives such as more structured employee and management development plans, performance management innovations, new competency based systems, peer group or other forms of learning groups. Continuous professional development (CPD) systems and revised management education programmes continue to illustrate that there are issues about the basic worth of the idea of mentoring.

The nature of and issues arising with perspectives on modern mentoring can be explored using social psychology, drawing upon the analysis of helping relationships. Social psychology deals with explaining and analysing the behaviour of individuals in social situations (Brehm and Kassin 1993). The analysis of helping relationships presents two contrasting explanations for helping behaviour of which mentoring can be taken as an instance. These contrasting explanations are the communitarian and the social exchange theories. Mentoring is an example of individual behaviour in a social situation, as it involves a relationship between two people, a dyad, in a particular organisational context. Social psychology has a well developed set of concepts and frameworks for studying such relationships. The study of social perception, social interaction and social influence all have relevance to the analysis of modern mentoring relationships. Social perception can relate to how people see themselves, and present themselves in relationships. Social interaction involves factors related to interpersonal attraction and helping others. Social influence involves considering how people's attitudes can be changed.

From this range of general areas of study in social psychology the specific relevance of studies of helping provides the best theoretical focus. The social psychological study of 'helping' (Smithson 1983) can be reviewed to provide some purchase on the prospects for modern formal mentoring, to help develop a theoretical overview relevant to mentoring now and in the future.

The social exchange perspective interprets all relationships in terms of people attempting to maximise the benefits and minimise the costs of transactions. Some form of calculation of costs and benefits is integral to establishing and developing any and all relationships. In this approach mentoring is a relationship like any other. It will form and be based on calculations of the costs-benefits for the partners involved. Such calculation may be of a 'bottom-line' type, where one criterion is central, or they may be based on a more sophisticated 'balanced scorecard'. Negotiations would characterise this type of relationship, about clarifying costs and benefits, on a key criterion or on a balanced scorecard. This is the 'if you scratch my back I'll scratch yours' origin of the motivation for partnerships. The constant highlighting of 'mutual benefits' for mentors and protégés in the development of formal schemes clearly uses a language and a framework that suggest social exchange factors are uppermost in the business and management context. The fixation with identifying and measuring 'costs and benefits' in mentoring reflects this basic approach to helping.

The communitarian perspective would view modern mentoring as an example of altruism. Mentoring is a manifestation of a 'spirit of community' (Etzioni 1993). People are responsive to each other's needs because it is the right thing to do, not because they benefit from it. It is the 'if your back needs scratching, I'll do it' view:

> . . . there is, quite properly, in any relationship or community some vague sense of appropriate reciprocity, of the need to contribute to a climate of mutuality. But basically people help one another and sustain the spirit of community because they sense it is the right thing to do. (Etzioni, p 145)

Etzioni expands upon this central point:

> At the heart of the Communitarian understanding of social justice is the idea of reciprocity; each member of the community owes something to all the rest, and the community owes something to all its members . . . beyond self support individuals have a responsibility for the material and moral well being of others. This does not mean heroic self-sacrifice; it means the constant self-awareness that no one of us is an island unaffected by the fate of the others. (Etzioni, p 264)

Such concerns lead to a need to see formal mentoring in the context of 'community'. The idea of revitalising communities is indeed at the centre of much contemporary thinking concerned with overcoming social problems, including the alienation of many groups from mainstream society, the growth of crime and violence in society, and juvenile delinquency. The concept is also relevant to the study of mentoring because the mentor is seen by some as the modern 'spirit of the community' personified. The whole idea of modern mentoring practice in this view is bound up with the renewal of community, and of close knit relationships and bonds being redeveloped as part of a broader social change; this applies to geographical, non-geographical and 'cyber' communities. Whatever the focus, what proponents of this perspective argue is that no amount of rational social exchange, exhortation, education or enforcement can substitute for involvement in tight knit communities as a basis for developing moral behaviour.

With regard to organisations as communities the focus is on work-based and professional communities. People at work or in professional networks are seen as more than colleagues; they become friends, people who will play and party together, getting to know and care for one other. Joining a work organisation or being part of a professional network is not simply about doing job; it is about joining and belonging to a community. Organisations can provide some elements of the communitarian nexus. They tend to have a moral infrastructure that helps to provide the social foundations of morality that we consider essential to civil and human society. Neither technology nor non-geographical communities can substitute for the geographical community, and the family unit at its nucleus; but they are apparently growing in importance and relevance for the future.

CONCLUSION

The historical, theoretical and management context review of the mentoring process illustrates that mentoring is a significant relationship, that will be bound up with its times and the specific social and economic systems that exist, from 'warrior' making, through masters in guilds, to liberal humanism and people realising their full potential. The important features of the modern social and economic context, which provides a role for mentoring practice, are as distinctive: helping alienated young people, promoting equal opportunity policies, and developing managerial and professional talent. Exploring and explaining formal mentoring in the modern workplace there are perspectives embodying either a social exchange or a communitarian explanation. Both these explanations provide a perspective on the reasons why mentoring makes sense, and raise issues about the problems that will be encountered in implementing formal mentoring as an exemplary L&D initiative in modern organisations.

Investmentco

Mentoring has a role to play in encouraging individual learning and organisational development within modern companies. Current mentoring practice within InvestmentCo is limited to a formal mentoring within its two graduate programmes. A number of improvement opportunities have been identified to make objectives clearer, separate mentoring from performance appraisal and introduce evaluation. Beyond the graduate programme, three specific mentoring opportunities have been identified: team leader development, the new management development programme, and informal mentoring to help increase the representation of women at senior levels within the company.

Re-read the case study of InvestmentCo's mentoring in practice. As you read the case, consider:

- How does this use of mentoring reflect the different processes that can be seen in history: helping heroes, masters-apprentices and personal development?
- What steps could be taken to make further use of mentoring in the organisation?
- What perspective on mentoring would you argue needs to be adopted to overcome the problems of the past and better use mentoring in the future?

You are asked to provide guidance on the possible use of mentoring in the following areas:

- team leader development for existing and prospective team leaders
- graduate entrants in their first two years
- increasing women into leadership roles

Exercise 13.1 Reflections on mentoring

There is still considerable debate about what mentoring means, and what really counts as 'mentoring'. The point that mentoring 'means all these things and more' is still true today. In defining mentoring formal mentoring in the workplace as a form of learning partnership; the following characteristics are parts of my definition:

- Mentoring is a one to one relationship
- There will be a senior-learner differential
- It will be a 'confidential' relationship; what happens within it is known only to the individuals concerned
- It will be multi-functional; while there may be a focal concern, mentoring invariably involves a wide range of issues in knowledge, skill and behaviour
- It will go through set phases; from initiation, through 'work', to termination

It is important to be clear about one central division in particular when defining mentoring at this early stage. This is the distinction between 'natural mentoring' and 'formal mentoring'. Natural mentors are experienced individuals who are closely and personally concerned with someone's development as a person, where the relationship has developed organically. Formal mentors are individuals who have been assigned to that role in the context of a specific organisational setting and set of circumstances.

The existence of natural mentoring in the workplace is an integral part of the social and power networks which exist in workplace communities. People in positions of power and

CONCLUDING CASE STUDY (cont'd)

authority, senior and established people, will develop special relationships with some other employees. Whether these are a consequence of an 'old boy network', or of friendships formed in the course of work experience, organic and natural mentoring is a fact of organisational life. The establishment and uses of formal mentoring in the workplace are many and varied. They include providing support in the induction and socialisation of new graduate trainees, the support of employees participating in formal learning processes such as management and professional development, and being a support for career development, either in the form of 'grooming' talented stars for promotion, or in the pursuit of policies related to the realisation of policies of equal opportunity. The concern in modern L&D is most often with the use of formal mentoring, and this chapter has dealt with that aspect of mentoring as a learning partnership.

Concluding case study review

Process and practice

A combination of both formal and informal approaches to mentoring could have been recommended for use at different levels within the organisation.

Both approaches have validity, as they are addressing different needs and objectives at three levels within the organisation.

A formal mentoring structure is helpful to facilitate the integration of new entrants and develop succession planning. However informal mentoring, involving 'natural' relationships (such as self-selection of mentors) can be encouraged between these levels. This is shown in Figure 13.2.

Figure 13.2   Mentoring in InvestmentCo

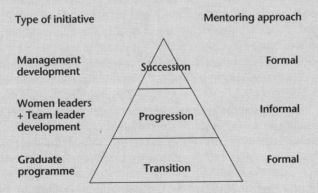

It is concluded that mentoring has a part to play in assisting with transition, progression and succession within the company.

However if mentoring is to be further developed within InvestmentCo, it will be essential to evaluate actual outcomes delivered by the different approaches. In this respect, it will be vital to quantify the benefits returned by mentoring. Without this, it will not be properly supported by the organisation or by individuals who are asked to play a role in future mentoring relationships.

CONCLUDING CASE STUDY (cont'd)

Perspectives

The focal point here is using the communitarian and social exchange perspectives to anticipate and explore principles and problems. Modern communitarians believe that the roots of the traditional community spirit, doing things for others because it is the right thing to do, still exist in modern societies. These roots need to be nurtured in order to help overcome the persisting problems of mass society: alienation, crime, and amoral behaviour. But in order for these roots to be nurtured people must *act themselves*, in their own lives and in their own circumstances. While such arguments can be developed into a political position with implications for government, education, and business, the heart of it all is this emphasis on individual action. It is, in other words, a recipe for mentoring; voluntary individual action, building relationships between people, in order to promote the involvement of wiser, experienced senior people in the development of inexperienced junior people.

Formal mentoring in the workplace is a form of organised altruistic 'volunteering' for which there is no financial reward, and mentors can stress their altruism in adopting the role. It links to broader ideas about recovering the virtues of communities and a positive morality around social justice, for example equal opportunities, in circumstances where both theses elements are desired. It is a moral process as much as a technical process. It is occurring within a social context and contributing to it. The communitarians would see mentoring as exemplifying the spirit of community and would want to encourage that.

The social exchange perspective sees matters differently. Against the claimed benefits there are costs involved in mentoring, the costs of time, effort and emotions. In work organisations people would seem to want 'equity' as they do not see workplaces as sites of classical community relationships. It is organisations that institute schemes, not individuals; as such schemes have specific aims and objectives and mentors are signing up to achieve those rather than simply helping individuals. They are, in fact, helping the organisation. There must be some calculation of reciprocity in mentoring as in any relationship, particularly in the workplace. There is a strong emphasis on mutual benefits, not just benefits for the learner. There are obvious rewards for mentors, ranging from status and personal profile to getting the help of learners as assistants. All volunteers will have calculated the opportunity costs in some way.

As our broader society is based on social exchange principles it is difficult to see how mentoring in the workplace can operate in contrast with those. People are calculators of reciprocity, making decisions based on such calculations rather than because they are bound to specific roles. Against this is the argument that there are always more costs than benefits for mentors. On a cost-benefit calculation no-one would become a mentor. In addition mentors report that they do not want financial rewards. The social exchange proponents would want to bring 'realism' to the development of mentoring, by ensuring reciprocity and mutual benefits.

General points about L&D processes, practices and perspectives

Some more general learning points about the L&D process would be around how to assess needs that mentoring might meet or indeed raise, designing relevant interventions in a variety of ways, delivering these and evaluating them:

■ It is easy to assume that corporate mentoring is a 'good idea' without fully appreciating some of the potential obstacles and issues that can arise. The need is to assess L&D needs, on the part of the organisation, people and work.

CONCLUDING CASE STUDY (cont'd)

■ Design issues; being flexible in design, but still having clear aims and objectives. What are the issues that mentoring can deal with in terms of cognitive capacities, capabilities and behaviours?

■ The issues involved in delivering through formal mentoring alliances; what development and guidance are to be provided to learners and mentors? The organisation already liaises with an external partner for one part of its development; do they need to be more involved?

■ Taking it for granted that mentoring operates successfully, and failing to monitor and evaluate actual outcomes.

In terms of practice there is indeed scope for different types and levels of mentoring, extending opportunities for individual career advancement beyond the graduate programme. But what are the costs and benefits? What kind of L&D strategy is the formal mentoring part of? Does it have to be consistent with a self-development or a systematic training approach? Which external partners could be involved? Could someone else provide mentor training? Could an external organisation even provide the mentors? What aspects of ICT could be used to support mentoring?

In terms of broader perspectives, what theories of learning are being used to understand the principles and problems of mentoring? Communitarian and social exchange perspectives are discussed here, but others could be used. How does mentoring fit with NVET? At the moment the UK Government is promoting and funding support for mentoring in a number of areas. And how does mentoring fit with learning organisation or knowledge management goals? It seems to have promise, but is this evident and understood and managed?

REFERENCES

Black, A. (1984) *Guilds and Civil Society in European Political Thought*, London, Methuen.

Billett, S. (2000) 'Guided learning at work', *Journal of Workplace Learning*, Vol. 12. No, 7.

Brehm, S. and Kassin, S. (1993) *Social Psychology*, Boston, Houghton Mifflin.

Brentano, L. (1969) *History of Guilds and Trade Unions*, New York, Burt Franklin.

Clawson, J.G. (1985) 'Is mentoring necessary?', *Training and Development Journal*, April.

Cluttterbuck, D. (1992) *Everyone Needs a Mentor*, London, IPM.

Dryden, W., Charles-Edwards, D., Woolfe, R. *et al* (1991) *The Handbook of Counselling in Britain*, London, Routledge.

Dymock, D. (1999) 'Blind date: a case study of mentoring as workplace learning', *Journal of Workplace Learning*, Vol. 11. No. 8.

Etzioni, A. (1993) *The Spirit of Community: Rights, Responsibilities and The Communitarian Agenda*, New York, Crown Publishers.

Garvey, B. (1994) 'A dose of mentoring', *Education and Training*, Vol. 36, No. 4.

Gibb, S. and Megginson, D. (1993) 'Inside corporate mentoring schemes: a new agenda of concerns', *Personnel Review*, Vol. 22, No. 1.

Gibb, S. (1999) 'The usefulness of theory: a case study in evaluating formal mentoring schemes', *Human Relations*, Vol. 52, No. 8.

Homer (trans. Rieu, E.V.) (1946) *The Odyssey*, Harmondsworth, Penguin.

Kram, K. (1985) *Mentoring at Work: Developmental Relationships in Organizational Life*, Glenview, IL, Scott Foresman.

Lahtinen, H. and Wilson, F. (1994) 'Women and power in organisations', *Executive Power*, Vol. 7, No. 3.

Levinson, D., Darrow, C., Klein, E., Levinson, M. and McKee, B. (1978) *The Seasons of a Man's Life*, New York, Alfred Knopf.

Mackenney, R. (1987) *Tradesmen and Traders*, Totowa, NJ, Barnes and Noble.

Roche, G. (1979) 'Much ado about mentors', *Harvard Business Review*, January-February.

Rogers, C. (1983) *Freedom to Learn*, Columbus, Ohio, Charles E Merrill.

Shapiro, E., Haseltine, F. and Rowe, M. (1978) 'Moving up: role models, mentors and the patron system', *Sloan Management Review*, Vol. 19.

Smithson, M., Amato, P.R. and Pearce, P. (1983) *Dimensions of Helping Behaviour*, Oxford, Pergamon.

Stewart, W. (1992) *An A-Z of Counselling Theory and Practice*, London, Chapman & Hall.

Thomas, D. (1993) 'Racial dynamics in cross race developmental relationships', *Administrative Science Quarterly*, Vol. 38.

Zey, M. (1991) *The Mentor Connection*, New Brunswick, Transaction.

chapter fourteen

The Future of L&D at Work

Learning outcomes

- Review key themes and issues of L&D at work using a force field analysis method
- Critically evaluate the prospects for L&D at work

INTRODUCTION

L&D at work has been reviewed here as having three interrelated aspects. First is L&D as a process, a series of phases to achieve the goals of L&D at work. There is a core process, of observing, planning, acting and reviewing, associated with performance management. The L&D process runs in parallel with the performance management of organisations (Casey 1993). It is concerned with managing cognitive capacities, capabilities and behaviours to achieve effective performance. Second is L&D in practice, involving the achievement of these goals through various means. What happens in L&D practice has been explored in terms of organisational strategies, partnerships with providers, the use of IiP, and the increasing use of new technologies. Third is various perspectives on L&D at work, which provide arguments and debates illuminating L&D at work. The relevance of perspectives, different points of view on L&D at work, were described: theories from human sciences, the role of NVET policy, and the increasing concern with knowledge management were all discussed as perspectives on exploring L&D at work.

When cases like those that opened the text, the Ladbroke Grove disaster, are revisited and reviewed it should be possible to see how to apply the concepts and models described in this text in terms of processes, practices and perspectives to understanding these cases. The mistakes made in practice reflect mistakes about the core processes; to learn from those and remedy matters so that performance is improved requires the sensitive and informed application of perspectives – what can theories tell us, what can Government do, what are the KM implications? Other cases, like the concluding one on mentoring, again illustrate how the use of ideas from processes, practices and perspectives can all be used to describe, explore and animate the challenges of L&D at work.

This analysis of L&D processes, practices and perspectives should not be seen to exist in isolation from the broader world of HRM, and from forces for change in HRM which lead to L&D mattering as much as it does (CIPD 2000). It is a commonplace to assert that people live and work in a volatile socio-economic environment, where as individuals, organisations, nations and regions they have to constantly deal with forces for and against change. L&D is a part of that. By investing in the right recipe for L&D, there is a better prospect of success. There is also the fear, that the failure to get L&D right will leave individuals, organisations, nations or regions struggling.

WHY L&D AT WORK MATTERS

L&D at work matters so much because it is the means that give some individuals the pick of career choices, the capacity to get on rather than being stuck going nowhere (King 1998). L&D counts so much because it is a world where, other things being equal, organisations with the capacity to develop their intellectual capital, capabilities and behaviours consistent with core values will provide products and services at the quaity and cost customers seek. Examples range from the spectacular success story of Microsoft, based on their 'intellectual property' control of computer operating systems and their continued tapping of the knowledge and skills of their workforce, to the many businesses where failure in tapping knowledge, increasing capabilities and behaviours contrary to core values has contributed to, or even caused, their decline and fall. The problems faced by the accounting firm Arthur Andersen as a consequence of the ENRON scandal are an example. A good example of this latter is the UK rail infrastructure company Railtrack, where an in-ability to address the customer and health/safety concerns of users and key stakeholders led to the organisation being put into administration and wound up.

L&D also counts so much because it is a world where the process of globalisation accelerates and increases the pressures to learn and develop that have always been inherent; as it requires, for example, nations to compare themselves with the best and compete with each other for inward investment from the major multinationals. Economic miracles from recent history, such as the successes of the German and Japanese economies, are attributable to a range of factors; among them are effective systems for education, training and development. Economic imperatives among both developed and developing nations tend to highlight the roles of development and learning in creating and using knowledge, capabilities and behaviours consistent with employment in modern jobs and organisations.

All these levels of development and learning interact, producing either a virtuous or a vicious cycle. In the virtuous cycle the net effect is that of investment in L&D to provide economic and social returns, creating a dependence upon development and learning, forcing further and greater levels of cognitive capacity, capability and behaviour. In the vicious cycle a failure at any one level will feed into all others; as individuals, for example, fail to learn, causing knowledge gaps, capability shortages or behavioural mismatch for organisations, or as existing organisations with low knowledge and skill requirements do not provide opportunities for educated and capable individuals, leading to frustrations.

THE UK: PRESENT AND FUTURE

Where then does the UK stand at the moment, and what are the prospects for the future? The perceptions of where the UK stands with L&D, and therefore what the prospects are in the UK, are split. One perception has clearly been for some time that there is now a greater concern with effective L&D at work. Great economic and social advantages and benefits are to be gained from effectively and efficiently developing the kinds and levels of cognitive capacity, capabilities and behaviours required in the jobs and organisations that are the foundations of a changed, and still changing, world of work. The levers of L&D, from access to greater learning opportunities, through reforms within national education and training systems, to persuading employers to spend more on training, offer areas for action where the most powerful stakeholders, employers, Government, educationalists and employee organizations, can work together on common interests in developing and implementing schemes and initiatives. And in a context where commitments to improved HRM in the workplace are taken for granted, the rationale for 'investing in people' as an integral part of a people friendly business strategy creates circumstances in which support for L&D will be natural and strong.

What cannot be ignored, however, is a contrary perception: that there is still a constant, systemic deflection and diversion away from effective L&D at work. There are uncertainties and difficulties with responding to a changed and changing world of work by seeking, through supporting L&D, to achieve economic and social change of the scale and quality apparently required. And breaking free of the existing economic and social 'status quo', of low skills, low participation in learning and often inefficient systems, is no easy option that can provide overnight returns. Then the debate about pulling the right levers to affect the policies of key institutions, the investments of thousands of organisations and the motivations of millions of people becomes one that divides stakeholders rather than uniting them. Who pays, and where does the money go? Finally, there is the question of the extent to which commitments to L&D can be an integral part of HRM when it seems that a 'new deal' in employee relations can lead to under-investment in staff; because long term, mutually beneficial relations are a thing of the past. If employees may not be within the organisation for any length of time, why develop them? If an organisation cannot provide a career path for an employee, why should they bother to work at learning over time for the benefit of the organisation?

It is not necessary to think in terms of one of these perceptions about L&D being right and the other being wrong. They can be represented as, broadly speaking, describing forces for more and more effective L&D and forces against more and more effective L&D. Figure 14.1 represents these split perceptions as the two sides of a force field diagram. Force field diagrams are used to visualise situations in which an equilibrium exists between forces for change and forces against change. These perceptions are neither right nor wrong.

It is possible to see the prospects for L&D as fluctuating about this status quo. It may be desirable to change this equilibrium, to seek more and more effective L&D at work. And there may be things that individuals, employers, governments, and others can seek to do to achieve that change. However, this is the situation that currently prevails. To learn about L&D at work, from the individual struggling to master a subject in a training room (Chalofsky and Reinhart 1988) to the billions spent by employers and Government (DfEE 2000), is to develop an understanding of this situation, and how it shapes and influences what is and what is not done, and what is done well and what is not done well, in the contemporary UK context. There is a great span and great depth to the questions raised by contemporary L&D at work; ranging from how best to manage a one day course in an organisation, to the development of policy by Government to achieve economic and social goals, and from the evolution of knowl-

Figure 14.1   *A Force Field Analysis for Employee Development*

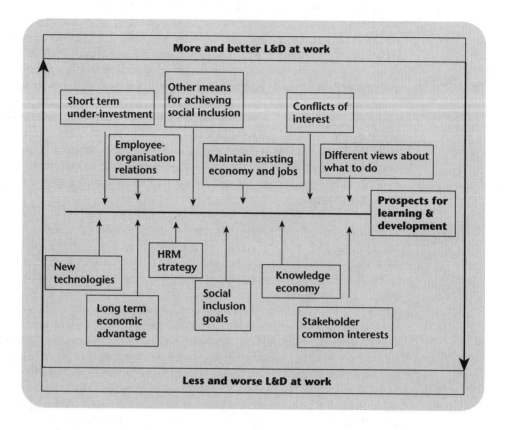

edge management in multinational organisations to the improvement of skills in a medium sized organisation improving its productivity. Authoritative answers to these questions cannot be found in any text, they need to be researched by thoughtful performers (Thody 2001). But a way to finding answers to these questions can be given: developing a sophisticated understanding of L&D process (Peterson 1992), exploring L&D in practice (Wilson 1999), and using different perspectives to help illuminate rather than obscure the realities of L&D at work.

REFERENCES

Casey, D. (1993) *Managing Learning in Organizations*, Milton Keynes, Open University Press.

Chalofsky, N. and Reinhart, C. (1988) *Effective Human Resource Development: How to Build a Strong and Responsive HRD Function*, San Francisco, Jossey-Bass.

CIPD (2000) *Success Through Learning: The Argument for Strengthening Workplace Learning*, IPD Consultative Document.

DfEE (2000) *Skills for All: Research Report from the National Skills Task Force*, DfEE.

King, S. (1998) 'Putting people at the heart of the learning process', *Education and Training*, Vol. 40, No. 4.

Peterson, R. (1992) *Managing Successful Learning: A Practical Guide for Teachers and Trainers*, London, Kogan Page.

Thody, P. (2001) *Researching Human Resource Development: Philosophy, Processes and Practices*, London, Routledge.

Wilson, P. (1999) *Human Resource Development: Learning and Training for Individuals and Organizations*, London, Kogan Page.

Appendix

Additional Internet Links for L&D at Work

'Train the Trainers' net	http://www.surrey.ac.uk/Education/TTnet/intro.htm Resources and connections to L&D issues focussed on 'training the trainers'
Training Zone	http://www.trainingzone.co.uk/ Resources and links site
National Training Organisation for Employment	http://www.empnto.co.uk/ Work standards and related material for 'people who work with people'
E-learning Network	http://www.elearningnetwork.org/
ESPRIT	http://www.kalif.org
Learning and Training in Industry (LTI)	http://www.lti-portal.org/
National Grid for Learning	http://www.ngfl.gov.uk
Ofsted	http://www.ofsted.gov.uk/
PIU	http://www.cabinet-office.gov.uk/innovation/ home/homef.html
Electronic Training Village	http://www.trainingvillage.gr/etv/ Resource on NVET policy in various countries
National Institute of Adult Continuing Education	http://www.niace.org.uk/ Resources and links about adult learning
Centre for Labour Market Studies	http://www.clms.le.ac.uk/ Links to CIPD annual survey
European Consortium of the Learning Organization	http://www.eclo.com
Discussion page and archive of mailings	http://www.learning-org.com/

Index